MASTERING
TURBO C

MASTERING TURBO C®
Second Edition

STAN KELLY-BOOTLE

SYBEX®

SAN FRANCISCO • PARIS • DÜSSELDORF • SOEST

Cover design by Thomas Ingalls + Associates
Cover photography by David Bishop
Book design by Julie Bilski
Illustrations by Jeff Giese
Screen reproductions produced by XenoFont

To my wife, Iwonka

► ACKNOWLEDGMENTS ►

I would like to thank a wonderful crew at SYBEX who used sticks and carrots in the gentlest fashion. Dr. Rudolph Langer, one of those rare executives in computer-book publishing who knows computers and loves all books, first trapped me into this project. Now that it's complete, I am glad he was so persuasive.

Vincent Leone was my developmental editor; my thanks to him for his constant support and guidance, not excluding the spotting of all my missing semicolons (I hope) and unwanted commas.

A word of praise to artists Julie Bilski and Charlotte Carter, Cheryl Vega in typesetting, and Sylvia Townsend for proff-redink. Appendix G received special help from Michael J. Young, whose own SYBEX book, *Systems Programming in Turbo C*, is a natural sequel to mine. I am grateful to Rhoda Simmons, Eric Stone, Hilda Van Genderen, and Nancy O'Donnell for their copyediting and proofreading and to Ted Laux, king of the DP indexers. Wayne Black was the technical reviewer for this book, Chris Mockel provided timely typing, and Jocelyn Reynolds and Bob Myren did the word processing.

The SYBEX people who worked on the second edition were Vincent Leone, developmental editor; Rhoda Simmons, copy editor; Chris Mockel and Jocelyn Reynolds, word processors; Olivia Shinomoto, typesetter; Ami M. Knox, proofreader; Helen Bruno, artist; Jon Forrest, technical reviewer; and Ted Laux, indexer.

Finally, I want to thank the good people at Borland International, Brad Silverberg, Pat Williams, and Nan Borreson in particular, for their fine products and unfailing support.

► CONTENTS AT A GLANCE ►

► *TABLE OF CONTENTS* ►

► CHAPTER 8: File I/O: Full Stream Ahead ►

► *FOREWORD* ►

We welcome Stan Kelly-Bootle's *Mastering Turbo C* to the library of books supporting Turbo language products from Borland International. Such books help users at every experience level derive optimum benefits from their software investments.

In this most readable exposition, Kelly-Bootle gently and logically acquaints the novice user with the power, versatility, and simplicity of the Turbo C integrated environment. Although *Mastering Turbo C* is written specifically for readers who have never used a C, or perhaps any structured language, the author provides chapter summaries and appendices that help more advanced users quickly find valuable information. Particularly helpful to all readers are a complete guide to using the graphics of Turbo C and information on the Turbo C Runtime Library.

It is a pleasure to recommend *Mastering Turbo C* as an introduction to the powerful Turbo C programming environment.

Philippe Kahn
President
Borland International, Inc.

► *INTRODUCTION* ►

There are three reasons for learning the C language: fun, profit, and everybody is doing it. The recent surge in popularity is largely due to Borland International's president, Philippe Kahn, who pioneered the unheard-of notion that professional-quality compilers and language-support products should not require you to get a second mortgage.

► *HISTORY LESSON* ►

While hardware costs had been declining dramatically since the first UNIVAC sale, the unquestioned assumption was that software, being human-labor intensive, was bound to move as rapidly in the opposite direction, if only to ensure that your total data-processing budget remained comfortably stable!

Kahn's counterexample to this hypothesis rests on the simple notion that you can amortize the considerable costs of developing sound, easy-to-use software by expanding the customer base with aggressive pricing and marketing. The latter is required, initially at least, to overcome the fixation that decent systems software is expensive and accessible only to computer-science graduates. The size of the potential user base, of course, had expanded rapidly during the early 1980s with the advent of the IBM PC and its many bandwagoneers.

► *Success* ►

The legendary success of Borland's Turbo Pascal proved that there was indeed an untapped market for professional compilers for personal computers outside the traditional software-development houses. That market, perhaps, had been resigned to the fact that at one end of the spectrum compilers were slow, free, suspect, and unsupported, while at the other end they were competent and desirable but priced for the full-time, $50-an-hour programmer. The scene changed suddenly and irreversibly when Turbo Pascal appeared in 1983, breaking the $100 barrier and earning all the magazine "product of the year" accolades.

► *Turbo Pascal Rules OK!* ►

Turbo Pascal's success (hundreds of thousands of copies have been sold and Version 5.0 maintains the momentum) was due not only to the price/performance bargain but also to the fact that a new integrated development environment had been created for it. Source-code entry and editing, syntax checking, compiling, linking, running, and debugging were all brought into the one package and made available through easily navigated pop-up menus. These activities had traditionally called for separate specialized software packages, which were often supplied by different vendors.

► *But C Is Different...* ►

Some cynics reacted by saying, "Ah, well, Pascal is just an educational toy, not a real production language. I am wed to my $600 C compiler—the only serious language for systems programming. In any case, C is so dangerous in the wrong hands, let's be grateful that the proletariat can't afford the real thing. If they want to play with C, there are plenty of freeware tiny C's to paddle in."

► *The C Mystique* ►

Among all the computer languages, dead and alive, C holds a unique place—people either love it or detest it to distraction. There are no neutral parties here! UNIX, the operating system closely associated with C (indeed, UNIX is largely written in C), has engendered the same dichotomy since it emerged with C from Bell Labs in the mid-1970s and migrated to the world's best campuses. UNIX and C have become de facto standards in many government and engineering fields, and they have gradually moved from minicomputers and mainframes into the microcomputer arena as CPUs have become more powerful and capable of supporting larger memories.

► *Why C?* ►

The portability of C programs stems from C's use of function libraries for such machine-dependent operations as I/O—an area that bedeviled the growth of a single Pascal standard. Since C is a small-core language (unlike, say, PL/1 or Ada), there are surprisingly few keywords to learn. On the other hand, C is richer in operators than most languages (there are several operators that work at the bit level).

The critics cannot gainsay C's success. The snipers usually overlook the fact that you cannot have a powerful systems programming language without some attendant dangers. C offers you access to the machine level with a rare blend of efficiency and elegance, but sometimes the conciseness of the language encourages a cryptic cleverness that hinders maintainability. Despite its dangers, C is undoubtedly the language of choice for most systems programmers.

The migration of C to the PC-DOS/MS-DOS environment has not been easy. The architecture of the Intel 8088/86 family is not ideally suited to a language like C, in which pointers play a leading, some say frightening, role. To keep the pointer arithmetic clean and tidy, pointers should point to large, linear memories. The segmented memory space of the PC forces compiler writers to provide different memory models for different pointer dispositions.

Another cloud on the horizon became visible as C moved away from UNIX to other environments and increasing progress was made on software in general. Compilers were emerging with slight but disconcerting differences in their interpretations of the syntax and semantics of C, which had been spelled out by Brian W. Kernighan and Dennis M. Ritchie in 1978. Because these specifications were the work of a few talented individuals rather than the tedious output of a committee of *t*-crossers and *i*-dotters, ambiguities came to light that led to diverse dialectic offshoots, threatening the prized portability of C.

A committee of the American National Standards Institute (ANSI) was formed to resolve these differences. The task of Technical Committee X3J11 was and is to draw up a set of standards for C. As I write, ANSI C is not yet formally carved in stone, but enough data have emerged to point C compiler writers and C programmers in the right direction. Unfortunately, many developers of new C products have played a waiting game because they were unwilling to take the plunge until ANSI C was formally ratified.

For all these reasons, there was pessimism that a fast, inexpensive development package conforming to ANSI C would ever become available for the IBM PC family.

► *Enter Turbo C* ►

The release of Turbo C in May 1987 put an end to this pessimism. Borland had again achieved the improbable—it brought to market a professional C-language development system for the PC packaged with the familiar integrated development environment that is demonstrably superior to C packages costing three or four times as much. For the traditional UNIX-style C programmer, Turbo C has a completely independent command-line compiler free from mollycoddling menus and windows.

Turbo C, like its Turbo predecessors, comes complete and ready to go. You get an ANSI-C compatible, 7000-lines-per-minute, one-pass compiler that generates linkable object modules compatible with the PC-DOS linker; a fast linker; support for six memory models; math coprocessor support or FP emulation; and a full-screen syntax-checking editor, complete with pull-down menus and windows. Turbo C also includes Project and Make options that check on file interdependencies and automate the compilation/linking process following changes to one or more component source files. There is also a more powerful, stand-alone MAKE utility that watches over file interdependencies.

In addition, Turbo C allows you to link mixed modules written in assembly language, Turbo Pascal, and Turbo Prolog.

The immediate success of Turbo C encouraged Borland to "gild the lily." Within six months of launching Version 1, the company announced Version 1.5. The main enhancement of the latter version was a sophisticated graphics toolbox that provided facilities similar to those in Turbo Pascal.

In August 1988 Borland issued another major update, Turbo C Version 2, with an integrated source-level debugger; improved Make utility; and several speed enhancing tweaks to the compiler, linker, and graphics routines. With minor exceptions, all these improvements are upwardly compatible: As you move from Version 1 to 1.5 to 2, you will not have to do any major recoding—in the worst case, your programs will have to be recompiled/relinked under the new regime. For serious systems programmers, Borland now offers a package called Professional Turbo C 2 that contains the new Turbo C as well as TASM (the new Turbo macro assembler) and the freestanding Turbo Debugger. There are various upgrade deals available—check with your supplier.

This second edition of *Mastering Turbo C* discusses various enhancements of Version 2 in Chapter 10 and covers the new version's debugging facilities in Chapter 11. Although the phrase *Chapter 11* has depressingly bankrupt overtones, I assure you that the debugging features described therein will spell *profit* to all Turbo C users.

► *JOIN THE ELITE* ►

Turbo C has already attracted a wide range of programmers, including amateur "hobbyists" as well as professional software writers. If you have bought Turbo C, then this book will help you exploit its many features. If you haven't, perhaps you will be encouraged to join the club.

Of course, many Turbo C users are hardy types to whom C is the native tongue. My book will help them pick out the features specific to Turbo C, but the gentle pace of most of the exposition is geared toward the thousands of newcomers to the big wide world of C. I therefore assume that you have only a few basic DOS skills and no prior exposure to C or any other structured language.

The ever-nagging problem facing many computer-book authors is how to enlighten the uninitiated without boring the socks off the cognoscenti. As a possible solution, each of my chapters ends with a summary so that readers can quickly find the sections most appropriate to their needs. All the program examples have been kept short and sweet to focus your attention on a particular aspect of C. My experience is that long examples are counterproductive.

This book is really part one of "mastering" Turbo C. You and your creativity form part two. Turbo C provides the paint and brushes for your PC canvas; this book lays out the palette and tells you which end of the brush goes into the paint. To become a master of C in the tradition of a Ritchie, Kernighan, Bourne, Holub, or Plauger, you need to start daubing away as soon as possible.

Here's to your ever-growing fluenC!

Stan Kelly-Bootle
Mill Valley, California and Bargemon, Provence

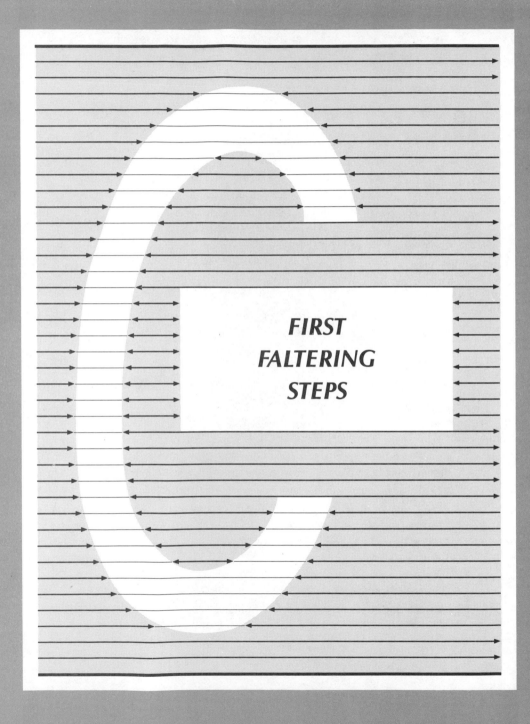

FIRST
FALTERING
STEPS

► *CHAPTER 1* ►

Learning how to create a sequence of statements that your Turbo C compiler will accept as valid is clearly a good starting point. There are two aspects to this.

First you'll learn the mechanics of the Turbo C integrated environment, how to navigate the menus, select options, enter and edit your source code, and invoke the compiler and linker.

Then there are the syntactical rules of the C language, which spell out with precision exactly which strings of symbols are permissible.

I will first cover briefly the major steps needed to create and run a Turbo C program. Some basic vocabulary will be established, so feel free to skim and skip according to your level of experience. The key points will be amplified later, so beginners should not be discouraged if new words and concepts fly by in rapid succession.

► *SOURCE CODE—EXTENSION .C* ►

The text of a program, called its *source code*, is a sequence of statements spelling out in fine detail the actions you want the machine to take. Before a program can be run it must be translated by the Turbo C compiler and then linked using the Turbo C linker.

C source code is usually stored in files with the extension .C. So, to find out what source code files you have in your current directory, you can type DIR *.C and press Enter to get

```
C>DIR *.C
TEMP       C       352      9-11-87  7:12p
HELLO      C        89      9-20-87  4:48p
FILECOMP   C     11185      9-20-87  1:38a
GETOPT     C      4228      5-13-87  1:00a
        4 file(s) 6660096 bytes free
```

which shows the names, sizes (in bytes) and date/time stamps of each file. Each of these files contains sequences of ASCII characters that can be displayed, printed, or edited, hence the general term *text* files. The full ASCII code is given in Appendix A.

The ANSI C standard does not specify how the character set should be encoded, but most implementations, including Turbo C, have opted for the ASCII set, so characters are stored and manipulated by their numeric ASCII codes. For now, simply note that the 7-bit ASCII code gives 128 combinations, including both printable symbols and nonprintable control codes.

► *DIRECTIVES AND INCLUDE FILES* ►

In addition to the normal program statements that you enter in the .C files, there are several *directives* you can provide. They are readily recognized since they usually appear at the start of the .C file with the prefix # followed by the particular directive's name and its *arguments*. As you might guess, directives direct the compiler in various ways. In fact, there is a *preprocessing* phase that handles all the directives before the compilation itself gets under way.

An important example, familiar to most BASIC users, is the **include** directive with a file name as its argument.

#include <*filename*>

tells the preprocessor to load the contents of the text file *filename* as though it formed part of your .C file at that point. Your .C file itself is not physically changed. You can set up your own **include** files to avoid repetitive typing. Initially, though, you will be using **#include** with some of the twenty-five special files provided by Borland for your convenience. These have the extension .H (for *header*) and they supply frequently needed definitions and declarations in accordance with ANSI C standards. Before too long you will come to know and love these .H files—they not only save you much drudgery, they also serve in the great cause of endowing C programs with their widely acclaimed portability.

Include files can be *nested*, that is, an include file may contain further include files, and so on, to a depth of sixteen.

You can picture the process as follows:

HELLO.C → preprocessor → HELLO.C + <*included-files*>

► *OBJECT CODE—EXTENSION .OBJ* ►

The compilation process, applied to your .C and .H files, produces *object code* files with the extension .OBJ. These files contain binary code that cannot be meaningfully displayed or printed, although you might find some recognizable ASCII characters embedded therein.

Object files contain machine language instructions that make sense only to the Intel 8088/86, 80286, or 80386 microprocessor that powers your PC. Unless told otherwise, the compiler will produce a .OBJ file with the same name as your principal source file as follows:

HELLO.C + <*included-files*> → Turbo C compiler → HELLO.OBJ

You can give the compiler a different name for the .OBJ file—but why add to the confusion?

► *EXECUTABLE CODE—EXTENSION .EXE* ►

The linking process takes one or more .OBJ files and, true to its name, *links* them together to produce one *executable* file with the extension .EXE. The linker can also automatically pull in code from standard precompiled *libraries* provided by Borland (or specialist libraries offered by a growing number of software vendors) to make programming easier for you. You are also allowed to create your own libraries. Your program can use any of these precanned library *functions* and leave it to the linker to incorporate their .OBJ code into the final product, namely, the .EXE file.

In simple cases with one .C file and one .OBJ file, the .EXE file is usually named accordingly.

HELLO.C → preprocessor → HELLO.C + <*included-files*> →
compiler → HELLO.OBJ + <*library-code*> → linker → HELLO.EXE

Again, you are free to rename the .EXE file, but life is more pleasant if the .C, .OBJ, and .EXE files are all called HELLO. You can then talk about the HELLO program without ambiguity.

When you are linking several .OBJ files, you will normally find that one of them has the key name that naturally goes with the final .EXE file name.

FILECOMP.OBJ/GETOPT.OBJ + <*library-code*> → linker → FILECOMP.EXE

Later on, you'll see how .PRJ or *project* files are used to tell the linker which .OBJ files to link and how to name the final .EXE file. Turbo C offers flexibility for professional developers in areas where the beginner might prefer to have no choice! We will often dogmatically insist on certain default actions until the reasons for the alternatives emerge.

Readers with wider DOS experience may want to know here that the linker supplied with Turbo C is compatible with and faster than the standard DOS linker. Also, if your program meets certain size restrictions, you can use the DOS EXE2BIN utility to translate your .EXE files into the faster, more compact .COM format.

► THE MANDATORY FIRST PROGRAM ►

Brian W. Kernighan and Dennis M. Ritchie, in their canonical book *The C Programming Language* (Englewood Cliffs, New Jersey: Prentice-Hall, 1978) started a tradition that most of the ten-thousand subsequent C books have followed. K&R (as the book is widely known) offers as its "Getting Started" program HELLO.C, the sole purpose of which is to display **hello, world** on the screen.

Simple though it is, HELLO.C actually illustrates nine major elements of the C language. Before you get to this exciting demonstration, I'll take you on a quick tour of the Turbo C integrated environment and show you the basics of program loading, editing, and running.

► INSTALLATION REMINDER ►

You will find the file HELLO.C on your Integrated Development Diskette. If you have followed the hard-disk installation procedures given in the *Turbo C*

User's Guide, this file should now be in your working directory C:\TURBOC. In or under the same directory, you will also have:

1. TC.EXE (the integrated development compiler), TCINST.COM (the installation program), and TCHELP.TCH (the help files). (TCC.EXE, the command-line version of TC.EXE, will also be here, but we will not be using it until later.)

2. All the *.H (include) files from Diskette 3 in directory C:\TURBO-C\INCLUDE.

3. All the *.LIB (library) files from Diskette 4 plus all non-.H files from Diskette 3 in directory C:\TURBOC\LIB. (To avoid tedious digressions, I am assuming the recommended hard-disk installation setup. If you have different drive or directory names, simply adjust the following instructions accordingly. For details on the TCINST installation program, see Appendix B.)

► EXPLORING THE INTEGRATED DEVELOPMENT ENVIRONMENT ►

The Integrated Development Environment (IDE) is only three keystrokes away. Type TC or tc at the C> prompt and press Enter, and you will soon see the screen shown in Figure 1.1, the Turbo C main menu screen. Press F10 (or Shift-F10 in Version 2) to call up the Borland copyright notice.

► *The Small Print Enlarged* ►

Carefully read the Borland version number and copyright notice in the central window. If you have not studied and understood Borland's No-Nonsense License Statement at the front of the *Turbo C User's Guide*, now is the time to do so. Borland International has removed any of the so-called excuses and rationalizations for piracy. If you are violating any of their conditions, you should rectify the situation before proceeding. More specifically, erase any illegal copy diskettes and purchase your own Turbo C—you will sleep soundly tonight, and in the morning your acne will have disappeared.

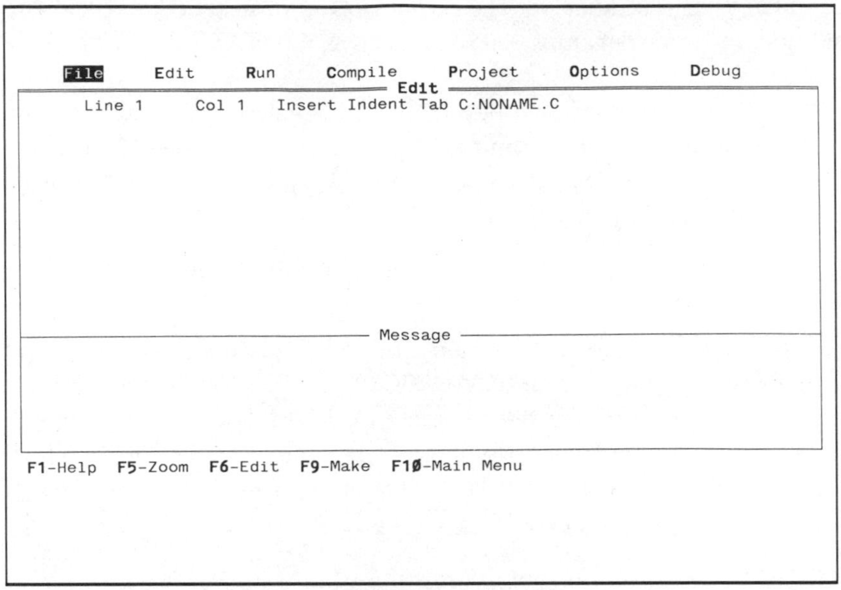

```
    File      Edit     Run    Compile    Project    Options    Debug
                               ───────── Edit ──────────
       Line 1      Col 1    Insert Indent Tab C:NONAME.C




                           ──────── Message ────────




  F1-Help  F5-Zoom  F6-Edit  F9-Make  F10-Main Menu
```

► **Figure 1.1:** *Turbo C main menu screen (Version 1.5)*

Pressing any key removes the version/copyright notice. Note that there are five basic areas in the main menu screen:

1. Main menu strip

2. Editor status strip

3. Editor window

4. Message window

5. Hot-key quick reference strip

► *Keys—Hot and Cold* ►

At any time Alt-F10 will redisplay the version/copyright window. (*Alt-F10* means hold down the Alt key while you press the F10 function key.) Alt-F10 is one of the many *hot-key* combinations you'll encounter. A hot key is one that works consistently wherever you are in the menu hierarchy, as opposed to those keys for which the function depends on the particular mode or screen position you happen to be in. Some hot keys are single F (function) keys, others are Alt plus a function key.

The bottom *quick reference* line of the main screen normally shows the most appropriate hot function keys for your current situation. If you hold down the Alt key by itself for a few seconds, the quick reference line will switch to show you what Alt plus the function keys will perform. Table 1.1 gives a partial list of hot keys. A tiny warning: In most error and verify conditions, the hot keys are disabled until you take the indicated recovery action. This is for your own good.

Key(s)	Versions 1, 1.5	Version 2
F1	Context-sensitive Help	" "
F2	Save the current file to disk	" "
F3	Window to enter file name for loading	" "
F5	Toggle: Zoom or Unzoom active window	" "
F6	Switch to the active window	" "
F7	Move to previous error	Trace
F8	Move to next error	Step
F9	Invoke Project-Make	" "
F10	Toggle: Main Menu or active window	" "
Alt-F1	Redisplay previous Help screen	" "
Alt-F3	Pick file window	" "
Alt-F5	—	Toggle: TC screen or User screen
Alt-F6	—	Toggle: Message or Watch windows; current or previous file
Alt-F7	—	move to previous error
Alt-F8	—	move to next error
Alt-F9	Compile current file to .OBJ	" "

► **Table 1.1:** *Main Turbo C hot keys*

Key(s)	Versions 1, 1.5	Version 2
Alt-F10	Display version/copyright screen	—
Alt-B	—	Pull down Break/Watch window
Alt-C	Pull down **C**ompile menu	" "
Alt-D	Pull down **D**ebug menu	" "
Alt-E	Go into **E**dit mode	" "
Alt-F	Pull down **F**ile menu	" "
Alt-O	Pull down **O**ptions menu	" "
Alt-P	Pull down **P**roject-Make menu	" "
Alt-R	**R**un the current menu	" "
Alt-X	e**x**it from Turbo C to DOS	" "
Shift-F10	—	display version screen

► *Table 1.1:* Main Turbo C hot keys (continued)

Note that Esc, the escape key, is *almost* hot! Esc is a general menu-exit key that steps you up from a sub-submenu to the previous submenu, from a sub-menu to its main menu, or from a main menu to an active window. However, Esc is not a true-blue-blooded hot key since it is inactive unless you are in a menu or help screen.

Esc and the hot keys will quickly become your close friends. For now, try Alt-F10 to bring up the Version/Copyright screen, then press any key to remove it.

► *Help!*

Press F1 to explore the on-line Help package. If F1 gives you an error message, you have probably failed to copy the TCHELP.TCH file into your working directory. The Help displays are *context-sensitive*, that is, the first F1 display will helpfully vary according to where you are in the system. Esc *always* clears the help box and restores the status quo.

Help is not confined to your context. Wherever you are, you can browse around for guidance on any other topic. Once you are in a Help screen, for example, a second F1 brings up a Help index from which you can select topics. Also, Alt-F1 at any time will redisplay the last Help screen you accessed. Repeating Alt-F1 keeps recalling past used Help screens up to a maximum of twenty. Some Help screens will show highlighted *keywords*, indicating topics for which amplified help is available. The arrow keys and the Home and End keys can be used to select keywords; once a topic has been selected, pressing Enter will bring up the relevant help.

► Leaving Already?

Next, try Alt-X to exit from Turbo C to DOS, then enter TC again to recover the main menu. This early exit practice is not as bizarre as you may think! There is nothing in the whole of computerdom as frustrating as the inability to withdraw gracefully from a program. The lack of "exit standards" has driven more users insane than anything else. The many signing-off ploys in use today include logoff, logout, bye, system, end, Ctrl-C, Ctrl-D, Break, and, the last resort, turning the power off. If you forget Alt-X, Turbo C has another mnemonic for quitting—type Q from the File menu.

► Back to TC

Entering TC invokes TC.EXE, the main Turbo C IDE program. Since you have not yet specified a .C file name, Turbo C assumes that you are going to edit a default program called NONAME.C, which explains the legend appearing at the end of line 2, the *editor status strip*. When you load a specific file into the editor, the NONAME.C legend will be replaced by the new file name. Later on, when you want to save your edited program, you are free to rename it.

You can load a file and invoke TC by typing TC *filename*, or TC *filename*.C, or TC *filename*.*ext* at the C> prompt, where *filename* may include full or partial path information. In the absence of a specific extension, TC assumes the default extension .C. If TC finds the file name, the file will be loaded for editing; otherwise you'll get a virgin *edit window*. The edit window is the large upper window. When you are in edit mode, this is where the source text appears as you type. The name of the current file is always displayed on line 2.

For much of this chapter you will be learning your way around the features of the IDE main menu screen. It allows you to load, enter, save, and edit source text, get help, switch and zoom windows, set countless options, then compile/link/run your program. You can even return temporarily to the

DOS level, do some DOS stuff, then type exit to return to where you left off in Turbo C.

At various times temporary windows will appear that contain progress reports and instructions about what to do next. Detailed error messages and warnings appear in the bottom *message window*.

► Window Switching and Zooming

The normal screen disposition shows a split between the upper edit window and lower message window. If you are in edit mode with the cursor in the edit window, the edit window is the *active* window. During debugging sessions, for example, the message window may become the active window. You can switch the active window at any time using the hot key F6. This action is known as *toggling*, named for those familiar lamp switches that switch on-to-off or off-to-on with each toggle. So F6 will switch from edit-window-active to message-window-active or vice versa with each application. The active window is visibly marked by the presence of a double bar on top.

Another hot-key toggle is F5, which will Zoom and Unzoom the active window with each depression. Zooming when the edit window is active expands the edit screen to fill the whole screen, temporarily removing the message screen. Pressing F5 again Unzooms, restoring the split screen and redisplaying any previous messages. Similarly, you can Zoom the message screen when it is active, temporarily losing the edit screen (but not, of course, losing any data). Incidentally, when you come to the editing features you'll see that you can scroll around the edit screen like a conventional word processor whether the screen is Zoomed or not.

Summing up this section:

F5 to Zoom/Unzoom active window

F6 to select active window

Let's now look in detail at the main menu, the key to further progress.

► The Main Menu ►

The essential maneuvers to learn are the following:

1. Hot key F10 takes you from the active window to the main menu.

2. Esc takes you from the main menu back to the active window.

3. Alt+*letter* gets a main menu selection at any time.

The *main menu* is the very top line showing the seven main options (which are cleverly named so that each starts with a unique, bold letter). This allows selection by keying the appropriate letter (together with the Alt key if you are outside the menu) or by highlighting each option in turn using the left/right arrow keys.

Once you have illuminated your choice, pressing Enter does the selection. This convenient and contemporary method is used throughout Turbo C and is easier to do than to explain. From now on, when I give an instruction such as "Select File menu" I will leave it to your own good taste which selection method you use: keying the letter F (or f) or highlighting the File legend and then pressing Enter. Either will pull down the File submenu.

Five of the seven main selections operate their own pull-down menus to offer further subselections, many of which sprout further multichoice displays. The two exceptions are the following:

Edit moves you directly to edit mode with edit window active.

Run immediately starts trying to run the current program (it may have to compile/link first, but this is automatic). In Version 2, selecting Run brings up the Run menu, at which you type R.

Another neat trick to remember is that while a menu option is pulled down the left/right arrow keys can be used to invoke the adjacent menus.

Table 1.2 gives a brief summary of the main menu selections.

When you add up all the combinations of menu and submenu choices, you have what Philippe Kahn would call "*un embarras de choix*." For the time being, though, you will be concentrating on the File and Edit menus.

► *LOADING YOUR FIRST PROGRAM* ►

If you are not in the main menu, use F10 to get there. You can always tell if the main menu is active because one of the seven top-line legends will be highlighted if it is.

From the main menu, select F for File. Your screen will appear as in Figure 1.2, with the pull-down File menu ready for your selection. You can highlight selections using the up/down arrow keys, or you can type the unique letter for each option, as listed in Table 1.3.

File	Load, Pick+, New, Save, Write to, Directory, Change Dir, OS, shell, Quit
Edit	Go to Edit mode
Run	Run current program, [Program reset, Trace-into, Step-over, User screen]
Compile	Compile to .OBJ, Make .EXE, Link .EXE, Build all, Primary C file, [Get info]
Project	Project name, Break make on+, Clear project, [Auto-dependencies, Remove messages]
Options	Compiler+++, Linker++, Environment+, Args, Retrieve options, Store options, [Directories+]
Debug	Track messages, Clear messages, Keep messages, Available memory, [Replace by evaluate, Call stack, Find function, Refresh display, Display swapping, Source debugging]
[Break/watch]	[Add watch, Delete watch, Edit watch, Remove all watches]

► **Table 1.2:** *Main menu selections. Items in brackets are only available in Version 2. Each + indicates a lower level of submenu.*

Test the up/down arrows by illuminating some of the File options. You now have three ways of invoking the Load option:

1. Type L.

2. Highlight the Load box and press Enter.

3. Press F3 (this works from anywhere).

A small window appears, prompting the entry or selection of a file name to be loaded. The window defaults to the mask *.C, so pressing Enter will bring up a directory window showing all your *.C files. You can also enter a specific file name or your own search mask, e.g., H????O.C or H*.*. While in the directory window you can

1. Use the arrows to mark the target file.

2. Press F4 to change the mask.

```
  File      Edit     Run     Compile    Project    Options    Debug
┌─────────────────────────────── Edit ──────────────────────────────
│ Load       F3  1 1    Insert Indent Tab C:NONAME.C
│ Pick   Alt-F3
│ New
│ Save       F2
│ Write to
│ Directory
│ Change dir
│ OS shell
│ Quit    Alt-X
└──────────────



                         ─────── Message ───────




───────────────────────────────────────────────────────────────────
 F1-Help  F5-Zoom  F6-Edit  F9-Make  F10-Main Menu
```

► *Figure 1.2:* File menu

Load	F3	Load a file into Editor
Pick	Alt-F3	Load a file from Pick list
New		Edit a new NONAME.C file
Save	F2	Save current file to disk
Write to		Save current file under new name
Directory		Display directories
Change dir		Change drive/directory
OS shell		Temporary escape to DOS
Quit	Alt-X	Leave Turbo C

► *Table 1.3:* File menu options

For now, type HELLO.C (or just HELLO or hello since .C is the default) as shown in Figure 1.3.

Note that ◄— and Del allow you correct your input in the usual way. The text of HELLO.C will now appear in the edit window as in Figure 1.4. You are

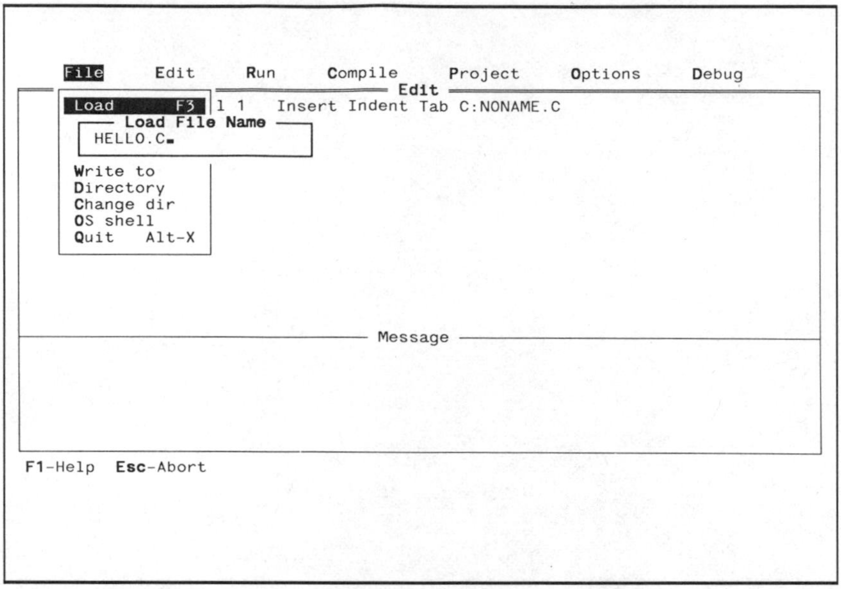

```
     File      Edit      Run      Compile      Project      Options      Debug
                                    ═══ Edit ══════
   ┌─────────────────┐ 1 1   Insert Indent Tab  C:NONAME.C
   │ Load       F3   │
   │  ── Load File Name ──
   │  │ HELLO.C▁                    │
   │  └───────────────────────────┘
   │ Write to        │
   │ Directory       │
   │ Change dir      │
   │ OS shell        │
   │ Quit    Alt-X   │
   └─────────────────┘


                           ─── Message ───




F1-Help  Esc-Abort
```

► **Figure 1.3:** *Selecting a file for loading*

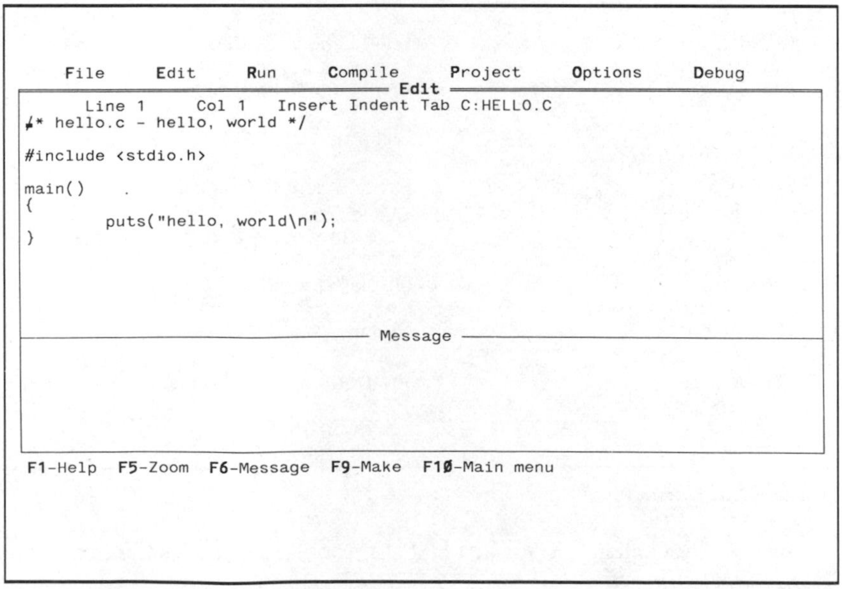

```
     File      Edit      Run      Compile      Project      Options      Debug
                                    ═══ Edit ══════
      Line 1      Col 1   Insert Indent Tab  C:HELLO.C
╱* hello.c - hello, world */

#include <stdio.h>

main( )    .
{
       puts("hello, world\n");
}




                           ─── Message ───




F1-Help  F5-Zoom  F6-Message  F9-Make  F10-Main menu
```

► **Figure 1.4:** *Loaded file ready for editing*

in edit mode with the cursor poised for action in the top left-hand corner. Note the top row of double lines indicating that the edit window is active.

The main menu is inactive but can be revived with F10 or invoked directly with Alt-*letter*.

► *Other Loading Options* ►

Before we tackle HELLO.C, let's briefly review the loading operations available. In later sections, I'll just tell you to load a given file, leaving you to choose your favorite method.

Loading is such a common operation that Borland has given you some shortcut methods. The hot key F3 always gets you the load entry box without your having to go through the File menu.

Typing P for Pick or using the hot-key combo Alt-F3 offers yet another loading method. Pick will display up to eight file names representing previously loaded files. You then select from this *pick list* to reload a file—the cursor will even be positioned to where it was when you last edited that file. At the end of the pick list you'll see an entry, " – load file – ," which works just like the normal L for Load submenu. So, if the pick list does not contain the target file you don't have to go back to the Load menu. You can even save your pick list from one TC session to the next by using the load/save-pick-list option in the TCINST installation program (see Appendix B).

► *Editing and Saving a File* ►

While you are editing, your changes are made to a copy of your file in RAM, which is notoriously *volatile*. Power outages and other catastrophes may nullify hours of effort, so regularly saving to disk is a sanity-preserving habit worth developing. You can either go to the File menu and select S for Save or use the hot key F2 from anywhere. You save your current changes in the file being edited unless you are editing NONAME.C, in which case Turbo C will kindly prompt you to rename before saving.

The Write to option in the File menu gives you yet another way of saving your work. This allows you to save the contents of the editor into any new or existing file, whether you are editing NONAME.C or not.

► *Warning Before Load*

Another helpful feature is that if you have a file already in the editor that has been modified since it was last saved, you will be asked to verify if you wish to save it before loading a new file. Replying Y for Yes will save your changes. Answering N for No will mean losing any changes made on the current file since Load clears the editor RAM when the new file is loaded.

► *Directory and Change Dir* ►

You can load a file from any drive or directory by entering the full path file name, or you can use Change dir to change your current drive/directory to that of your target file. The Directory option is useful for checking which directory is current and also for listing your files. As with the DOS DIR command and the Load entry box, you can create a *mask* using the wildcards * and ? to display sets of file names. As with Load, you can then select a particular file with the arrow keys, or use F4 to change the mask.

► *Setting/Saving the Compiler/Linker Options* ►

There are three simple but essential chores to complete before you play with HELLO.C. You need to tell Turbo C where your include and library files are located and then save this data in the configuration file TCCONFIG.TC. Use Alt-O to get from the edit window to the Options menu. The screen will look like Figure 1.5.

```
    File      Edit      Run    Compile    Project   Options     Debug
                                      Edit
       Line 1      Col 1   Insert Indent Tab C:HELLO.C  Compiler
/* hello.c - hello, world */                           Linker
                                                       Environment
#include <stdio.h>                                     Directories
                                                       Args
main()                                                 Retrieve options
{                                                      Store    options
        puts("hello, world\n");
}




                              Message




   F1-Help  F5-Zoom  F6-Edit  F9-Make  F1Ø-Main Menu
```

► *Figure 1.5:* Options menu display

Most of the Options offer submenus that show you the existing status of the particular option and offer you the means of changing it.

For reference, all the Options selections and submenus are listed in Table 1.4 and Table 1.5.

Compiler	Model, Defines, Code Generation, Optimization, Source, Errors, Names
Linker	Map file, Initialize segments, Default libraries, Warn duplicate symbols, Stack warning, Case-sensitive link
Environment	Include dirs, Output dir, Library dir, Turbo C dir, Auto-save edit, Backup source files, Zoomed windows
Args	Supply command-line arguments
Retrieve options	Load saved configuration file
Store options	Save options in configuration file

► **Table 1.4:** *Options menu selections in Versions 1 and 1.5*

Compiler	[same as Versions 1., 1.5]
Linker	[same as Versions 1., 1.5] Graphics library
Directories	Include dirs, Library dirs, Output dir, Turbo C dir, Pick file name, Current pick file
Environment	Message tracking, Keep messages, Config auto-save, Edit auto-save, Backup files, Tab size, Zoomed windows, Screen lines+
Args	[same as Versions 1., 1.5]
Retrieve options	[same as Versions 1., 1.5]
Save options	Save options in configuration file

► **Table 1.5:** *Options menu selections in Version 2. (+ indicates a lower level of submenu.)*

► *Setting the Include Directories*

Type E to get the Environment submenu (or D for Directories in Version 2), then select I for Include. You then enter the directory, usually C:\INCLUDE, where your standard include files are stored. In particular, the first include directive in HELLO.C is

```
#include <stdio.h>
```

When you compile HELLO.C, the Turbo C preprocessor will search for the header file C:\INCLUDE\STDIO.H. If found, it is loaded into memory with HELLO.C, making available a series of macro definitions and function declarations that form part of the C standard I/O routines.

If you fail to set an include directory, Turbo C will look in the current directory, and in the likely event that STDIO.H is not found you will get an error message if and when the compiler encounters a reference to an object defined in STDIO.H. Recall that the .H files are really a convenience that save you from entering commonly needed source text. Certain common .H files often get #included as a matter of habit, whether needed or not, on the grounds that there is little or no overhead and it's better to be safe than sorry!

For more advanced users, there is the possibility of setting up multiple include directories. For example, C:\INCLUDE;C\SPECIAL lets the preprocessor search both directories for include files.

► *Setting the Library Directory*

Next, select L for for Library directory and enter C:\LIB (or wherever you have your start-up CO?.OBJ and run time library routines, *.LIB).

► *Saving Your Options*

Now escape back to the Options menu and select S for Store options. The default file where your options are stored (and retrieved by Turbo C when it fires up) is TCCONFIG.TC. This file name will appear in response to selecting S, so just press Enter to save the options there. Later on, when you encounter the host of options available, you will appreciate the advantage of being able to store several different configuration files. By using the Retrieve menu, you can switch configurations without going through a lengthy options session each time.

► *RUNNING HELLO.C* ►

From the main menu select R for Run (or press Alt-R from anywhere). In Version 2 you must make an additional selection from the Run menu. If you've been following closely you may ask, How can Turbo C possibly run HELLO unless it finds HELLO.EXE? And how can it produce HELLO.EXE without HELLO.OBJ? HELLO.C by itself certainly cannot be executed.

The answer is that Turbo C is smart enough to check around and decide on the steps needed to carry out the Run command. In the present situation Turbo C quickly determines that HELLO.OBJ and HELLO.EXE are both missing, so it invokes the preprocessor/compiler/linker sequence discussed earlier:

HELLO.C → preprocessor → HELLO.C + *<included-files>*
→ compiler → HELLO.OBJ → linker → HELLO.EXE

(The output .OBJ and .EXE files appear in the current directory and are named HELLO by default. The menu options allowing you to change the output directories and/or the names need not detain us here—see Environment under Table 1.4.)

► *The Run Itself* ►

The Run menu triggers a burst of activity: Progress windows show you each phase in the creation of HELLO.EXE, and it is then immediately run (providing there are no errors). The screen will clear and display **hello, world**, as promised ten pages ago. Hit any key and you will return to Turbo C. (In Version 2 you use Alt-F5 to toggle between the IDE and the user screen.)Now press Alt-X to give Turbo C a well-earned rest.

Entering DIR HELLO reveals that you have HELLO.OBJ and HELLO.EXE in addition to HELLO.C. Type HELLO and press Enter to prove that HELLO.EXE performs as it did from inside Turbo C (apart from the screen clearing, which is performed by Turbo C not by HELLO.C).

If you immediately returned to Turbo C, loaded HELLO, and invoked Run, Turbo C would naturally find no need to compile/link, and HELLO.EXE would be executed posthaste.

► *HELLO.C—ANATOMY LESSON* ►

We leave Turbo C, per se, to study line by line the text of HELLO.C (Program 1.1). It reveals several major facts about every C program.

```
/* hello.c--hello, world */
#include <stdio.h>
main()
{
        printf("hello, world\n");
}
```

► *Program 1.1:* HELLO.C

► *Comments (Line 1)* ►

► */* hello.c—hello, world */* You are free, nay, encouraged, to sprinkle your source with *comments*. Any text you care to enter between */* and */* is ignored by the compiler (it is treated as white space). Like a **REM** line in BASIC, this text is there to help you and your next of kin. Since C allows many compact, unobvious expressions, commenting the obscurities is more necessary than with "verbose" languages such as Modula-2. Comments also provide a method of declaring version numbers, dates, authorship, and copyright. Remember, too, that statements that might appear crystal clear today can become obscure as time goes by.

Unlike BASIC's **REM**, C comments can straddle lines.

```
/*
    this is a comment
    so is this */
```

Standard C does not permit the *nesting* of comments. In other words, you cannot insert comments in a piece of code that already contains comments. If you added */* and */* as follows, hoping to effectively remove the **#include** line, it would not work.

```
/*
/* hello.c—hello, world */

#include <stdio.h> */
```

The first */* encountered would be matched with the opening */*, and commenting would cease prematurely. Turbo C offers a nesting comment option via the **O**ptions menu, but using it can jeopardize program portability. You'll meet a safer way of *commenting out* when we discuss the #if directive.

► *White Space (Lines 2 and 4)* ►

The empty lines form *white space* that is ignored by the compiler. Generally speaking, carriage return, line feed, space, and tab codes, apart from serving as possible identifier separators, have no syntactic significance. In other words, if one space is needed after an identifier then several spaces or tabs are acceptable. The physical layout of a C program can be arranged for maximum legibility without affecting its meaning. C contrasts sharply with BASIC, say, in which a new line is always syntactically significant. HELLO.C would not be compiled differently if you retyped it as

```
/* hello.c—hello, world */
#include <stdio.h>
main( ) {printf("hello, world\n");}
```

You *must* move to a new line after a directive, by the way, to prevent possible parsing problems with the preprocessor.

► *Include Directive (Line 3)* ►

► *#include <stdio.h>*   As explained earlier, the # symbol indicates that the following identifier is a preprocessor *directive*. In this instance, **#include** directs the preprocessor to add the source code of the file stdio.h to the rest of HELLO.C prior to compilation.

You can tell the system where to find stdio.h by using full drive/path information, or you can use angle brackets, as in **<stdio.h>**, meaning "look first in the \include directory as preset in the Options menu."

You can also write **#include "stdio.h"** using double quotes. This says, "look first in the working directory." For our purposes the *<filename>* method will suffice.

We'll return to study the contents of stdio.h after we've looked at functions and definitions.

► *The main( ) Function (Line 5)* ►

► *main( )*   A C program consists of a series of *functions*. In C the word *function* is used in a wider sense than in most other languages. C functions subsume the notions of subroutine and procedure as well as the "conventional" function of BASIC or Pascal.

With C almost any block of statements can be lumped together to *define* a function to which a unique name is assigned. When that name is encountered anywhere in a program, the function is *called* or *invoked*, and the statements used to define the function are obeyed.

The block of statements defining the action of a function can include calls to other previously defined functions (including itself, *recursively*, as we say), which in turn may contain calls to other predefined functions, and so on.

Functions are therefore the heart and soul of C, and much of this book is devoted to showing how functions are built up from more primitive elements, including libraries of machine-specific functions used for I/O and memory management, for example.

When a function needs input data, referred to as *arguments* or *parameters*, they appear within parentheses after the function name and are separated by commas.

function name(arg1, arg2, arg3,...);

You can picture the above statement as an instruction to the system to perform the previously defined function, *function name*, using the given values *arg1*, *arg2*, and so on. Some functions take a fixed number of arguments (including none), while others can take a varying number (including none), depending on the circumstances.

A familiar example from mathematics would be the function, **cube(N)**, which calculates the cube of the single argument *N*. Calling **cube(3)** would *return* **27**. *N* is called a *formal parameter* to distinguish it from the **3**, which is the *actual* or *real* parameter used when calling cube. Much more on this important subject anon.

The action of a function will depend entirely on the statements used in its definition and the particular values of the arguments supplied, if any. The result may be a useful *returned* value, as with conventional functions, or it may simply be an action such as displaying a message on the screen, as with conventional procedures.

You soon learn to look on functions as black boxes—you shove values in and get values or actions out. Life is too short to know exactly what goes on inside every black box. Have faith!

When a function requires no arguments, C notation still requires that you put parentheses after the function name even though there is nothing within them. In some circumstances to be discussed later, the absence of arguments is made more explicit by writing *function name* (void). The parentheses convention makes it easier for you *and* the compiler to spot the functions in any piece of source code! Note that we will often write *name*( ) without bothering to spell out the arguments to indicate that we are discussing a function rather than some other object called *name*.

You can now rightly deduce that in HELLO.C **main( )** is a function called with no arguments, whereas **printf( )** is a function called with one *string* argument. In HELLO.C the string argument happens to be a *string constant* or *string literal* for the obvious reasons that its value, **hello, world\n**, remains fixed and is expressed "literally." Later you'll meet *string variables* that can assume different string values at the whim of the programmer. The function **printf( )** can accept both kinds of string arguments and other types of arguments, by the way.

A string constant in C is any sequence of characters between double quotes, as in "**hello, world\n**". In technical parlance a string is an *array* of characters terminated by the ASCII NUL character (value 0). You don't ever "see" this NUL, but it's stored at the end of every string, or, to be more accurate, it *is* the end of every string (hence the song "Without A NUL, That String Would Never End!").

The strange looking \n provides a *newline character* and will be explained later in this chapter.

Note in passing that under different circumstances, **main( )** and **printf( )** might be invoked with a different number of arguments.

The function **main( )** has a unique role to play in all C programs. Since a C program consists of sequences of functions, you may wonder which one fires up first. The answer is that **main( )**, wherever it is placed physically in the source code, is the "leader." Every complete C program must have just one **main( )** somewhere, and this is where C starts off when executing the compiled/linked code. To see what **main( )** does, you need to look at the block or body of code following it. This leads us to the next feature of HELLO.C, *block markers*.

► *Block Markers (Lines 6 and 8)* ►

► { }   Curly braces are used to signal the start and end of a block of code. They play the same role as **BEGIN** and **END** in other structured languages.

To discover what **main( )** does, you need to check out all the statements lying between the first { following **main( )** and its matching final }. This is quite simple in the case of HELLO.C since you find only the single statement

```
{
    printf("hello, world\n");
}
```

In real-world programs, **main( )** could have many other blocks *nested* inside the outer, or principal, { and } block markers. The number of {'s must always match the number of }'s, of course. There are typographical conventions to help the eye in detecting nested blocks, and these will emerge as we proceed.

The key point here is that any lump of code placed between matching pairs of curly braces represents a block that tells the compiler how to break down and process "units" of the program. In simple terms, a group of statements within { and } acts like a single, compound statement. The block concept will be clarified when you see more complex situations.

► *The printf( ) Function Call (Line 7)* ►

► *printf("hello, world\n");*   As you've seen, the body of **main( )** contains the single line shown above, which is a call to the function **printf( )** with a string constant as argument.

printf( ) is a precompiled library function supplied with Turbo C (and all other conforming C compilers) that displays formatted (hence the *f* in *printf*) strings of characters on your *standard output* device, which for the moment simply means your monitor screen.

The name *print* is a well-entrenched archaism dating back to those sybaritic days when output terminals were teleprinters or Flexowriters. Nowadays we have CRT's (also known as *glass teleprinters*) but the verb "print," meaning "display," still survives.

The particular version of **printf( )** supplied with the Turbo C library has been written specifically for the computers in the IBM PC family (or compatibles) running under DOS. The C language achieves portability by not getting involved directly with all the machine- and OS-dependent tricks needed for device and file I/O. Your HELLO.C would compile and run on a Cray or

VAX because their libraries contain a **printf( )** written specially for their respective hardware and operating systems.

    printf( ) turns out to be quite a complex function, able to accept a variable number of parameters. Its usage in HELLO.C hides the fact that it can be used to display both numbers and strings in a wide range of formats. To display a single string like **hello, world** you can actually use a much simpler function called **puts( )**. You'll see this shortly in an exercise with the Turbo C editor.

► *The Escape Sequence (Line 7)* ►

    ► **\n**   The escape character \ (familiar to UNIX users) is used to solve the problem of inserting nonprintable control codes or difficult characters into a string. For example, it's clearly impossible to plant a new line after **hello, world** by pressing Enter as in

    printf("hello, world<Enter>");

The Enter key does give a new line on the screen during input, but the compiler ignores it! To get a true new line you type the escape sequence \n.

    Similarly, there is a problem if you want to display a string containing *real* double quotes. In

    printf("I am saying "Hello"");

Turbo C would take the second " as an end to the string "**I am saying** ". What to do? You use the escape sequence \" for the internal double quotes as in

    printf("I am saying \"Hello\"");

which will display, **I am saying "Hello"**.

    The escape character \ tells the compiler to treat the following character(s) in an unusual way, i.e. *escape* from the normal interpretation. Such characters are sometimes called *metacharacters* since they have significance outside the normal set. Table 1.6 indicates how Turbo C translates the escape sequences.

Sequence	Value	ASCII	Function
\0	0	NUL	String terminator
\a	0x07	BEL	Audible bell ("attention")
\b	0x08	BS	Backspace
\f	0x0C	FF	Form feed
\n	0x0A	LF	New line (line feed)
\r	0x0D	CR	Carriage return
\t	0x09	HT	Horizontal tab
\v	0x0B	VT	Vertical tab
\\	0x5C	\	Backslash
\'	0x27	'	Single quote (apostrophe)
\"	0x22	"	Double quote
\?	0x3F	?	Question mark
\ddd	0ddd	any	1 to 3 digit octal value
\xhh	0xhh	any	1 to 2 digit hex value

► *In the Value column, octal constants start with 0 and hex constants start with 0x. This 0 is not needed after \.*

► **Table 1.6:** *Escape sequences*

► *Escape with Special Characters*

Because the single apostrophe has the special function of designating single character constants, you can see why \' is needed to express a literal '. Similarly, \\ must be used to get a single literal \. The first \ protects the following character from being treated as a metacharacter, so '\'' means the ASCII character 047 or 0x27 (''' is illegal), and '\\' means the ASCII character 0134 or 0x5C ('\' will not work!).

► *Back to \n*

Coming back to \n, note that in place of

```
printf("hello, world\n");
```

you could achieve the same result with

```
printf("hello, ");
printf("world");
printf("\n");
```

The first statement displays **hello,** and leaves the cursor sitting after the space, waiting for something to happen. Then **world** is displayed, and, finally, **printf("\n");** provides a new line on the screen. Yes, **printf("\n\n\a\a");** would give two new lines followed by two ringy-dingies (ASCII BEL character).

Once you've mastered the Turbo C editor, you can "ring" the changes on HELLO.C with such variants as

```
printf("\t\\hello\t\a\aworld\n\n");
```

This would display a tab indent followed by \hello. You would then get two rings, and **world** followed by two new lines would be displayed.

► *A Detour into Data Types* ►

Individual character constants, as opposed to strings of them, can be expressed with single quotes: '**A**', '\101', '\x41', and '\X41' all represent the same ASCII character.

You may be wondering if there is any difference between the single character '**A**' and the one-character string "**A**". There are two differences worthy of a slight detour.

1. '**A**' and "**A**" are different *data types*. '**A**' is of type **char**, stored and treated numerically as an integer, whereas "**A**" is of type *array of* **char**. It just happens that in this example the array holds one significant character.

   As in Pascal (but unlike BASIC) C requires that the data type of each identifier be *declared* before it is used in a program.

   The "why" of declarations is quite simple: The compiler can use them to efficiently allocate memory for each constant and variable and possibly check that your statements make sense (adding chalk and cheese may not be allowed). The "how" of declarations is not so easy and will be revealed as time goes by.

2. Since "**A**" is a string, it requires a final NUL, so it's stored in two bytes—"**A**" and NUL. Single character constants strictly need only

one byte, but C treats them as integers as a matter of arithmetical convenience (permitting such tricks as (**'A'** + **1**) to give **'B'**). Turbo C stores **int** type integers in two bytes, reflecting the 16-bit registers of the IBM PC microprocessor. So, when you store a single character constant as a 2-byte integer what happens to the other byte? In the case of **'A'**, the lower byte would contain 0x41 with the upper byte usually *sign extended*, i.e., filled with 0's or 1's, depending on the value of the eighth (most significant or sign) bit of the lower byte. For characters in the standard ASCII range (decimal values 0–127), the sign bit is 0, so the upper byte is 0x00.

► *Statement Terminator (Line 7)* ►

► **;** The semicolon at the end of the **printf( )** line indicates the end of a *statement*. It is officially called a *statement terminator* in C to distinguish it from statement *separator* symbols used in other languages.

In C a line of text can contain several statements, and a statement can straddle several lines, so the **;** plays a vital role in telling the compiler how to translate your code correctly. Note, however, that no **;** is needed after the final **}** block marker. The compiler already knows the statement is ended.

You *can* legally enter a **;** without having a prior statement. This represents a nul or *empty* statement, which sounds rather Zen but does prove useful in situations in which the syntax demands a statement but there is no action required. (Compare this with **NOP**, the *no operation* instruction found in assembly languages.)

Note also that no semicolon is needed after the **#include** directive. The preprocessor has its own set of rules, one of which is that directives are terminated by a new line.

► *Statements and Expressions—Another Necessary Detour* ►

A C program normally runs by executing each of its statements in sequence, just as you would read them on the page. This sequential execution can be altered using various *control flow* or *conditional* statements, such as

    if *(expression)* {*statement(s)*}

which says, "carry out {***statement(s)***} only if (***expression***) is true. Another example is

   while (***expression***) {*statement(s)*}

which says, "keep obeying {***statement(s)***} while (***expression***) is true. There are no special Boolean data types in C, by the way. False simply means 0, and true means nonzero (usually 1).

   These concepts are introduced briefly here to illustrate the use of the statement terminator. (The whole of Chapter 4 is devoted to C's armory of control flow constructs—without which, of course, programs would be confined to dull slogging through fixed sequences.) Informally, we can offer the approximate hierarchy of C language constructs shown in Table 1.7.

C	English	Examples
operands (variables & constants)	words	sum, total, flag "hello", 'A', 3
operators (arithmetic, logic, etc.)	verbs	== , = , * , +
expressions	phrases	(sum == total) flag = 1 total = sum + 3
statements	sentences	flag = 1; total = sum + 3;
complex statement	long sentence	if (sum == total) flag = 1;

► *Table 1.7:* C constructs with approximate English equivalents

The last example means, "if the values represented by sum and total are equal, then set flag to value 1." Note that the *assignment* operator (=) and the *equality* operator (==) are different. In the example of a complex statement, there is no ; after the *expression* (**sum == total**)—the whole statement does not terminate until after the *statement* **flag = 1;**.

   Expressions in C are unusually active creatures: They not only trigger the appropriate activity according to the operands and operators found therein but are also *evaluated* in the sense that they actually acquire a value that reflects the operation.

This is so unlike BASIC and Pascal that it can be somewhat disconcerting to the beginner. The expression **flag = 1** not only assigns the value 1 to **flag** but also "takes on" the value of **flag**, namely 1. So, you can find busy statements like

total = (sum = 2) + 3;   /* set sum to 2 and total to 5 */

or

total = sum = 3;   /* set sum and total to 3 */

Expressions that pack a lot of punch give C its unique flavor but can lead to over-compact, hard-to-read code if taken to extremes.

As soon as you add the magic semicolon you complete that particular statement. Turbo C will pause to digest, as it were, all the rubbish since the previous ; or }, and all the expressions in the statement will be obeyed and evaluated according to the precise rules of *precedence* and *associativity*. Depending on any conditionals encountered, execution will resume with the next or some other statement.

► *HELLO.C Summary* ►

I seem to have been continually sidetracked while trying to divine the modus operandi of my naive example, so I'll recapitulate. The key points can be summarized as follows:

1. Source code HELLO.C plus STDIO.H compiles to form HELLO.OBJ. HELLO.OBJ is linked with object code in the Turbo C library to give us the executable file HELLO.EXE.

2. You learned how to set up options on the Turbo C Integrated Development Environment and load and run a program from the main menu.

3. The anatomy of HELLO.C:

   /* */ for comments
   directives: #include <stdio.h>
   new line after directives—no semicolon
   white space for pretty layout
   the **main( )** function
   the function body and block markers {}

printf( ) and function arguments
string constants: "**hello, world\n**"
escape sequences: **\n** for a new line
statement terminator: semicolon

► ERRORS ►

Having successfully reached the stage when an .EXE file is produced, your program is ready to run. Congratulations! Your source code has passed the inexorable Turbo C syntax checker built into the compiler. Rest assured that you will see Turbo C's reaction to illegal or doubtful statements before many moons have passed.

► *Compile-Time Errors* ►

Unlike the BASIC interpreter you may be used to, Turbo C does not immediately spot syntax errors on a line-by-line basis. Rather, being a compiler, Turbo C inspects as much of your complete source code as possible before reporting your errors and inviting corrections. Such errors and warnings are referred to as *compile-time* problems.

Warnings are usually nonfatal, whereas errors must be corrected and the program recompiled and relinked before further progress is possible. The Make utility is a clever aid in such situations; using the project files mentioned earlier, it can help automate the recompiling and relinking process depending on *which* files have changed since the last compilation.

Several C interpreters or combined interpreter/compilers are now available. The trade-off is traditionally between the higher execution speed of compilers and the immediate error detection of interpreters. In fact, Turbo C compiles quickly enough to settle such arguments.

Some errors may surface during linking, such as missing or misplaced .OBJ files, but these are easily corrected by telling the linker where to look. The linker may also uncover discrepancies between the modules. I'll tell you more on this when I discuss the Turbo C menus.

► *Run-Time Errors* ►

The completed .EXE file contains all the machine code required for loading and execution by your operating system (PC-DOS or MS-DOS). Just like the many .EXE files provided with DOS, your newly created .EXE file can be invoked at any time by simply typing HELLO at the C> prompt and pressing Enter.

The fact that your code is free from syntax and other compile- and link-time errors does not guarantee that the .EXE program will run as expected or at all! *Run-time* errors come in many delicious flavors, ranging from endless loops to total system crashes, from polite error messages to getting the wrong results without a warning.

As with natural languages, you need to distinguish *syntax* (superficial conformity) from *semantics* (the deep meaning, if any). Legal statements, alas, may compile into nonsense that the system cannot usefully execute or even survive. The C language, you'll discover, is not especially mollycoddling as are Ada, Pascal, or Modula-2. In providing the power and compact notation to let you operate efficiently and close to the "machine level," the C syntax places fewer restrictions on the dumb and dangerous things you can do if you really try. C, as it were, is like assembly language in that it assumes you can handle a loaded shotgun without a safety catch. Other languages worry about your competence and make you line up for firearm permits.

Another real possibility is that your program might run to completion but fail to reflect your intentions. Either your original problem analysis, input data, or algorithms are faulty, or there are errors in your coding (or all of the above). An essential part of mastering Turbo C (and any other programming language) is to develop debugging skills to track down and fix such problems. Some guidance on this vast subject will be provided in later chapters, but don't expect any magical sesames. Chapter 11 explains the tools that Version 2 provides to help you zap those elusive insects.

Finally, with software as complex as DOS and the Turbo C package, you cannot entirely rule out bugs (also known as unpublished features) in the systems software. Since the latter probably have been subjected to more testing than your own programs, it is wise to double-check your work before blaming others. If you feel certain that the systems software is at fault, your report to the software vendor *must* be precisely documented with your program listings, screen printouts, hardware configuration, DOS level, and the serial numbers of your package. Unless your reported bug can be repeated under your exact configuration and environment, it will be virtually impossible to fix.

► *USING THE TURBO C EDITOR* ►

Because .C and .H files are ASCII text files, you can use almost any text editor to create and modify your source files. Most word processing packages offer a *nondocument* option that avoids peculiar formatting and typesetting codes that might upset the compiler. Since Borland includes a very flexible text editor with Turbo C that is specially equipped to produce readable .C files, it makes sense to try it out. This editor arrives set to work almost exactly like the nondocument mode of the popular WordStar package from MicroPro International, but the TCINST installation program, detailed in Appendix B, allows you to customize the editor to suit your own bizarre prejudices.

I will not, therefore, confuse (or bore) you with a key-by-key account of the editing process itself. When I do refer to specific editor control keys, I will use the standard Turbo C versions. If you are new to any form of text editing, the only way forward is constant practice and experiment with the following basic maneuvers:

► *Basic Editing Features* ►

► ***Cursor movement*** Moving right/left/up/down; moving to end/start of words, lines, screens, blocks, and files. Scrolling and paging up and down. Note that the line and column numbers are displayed dynamically on the top line of the edit window, known as the edit window status line.

► ***Auto-indent*** Toggled on/off by pressing Ctrl-O I. When off, pressing Enter gives a new line without indenting. When on, pressing Enter positions the cursor on the next line but aligned under the first character of the previous line. Auto-indent makes it easier to produce legible "structured" text, since indents clearly indicate the relative level of nested blocks. The edit window status line displays **Indent** when auto-indent is on.

► ***Insert on/off*** Toggled with the Ins key, determines whether your typing will write over (insert off) or "push" (insert on) existing text. Watch for the **Insert** legend on the editor window status line.

► ***Tab mode*** Toggle with Ctrl-O T. Again, the status line indicates the mode in force. With tab mode on, the tab key inserts tab codes in the text (white space) and tabs the cursor modulo 8 spaces. With tab mode off, the cursor spaces to positions determined by the words of the previous line.

► ***Deleting*** Use Del and backspace to remove a character under or to the left of the cursor. Use control combinations to erase words, whole or part lines, or blocks.

► *Block marking*   Move, copy, delete, write-to-disk marked blocks.

► *Search and replace*   Hunt for a target string with or without a replacement string. Many options, allowing forward and backward searches with or without case sensitivity, with or without prompted replacements, with or without counted matches, with or without whole word matching, and so on.

► *Saving, renaming, and quitting*   It is worth stressing the importance of the hot key F2, which allows you to save work in progress during an editing session. You can also quit without saving.

► *HELLO.C VARIATIONS* ►

To give you some useful practice with the built-in Turbo C editor (as well as to extend your knowledge of C) make a copy of HELLO.C called HELLO1.C. Load HELLO1.C into the editor and try the following:

1. Alter the opening comments, changing **printf** to **puts** and removing the \n from the "**hello, world**" string. Use F2 to save your changes. Your program should now look like Program 1.2.

The function **puts( )** means, "put string." Like **printf( )**, it is declared in **stdio.h**. **puts( )** is a simpler version of **printf( )**, taking only a single string argument and performing no formatting. **puts( )**, unlike **printf( )**, automatically appends a new line after displaying the string. *Put*, like *print*, is a common synonym in C for outputting *to* some device or file.

To gain familiarity with the menus, follow the procedure outlined below.

```
/* hello1.c--hello, world variation */
#include <stdio.h>
main()
{
    puts("hello, world");
}
```

► *Program 1.2: HELLO1.C*

► *Compiling HELLO1.C* ►

Press Alt-C for the compile menu. Select C (Compile to .OBJ) to produce HELLO1.OBJ. You can follow the progress of the compiler in the compile window. If all is well, a flashing **Press any key** message appears alongside the **success** message, and you can pass to "Linking HELLO1.C," below.

► *Error Correction (If Any)* ►

If you have mistyped, the compile window tells you how many errors and warnings have been generated. Hitting any key takes you to the message window where you get a highlighted error message indicating your first mistake. Any other errors will be listed below the highlighted one. The arrow keys can be used to highlight such errors. As you move around the message window, the corresponding error in the source code is *tracked*, i.e., highlighted in the edit window. Hitting Enter takes you to the offending line so you can correct it. You then press F6 to get back to the message window, select another error, and so on. Alternatively, you can press F8 (next error) or F7 (previous error) while in the edit window, and the cursor will move to the appropriate error. Version 2 uses Alt-F8 for next error and Alt-F7 for previous error.

When all the errors appear to have been corrected, you must recompile, recorrect, and re-recompile until you get it right! You will soon discover that a single source code error can often generate a host of apparently unrelated error messages. The reason for this disconcerting phenomenon will emerge as you learn more of the C syntax.

► *Linking HELLO1.C* ►

Select L (Link EXE file) in the Compile menu to produce HELLO1.EXE. Notice the progress window showing the linking process. Turbo C is busy looking in the LIB directory for any referenced library functions. Again, success is signaled with a **Press any key** message. You can now select Run in the main menu (or Alt-R directly). Since HELLO1.EXE exists, Turbo C runs it immediately. The action of HELLO1.EXE is exactly the same as HELLO.EXE.

► *Making HELLO1.EXE* ►

Now select M (Make .EXE file) from the Compile menu to invoke Project-Make. Note the name HELLO1.EXE appearing alongside the Make legend.

Turbo C quickly checks that HELLO1.C and HELLO1.OBJ have not changed since HELLO1.EXE was formed, so you get a message saying that the *dependencies* check out OK, and no further action is taken.

You could have used Project-Make initially in place of separate Compile and Link operations, but I wanted to give you some exercise. The Make option is the simplest and safest path to the .EXE file, since in the absence of either a .OBJ or .EXE file (or if they are relatively antiquated) the compiler/ linker will be invoked for you.

Of course, if you want to *run* your program immediately, the Run menu also invokes Project-Make, checks the dependencies, calls the compiler/ liner as needed, and then executes the .EXE file.

► *HELLO2.C* ►

The next variation to try is shown in HELLO2.C, (Program 1.3). It introduces the **#define** directive, which is C's basic mechanism for creating *macros* and *aliases*.

The line added to HELLO1.C is

#define GREETING "hello, world"

and the argument for **puts( )** is changed to **GREETING**.

As with the **#include** directive, the # before **define** triggers action by the preprocessor. Each subsequent appearance of the *identifier* **GREETING** anywhere in your source code will be replaced by the string "**hello, world**" *before* compilation commences. So, when the preprocessor meets **puts (GREETING)**, the function call is changed to **puts("hello, world")**. We have concocted yet another way of achieving K&R's original goal!

```
/* hello2.c--hello, world variant */
#include <stdio.h>
#define GREETING "hello, world"
main()
{
     puts(GREETING);
}
```

► *Program 1.3: HELLO2.C*

If the preprocessor encounters the sequence **GREETING** *inside* a string, no substitution takes place. For example,

    puts("GREETINGs dear friend");

will *not* be affected by the definition.

The use of **#define** here is somewhat artificial, but suppose that for some obscure reason you wanted to write a longer program peppered with occurrences of the string **"hello, world"**. The one **#define** directive would eventually pay off in terms of reduced keystrokes. Before we assess the other advantages of **#define**, let's review the syntax involved. The general format for simple token substitution or aliasing is

    #define *identifier string*

where you need at least one space or tab between each section and a final new line immediately after **string**. If the string is too long to fit a single line, you can use the escape character (backslash) before the new line, then continue typing the rest of the string on the next line as in

    #define WARNING "This is a very long warning, so I need a \
    to avoid going off the screen"

Remember that a semicolon is a *statement* terminator, so you don't need one at the end of a directive.

► *IDENTIFIER RULES* ►

The identifier in the **#define** line (called the *macro name*) must conform to the basic rules for all C identifiers:

1. Identifiers must start with an uppercase or lowercase letter or an underscore (_).

2. After the initial letter or underscore, you can have any number of characters from the following set: A–Z, a–z, underscore, slash (/), or the digits 0–9. Turbo C actually uses only the first thirty-two characters of an identifier, however, so you should really show some

restraint. The following two identifiers would not be distinct:

```
This_is_long_variable_numbered_10
This_is_long_variable_numbered_11
```

3. Because C is case sensitive, **Greeting** and **greeting** are distinct from **GREETING** and would not be affected by our **#define** directive.

4. It is customary but not mandatory to use all uppercase letters for macro-name identifiers simply to give a visual clue that they are not ordinary identifiers.

5. There are fifty-eight *keywords* in Turbo C that have preassigned meanings (see Table 1.8). These either cannot or should not be used as identifiers. Some reserved words may be used legitimately as macro names under special circumstances (usually to allow compatibility with pre-ANSI compilers), but the novice should accept the fact that keywords should only be used as nature intended. By the end of this book you will know the purpose of each of these keywords!

6. An initial underscore is traditionally reserved for *external* identifiers. You should avoid using such identifiers for your own internal objects.

► SUBSTITUTION STRING RULES ►

There are none! You can enter any sequence of characters, and they will be literally and exactly inserted in your source text, wherever the given identifier is found. The only exception is the line-continuation trick using a backslash in which the backslash is not really part of the string.

Whether the substitution makes contextual sense will be determined by the compiler, not the preprocessor. This turns out to be an important issue when you meet more complex situations. A good safety-first rule is to enclose the string in parentheses to give it "syntactical" protection. The parentheses can do no harm, and they often prevent calamitous side effects due to C's precedence rules when evaluating complex expressions.

► DEFINING MACROS ►

The **#define** directive offers more than the simple substitution operation. Used as a *macro*, it allows arguments to be supplied, rather as you saw with

*asm	if	− cs
auto	int	− ds
break	*interrupt	− es
case	long	− ss
*cdecl	*near	− AH
char	*pascal	− AL
const	register	− AX
continue	return	− BH
default	short	− BL
do	signed	− CH
double	sizeof	− CL
else	static	− CX
enum	struct	− DH
extern	switch	− DL
*far	typedef	− DX
float	union	− BP
for	unsigned	− DI
goto	void	− SI
*huge	volatile	− SP
	while	

► *Keywords marked with an * are exclusive to Turbo C, as are the special register symbols (in column 3).*

► **Table 1.8:** *Turbo C keywords*

functions. As with functions, you use (and) immediately after the macro name as in

```
#define cube(x)    ((x)*(x)*(x))      /* x is formal parameter */
/* "*" is the multiplication operator */
```

The string now defines how the formal parameters (just **x** in this case, but there may be more than one) are applied when the preprocessor encounters the token **cube** in the source text. So, **cube(3);** would be converted to ((3)*(3)*(3)) in situ before compilation, and **cube(a + b);** would become ((a + b)*(a + b)*(a + b)), which may help you see the need for the parentheses in the **#define** line! Without them, you would get an ambiguous or erroneous result since a + b*a + b*a + b equals a + (b*a) + (b*a) + b because C places * higher in precedence than +. More on this anon.

► ON YOUR OWN ►

Write and compile Program 1.4 as a tribute to Philippe Kahn, the president of Borland International.

```
/*   BONJOUR.C -- Hello, Philippe */
#include <stdio.h>
main()
{
     puts("Bonjour, joli monde!\n");
}
```

► *Program 1.4:* BONJOUR.C

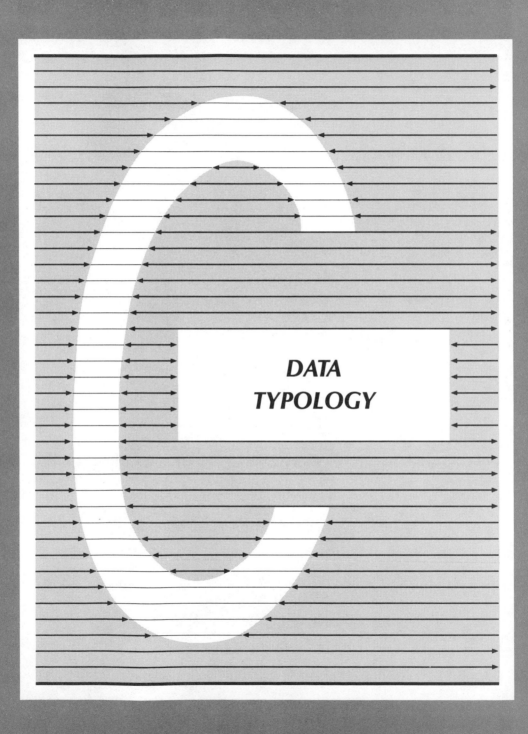

DATA
TYPOLOGY

► *CHAPTER 2* ►

In Chapter 1, I introduced informally the concept of *data types*, explaining that Turbo C needs to allocate appropriate amounts of memory to store different classes of objects. To keep my initial programs simple, I used only a special and rather limited class of data types known as *constants*. (I used character and string constants.) In this chapter you'll meet the arithmetical constants known as integers, but first you'll learn how to use integers as *variables*. There will be a certain amount of essential theory supported with examples before you return to the fun of TC.EXE.

To avoid repetition, many of the examples will be extracts rather than complete, compilable programs. Such snippets will not have the proper header files with a **main( )** function, and so on. Complete programs are given file names and program references, e.g., Program 2.3 is the third full program in Chapter 2.

► *WHY DATA TYPES?* ►

Now the compiler can determine the data types and memory requirements of constants from their actual typographical formats as they are encountered in the source text. However, when we use variables, the system needs some prior warning as to which data type we intend. Each data type has predetermined memory requirements and an associated range of legal values. This advanced warning is known as a data type *declaration*.

Data typing separates the identifiers used to denote variables into more or less immiscible categories, allowing the compiler to detect certain errors (like the proverbial adding of apples to pears or dividing chalk by cheese).

In *strongly typed* languages like Modula-2 and Ada, the data typing is strictly enforced so that even closely related data types cannot be intermixed without the programmer giving specific permission (or *type casting*). C is a *weakly typed* language, meaning that in many situations the compiler will quietly convert your data types to achieve compatibility within a mixed expression. It is rather like achieving *apples* + *pears* by first changing both to *fruit*.

Is strong typing better than weak typing? Each language has its own rationale and its own band of voluble fans. C expects you to know its internal data-type conversion policy and wastes little space or time in policing your assignments and arithmetic. The strongly typed language supporters prefer security even at the expense of compiler size and runtime efficiency.

► INTEGER VARIABLES ►

Integers, or *whole* numbers, are either positive, negative, or zero.

With Turbo C (and other IBM PC C implementations), integer variables (and constants) end up in 16 or 32-bit two's-complement form, which is the natural arithmetical mode of the 8088/8086/80286/80386 instruction sets. Because different computers have different register widths, though, C does not set standard bit sizes for objects like integers, nor does it dictate how numbers should be internally represented, for example as one's-complement or two's-complement. (I'll explain two's complement shortly.) Outside the mainframe world, 16- and 32-bit integer representations are the general rule, so Turbo C will give you widely portable code.

► int and long ►

By declaring an identifier (**sum**, for example) as an **int** (integer data type) you warn the compiler ahead of time that **sum** will need 16 bits to represent its legal range of values (from − 32,768 to + 32,767 for Turbo C). Exactly when the actual allocation takes place depends on factors to be discussed later.

Declaring **sum** as a **long** (or, equivalently, **long int**), tells the compiler that 32 bits will be needed, giving **sum** a legal range of − 2,147,483,648 to + 2,147,483,647.

Officially, C does not insist that **long** be longer (have more bits) than **int**—it insists only that **long** must not be shorter (have fewer bits) than **int**. For Turbo C, just remember that **int** is 16-bit and **long** is 32-bit. Other systems may have both **int** and **long** as 32-bit values, so some care is needed.

► *Short Integers* ►

C officially recognizes a third integer data type called **short int** (or **short** for short). As with **int** and **long**, the ANSI standards leave it up to each individual implementor to choose a suitable bit size for **short**, provided only that **int** is not shorter than **short**. The rules for the three integer types can be expressed informally as **long** >= **int** >= **short** where >= means "bit size is greater than or equal to."

You'll be relieved to learn that in Turbo C **short** and **int** are indeed the same 16-bit entities. For the moment, then, we will concentrate on **int** and **long**. If you come across **short** or **short int** while reading a non-Turbo C program, make a mental note that for some systems it *may* be smaller than **int**. In the big, wide world of C, the choice of integer data types can affect program portability.

► *Signed Integers* ►

Note that **int** and **long** are known as *signed* data types because they are stored and manipulated using the two's-complement convention whereby the leftmost or most significant bit (MSB) acts as a sign bit. The MSB for positive integers is 0, and for negative integers it is 1.

Under this regime, the **int** value − 1, for example, is written and stored as binary

    1111111111111111

(hex 0xFFFF, decimal $2^{16} - 1$), while − 32,768 is stored as

    1000000000000000

(hex 0x8000, decimal 2^{15}). The **long** version of − 2 would be binary

    11111111111111111111111111111110

(hex 0xFFFFFFFE, decimal $2^{32} - 2$). (If this section and the following one are not absolutely clear, you should read Appendix D, Computer Math

Roundup. You need to understand signed and unsigned binary arithmetic since C assumes that you know what you are doing—there are few checks on range overflow!)

► *Unsigned Integers* ►

Each of the signed integer types has a corresponding *unsigned* version—**unsigned int** and **unsigned long**. These types give non-negative ranges: 0 to +65,535 and 0 to +4,294,967,295, respectively. Unsigned integers treat the MSB as 2^{15} or 2^{31}, not as a sign bit. Table 2.1 summarizes the integer data types for Turbo C.

► *INTEGER DECLARATION SYNTAX* ►

If the compiler meets the identifier **sum** *before* its declaration has been made, an **undefined symbol: 'sum'** error message will be generated.

The simplest integer declarations take the following forms:

```
int sum;                    /* sum is declared to be of type int */

long grand_total;           /* grand_total is of type long int */
long int salary;            /* longwinded version of long salary */

unsigned int count;         /* count is an unsigned integer */
```

Specifier	Bit Size	Range
int short [int]	16	−32,768 to +32,767
unsigned int unsigned short [int]	16	0 to +65,535
long [int]	32	−2,147,483,648 to +2,147,483,647
unsigned long [int]	32	0 to +4,294,967,295
► *[int] means int is optional.*		

► *Table 2.1:* Integer data types

```
unsigned long big_count;        /* big_count is unsigned and long */
unsigned long int Big_Count;    /* so is Big_Count */
```

For the moment, I will make no distinction between *declaring* and *defining* an identifier. Technically, a declaration simply notifies the compiler of the name and nature of the beast (size and type), while a definition actually triggers the allocation of memory. In most cases we can gloss over the distinction since the declaration also defines the variable. Later, when you start creating your own functions, you will be declaring objects that may have already been defined elsewhere.

► *Type Specifiers* ►

The keywords **short**, **int**, and **long** are known as *type specifiers*. The optional specifier **unsigned** can precede and modify these type specifiers, as shown. (**Signed** is assumed in the absence of **unsigned**.)

The general syntax of simple integer declarations is

[unsigned] type-specifier identifier;

where the brackets around **unsigned** indicate that it is optional. I use italics here to indicate a lexical unit that can be replaced by an appropriate set of characters in the source code.

The identifier being declared follows the rules discussed in Chapter 1 (start with a letter or underscore, follow with up to 31 letters, numbers, or underscores, and avoid reserved keywords). This identifier is called a *simple declarator* to distinguish it from more complex forms used to declare pointers and arrays.

You need some white space (at least one space or tab) between the various elements like **unsigned** and **int**, and **int** and **sum**, and a final semicolon as a terminator. Although a declaration is not, strictly speaking, a C statement, it is terminated in the usual manner.

► *Multiple Declaration* ►

You can save keystrokes by declaring several identifiers of the same type using commas as separators.

```
int sum, total;              /* sum and total are of type int */
long grand_total, bignum, X;  /* three long ints */
unsigned int a, b, c, d;      /* four unsigned ints */
```

The first line is entirely equivalent to

```
int sum;
int total;
```

Now that you know how to declare an integer variable, let's look at some of the things you can do with it in a Turbo C program.

▶ INTEGER VARIABLE ASSIGNMENTS ▶

Having been declared, the above identifiers are hereinafter known to the program as integer *variables*, meaning that at any time during the course of the program they can be *assigned* different values within their particular integer range. Contrast this with constants, which normally remain saddled with their original value throughout the program. In the following, **sum** is a variable:

```
sum = 1;          /* sum now holds the value 1 */
sum = -356;       /* and now, -356 */
sum = 269;        /* sum changed to 269 */
sum = sum + 1;    /* sum becomes 270 */
```

In C, the assignment operator (=) works from right to left. In

left-value = right-expression;

the *right-expression* is evaluated first, then the result is assigned to the *left-value*. There are strict rules in C governing the kinds of objects you can legally use on the left and right sides of an assignment. For the moment, you need only these obvious rules:

1. The left-value must be a variable of some kind, able to "receive" the new value coming in from the right. Such variables are officially

known as *lvalues* (pronounced "el-values"). Only lvalues are legal on the left, receiving end of an assignment.

2. The right-expression must be capable of providing a value compatible with the lvalue, whatever that means. In cases where right and left are of different data types, C has its own strict rules whereby silent, internal conversions are applied to the right-expression, if possible, to make it compatible before making the assignment. Later you'll see that the programmer can intervene with *type casts* and *force* nonstandard conversions.

► *The Assignment Symbol* ►

In spite of appearances, the C assignment symbol must not be confused with that of the conventional algebraic equals sign. For example, writing the last statement of the previous example as the algebraic equation

sum = *sum* + 1

has no finite solution, while the valid algebraic lines

5 = *sum* + 1
sum + 2 = 35

would not make sense in C, since neither 5 nor *sum* + 2 are lvalues.

C uses two adjacent equals signs to distinguish the two concepts, equality (= =) and assignment (=):

if (sum == total) ....

is read as "if **sum** equals **total** ...." whereas

sum = total;

is read as "assign the value of **total** to the variable **sum**."

A popular mental model is to picture variables as labeled boxes. To find the current value of **sum**, you open the box marked **sum**! The assignment

```
sum = sum + 1;
```

means: "Look in the **sum** box, grab the value, add one to it, and put the new value back in the box." Other readers may be more comfortable with the image of **sum** as a 16- or 32-bit word in RAM being incremented via the 8088/8086 **ADD** instruction.

► INCREMENTS AND DECREMENTS ►

Incrementing (and decrementing) by 1 is such a common computing pastime that C offers several shorthand versions of the above type of assignment. To whet your appetite:

```
total = sum ++ ;         /* set total to sum, then inc sum by 1 */
total = sum -- ;         /* set total to sum, then dec sum by 1 */

total = ++ sum;          /* set sum to sum + 1, then set total to new sum */
total = -- sum;          /* set sum to sum - 1, then set total to new sum */
```

The double symbols **++** and **− −** after **sum** are called the *postincrement* and *postdecrement* operators respectively, implying that **sum** is increased or decreased by 1 *after* the assignment to **total**. The general term *postfix* is used for such operators.

Similarly, the *prefix* operators **++** and **− −** appearing before **sum** are known specifically as *preincrement* and *predecrement* operators. With these, the increment or decrement by 1 is performed on **sum** *before* the assignment to **total** is made.

To illustrate these operations, consider the following snippet:

```
int sum, total;          /* declare */
total = 5; sum = 3;      /* initialize */

total = sum ++ ;         /* total now = 3 and sum = 4 post-inc */
total = ++ sum;          /* total now = 5 and sum = 5 pre-inc */
total = sum -- ;         /* total now = 5 and sum = 4 post-dec */
total = -- sum;          /* total now = 3 and sum = 3 pre-dec */
```

If you just want to increment or decrement without any assignment, the postfix and prefix methods are effectively equivalent.

```
sum ++ ;              /* set sum to sum + 1 */
++ sum;               /* set sum to sum + 1 */

sum -- ;              /* set sum to sum - 1 */
-- sum;               /* set sum to sum - 1 */
```

What you cannot do is use **sum ++** (or the other three variants) on the left side of an assignment. **sum ++** is not an lvalue, so **sum ++ = total**, for example, is not allowed.

These postfix and prefix operators, by the way, can be used with variables other than integers, but the increment or decrement produced may be other than 1. (See Pointer Arithmetic, Chapter 6.)

► *COMPOUND ASSIGNMENTS* ►

Another useful convention in C is the *compound assignment*, which simplifies statements like **total = total + sum** as in

```
total += sum;         /* increase total by sum */
                      /* i.e. total = total + sum */

total -= sum;         /* decrease total by sum */
                      /* i.e. total = total - sum */
```

Here the operators **+=** and **-=** use the two symbols shown to form a compound assignment. These are two forms of a more general compound assignment trick,

left-value op= right-expression;

where *op* can be any one of the ten C compoundable operators shown in Table 2.2 (these operators will all be explained in due course).

This general form translates into

left-value = left-value op right-expression;

Arithmetical	+ (add), − (subtract), * (multiply), / (divide), % (integer remainder or modulus)
Shifts	<< (left shift), >> (right shift)
Bitwise	& (AND), ¦ (OR), ^ (XOR [Exclusive OR])

► *Table 2.2:* Compoundable operators

assuming, of course, that *op* makes sense with the right and left sides of the assignment. For example, the following pairs of lines are equivalent:

```
sum = sum * factor;              /* multiply */
sum *= factor;

sum_of_all_sums = sum_of_all_sums / factor;          /* divide */
sum_of_all_sums /= factor;

rem = rem % divisor;            /* integer remainder or modulus */
rem %= divisor;
```

The compound assignment is one of the many features that makes C popular with programmers. If the left-value is long-winded (as in the second example above), the notation saves much typing, reducing the chance of error without obscuring the meaning.

► ASSIGNMENT VALUES AND MULTIPLE ASSIGNMENTS ►

C also allows you to "chain" assignments as in

```
answer = total = sum = 0;       /* clear them all */
```

The above *multiple assignment* starts at the right, setting **sum** to zero, and then assigns the value of the statement (**sum = 0**) to **total**. C is rather unusual in that assignment statements not only assign but also have a value that can be used just like a right-expression. What, then, is the value of (**sum = 0**)? It is simply the lvalue received by **sum** as a result of the assignment. So what we pass on to **total** is 0 (the new value of **sum**). Likewise, the value of (**total** = (**sum** = 0)) is the new value of **total**, namely 0, and this is passed to **answer**.

To cut a long story short, all three variables are set to 0, just as if we had made the three separate statements

```
sum = 0; total = 0; answer = 0;
```

In the above example, the whole multiple assignment itself has the value 0, but we make no use of this fact.

Rather than being an abstruse quirk of the language, this value property of assignments is yet another reason for C's reputation for compactness. Consider the following snippet:

```
answer = total + (sum = 4);
```

This statement is equivalent to the more verbose

```
sum = 4;
answer = total + sum;
```

► *PRECEDENCE AND ASSOCIATIVITY* ►

Can you guess why the parentheses are important in (**sum** = 4)? I have not yet broached the topic of operator *precedence*, mainly because only a few operators have been discussed! However, now that we have + and = rubbing shoulders, we must consider the problem.

All mathematical texts, whether for human or computer consumption, need to have conventions for grouping operands with operators and possibly for deciding the order in which they should be evaluated. For example, $2 \times 3 + 1$ is ambiguous ($6 + 1 = 7$ or $2 \times 4 = 8$?) unless you lay down a few rules. One simple rule is that operations enclosed in parentheses are completed separately: $(2 \times 3) + 1$ or $2 \times (3 + 1)$ removes the ambiguity. You may also decree that multiplication has higher precedence than addition, i.e., $2 \times 3 + 1$ means $(2 \times 3) + 1$. In this case, you needn't use parentheses, but they help the eye and do no harm. If you really want $2 \times (3 + 1)$, then parentheses are essential to override the precedence rules.

Certain commutative operators, like + and −, can have equal precedence from a purely mathematical standpoint. When calculating $x + y - z$, for example, you get the same answer, in theory, whether you do $(x + y) - z$ or $x + (y - z)$ or even $(x - z) + y$. The same is true for $x \times y/z$ (using / to indicate division).

However, the grouping of the operands may be relevant in practical terms since the computer may not be able to store intermediate results with complete accuracy. For example, **(x * y) / z** might lead to overflow before the division is reached, whereas the grouping **x * (y / z)** might avoid this problem. You can see that in more complex computer work both the grouping and order of evaluation can be relevant even if the pure mathematics reveals no problem.

Some C operators, like **++** and **−−**, offer a challenge in that the *sequence* of evaluation, as opposed to the grouping, can affect the result. Take, for instance,

```
total = 0;
sum = (total = 3) + (++total);    /* poor but legal code */
```

Which group, **(total = 3)** or **(++total)**, should be evaluated first? It does make a difference: **sum** will equal 7 if we evaluate **(total = 3)** first (i.e., from left to right) but 4 if we evaluate **(++total)** first (i.e., from right to left).

It is *vital* to know that the order of evaluation is *not* decreed by any C standards committee—each compiler writer is free to choose any convenient evaluation sequence (there are, though, four specific operators that require the leftmost operand to be evaluated first). For maximum sanity and portability, therefore, you must avoid code like the above example, legal though it is. A general rule is that if you assign to a variable, avoid reusing that variable in the same expression. Safer versions of the example would be

```
total = 3;
sum = total + (total + 1);
++total;
```

or

```
total = 0;
temp = ++total;                 /* a temporary variable often */
                                /* solves the problem */
sum = (total = 3) + temp;
```

depending on your original intentions.

The pecking order for C's forty or so operators is shown in full in Appendix E. Don't rush to memorize them all just now. In fact, it pays to be more rather than less generous with your parentheses for ease of mind and legibility, though you must remember that parentheses alone will not remove the order of evaluation problem typified by the ++ example above.

► *Precedence Categories* ►

There are fifteen precedence categories, some of which contain several operators, while others contain just one. A lower category number indicates higher precedence.

When C is faced with a sequence of operators of the same precedence and no guiding parentheses, it follows certain grouping or *associativity* rules. These rules effectively supply default parentheses. The rules, alas, vary according to the precedence categories.

Most of the categories have left-to-right associativity, so it's easier to remember the three precedence categories that associate from right to left: categories 2, 13, and 14 in Appendix E.

Category 14 contains the assignment and all the compound assignments (the most common right-to-left associative operators).

Now the example

```
answer = total = sum = 0;      /* clear them all */
```

given in the section on multiple assignments makes more sense. It is evaluated as

```
answer = (total = (sum = 0));    /* clear them all */
```

I'll point out the other right-to-left operators as they arise.

I stress again that associativity dictates how operands and operators are grouped, not necessarily the order in which each group will be evaluated. For example, the three operators *, /, and % all belong to precedence category 3, which associates from left to right. A statement such as

```
x = total * temp / price * rate % factor;
```

would be treated as though you had typed

    x = (((((total * temp) /) price) * rate) % factor);   /* not LISP */

Note the low precedence of = (category 14).

Whether this is the optimum grouping, considering accuracy or overflow, is another question. Your own parentheses, of course, could force a different grouping.

On this occasion, the grouping happens to dictate a unique sequence of evaluation: **(total * temp)** must be calculated first, the result divided by **price**, and so on.

If **price** were replaced with **price + extras** without parentheses as in

    x = total * temp / price + extras * rate % factor;

you might be in for a surprise, since * (category 3) is higher precedence than + (category 4). The compiler supplied grouping would give you as step 1

    x = (total * temp / price) + (extras * rate % factor);

and as step 2

    x = ((total * temp) / price) + ((extras * rate) % factor);

We don't know which inner piece might be evaluated first.

Here again is the example that triggered the discussion on precedence.

    answer = total + (sum = 4);   /* why the parentheses? */

Let's see what happens when we remove the parentheses.

Since + has a higher precedence than =, and since = associates from right to left,

    answer = total + sum = 4;

would be grouped by the compiler as follows:

    answer = ((total + sum) = 4);

resulting in a *syntax error* (or maybe two). Why? Because, **(total + sum)** is not an lvalue, so you can't assign anything to it. The error message would be **lvalue required in function....**

Summing up, the parentheses are essential to override C's natural associativity rules, since the latter would lead to a syntax error.

► *WARNING ON THE LACK OF WARNINGS* ►

Before you become complacent, here are some situations in which macho C will fail to protect you. Consider the following snippet:

```
unsigned int count, result;      /* declare */
int sum, total;

count = 0;                       /* initialize */
sum = 32767;

count -- ;                       /* decrement count? */
++sum;                           /* increment sum? */
total = count;                   /* what will total be? */
result = sum;                    /* what will result be? */
```

We have declared **count** as **unsigned**, so you might expect some complaint from the compiler when **count** is decremented by one "below" 0. In fact, C will not protect you. After going through the motions of decrement (0 − 1), the value placed in **count** is the erroneous bit pattern 0xFFFF (2^{16} − 1 or 65535), which is the *largest* unsigned int value.

In the statement **total = count;** the erroneous bit pattern in **count** is transferred, as is, to the signed integer variable, **total**. C allows such assignments between different integer types because of its weak data typing, and, as luck would have it, **total** now holds the value − 1 in signed two's-complement format! I use the word *luck* somewhat cynically, but computers not using two's-complement arithmetic would find it more difficult to preserve the correct value, − 1, from an unsigned variable.

Incrementing **sum** by one "beyond" its maximum limit of 0x7FFF (32,767 or 2^{15} − 1) is also performed without an overflow error message. The *signed* result left in **sum** would be − 32,768 (internally represented as 0x8000 or 2^{15}). This great shift in value can produce bizarre results for the unwary.

The final assignment, **result = sum**, is made by transferring − 32,768 to an unsigned variable without flinching, so **result** ends up with an unsigned value of 2 ^ 15.

Similar considerations apply when assigning between **long** signed and unsigned variables. Assigning from **int** to **long** when both are signed or both are unsigned is always safe since the latter's lvalue range is greater. Going the other way, from **long** to **int**, however, must be done with care. If the value in the **long** happens to be within **int** range, the correct transfer occurs and no harm is done. On the other hand, if the **long** source exceeds the destination **int** range, you will lose the upper 16 bits of the **long**.

```
long stretch;
int sum;
stretch = 0xFFFFFFFF;
sum = stretch;                    /* sum = 0xFFFF!! */
```

These are known as *silent truncations* and must be avoided like the plague (as with cliches).

The moral is to declare integer variables according to their expected ranges.

► INITIALIZATION OF VARIABLES ►

Another time saver in C is the ability to *initialize* a variable (give it a starting value) during its declaration. For example,

```
int sum = 25;                     /* declare sum as int with initial value 25 */
```

is equivalent to

```
int sum;                          /* declare */
sum = 25;                         /* initialize */
```

You can also declare and initialize a series of variables of the same type without repeating the type specifier as in

```
short int sum = 0; total = 0; result = 0;   /* all shorts */
```

The value used to initialize is naturally known as an *initializer*. For most of the numerical variables used in this chapter, the initializer can be either a constant or a numerical expression containing previously declared and initialized variables. (Later on you'll see some restrictions depending on storage classification.) Here are some declaration and initialization examples:

```
int sum = 25;                  /* declare and initialize */
int total = sum*2;             /* declare and initialize to 50 */
long grand_total = total + sum;  /* declare and set to 75 */
```

Note that in the third line, because **total + sum** is within **int** range, a safe, silent conversion from **int** to **long** takes place before **grand_total** is initialized. Be aware of the fact that a right-expression containing only **int** values could conceivably exceed the **long** range, leading to silent truncation.

Although there are exceptions, simply declaring a variable usually will not give it an initial, predictable value such as 0. It is safer for the beginner to initialize each variable in some way before using it in the right-expression of an assignment.

► INTEGER CONSTANTS ►

In many of the previous examples we used *integer constants* like 1, −1, and 269 without much ado. Remember, though, that the compiler needs to translate the ASCII symbols, **1, 2,** −, and so on, as found in the source code, into binary before expressions like **sum = 1** or **sum + 269** can be evaluated. Since we have not declared these constants explicitly as **short, int,** or **long**, you may wonder how the compiler knows how many bits, 16 or 32, to use in the conversion. The answer is that the compiler takes account of the value of the constant. Constants with values between 0 and 32,767 become 16-bit **int** types, while those with values between 32,768 and 2,147,483,647 take the 32-bit **long** format.

► Hexadecimal, Decimal, and Octal Constants ►

Constants can be expressed in hex (base 16), decimal (base 10), or octal (base 8) by following a few simple rules:

1. Octal constants must start with a **0** as in

   mask = 017777; sum = 012345;

   An error will occur if you use the numerals 8 or 9 in an octal integer.

2. Hex constants must start with **0x** or **OX** as in

   mask = 0XFFFFE; sum = 0x12345; tot = 0Xabcdef;

   An error will occur if you use illegal characters in a hex constant. After the **0x** or **OX**, only 0–9, A–F, or a–f are permitted.

3. Decimal constants are written conventionally with no leading **0** (otherwise they would be taken as octal).

   sum = 1; total = 269;

The number 0 presents no contradiction. Whether it is octal or decimal does not merit much angst.

The unary operator − in front of an integer constant tells the compiler to reverse the sign by subtracting the value from 0. Constants outside the upper limit will be silently truncated as we saw with integer variables. *Constant expressions*, that is, combinations such as **(1 + 3)** or **(4 − 6 * 34)** are allowed and are evaluated according to the normal operator precedence rules.

Summing up, a constant acquires both a value and a data type from the way it appears in the source text.

The use of explicit constants as "magic numbers" should be avoided where possible. If a disk block contains 512 bytes, say, it is better to use **#define BLKSIZE 512** (as in the following snippet) than to have the source text sprinkled with references to the constant 512:

```
#define BLKSIZE 512

unsigned int rec_size = 300;
unsigned int byte_count = rec_size*BLKSIZE;
```

The resulting code is more legible and can be more quickly updated should **BLKSIZE** change in value.

► *DISPLAYING INTEGERS* ►

It is time to run a few programs that will help you see the various integer types and operators in live action on your screen rather than as dry abstractions on the page. We will use SHOWNUM.C, listed in Program 2.1, as a test bed. Later you can experiment by editing it with values and data types of your own choice.

Fire up by typing **tc SHOWNUM.C** at the C> prompt and enter the text as shown. Use Alt-C and select the Make option from the Compile menu. After a successful compile/link, use the ← to access Run in the main menu. Let's see how SHOWNUM works.

► *printf( ) Format Control Strings* ►

Until now, **printf( )** has been used with a single string constant as an argument. SHOWNUM uses a variation allowing you to display formatted integers.

Here, the first **printf( )** has two arguments, separated by a comma. The first argument, "**The value of inta is %d\n\n**", represents a *format control string*, the function of which is to control the conversion and formatting of the following argument (or arguments). This string contains two distinct

```
/* shownum.c - display various integers */

#include <stdio.h>

main()
{
    int inta = -1, intb = 3;
    unsigned long uninta = 65535;
    printf("The value of inta is %d\n\n",inta);
    printf("Sum inta+intb = %d\n\n",inta+intb);
    printf("The value of uninta is %u\n\n",uninta);
    printf("uninta squared is %lu, (inta - uninta) is %ld\n",
            uninta*uninta, inta-uninta);
    printf("Net Profit is %d%%",intb);
}
```

► *Program 2.1:* SHOWNUM.C

classes of characters:

1. *Plain characters* such as the familiar text and newline escape characters that are displayed without change as in the HELLO.C of Chapter 1.

2. *Conversion specifications* such as **%d**. These are not displayed as part of the text but act as "templates" for the following arguments of **printf( )**.

Each conversion specification must start with a percent sign. This tells the compiler where and how to display an argument. Each argument to be displayed by **printf( )** will have an appropriate specification like **%d** embedded in the format control string. The concept is similar to the **PRINT USING MASK$** construct found in most BASICs.

There are many possible conversion specifications, offering conversions (with specified precision) from all the arithmetical data types to ASCII displays in decimal, hex, octal, and floating-point scientific (or exponentional) notation, with or without left or right justification, with or without zero fill, ad nauseam. Appendix C lists all these for reference, but for now we'll concentrate on the following simpler formats used to display integers, strings, and characters with no frills:

%s   for any matching string argument

%c   for any matching single character argument

%d   for decimal **int** (signed)

%u   for decimal **unsigned int**

%o   for octal **unsigned int** (note: leading 0 not displayed)

%x   for hexadecimal **unsigned int** (note: leading 0x not displayed)

%X   for hexadecimal (as above but giving A–F rather than a–f)

Each of **d**, **u**, **o**, **x** or **X** can have a lowercase letter **l** prefixed to give the corresponding **long** data type conversion or a prefixed **h** to give **short int** conversion as in

%ld   for decimal **long** (signed)

%hd   for decimal **short** (signed)

%lu   for decimal **unsigned long**

%ho   for octal **short** (unsigned)

To display a real percent symbol from a format string, you need to use two of them, that is, enter "%%" as in the old '\\' escape character trick. Only the second % will appear.

Referring back to SHOWNUM.C, the second argument in

printf("The value of inta is %d\n\n",inta);

is the **int** variable **inta**. This gets matched with the **%d** in the format string so that when you run SHOWNUM the top line should display

The value of inta is − 1

followed by two new lines. The **%d** interprets the bit pattern in **inta** as a **signed int** and converts to the ASCII pair − 1 for the display.

The next **printf( )** in SHOWNUM,

printf("Sum inta + intb = %d\n\n",inta + intb);

illustrates how the second argument can be a compound arithmetical expression. The **%d** is here replaced by the sum **inta + intb**, again interpreted as an **int** (signed of course). However complex the expression is, it will be evaluated and *then* matched by a single conversion specification such as **%d**. The second line displayed by SHOWNUM will therefore be

Sum inta + intb = 2

followed by two new lines.

The **%u** in the third **printf( )** converts the **unsigned long** variable **uninta** to an unsigned int and displays

The value of uninta is 65535

without error. Try changing the **%u** to **%lu** and **%d** and see if you understand the results.

The fourth **printf( )** statement shows two control specifications **%lu** and **%ld** embedded in the format string

```
printf("uninta squared is %lu, (inta – uninta) is %ld\n",
       uninta*uninta, inta – uninta);
```

Don't be fooled by the comma in the format string—it is inside the string, so it does not act as an argument separator. The following two arguments are arithmetical expressions, and they will be matched in turn by the **%lu** (long unsigned conversion) and **%ld** (long signed int conversion). The display will be

uninta squared is 4294836225, (inta – uninta) is – 65536

Reversing the conversion specifications will teach you some of the quirks of mixing signed and unsigned integer types.

SHOWNUM.C ends with a simple demonstration of the "%%" trick. You should see

Net Profit is 3%

on the final line of the display.

You should play with SHOWNUM, altering values, data types and format strings, until you are familiar with the simple conversion specifiers. Try displaying in short and long hex and octal. It will increase your knowledge of number representation as well as giving you practice with the Turbo C editor and menus.

▸ *MAKING YOUR OWN FUNCTIONS* ▸

Now that you have seen a library function in action, let's examine the problem of creating our own personal functions. Functions arise quite naturally when you find that your program is regularly doing the same or similar things. The obvious question is, Can I avoid repetitive typing in my source code? Let's take SHOWNUM as a simple example. Rather than entering several similar **printf( )** lines, we want to create a function called **dispnum( )** that can take an integer argument, say **n**, and display

   The value of n is *value*

At the same time, we'll introduce another function called **cube( )** that takes
an integer argument and returns its cube.

   SHOWNUM1.C (Program 2.2) illustrates the basic mechanics of declaring, defining, and invoking these naive functions. A new type modifier called

```
/* shownum1.c - display and cube integers */

#include <stdio.h>

main()
{
     const int nymph = 40;

/* this int identifier is frozen by the const modifier */
/* nymph behaves like a constant and cannot be changed */

     int sum, inta = -1, intb = 3; /* automatic variables */

/* these variables are of storage class auto by default */
/* i.e. they are automatically created when main starts */
/* and vanish when main ends. They are inaccessible     */
/* outside their own function. More in Chapter 3.       */

     dispnum(inta);         /* call dispnum with real var arg */
     dispnum(intb);
     dispnum(3*intb+inta);
     sum = cube(5);         /* call cube with real const arg */
     dispnum(sum);

     dispnum(sum++); dispnum (sum);
     dispnum(-sum); dispnum (sum);
     sum += intb; dispnum(sum *= inta);
/* can you forecast the resulting displays? */

     dispnum(cube(inta));
     dispnum(cube(intb+1));
     dispnum(cube(cube(inta)));
}

dispnum(n)        /* declare dispnum with dummy arg */
                  /* A returned value of int is assured by default. */
                  /* However, dispnum() does not return a value. */
int n;                      /* declare dummy arg */
{                           /* body of function */
     printf("The value of n is %d\n\n",n);
}
int cube(n)                 /* cube() returns an int */
int n;
{
     return n*n*n;          /* the value returned by cube() */
}
```

► *Program 2.2: SHOWNUM1.C*

const is introduced and explained within comments. The topic of *storage classes* is touched on and will be further amplified in Chapter 3.

► *Anatomy of the dispnum( ) Function* ►

There are three parts to dispnum( ):

1. The declaration line, dispnum(n), giving the function name and its argument list—the single identifier n in this case. If there were no arguments, the list would be empty [as in main( )], or you could write dispnum(void). If there were two arguments we would need dispnum(n,m), and so on. Note that no statement terminator is needed. The argument n is called a *dummy* or *formal* argument. It serves as a place marker when the function is actually called with a real argument, as you'll see presently.

2. The declaration giving the data type of the dummy argument: int n;.

3. The body of the function between { and }, similar to the body of main( ), which determines (defines) the action of the function. Here the function just performs the one action,

    printf("The value if n is %d\n\n",n);

    and then ends because the final } has been reached.

► *Calling the dispnum ( ) Function* ►

The function dispnum( ) is called (or invoked) several times from within main( ) by simply naming it with a particular *real* or *actual* argument that matches the type of the dummy argument as in

    dispnum(inta);   /* call dispnum with real arg */

We say that the real argument inta is *passed* to the function dispnum( ), just as the real argument "hello, world" was passed to printf( ) in HELLO.C

(Chapter 1). The result of the call, then, is the same as that of

```
printf("The value of n is %d\n\n",inta);
```

In fact, **dispnum( )** does not operate directly on **inta** but on a temporary *copy* of **inta**. In C, all function arguments are passed by *value*, so that normally a function cannot alter the real argument—it knows only the copied value of **inta**, not the memory location where **inta** resides. Even if **n**, the dummy argument, is changed by **dispnum( )**, this change cannot "get back" to **inta**.

Unlike more fussy languages, C traditionally does not engage in tedious checks to see that functions are called with matching arguments—later we'll see how ANSI C offers some help in this direction.

► *The cube( ) Function Analyzed* ►

Like **dispnum( )**, the function **cube( )** also has three parts: function declaration, argument declaration, and body, though there are a few differences: **cube( )** returns a value, as indicated by the keyword **return** in the function body. The expression (**n*n*n**) after **return** represents the value returned when the function is called. If a function does not return a value, as in the case of **dispnum( )**, then no **return** statement is needed or you can write **return;** to indicate that nothing is returned. A function like **cube( )** that does return a value can be considered as having that value when used as part of an expression in **main( )** (or anywhere else it gets called). The declaration of **cube( )**, in fact, indicated that its returned value would be of type **int**. In the absence of a type specifier in the function definition, an **int** return value is assumed.

All of this explains why **cube( )** can legally be used in assignments such as

```
sum = cube(5);
```

and the use of **cube(inta)** as a real argument to **dispnum( )** in

```
dispnum(cube(inta));
```

The latter works because **cube(inta)** is in fact an **int** derived from the evaluation of **n*n*n** using the **int** value of **inta** as the **int n**.

Similarly, **cube(inta)** is a valid int argument for **cube( )** itself as in

    dispnum(cube(cube(inta)));

So, **cube(inta)** can be used in any situation where a non-lvalue **int** can be used.

► *Unused Variable Warnings* ►

I deliberately refrained from using the **const int** identifier **nymph** in SHOWNUM1.C in order to reveal a neat feature of Turbo C. It will issue a friendly, nonfatal warning for each identifier declared but not referenced in the program. This can help you clear out any deadwood at the end of a long development session.

If you enter and run SHOWNUM1.C, your screen should look like Figure 2.1.

```
The value if n is -1
The value if n is 3
The value if n is 8
The value if n is 125
The value if n is 125
The value if n is 126
The value if n is 125
The value if n is 125
The value if n is -128
The value if n is -1
The value if n is 64
The value if n is -1
Press any key to return to Turbo C . . . .■
```

► *Figure 2.1:* SHOWNUM1 result screen

As with SHOWNUM, you should experiment with other values in SHOWNUM1. Note that **cube( )** can quickly exhaust the range of **int**, so try using **long** and **unsigned long** to find the maximum **n** before these ranges are exceeded. Remember to alter the format strings in **dispnum( )**!

► *Duplication of Variable Identifiers* ►

You may have noticed that the identifier **n** was declared twice in SHOWNUM1.C. Can you declare the same identifier more than once? A useful general answer is, "No, not for variables within the same block"; a more accurate answer for all identifiers is, "It all depends!" Take the following snippet:

```
{
   int sum;
   long sum;                     /* ERROR – sum as int still active */
}
```

sum is already declared as **int** and is still active. To understand when and where variables are active requires a discourse on the vital topics of *storage classes*, *scope*, and *visiblity*. We will introduce some of the basic concepts now, leaving a detailed study for later.

► *Storage Classes—First Steps* ►

Without realizing it, perhaps, you have been using a storage class called *automatic* in all your variable declarations so far. The keyword **auto** can be used explicitly as a storage-class specifier placed before the type specifier as in

```
auto int sum;
```

However, in the declarations used to date, **auto** has been the default, implied by the context, as it were. The comments in SHOWNUM1 indicate the flavor of automatic identifiers. They correspond to the local identifiers of languages like Pascal. The adjective *local* is perhaps more suggestive of their property than *auto* since variables like **sum** and **inta** are local to **main( )**. The

n that is local to **dispnum( )** does not clash at all with the **n** that is local to **cube( )**. Local variables are safer in the sense that changes to them are confined to their own backyard. Imagine the chaos if the **n** being altered by **cube( )** somehow managed to infiltrate into the **n** of **dispnum( )**. Such nightmares are known as *side effects*, or rather *unwanted* side effects. Some side effects turn out to be beneficial when used with care.

In contrast with local or automatic variables, most languages need *global* variables, which are accessible from all parts of a program and therefore at risk to the side-effects problem. In C the globals are sometimes called *external* because they "exist" outside the functions. The storage-class specifier **extern** can be used to declare a global variable as in

```
extern int sum;
```

but like **auto** it is often implied by the context and can be omitted.

C offers a rather daunting selection of storage classes and default rules that determine where a variable exists (scope) and where it is accessible (visibility). These will be gradually revealed in the following chapters as we encounter more complex function schemas.

► *SUMMARY OF CHAPTER 2* ►

Here are the main points covered in this chapter.

◄► Data typing allows the compiler to allocate the correct memory space for constants and variables and also guides the compiler as to what arithmetical operations and ranges of values are legal. C is not strongly typed: it often allows different types to be mixed in expressions and will often "silently" convert one type to another.

◄► The three basic integer data types are **short**, **int**, and **long**. They are treated by default as **signed** unless explicitly declared as **unsigned**. **short** and **int** each take 2 bytes. They are the same types in Turbo C but may be different on other implementations. **long** takes 4 bytes. Turbo C uses conventional two's complement arithmetic, so negative signed numbers look just like large unsigned numbers! (The sign bit is the most-significant bit.)

◄► Declarations need a data-type specifier followed by one or more identifier names:

```
int i;
int j, k;
long I, J, K;                    /* or long int I, J, K; */
unsigned int m, n, o;
unsigned long salary;            /* or unsigned long int salary */
```

◄► Variables can have values assigned to them at various stages of a program; constants are fixed in value. Assignment is accomplished via the = operator:

```
i = j;                          /* assign value of j to lvalue, i */
salary = 10000;                 /* assign a constant to lvalue, salary */
```

The above lines are called assignment statements. Certain objects are called lvalues because they can legally exist on the left side of an assignment. No constants are lvalues, and not every expression containing a variable is an lvalue.

◄► C may make internal conversions during assignments, either promoting an **int** before assignment to a **long** or truncating a **long** before assignment to an **int**. The latter conversions are dangerous.

◄► Multiple assignments are allowed:

```
i = j = k = 20;                 /* all vars now equal 20 */
```

This is possible because the expression **k = 20** itself takes a value equal to its left-hand member, which it then passes on to **j**. The expression **j = k = 20** has a value that it passes to i. The value of the whole expression is also 20, but it is not used in this example. C is unusual in having expression-statements and evaluated expressions. Any C expression can become a statement by appending a semicolon. The value of an expression is simply discarded in most cases.

◄► C has elaborate precedence and associativity rules that dictate how operators are grouped in compound expressions. Appendix E lists the fifteen categories. Parentheses can be used to override these rules—but the order in which terms are evaluated depends on the individual compiler. ANSI C allows for the unary operator + that gives some control over evaluation sequence.

◄► Variables can be initialized during a declaration:

int i = 3; long L = 279;

For the moment, assume that variables contain garbage until intialized or assigned in some way.

◄► The post- and preincrement and post- and predecrement operators (++ and −−) let you add or subtract 1 from all integral variables. The postfix operators return the old value before the change; the prefix operators return the changed value:

```
int p = 0, q = 1;
p = q++;              /* p = 1 and q = 2 */
p = ++q;              /* p = 3 and q = 3 */
p = q−;               /* p = 3 and q = 2 */
p = −q;               /* p = 1 and q = 1 */
```

◄► The compound operators, += , *= , and so on, simplify assignments by combining them with some other operation:

```
i += 4;               /* same as i = i + 4; */
j − = i;              /* same as j = j − i; */
k *= 3;               /* same as k = k*3; */
```

◄► Integer constants can be expressed as decimal, hex, or octal. Their size dictates their data types unless overridden with a suffix:

```
    i = 34;                   /* 34 is decimal and type int */
    i = 34U;                  /* 34 forced to be unsigned int */
    i = 34L;                  /* 34 forced to be long int (signed) */
    i = 34UL;                 /* 34 forced to be unsigned long int */
/* lowercase u, l also allowed */
    i = 034;                  /* 034 is octal */
    i = 0x34;                 /* 0x34 or 0X34 are hexadecimal */
```

◄► printf( ) can display formatted variables, expressions, and constants of different data types. A format string is used to control where and how each matching expression argument appears. Simple examples are

%d, %u, %ld, %lu

which format signed, unsigned, long, and unsigned long numbers.

◄► The declaration, definition, and calling syntax for simple functions was hinted at with examples.

```
        [type] func([arg1, arg2,...]);   /* declaration only */

        [type] func([arg1, arg2,...])    /* declaration/definition */
            [parameter declarations]
        {
/*      body of function         */
        [return] [result];
        }

main( )
{
    ...
[result =] func([real_arg1, real_arg2,...]);                /* call the function */
...
}
```

◄► Real arguments in the function call are passed by value to the function via copies to the dummy arguments used in the definition. A function may or may not return a useful value using the **return** statement.

◄► Two common storage classes were mentioned briefly: **auto** (local) and **extern** (global).

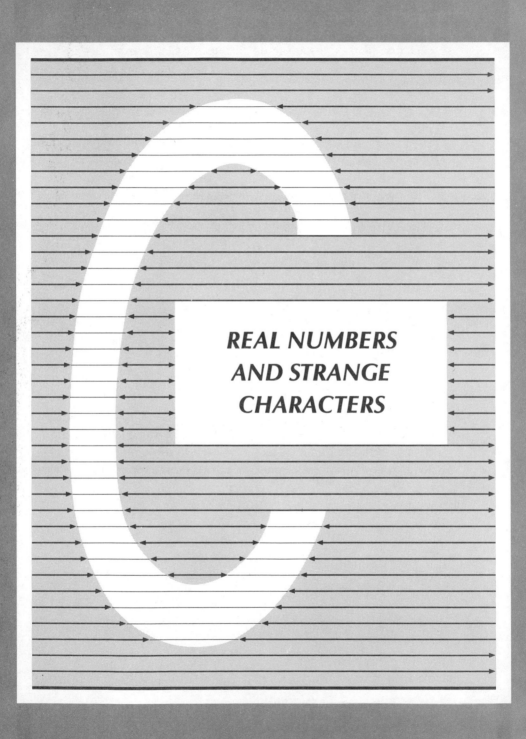

**REAL NUMBERS
AND STRANGE
CHARACTERS**

► *CHAPTER 3* ►

This chapter introduces two more basic data types that allow you to work with *floating-point* and *character* variables. I'll explain the motivation for these types and extend the use of **printf( )** to format and display them.

Character variables lead naturally into C's unusual treatment of strings as *arrays* of characters referenced via *pointers*, so you'll get your first, gentle exposure to this central *bete noire* of the C language. Other languages reluctantly offer pointers in various guises and then strive to protect the programmer from the dangers of misuse. In C pointers are the primary weapons, designed to butcher both friend and foe. You'll love them!

You will also start using simple *control* structures, allowing your program to select alternative courses of action depending on the results of various conditional tests.

► BEYOND THE INTEGERS ►

The integer types introduced in Chapter 2 have the merit of complete, whole-number accuracy, provided that you keep within their acknowledged ranges. Although the computer works internally in binary, the conversions to and from decimal are exact for integer values. Problems can arise, though, when your calculations involve numbers or results with fractional parts. Computing, say, 3.87675×10.00234 or $1/7$ cannot be readily accomplished with integer data types unless you are happy with integer approximations such as $3.87675 \times 10.00234 = 40$ to the nearest whole number and $1/7 = 0$.

► Integer Accuracy ►

If you are willing and able to scale all your calculations, you can actually handle all *rational* numbers with integer data types. (A rational number is one that can be expressed as the ratio of two integers, p/q, where q is non-zero. The number 0.99 is rational since 0.99 = 99/100.) For example, it is common to treat $199.99 as 19,999 cents (scaling by 100) thereby removing the problem of decimal fractions.

Even if you need to divide or take percentages of such amounts, you can scale up again by 100 or 10,000 or whatever, depending on the accuracy needed, and keep your intermediate results as integers until the final answer is scaled back and possibly rounded as appropriate. However, the scaling is a nuisance in all but the simplest cases, and, worse still, even the **unsigned long** limit of ten significant digits can easily be exceeded.

Accuracy in all types of computation boils down to how many significant figures you can retain at each step. The position of decimal (or binary) point is irrelevant.

Note that you can concoct programs that can achieve any given degree of precision, subject only to storage limitations. For example, the extended multiply equation

$$(10 \times a + b) \times (10 \times c + d) = 100 \times a \times c + 10 \times a \times d + 10 \times b \times c + b \times d$$

is an example of how you can multiply two extra long numbers without overflow by using the proper software gymnastics. There is also the BCD (Binary Coded Decimal) approach that allows exact arithmetic on strings of digits of arbitrary length.

► THE FLOATING-POINT SOLUTION ►

C, and most other languages, offers a more compact solution: the *floating-point* or *FP* data types. In the following sections, you will see how they let you handle fractions, such as 3.14159 and − 0.00001, as well as integers outside the **long int** range. Internally, FP does a form of scaling for you automatically. (Appendix D explains the basic rules for FP notation and manipulation.)

FP is not a general panacea. Even though FP operations extend enormously the range of values you can handle there are inherent problems of precision that require constant attention. As a simple example, the fraction 1/3 (= 0.3333... recurring) cannot be exactly represented in FP format using a finite number of binary bits. Even if there are clever ways of storing such rational numbers, transcendental numbers such as pi can only be stored as approximations. Long before the electronic computer arrived, the branch of mathematics called numerical analysis had evolved to study the problems of reducing the errors that accumulate when you are forced to round off and approximate at various stages of a long calculation.

Let's review the basic arithmetical operators and, in particular, study the quirks of / (division) and % (integer remainder)—these are relevant to a proper understanding of floating-point operations.

► ARITHMETICAL OPERATIONS ►

You have already met the arithmetical operators + (add), − (subtract and also unary minus), * (multiply), / (divide), and % (integer remainder) as applied to integers (variables and constants).

We call % the integer remainder operator to remind you of the fact that it can be used only with integer types. The other operators can be used with both integer and FP numbers (variables and constants).

There are no problems with precision or rounding when you add, subtract, and multiply positive or negative integers unless the results go out of range. Integer division and its associated operation, integer remainder, though, have some anomalies to be discussed in the next section.

► Integer Division, Remainder and Modulus ►

Dividing an integer by an integer in C using / gives you only a whole number quotient (usually truncated and therefore incorrect), while the % operator does not always give the expected integer remainder. The normal classroom paradigm for integer division is

dividend/divisor = quotient with remainder

or

dividend = quotient×divisor + remainder

where the absolute value of the remainder is less than the absolute value of the divisor. If the latter is not true, you have clearly not completed the division process! The absolute value of x is written **abs(x)** or $|x|$, and is defined as follows:

If x ≥ 0 abs(x) = x
If x < 0 abs(x) = −x

In other words, if *x* is signed and negative, just reverse the sign to get abs(*x*); otherwise *x* and abs(*x*) are the same. (C provides such a routine, **abs( )**, in **stdlib.h**.)

We must also rule that the divisor is nonzero. For a zero divisor, the operation is simply *undefined* (so forget all that 1/0 = infinity nonsense).

In C notation, with integers **a** and **b** (**b** being nonzero), this equation can be written

a divided by *b* = *(a/b)* with remainder *(a%b)*

so you would expect that

a = *(a/b)*b* + *(a%b)* with abs(a%b) < abs(b)

would always be true (excluding overflow problems). Unfortunately, if either **a** or **b** or both are signed you have ambiguities if either or both go negative. Unsigned **a**'s and **b**'s, by definition, of course, cannot go negative, and no problems arise. Look at the following examples:

```
1/0 illegal     1%0 illegal
0/1 = 0         0%1 = 0 check: 0 = 0*0 + 0 and 0 < 1 OK
4/2 = 2         4%2 = 0 check: 4 = 2*2 + 0 and 0 < 2 OK
3/2 = 1         3%2 = 1 check: 3 = 1*2 + 1 and 1 < 2 OK
1/2 = 0         1%2 = 1 check: 1 = 0*2 + 1 and 1 < 2 OK
10/3 = 3        10%3 = 1 check: 10 = 3*3 + 1 and 1 < 3 OK
```

So far, with both **a** and **b** positive, there are no surprises. The **%** gives you the conventional *mod* (or *modulo*) operation, which yields the remainder of a division process. Let's see what happens if **a** goes negative.

− 12/3 = −4   − 12%3 = 0 check: − 12 = (−4*3) + 0 and 0 < 3 OK

No problem here, but perhaps we were lucky since − 12 is divisible exactly by 3. Let's try again.

$$-10/3 = -3 \quad -10\%3 = -1 \text{ check: } -10 = (-3*3) + (-1)$$

and

$$abs(-1) < 3 \text{ OK}$$

Note that the unary − has higher precedence than / and %, so −10/3 means (−10)/3 not −(10/3).

This seems fine, but what if we write

$$-10/3 = -4 \quad -10\%3 = 2 \text{ check: } -10 = (-4*3) + 2 \text{ and } 2 < 3 \text{ ALSO}$$
OK!

Both answers for −10/3 and −10%3 meet the mathematical tests, so which set is correct? And what will C do? C officially says that the result is machine dependent, so for true portability you should avoid division and remainder operations with negative integers.

Most C compilers, including Turbo C, opt for the values in the first example by always taking as **a/b** the value nearer to zero and the **a%b** with the same sign as **a**.

For Turbo C then, −10/3 = −3 because −3 is nearer to zero than −4. This makes −10%3 = −1. Another way of looking at Turbo C's value for −10/3 is to think of the full answer −3.3333... and discard the fractional part (with no rounding).

The plot thickens if **b** is negative. Again, the official C reaction is that the results are implementation dependent. Turbo C gives the following result:

$$10/-3 = -3 \quad 10\%-3 = -1 \text{ check: } 10 <> (-3*-3) + (-1)?? \text{ NOT OK}$$

but

$$abs(-1) < abs(-3) \text{ OK}$$

So here we meet a potentially dangerous violation of the basic rule that $a = (a/b) \times b + (a\%b)$.

There is a similar problem with

$$-10/-3 = 3 \quad -10\%-3 = 1 \text{ check: } -10 <> (3*-3) + 1?? \text{ NOT OK}$$

but

abs(1) < abs(– 3) OK

The ambiguity stems from two distinct approaches to integer arithmetic: *Eulerian arithmetic,* as in C, and *modulo arithmetic,* as in many computer contexts. Fortunately, the two arithmetics agree for non-negative integral dividends (the **a**'s) and positive integral divisors (the **b**'s). The moral is to use unsigned and/or positive signed integers when using **%**.

C uses the one divide operator **/** for integers and floating-point numbers, but with the latter there is no ambiguity regarding sign or meaning. When both **a** and **b** are integer types, the quotient of **a/b** is also an integer type, with possible truncation. But if one or both of **a** and **b** are FP, **a/b** becomes FP. This is an example of a general rule in C that is invoked when expressions have mixed types: internal, silent conversions are made whenever necessary (and possible).

The function **fmod(***x,y***)** is provided in the Turbo C math library to calculate *(x mod y)* for floating-point ***x*** and ***y***.

► *FLOATING-POINT DATA TYPES* ►

C offers three FP data types to handle numbers with fractional or decimal parts. They also permit the use of numbers, both integral and fractional, outside the maximum **long int** range.

The three types, **float**, **double**, and **long double**, correspond to the *single, double,* and *extended* precision formats available on many current computers and math coprocessors. Table 3.1 shows their bit allocations and legal ranges as assigned in Turbo C.

Type Specifier	Bit Size	Range
float	32	– 3.4e – 38 to + 3.4e + 38
double	64	– 1.7e – 308 to + 1.7e + 308
long double	64	– 1.7e – 308 to + 1.7e + 308

► *Table 3.1:* Floating-point data types

► *Floating-Point Declarations* ►

You declare FP variables in the usual way, using a type specifier.

```
float x, y, z = 2.0;         /* 3 floats – one initialized */
double pi, eps;              /* 2 doubles */
long double scotch;          /* 1 long double */
```

As with integers, ANSI C leaves it to the implementor to decide exactly how these FP types should be internally represented, provided only that

```
long double > double > float
```

where $>$ is used informally to indicate "greater than or equal precision."

Just as you saw with **short** and **int**, Turbo C's **double** and **long double** turn out to be identical in format and range. Other C systems might have an 80 or 128-bit **long double**, so some care is needed to ensure complete portability. We will use only **float** and **double** in this book.

Note that there are no **signed** or **unsigned** versions of the FP data types—they are all implicitly **signed** by definition.

The ranges shown in Table 3.1 use *scientific* notation (also called *E* or *signed exponent* notation). Symbolically,

$$Mex = M \times 10^X$$

where M is the fixed-point part or *mantissa* and X is the *exponent*. The **e** can also be written as **E**.

A positive exponent shifts the decimal point to the right (multiplying by a power of 10), and a negative exponent shifts the decimal point to the left (dividing by a power of 10). A zero exponent does not affect the mantissa, since $10^0 = 1$ by definition. Some examples of scientific notation are shown in Table 3.2. As you can see, there can be many different FP expressions (and internal bit patterns) representing the same number. (Zero is an exception because it has a unique FP bit pattern.)

► *Floating-Point Pros and Cons* ►

The FP format is most economical. For instance, the maximum number of type **double** would take 309 decimal digits to write out in full and over 1000

$$120.0e+0 \quad = \quad 120 \times 10^0 \quad = \quad 120$$

$$12.0e+1 \quad = \quad 12 \times 10^1 \quad = \quad 120$$

$$1200.0E-1 \quad = \quad 1200 \times 10^{-1} \quad = \quad 120$$

$$1.2e+2 \quad = \quad 1.2 \times 10^2 \quad = \quad 120$$

► **Table 3.2:** *Scientific notation examples*

bits if stored in conventional binary. This enormous range, however, does not indicate the true precision available with **double**. Precision is a function of the mantissa width (52 bits), which gives "only" 15 or 16 significant digits. (Appendix D explains this in detail.)

Among the quirks of FP arithmetic are the following:

1. Adding a small number to a large one may have no effect. The significant bits of the small number may be lost when it is aligned prior to addition to the larger number.

2. It can be misleading to test for equality between two FP numbers. Rather than testing for equality as in

    if (fp1 == fp2) { ... }

    it is better to test their difference as in

    if (fabs(fp1 − fp2) <= delta) { ... }

    where **delta** is a small constant reflecting the precision of the FP type, such as 1.0e−15. **fabs( )** is a standard library function giving the absolute value of an FP argument.

► *More Internal Conversions* ►

Because of the limited precision of **float**, the system always converts **float** to **double** internally, temporarily, and silently, before evaluating any expression containing **float**'s. If the final result has to be assigned to a **float** or **int** variable, another silent conversion from **double** to **float** or from **double** to

int takes place before the assignment, with possible loss of accuracy.

You may ask why **float** is used at all. The answer is memory conservation: each **float** variable uses only 32 bits compared with 64 bits for a **double**. If speed and precision are more important than RAM, use **double** variables to reduce the conversion time.

► *Speeding FP with Math Coprocessors* ►

All FP arithmetic performed by software is quite heavy on CPU cycles. This fact has motivated the invention of *math coprocessors*, chips specially designed to handle the FP chores faster by hardware. As the name implies, a coprocessor works in conjunction, and often in parallel, with the main CPU.

For the IBM PC range, the Intel 8087, 80287, and 80387 are a family of math coprocessors compatible with the 8088/6, 80286, and 80386, respectively. The improvement in performance is well worth the modest investment. Turbo C supports the 8087 and 80287 in a flexible way. If you do not have one of these fitted, you have two options:

1. Avoid FP numbers and tell Turbo C not to link in any of the special FP library routines. This speeds up the linking process. The Compile menu has a Code Generation submenu that contains a Floating-Point subsubmenu. This offers three choices: None, Emulation, and 8087/80287. Selecting None will inhibit the FP library linkage.

2. Use FP numbers and let Turbo C link in the *emulation* library (EMU.LIB). This is the default situation (Emulation on). All your FP work will be handled by software that emulates (imitates) the action of the 8087 or 80287. An added bonus is that if you run such programs on a system fitted with a math coprocessor, Turbo C is set by default to detect its presence, automatically enlisting FP hardware support and bypassing the emulation.

Normally, then, if you have a math coprocessor fitted, you can just let Turbo C's auto-detect mechanism do its thing.

To let you test programs that may run on systems with or without a math coprocessor, you can also force Turbo C to ignore a fitted 8087/80287 and emulate by software.

```
C > SET 87 = N
```

sets the DOS environment variable **87** to **N** for No, which turns off the auto-detect and tells Turbo C to emulate. Similarly,

    C> SET 87 = Y

tells Turbo C to use the 8087/80287 whether it's there or not! Expect big trouble if **87** is set to **Y** without the physical presence of the math coprocessor. You can unset **87**, restoring auto-detection, by typing

    C> SET 87 =

with a ◄─┘ immediately after the = .

► *Floating-Point Constants* ►

Unless followed by an **F**, floating-point constants are always interpreted as **double** even if the value would fit in a **float**.

FP constants can be written in two different ways: normal decimal-point notation or scientific.

```
float w, x, y;                /* declare three floats */
double z;                     /* declare one double */

w = 3.14159; x = 4e + 5;      /* x = 400000.00 */

/* internal conversions: constant converted to double, then to float
   before assignment */

y = 1.0F                      /* F inhibits conversion to double */

z = −2.5e−12;                 /* z = −0.0000000000025 */
/* no conversions: constant and lvalue are both double */
```

You can use **e** or **E**, and the **+** signs are optional. Notice that if you use scientific notation, the decimal point is not essential: **4e + 5**, **4.e + 5** and **4.0e + 5** are identical.

For decimal-point (unscientific) notation of FP constants, the decimal point *is* needed: **4.**, **4.0**, **.0**, and **0.** are all FP, but **4** and **0** would be taken as **int**s.

The exponent must be a whole number and may be negative: **2.4e3.8** is illegal.

► *Floating-Point in Action with printf( )* ►

You may recall using the format-conversion code **%d** with **printf( )** to display signed integers. The corresponding trick for both **float** and **double** is to use **%f**. For example,

```
float height   = 2500.35;
double depth  = 3.12e5;
printf("Height is %f and Depth is %f\n",height,depth);
```

will display

Height is 2500.349854 and Depth is 312000.000000

(I'll cover the chief variants on **%f** in the following sections, but see Appendix C for the whole story.)

All values are converted to **double**, if necessary, before the **%f** conversion to ASCII takes place. This explains the slight error in the display of **height**. You'll see how to control the precision of the conversion shortly.

Using **%e** or **%E** in place of **%f** in the previous example,

```
printf("Height is %e and Depth is %E\n",height,depth);
```

will give

Height is 2.500350e + 003 and Depth is 3.120000E + 005

Note the choice between **e** and **E** on display. The exponent is always signed + or − and displayed with three decimal digits (padded with zeroes as required). The mantissa is always scaled to give *d.ddd...* but you can control the layout and precision, as you'll see anon.

Another useful variant is **%g**, which will display the shorter of the two versions **%f** and **%e**. (**%G** does the same but displays E rather than e.) The **%f** version is used if both formats take the same space. The **%g** variant is useful when you have no idea of the range of the results.

► *The Precision Specifier*

The default conversion for **%f** is rounded to six decimal places, whatever the argument type. You can vary this precision using a decimal point and a *precision specifier* as shown in Table 3.3.

Example	Displays Height As...
%f	2500.349854 (default = %.6f)
%.0f	2500
%.1f	2500.3
%.2f	2500.35
%.3f	2500.350

Example	Displays Depth As...
%e	3.120000e + 005 (default = %.6e)
%.3e	3.120e + 005

► **Table 3.3:** *Precision specifier examples*

► *The Width Specifier*

Whether or not you have a precision specifier you may supply a *width specifier*, **%wf** or **%w.pf**, where *w* is a number indicating the *minimum* number of columns to be allocated to the display and *p* is the precision number just described.

Leading spaces will normally be used to pad the display, but you can pad with leading zeroes by using **%0wf** or **%0w.pf**. Padding with leading spaces and zeroes is known as *right justification* since it effectively lines up columns of numbers to a flush right-hand margin. To indicate the layouts more clearly in the following examples, I will use the symbol *s* for space.

Using too small a width value will not lead to the loss of any characters—**printf( )** will simply override and take the space it needs. Examples are easier than descriptions—see Table 3.4.

The last example shows one use of the # modifier flag. In other situations it can modify the appearance of leading or trailing zeroes.

Width and precision specifiers work in a similar way with **%e**, **%E**, **%g**, and **%G**. With the integer conversion specifiers like **%d** and **%u**, of course, precision is not relevant (there are no decimal places), but you can use the width specifier to pad the field as shown above.

I have by no means exhausted the formatting possibilities, but I will conclude with just one more tweak—the use of − to force left justification within a given field width by padding with spaces (never zeroes) on the right. The − here can be confusing unless you think of it as reversing the normal right-justification! It has nothing to do with displaying a minus sign for negative values. Examples are shown in Table 3.5. (See Appendix C for much more.)

► SHOWNUMF.C ►

To try out some of these **printf( )** variations, enter SHOWNUMF.C as listed in Program 3.1. The entry **%%f** is needed to display **%f**—it is not a format

Example	Displays Height As...
%.2f	2500.35 (no width specified)
%6.2f	2500.35 (width ignored—too small)
%9.2f	*s s* 2500.35 (pad blanks to 9 columns)
%09.2f	002500.35 (pad zeroes to 9 columns)
%14f	*s s s* 2500.349854 (same as %14.6f)
%14.0f	*s s s s s s s s s s* 2500 (note no decimal point)
%#14.0f	*s s s s s s s s s* 2500. (unless you add a #)

► **Table 3.4:** *Width specifier examples*

Example	Displays Height As...
%.2f	2500.35 (no width specified)
% − 6.2f	2500.35 (width ignored—too small)
% − 9.2f	2500.35*s s* (pad right blanks to 9 columns)
% − 09.2f	2500.35*s s* (same! The zero is ignored)
% − 14f	2500.349854*s s s* (same as % − 14.6f)
% − 14.0f	2500*s s s s s s s s s s* (note no decimal point)
% − #14.0f	2500.*s s s s s s s s s s* (unless you add a #)

► **Table 3.5:** *Left justification*

```
/* shownumf.c - display fp numbers */

#include <stdio.h>

main()
{
        double fsquare();    /* declare a function */

        float height = 2500.35;
        double depth = 3.12e5;

        printf("%%f       height is %f\n",      height);
        printf("%%.2f     height is %.2f\n",    height);
        printf("%%9.2f    height is %9.2f\n",   height);
        printf("%%-9.2f   height is %-9.2f\n",  height);
        printf("%%09.2f   height is %09.2f\n",  height);
        printf("%%14.0f   height is %14.0f\n",  height);
        printf("%%-14.0f  height is %-14.0f\n", height);
        printf("%%#14.0f  height is %#14.0f\n", height);

        printf("%%e       height is %e\n",      height);
        printf("%%.3e     height is %.3e\n",    height);
        printf("%%g       height is %g\n",      height);

        printf("%%f       depth is %f\n",depth);
        printf("%%E       depth is %E\n",depth);
/* try your own format variants here, e.g. %10.4g etc. */

        printf("%%f depth squared is %f\n",  fsquare(depth));
        printf("%%e depth squared is %e\n",  fsquare(depth));
        printf("%%g depth squared is %g\n",  fsquare(depth));
}

double fsquare(n)    /* define the function */
double n;
{
    return(n*n);            /* the value returned by fsquare() */
}
```

► *Program 3.1:* SHOWNUMF.C

specifier. SHOWNUMF.C also introduces the simple function **fsquare( )** to advance your understanding of function declarations and definitions.

Check your results against Figure 3.1.

► *fsquare( ) Declaration and Definition* ►

The line

    double fsquare( );

in **main( )** is a function *declaration*, warning **main( )** that **fsquare( )** will return a **double**. The actual function *definition* comes later, spelling out in detail what arguments **fsquare( )** needs (just one **double** argument, **n**, in this case)

```
%f         height is 2500.349854
%.2f       height is 2500.35
%9.2f      height is   2500.35
%-9.2f     height is 2500.35
%09.2f     height is 002500.35
%14.0f     height is             2500
%-14.0f    height is 2500
%#14.0f    height is            2500.
%e         height is 2.500350e+003
%.3e       height is 2.500e+003
%g         height is 2500.35
%f         depth  is 312000.000000
%E         depth  is 3.120000E+005
%f depth squared is 97344000000.000000
%e depth squared is 9.734400e+010
%g depth squared is 9.7344e+010



Press any key to return to Turbo C . . .▄
```

► *Figure 3.1:* SHOWNUMF.C *screen output*

and how the function calculates its returned value.

Note that this particular style of function declaration, known as the classical C style, has empty parentheses—it is not concerned with function arguments, only with the data type of the returned value. Later you will meet the modern variant, in which the function declaration also indicates the argument types.

In the absence of such a declaration, **main( )** will assume that **fsquare( )** returns an **int**. In other words, unless told otherwise, **int** is the default data type returned by a function. Try omitting the **fsquare( )** declaration from **main( )**—you will get an instructive error message. Turbo C finds a clash between the implied **int** returned by its first encounter with **fsquare( )** and the **double** value called for in the subsequent definition.

Next, try moving the **double fsquare(n)** definition ahead of **main( )**. (Use the editor's Wordstar-like block moves ⁀ **KB/** ⁀ **KK/** ⁀ **KV/** ⁀ **KH**). You'll find that the **fsquare( )** declaration within **main( )** can now be omitted.

This explains why you often see programs with no function declarations within **main( )**: Either the function is defined first, or the nondeclared function encountered before its definition can be safely treated as though it returned an **int**. (I'll get deeper into this subject in Chapter 7.)

► *Conversion of Arguments* ►

As a further experiment, try calling **fsquare( )** with the **float** variable **height** in place of the **double** variable **depth**. Although **fsquare( )** officially asks for a **double** argument, you'll find it works equally well with a **float**. This is part of the grand internal conversion plan already discussed—passing real to formal arguments during function calls triggers promotions and conversions like those found in assignments and mixed-expression evaluations.

To return to more mundane matters, we next consider another basic data type called **char**, so far encountered only in constant forms.

► *DATA TYPE char* ►

The type specifier **char** is used to declare variables in the now familiar manner.

```
char c, ch, flag;   /* three char variables declared − not initialized */
```

The variables **c**, **ch**, and **flag** are each allotted one byte in memory and can be assigned values within this range at any point in the program from which they are visible.

► *The Hidden Truth about char* ►

Despite its name, the data type **char** is best considered as a special integer type representing the whole number values assigned internally to the computer's character set, in our case the ASCII set (see Appendix A). The ASCII set consists of 128 printable characters (0-9, A-Z, a-z, and punctuation marks) and nonprintable control characters encoded in seven bits. Hence the natural bit width for storing such characters is the 8-bit byte.

The IBM PC extends the ASCII set, providing printable characters for the control codes and taking advantage of the additional 128 bit patterns by assigning special symbols that use the eighth bit. This is the *IBM PC Extended ASCII character set*, full of hearts, clubs, sharps, flats, and happy faces. Some of my examples will refer to this enlarged set.

When I describe **char** as a numeric type, I mean that **char** variables can be manipulated just like integers.

```
c = 'a'; ch = c + 1;
```

will increase the bit value in **c** by 1 and move the resulting sum to **ch**. The ASCII code chart tells us that **ch** now holds the bit pattern for 'b'. A common example is the conversion of characters from lower to upper case or vice versa:

```
c = 'Z'; c = c + 'a' − 'A';    /* c now equals 'z' */
ch = c − 'a' + 'A'             /* ch equals 'Z' */
```

This trick works because the values of the uppercase and lowercase ASCII characters differ by a constant: 32 (decimal) = 'a' − 'A' = 'b' − 'B' and so on. You could write

```
c = c + 32;                    /* lowercase shift − possibly! */
ch = ch − 32;                  /* uppercase shift − with due caution! */
```

but this obscures the underlying logic and will reduce portability. 'a' − 'A' = 'b' − 'B' is true for most character sets, but the value of the constant difference may not be 32.

You can multiply and divide **char**'s even if the results defy any character logic ('!' times 2 equals 'B' for instance). C will go through the motions without complaint, possibly truncating in the process.

► *The Sign of a char* ►

The question immediately arises whether **c** and **ch** in the above example will behave like **signed** or **unsigned** integers. If **c** reaches the value 127 (01111111 in binary), would (**c** + **1**) represent 128 (unsigned) or − 128 (signed)? The answer is that, as with **int**, you have control over which interpretation the system will make. You can use the optional type modifiers **signed** and **unsigned**.

```
signed char c;                 /* c has the range − 128 to + 127 */
unsigned char ch;              /* ch has the range 0 to + 255 */
```

► *The Default Sign for char* ►

The default modifier, however, can be set as an option via the Turbo C Options menu. Select the Compiler submenu, then the Code Generation subsubmenu. There you will find the Default **char** type option. This toggles you between **signed** and **unsigned** as the default **char** type.

Au naturel, the factory setting is **signed**, whereby **char c;** is equivalent to **signed char c;**, and you would have to explicitly use **unsigned char ch;** for any unsigned character variables.

Contrariwise, if the Compile/Options menu were set to **unsigned**, the declaration **char c;** would be equivalent to **unsigned char c;**. In this case, a deliberate **signed char ch;** would be needed to beat the default. (If you use the command-line compiler TCC.EXE there is a − **K** switch option that does the same job as the Default char type menu toggle.)

► *More Arithmetic with char* ►

Thinking of **char**'s as numbers makes sense of the following type of manipulation you'll frequently encounter:

```
if (ch >= 'A' && ch <= 'Z') ch = ch + 'a' − 'A';
/* convert ch to lowercase ONLY if ch is an uppercase letter */
/* The parentheses around the if (condition) are essential */
```

► *BRIEF LOGICAL DETOUR* ►

The **&&** is C's logical AND operator, so **if** is testing to see if **ch** is both greater than or equal to 'A' AND less than or equal to 'Z'.

Expressions like **ch** >= 'A' are called *Boolean* to honor the English mathematician George "Kelly"-Boole (1815–64). Boolean expressions are two-valued, either true or false, and can be combined with the Boolean logical operators **!** (NOT), **&&** (AND), and **||** (OR) as listed in Table 3.6.

Simple and compound Boolean expressions are regularly tested in C to determine which course of action the program should take. Without such *program control* mechanisms, of course, programs would be reduced to predetermined, inflexible sequences. The **if** clause is just one method of setting up a control structure. You can also perform blocks of statements **while** a certain condition holds, or iterate blocks with a **for** loop until a certain condition is false. These and other constructs will be explained as we progress.

Operator	Meaning	Examples
!	NOT	If *X* is true then *!X* is false. If *X* is false then *!X* is true.
||	OR	If either *X* is true or *Y* is true (or both) then (*X* || *Y*) is true, otherwise (*X* || *Y*) is false.
&&	AND	If *X* is true and *Y* is true then (*X* && *Y*) is true, otherwise (*X* && *Y*) is false.

► **Table 3.6:** Boolean operators

► *The Truth about C* ►

C demands no profound wrestling with the real meanings of *true* and *false*. Mundanely, any expression that evaluates to zero is considered *false*, while any expression that evaluates to a nonzero value is taken as *true*. Unlike Modula-2, there is no specific **BOOLEAN** data type. You can legally write **if** (*X*) where *X* is any data type, variable, or constant that can legally be compared with zero. (Parentheses *must* surround the conditional portions of control statements.)

```
if (3) {....}                    /* legal but pointless */
```

means *always* perform the following block, since (**3**) is true (nonzero). More useful is

```
if (ch) {...}                    /* if ch is non-NUL */
```

where **ch** is a **char**. The ASCII NUL character is value zero, so the block after the **if** is performed only for non-NUL characters. More long-winded equivalents would be

```
if (ch != '\0') {...}            /* if ch is non-NUL */
```

or

```
if (ch != 0) {...}               /* if ch is non-NUL */
```

since **ch** is promoted to an **int**. You can reverse the logic with

    if (!ch) {...}   /* if ch is NUL */

If **ch** is non-NUL, **!ch** becomes zero (false), but if **ch** is NUL, **!ch** becomes one (true).

Here is the the character test example again.

    if (ch >= 'A' && ch <= 'Z') ch = ch + 'a' − 'A';
    /* convert ch to lowercase ONLY if ch is an uppercase letter */

If the first condition fails, C does not bother to test the second one since the compound expression must be false. If the first condition succeeds, the second one is tested. Only if both conditions hold will the statement

    ch = ch + 'a' − 'A';

be executed. The two conditions ensure that **ch** is indeed an uppercase letter. Note that >= and <= work with characters in a purely numerical way, just like the other *relational* operators listed in Table 3.7. For the ASCII set, you need to remember that '**a**' > '**A**' and that all the control codes are less than ' ' (a blank space).

► BACK TO DATA TYPE char ►

The next piece of the **char** jigsaw is knowing what C actually does when performing arithmetic on **char**s.

► From char to int and Back ►

Before evaluating expressions, any **char** encountered is quietly *promoted* to an **int**, and this is where the sign of the **char** comes into the picture.

For signed character types, the upper byte of the **int** will be *sign-extended*, thereby maintaining the sign and value of the 8-bit **char** in the 16-bit **int**. With unsigned character types, the upper byte of the **int** is cleared to zero. For example, the letter '**a**' (hex 0x61) is promoted to hex 0x0061 regardless of whether it is initially represented as a signed or unsigned **char**. On the other

Operator	Meaning	Examples
==	Equals	if (x == 1) {....}
!=	Not equals	while (ch != EOF) {...}
<	Less than	if (ch < 'z') {...}
<=	Less than or equals	while (i <= maxi) {...}
>	Greater than	if (j > blk*siz) {...}
>=	Greater than or equals	if (i%j >= k%l) {...}

► **Table 3.7:** *Relational operators*

hand, the Greek beta (hex 0xE1) is promoted to 0x00E1 if it is unsigned but becomes 0xFFE1 if it is signed.

Note that inner conversions and promotions are made in temporary registers or RAM before the evaluation. The actual sizes of the variables are unaffected.

► *The Constant char*

You can now see how Turbo C's 16-bit **char** constants, introduced in Chapter 1, fit into the grand plan. If you set Turbo C to the **unsigned** default, all single **char** constants will have their upper bytes clear. With the **signed** default, any **char** constants with values over 127 (decimal) would have all one's in their upper byte (0xFF hex). This conversion occurs during compilation as the constants are encountered in the source code.

With Turbo C's nonstandard, nonportable double character constants such as 'A\n', no sign extension takes place because all sixteen bits are occupied—the 'A' in the lower byte and the '\n' in the upper byte.

In the assignments

```
c = 'a'; ch = c + 1;
```

the 'a' is represented as two bytes (0x0061). The upper byte will always be zero since the eighth bit of 0x61 is zero. Whether **c** is **signed** or **unsigned** it will pick up the lower byte 0x61 via the assignment—internally, **c** is temporarily promoted to **int**, receives 16 bits, then sheds the upper byte (which is zero anyway).

The net result is that you can, with care, use **char** variables to store small integers (− 128 to + 127 or 0 to 255) when **int** might prove wasteful of RAM. However, you are not saving any CPU cycles!

► *Using int for Characters*

A more common requirement is using **int** when you might feel that **char** is more natural. This twist of fate occurs because of C's **EOF** (end of file) convention. When your program is pulling characters from a text file using a function such as **fgetc( )** (a popular maneuver that you'll learn in Chapter 8), you need to know when the end of the file is reached. And, preferably, you would like to detect this condition from the value returned by **fgetc( )** since the program is usually engaged in perusing each of these "character" values anyhow. The alternative would be having to test some other flag or condition before each **fgetc( )** call ("Are we there yet?"). What you need is some unique value from **fgetc( )** that says, "This is *not* a character because there are no more characters available!" It is clear that no unique character from the ASCII or extended ASCII set can meet this requirement. For portability, such a character would have to be universally agreed upon, and it would then be taboo except as an end of file marker. (You may know that the Ctrl-Z [ASCII value 26] EOF convention for DOS text files causes many headaches when handling non-DOS files.)

The conundrum is solved in C by having **fgetc( )** and similar file and stream I/O functions return an **int** rather than a **char**. The choice of a unique, non-clashing, readily detectable EOF value suddenly becomes easy. That value is traditionally − 1, but any noncharacter value would work. The price paid is that the variable receiving characters and EOF's must be of type **int**, not of type **char**. The price is not really high since most manipulations of the returned value would incur a promotion to **int** in any case. **EOF** is defined as − 1 in STDIO.H, so you will often find the following snippet:

```
#include <stdio.h>
    ...
    int ch;                              /* the char is really an int! */
    ...
    while ((ch = fgetc(stream)) ! = EOF)

    {
/* while ch is not equal to EOF...do something with ch */
/* Its bottom byte is a character from the file since you have
```

```
        not reached the end of file */
            ...
        }

    /* end of file here */
```

Generally speaking, library functions that require a **char** argument are written to accept an **int** argument. You saw a similar philosophy of silent promotion with functions taking **float** and **double** arguments.

► *Precanned char Aids* ►

The Turbo C library contains a set of useful routines declared in CTYPE.H (whether they are functions or macros need not bother us—the end result is the same) that help you classify a **char** variable. In fact, the test we examined earlier,

```
    if (ch >= 'A' && ch <= 'Z') {...}
```

can be written succinctly as

```
    #include <ctype.h>
            ...
            if (isupper(ch)) {...}
```

The macro **isupper( )** behaves very much like a function taking an **int** argument: when you "call" it with a **char** argument, an **int** within ASCII range, or an **int** with value EOF, **isupper( )** returns nonzero (true) if the argument is an uppercase letter. Otherwise it returns zero (false). I will use the expression *ASCII + EOF* to indicate the set of ASCII characters and equivalent ASCII integers (0–127), supplemented by the EOF value (−1).

There are twelve such **is**... *predicates* or properties returning true or false. One of them, **isascii( )**, can be called with *any* integer value—it tells you if the argument is a valid ASCII value (0-127). The others work with ASCII + EOF arguments only. Table 3.8 lists them and their properties.

► *ARRAYS* ►

There are many instances where you want to handle a number of related variables of the same type. Suppose you wanted to manipulate a group of

Predicate	Argument	Tests True If...
isascii(ch)	int	$0 < ch < 127$
isalnum(ch)	ASCII+EOF	**ch** is a letter or digit
isalpha(ch)	ASCII+EOF	**ch** is a letter
iscntrl(ch)	ASCII+EOF	**ch** is control character or DEL (0x00–0x1F or 0x7F)
isdigit(ch)	ASCII+EOF	**ch** is a digit
isgraph(ch)	ASCII+EOF	**ch** is printable nonspace character (0x21–0x7E)
islower(ch)	ASCII+EOF	**ch** is lowercase letter
isupper(ch)	ASCII+EOF	**ch** is uppercase letter
isprint(ch)	ASCII+EOF	**ch** is printable character or space (0x20–0x7E)
ispunct(ch)	ASCII+EOF	**ch** is punctuation symbol (all printable characters, excluding alphanumeric, spacing, and control characters)
isspace(ch)	ASCII+EOF	**ch** is white space, i.e., space, tab, CR, LF or FF
isxdigit(ch)	ASCII+EOF	**ch** is hex digit (0–9, A–F or a–f)

► *Table 3.8: Character tests*

eight characters with a view to creating anagrams. You could start by declaring them with individual identifiers as in

```
char ch0, ch1, ch2, ch3, ch4, ch5, ch6, ch7;
```

but before long this would prove quite restrictive and time consuming. A more convenient approach is to declare a single entity, called an *array*, with eight elements.

```
char ch[8];                    /* ch is an array of char with 8 elements */
```

The syntax is simple and suggestive if you have ever used vector notation.

The [*N*] immediately following the identifier tells the compiler that you are calling for an array of *N* elements where *N* must be a positive integer. You can now refer to the eight **char** elements of the array **ch** by using an *index* from 0 to 7.

```
unsigned int i; char ch[8];

ch[0] = 'a'; ch[1] = 'b';          /* initialize 1st two chars */
ch[6] = 'g'; ch[7] = 'h';          /* and last two chars of array */
i = 2; ch[i] = 'c';                /* set third char to 'c' */
ch[i + 2] = ch[0];                 /* set fifth char to 'a' */
```

You can treat each of the elements from **ch[0]** through **ch[7]** exactly as if you had declared them individually as type **char**. Also, as you can see, it is possible to use constants or integer variables and expressions as your indices (or indexes, if you prefer the modern, dubious spelling). In fact, you can use a type **char** as an index simply because **char** has the basic integral properties needed for counting 0, 1, 2,.... Indices can never be **float** or **double** unless you first force them into **int**'s. **ch[2.3]**, for instance, is verboten.

The first element of an array is *always* indexed with 0, *never* with 1. This simple fact is often overlooked, much to the amusement of the compiler. The *N*th element of an array is ***array_name[N − 1]***.

You can set up arrays for any of the data types discussed so far.

```
#define MAXVEC 1000

    float grid[100];               /* grid[0] to grid[99] are all floats */
    double vector[MAXVEC];         /* 1000 doubles */
    long salary[MAXVEC*2];         /* 2000 longs */
    vector[MAXVEC − 1] = 3.14159;  /* set last element of vector */
```

For the moment, we'll confine our attention to arrays of **char**. As I hinted earlier, arrays of **char** provide us with a natural and powerful mechanism for handling string variables.

► *Initializing Arrays* ►

In the earlier examples we declared an array and then set individual members of it using separate assignments. C allows a more concise way of declaring and initializing arrays.

```
char ch[8] = {'a','b','c','d','e','f','g','h'};
/* declare and initialize: ch[0] = 'a', ch[1] = 'b'.... */
```

The sequence of constants, with commas as dividers, is enclosed in curly braces. The resulting object is called an *initializer*. Each constant in the initializer is assigned in turn to the elements in the array. If you have fewer constants than array elements, the extra array elements are set to zero. Having more constants than array elements will trigger an error.

If you are exceptionally lazy, you can omit the number of elements inside the [ ]. C will then calculate this number for you from the number of constants in the initializer.

```
char name[ ] = {'S','t','a','n','\0'};
/* name becomes an array of 5 elements i.e. name[5] */
```

In the above example you can see that **name** is looking suspiciously like a string holding "**Stan**" with the final NUL that we discussed back in Chapter 1. In fact, the above initialization can also be achieved with either

```
char name[5] = "Stan";
```

or

```
char name[ ] = "Stan";          /* name[ ] becomes a name[5] */
```

using a string constant in place of an initializer. "**Stan**" as a string constant is stored with a final, invisible NUL automatically appended, so **name[]** receives five characters not four.

Quick quiz: What is the value of **name[4]**? Yes, it is NUL ('\0') because **name[4]** is the fifth, final character of the array **name**.

► *The Name of the Pointer* ►

Each of the expressions **name[*i*]**, as *i* ranges from 0 to 4, is of type **char**. However, the identifier **name** by itself (which you'll see used shortly) is *not* treated by C as either a string or as a **char** but as a special data type known as **pointer to char**.

Unlike **name[0]**, which is of type **char** because it is the first byte of the array, **name** itself represents the memory address of the byte **name[0]**. We say that **name** *points* to **name[0]**. You could find the address held in **name**, peek into the byte at that address, and confirm that is was indeed 0x53 (the ASCII character 'S') as placed in **name[0]** by our initialization. The actual value of **name** is seldom of importance.

► Pointer Size and Memory Models ►

For most of the programs we'll be considering, the **pointer** types can be considered to be simple unsigned 16-bit values that can address up to 64K of memory.

The 8088/8086/80286 has a complicated segmented memory-addressing scheme that is beyond our immediate scope. Briefly, Turbo C allows you to choose between six different *memory models*, ranging from *tiny* to *huge*. This choice dictates the pointer size, 16-bit or 32-bit, the compiler will use, and this in turn determines the maximum sizes of your program and data segments.

It turns out to be wasteful to use a larger model than you actually need since the pointer arithmetic becomes progressively more complex. I will assume the most efficient (tiny) model for the time being. It uses 16-bit pointers (known as *near* pointers) whereby all your code and data is assumed to occupy a 64K segment of RAM.

► Pointer Awareness ►

We will be returning regularly to the topic of pointers because they play a central role in C. Strangely enough, they can be used and enjoyed without an intimate knowledge of how RAM is addressed.

The symbolism employed by C allows you to manipulate pointers in an abstract, algebraic way, much as you get used to writing **a*b/c** without fretting unduly about how the machine is multiplying and dividing, provided that c is nonzero!

The two key symbols are **&**, meaning *address of*, and *****, meaning *pointed at by*. The two are complementary, as illustrated by the following informal definitions:

&var is the address in memory of the identifier **var**.

*ptr is the object found in memory at address **ptr** provided only that **ptr** is not the *NULL pointer*. If **ptr** has the value NULL (effectively zero, or false) ***ptr** is *undefined*.

So you can say that **&var** points to **var** and **ptr** points to ***ptr**.

The NULL exception for ***ptr** is extremely important (it corresponds to the "never divide by zero" injunction). Zero or NULL pointers are perfectly valid and legal; indeed they are as indispensible as the number 0 in arithmetic. However, NULL pointers do not point at anything, so you cannot use the * operator with them. Later you'll see a typical use of the NULL pointer as the terminator of a chain of linked lists rather as ASCII NUL is used to terminate a string.

& is known as the *address* operator. * is called the *indirection* operator because it expresses the idea that you get an operand indirectly by first getting its address and then accessing that address.

What data types are pointers? Well, if **var** is of type **int**, we naturally say that **&var** is of type **pointer to int**. Likewise, if **ptr** is of type, say, **pointer to float**, then ***ptr** must be of type **float** (unless **ptr** is NULL, of course).

► *The Big BUT...* ►

But, and herein lies the danger, in one sense all pointers are simply unsigned 16-bit (we confine our attention to near pointers) addresses with no distinguishing birthmarks. Some programmers get into the habit of using unsigned **int** or **long** variables as pointers. C does not always object, but portability suffers since there are computers with larger addressing ranges.

Pointers can be painlessly "corrupted" to point to places they shouldn't! You can take **&var**, do some pointer arithmetic, obtain a **ptr**, and then rashly assign something to ***ptr**.

```
int var, *ptr;              /* declare an int and a pointer to int */
                            /* this is explained below */
    ptr = &var;             /* ptr points to var */
    {play around with ptr}
    if (ptr) *ptr = 96      /* assign only if ptr is not NULL */
```

The **if (ptr)** screens out NULL pointers since NULL evaluates to zero (false).

But ***ptr** may, without due care, turn out to be part of your program or Turbo C or even DOS rather than part of your data. A crash or something worse may result!

► *Pointer Declarations* ►

I've said that when you declare an array **name[5]**, the identifier **name** is actually **&name[0]**, a pointer to the first element of the array. You do not have to declare **name** as a pointer to **char**—C does that for you as part of the array declaration.

C does allow you to explicitly declare pointers to any data type (except **void**) as in

```
int *int_ptr; char *char_ptr;
float *float_ptr; unsigned long *ul_ptr;
```

The presence of the * is sufficient warning to the compiler that the identifier following is a pointer to the type specified.

Although **int_ptr** now exists as a variable of type **pointer to int**, all you have is a 16-bit uninitialized allocation of RAM; **int_ptr** is not yet pointing to anything in particular, and no **int** variable has been created. As you saw with all the earlier declarations, it is possible to initialize during a pointer declaration. Consider the following snippet:

```
int i = 1, j = 2, *int_ptr = &i;
/* initialize int_ptr with the address of int i */
    printf("int_ptr points at %d/n",*int_ptr);
    int_ptr = &j;      /* reset pointer */
    printf("int_ptr now points at %d/n",*int_ptr);
/* what will display? */
```

► *Pointer Power* ►

In spite of the dangers, pointers provide C with a certain grace and power. One of the chief applications is when you want a function to change the value of one or more of its arguments. I explained that C passes all arguments by *value*—in other words, the function receives a copy of the argument and cannot normally alter the original argument variable. (Refer back to **cube( )** in Chapter 2 to refresh your memory on this.)

However, if you pass a pointer argument, **ptr** say, to a function, the function makes a local copy of **ptr** as it does with all arguments. Using this copy pointer, the function can actually access and alter *ptr (unless **ptr** is NULL).

So we effectively achieve what is known as *calling by reference*. This mechanism allows functions to return values in the usual way (as in **x** = **cube(y)**) and also alter the actual arguments passed to the function when desired.

The library routine **scanf( )** is a good illustration and one I have been dying to introduce since it allows you to get input from the keyboard. Its introduction has been delayed until now because it uses pointer arguments.

► KEYBOARD INPUT ►

printf( ) and **puts( )** allow you to display data on your screen (**stdout** or *standard output device*). So far these data have been embedded in the programs themselves, which hardly leads to realistic applications! We need to explore another, rather obvious source of data—your keyboard, also known as the *standard input device* or **stdin**.

► *Keyboard Input Using scanf( )* ►

scanf( ) uses a similar format control string to **printf( )**. Each element of this string determines how the elements read from the input device will be interpreted and where they will be stored. Take the following simple case:

```
int i;
char name[30];
printf("\n Enter your number and name:");
scanf("%d %s", &i, name);
```

If you respond to this by keying in the line

```
35 Stan
```

with any amount of white space between the two fields, the control string matches the **35** with the pair **%d** and pointer **&i** and then matches the string "**Stan**" with the pair **%s** and pointer **name**. As with **printf( )** the conversion specification **%d** causes a conversion of the ASCII characters "**35**" to **int**. The resulting number is stored at the address of **i**, namely **&i**. This is a fancy way of saying that the variable **i** is assigned the value 35. As explained in the previous section, C functions cannot alter **i** directly. Passing **i** rather than **&i** to **scanf( )** would not work: **scanf( )** would receive only a copy of i, and no change to i itself could be made.

Similarly, **%s** tells **scanf( )** to expect a string pointer, **name**, and the input string "Stan" is moved (with an appended NUL) to the array **name[30]**. Recall that **name** is a pointer to the first element of the array **name[30]**.

As with **printf( )**, **scanf( )** has wide choice of control specifiers, and they are best learned by osmotic exposure. Appendix C lists them all for reference. The most common conversions are **%f** (floating point), **%u** (unsigned integer), and **%c** (single character). **scanf( )** trudges along until all the conversion specifications in the control string have been matched by input items.

The key to **scanf( )**, and the cause of most frustration, is the need to pass pointers to the target identifiers. With **&i** this is visually obvious. The puzzle for beginners is that **name**, which looks like a normal identifier, is in fact a pointer to **char**, that is, **name** is an address. It therefore doesn't need a preceding **&** to turn it into an address. You do not write **&name** (illegal), but you can write **&name[0]** (which is the same as **name**—both are pointers to the string variable). From my definitions of **&** and ***** it should also be clear that ***name** would be a synonym for **name[0]** since **name** is the pointer and ***name** is a *pointee*, to coin a word.

I'll end this varied chapter with GETDAT.C (Program 3.2). The comments explain what is going on, and Figure 3.2 shows a typical screen that would result from running GETDAT.EXE.

```
/* getdat.c - simple keyboard input and outpt */

#include <stdio.h>

main()
{
    int i, j;
    char name[31]; /* declare array of char - 30 + NUL */

    printf("Enter your Name and Number!: ");
    j = scanf("%s %d", name, &1);
/* scanf also returns a value! The number of successfully */
/* matched input items */
    printf("Well, hello %s!\n",name);
    if (i > 99)
        printf("Your number is greater than 99!\n"0;
    else
        printf("Your number is less than 100!\n");
    printf("PS: You entered %d items\n",j);

}
```

► *Program 3.2:* GETDAT.C

```
Enter your Name and Number!: Rudolf 99
Well, hello Rudolf!
Your number is less than 100!
PS: You entered 2 items










Press any key to return to Turbo C . . .▪
```

► **Figure 3.2:** *GETDAT.C screen output*

► SUMMARY OF CHAPTER 3 ►

Here are the main topics covered in Chapter 3.

◄► Integer data types cannot handle decimal fractions or large numbers. Division and remainder with integers may lead to erroneous results.

◄► The FP (floating-point) data types extend the range and numerical precision available by storing numbers in two parts—a mantissa and an exponent.

◄► Three FP types are provided: **float**, **double**, and **long double** (although **long double** happens to be the same as **double** in Turbo C). These type specifiers are used in declarations in the same way as is **int**.

◄► **float**s are promoted to **double** internally during all FP calculations.

◄► The considerable software overhead in floating-point arithmetic can be reduced with a math coprocessor such as the 8087 or 80287. Turbo C can detect and utilize a fitted math coprocessor. If there is no coprocessor, Turbo C performs floating-point calculations with software (emulation with EMU.LIB).

◄► **printf( )** can format FP numbers with precision and width specifiers in conjunction with **%f**, **%e**, and **%g**.

◄► I provided more information about function declarations and function definitions—where they can be placed and what happens if they are missing. This big subject will occupy much of Chapter 7.

◄► The **char** data type is really a small integer—it can be signed or unsigned by default and later specified either way with an explicit **unsigned char** or **signed char** declaration. All **char**s are promoted to **int** (signed or unsigned as appropriate) during arithmetic. You can add 1 to 'A' to get 'B', subtract 2 from 'c' to get 'a', and so on.

◄► I introduced C's simple approach to logic: false is zero, true is nonzero. Almost any variable or constant can therefore be used in Boolean expressions. Typical conditionals such as **if** and **while** simply test the following expression for zero or nonzero.

◄► Compound Boolean expressions use **!** (NOT), ¦¦ (OR), and **&&** (AND) in any logical combination. Booleans can also be generated using the relational operators **==** (equals), **!= =** (not equals), **<** (less than), **<=** (less than or equals), and so on.

◄► Character constants take up 2 bytes. The upper byte is sign extended unless the compiler option default is **unsigned char**. Character constants can be expressed in various formats: 'A', '\t', '\007' (octal), or '\x1F' (hex). Turbo C allows nonportable double character constants, e.g., 'bG' or '\t\a', which are also held in 2 bytes.

◄► You should declare as **int** any characters read from streams and files since the EOF signal received at end of file is the non-**char** − 1.

◄► CTYPE.H contains many precanned **char** testing routines such as **isupper( )** and **isascci( )**.

◄► Arrays are collections of variables sharing the same base data type. They are declared as **base_type array_name[size];** where each variable **array_name[i]** is of type **base_type** for i = 0 to **size** − 1. The index i must be an integral type.

◄► Arrays can be initialized with = **{val1, val2,...valn}**; as part of their declaration.

◄► The identifier **array_name** is of type pointer to **base_type**. Hence, **array_name** is a constant pointer to the first element of the array, **array_name[0]**.

◄► I presented pointer notation: **&var** is a pointer to **var**, and ***ptr** is the object being pointed at by **ptr** unless **ptr** is NULL, in which case ***ptr** is undefined.

◄► Variable pointers to any nonvoid **data_type** can be declared and optionally initialized using

data_type *ptr_to_data_type [= &data_type_var];.

◄► Pointers are powerful and dangerous. Turbo C does its best to warn you by checking pointer and pointee types, but you can poke yourself to death if you wish. Pointers have their own arithmetical rules (which are covered in Chapter 4).

◄► Pointers allow functions to alter their real arguments (via a simulated "call by reference"), which is not otherwise possible with C's "call by value" regimen.

◄► Data from the keyboard (and other sources, as you'll see later) can be formatted and passed to variables using **scanf( )**. **scanf( )** uses format strings in the same way as **printf( )**. The arguments must be pointers to the variables receiving the keyboard input:

```
int number; char name[30];
scanf("%d %s",&number, name);
```

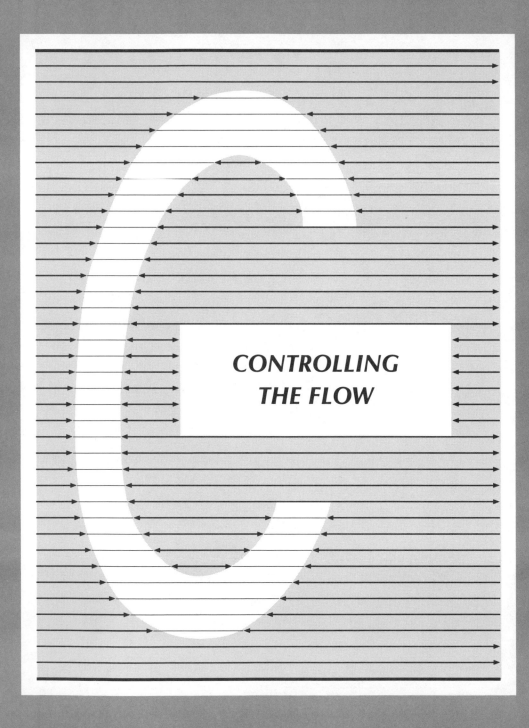

**CONTROLLING
THE FLOW**

► *CHAPTER 4* ►

The main topic in this chapter is the use of *control flow* statements, entailing a brief homily on *structure*. The program examples, en passant, will reveal other aspects of C, such as *type casting*, *conditional expressions*, *string manipulation*, and *pointer arithmetic*.

► *CONTROL FLOW STATEMENTS* ►

You have already seen some simple control flow examples using **if**, **else**, and **while**. These use the simple fact that an expression can be tested for true (nonzero) or false (zero), and, depending upon the result of the test, the flow of the program execution can be varied—blocks can be bypassed or performed repeatedly (looped).

In theory, you can get by with the plain vanilla **if**, from which the other control effects can be derived, howbeit at the expense of clarity and code size.

C offers many control flow variants and extensions: **goto**, **else if**, **do...while**, **continue**, **break**, the **case/switch** statement, and the **for** loop.

All of these except **goto** enforce the expression of algorithms in a logical and legible way—the approach now generally burdened by the name *structured* programming.

► *THE IMPORTANCE OF BEING STRUCTURED* ►

In a properly structured program, sets of actions are grouped together in units that are, in a certain sense, self-contained syntactically for the compiler and visually for the human reader.

At the top level, C encourages the division of a program into many small routines, called functions, with well-defined interfaces and an efficient calling mechanism. Functions can call other functions (including themselves).

Unlike structured languages such as Ada and Modula-2, however, C does not allow you to *define* a function within another function.

Within each function, the code is structured into blocks using { and } as block markers. Blocks can be nested to any level, but if you concentrate your attention on any given block, however large or small, the ideal is that control enters only at the start of the block and emerges eventually only at the bottom. I say "eventually" because sections of code within the block may be iterated many times via various looping constructs.

What is frowned upon is the anarchy of, say, BASIC (excluding the more recent structured versions) or assembly languages, in which a conditional or unconditional **GOTO** or branch instruction can pass control to or from any part of the program regardless of block structure, creating what is commonly known as spaghetti coding. Consider the following simple pseudo-code with an outer and inner (nested) block:

```
block A   label A1: initialize block A variables
          label A2: process them
           block B
            label B1: initialize block B variables
            label B2: process them
            label B3: exit block B
          label A3: more processing
          label A4: exit block A
```

For block A to work safely, it is essential that control starts at **label A1:**. It should be impossible to branch directly to **label A2:**, say, from outside A, bypassing the initialization code at **label A1:**. The nested block B, which is used in processing block A, should be completely inaccessible from outside A. Even from within A, B should be entered only via **label B1:**. Once control is in B, we should be free to iterate via **B1:** and **B2:** but forced to exit via **B3:**. Similarly, we should not be able to jump out of A except via **A4:**.

Hard-earned experience in programming has proved that accuracy and maintainability are greatly improved if these rules are either followed voluntarily or enforced by the language specification.

Summing up the structured paradigm: From outside of A only **A1:** is accessible. Within A, all A labels and **B1:** are accessible. Within B, only B labels are accessible.

Most of C's control flow statements enforce this regime, but there are some minor loopholes and one major one!

► *THE goto STATEMENT* ►

C (like BASIC and Pascal) has a **goto** and **label** control flow mechanism. The C **goto** can only transfer control within a function, but it can still violate the rules for a strictly structured programming language by allowing jumps in and out of blocks. The programmer, therefore, must use **goto** with extreme caution. Accidentally bypassing initializations and branching into and out of other control loops are the chief dangers.

In practice, **goto** is used sparingly, usually to exit from a deeply nested block when some calamity is detected that would be difficult to handle by a succession of exits from each enclosing block. Adding a **goto** to our earlier example illustrates this situation.

```
block A   label A1: initialize block A variables
          label A2: process them
            block B
              label B1: initialize block B variables
              label B2: process them
               if (ERROR) goto A4;
              label B3: exit block B
          label A3: more processing
          label A4: exit block A
```

► *The goto Syntax* ►

The **goto** syntax is rather like BASIC's:

```
goto label;
```

Anywhere in the current function, you can label the target statement as follows:

```
label: statement;
```

The net result is that if and when the **goto** is executed, control passes to the (possibly empty) statement appearing alongside the matching label. **label** can be any identifier unique within the scope of the function. Labels can never appear without a real or empty statement, so

```
goto error;
...
error:                          /* illegal – hanging label */
```

is illegal, but

```
goto error;
...
error:;                        /* OK — empty statement at label */
```

is legal.

In view of the **goto**, we can say that, in general, the constructs offered by C encourage structured programming but do not guarantee it!

We now goto the well-behaved control flow statements.

► THE if, else, AND else if STATEMENTS ►

Any expression that can be legally evaluated (with internal conversion when necessary) to give an integer or pointer value (zero or nonzero) can be used as the condition-expression in the following schema:

```
if (condition-expression) T-statement
[else F-statement]
TF-statement
```

(Recall that [ ] surround an optional element.)

As in plain English, the **if** suggests a testing of the following expression in order to determine a course of action. Many computer languages use the format **IF...THEN** to stress the idea of consequence, but in C the **THEN** is implied (as it often is in English: "If that's true, [then] I quit!"). Also, as you saw in Chapter 3, C takes a purely numeric view of Boolean variables, converting the conditions $(3 >= 2)$ to 1 (true) and $(3 = 2)$ to 0 (false). Any nonzero condition-expression will be interpreted as true, which is reflected in the object code with the branch-not-zero instruction found in all machine languages.

T-statement represents the piece of code (possibly the empty statement ;) that will be followed (obeyed) *only* if **condition-expression** is true (nonzero). If this code contains more than one statement, it will need block marker braces to distinguish it from any following code sequences. Curly braces are optional if the T-statement consists of just one statement as in

```
if (x == 1) y = 2*x;          /* T is a single statement */
if (z >= 5.1) { x = 0; y = 3; }  /* T is a multiple statement so braces
                                    are needed */
if (n < *ptr) {ch[n + 1] = '\0';} /* braces harmless – not really needed */
```

If your condition-expression is false (zero), the whole T-statement is bypassed, ignored and forsaken. The layout of your source code should therefore make it as clear as possible exactly where T-statements start and end. This is by no means a trivial problem since T-statements often contain many lines (and possibly pages) of complex code with embedded (nested) conditions. In such cases, indents and comments should be used to indicate the different nesting levels. (Examples will follow shortly.)

Returning to the basic paradigm,

```
if (condition-expression) T-statement
[else F-statement]
TF-statement
```

if *T-statement* is executed, control passes to *TF-statement* whether there is an **else** clause or not, and we are back into the main program sequence again.

If *condition-expression* evaluates to false, *T-statement* is ignored, and if there is an **else** clause *F-statement* will be executed. After *F-statement*, which may be empty, single, or multiple, we continue normal service with *TF-statement*. In summary,

- ► T-statement is obeyed only if the condition-expression is true.
- ► F-statement (if any) is obeyed only if the condition-expression is false.
- ► TF-statement is obeyed if condition is true or false.

(To be super pedantic, of course, the program may actually terminate rather than meet a TF-statement.)

► *Poor Dangling Else—The if...else Pitfall* ►

Since the T- and F-statements may contain further **if** and **else** clauses, great care is needed to avoid faulty logic. The problem is in deciding which **else** belongs with which **if**.

The golden rule is that an **else** matches the previous innermost unmatched **if** that is nearest. This matching may not always be immediately apparent. Take the following snippet:

```
if (x == 1)
   if (y == 1) puts("x = 1 and y = 1");
else puts("x != 1");                /* wrong conclusion */

/* reminder: puts( ) displays arg string plus newline */
```

At first sight you might be misled by the indentation to think that the **else** branch is taken only if **x** is not equal to 1. However, the **else** syntactically "belongs" to **if (y == 1)**.

Recall that the C compiler is unaware of your pretty (but possibly pretty wrong) indents. Correct versions, both logically and typographically, are

```
if (x == 1)
   if (y == 1) puts("x = 1 and y = 1");
   else ;                             /* an empty F-statement is
                                          legal but wasteful */
   else puts("x != 1 and y = don't care");  /* correct conclusion */
```

or

```
if (x == 1)
   if (y == 1) puts("x = 1 and y = 1");
   else puts("x = 1 and y != 1");      /* good conclusion */
else puts("x != 1 and y = don't care"); /* also good */
```

or

```
if (x == 1) {
   if (y == 1) puts("x = 1 and y = 1");
}                                       /* note: the added braces
                                           make a difference here */
else puts("x != 1 and y = don't care"); /* correct conclusion */
```

depending on your intentions.

In the third version, **if (y == 1)**... is surrounded with braces and becomes a complete block with no **else** option. C therefore matches the **else** with the **if (x == 1)**... condition. Curly braces are optional in the second version since the T- and F-statements are both single statements.

Mismatched or dangling **else**s often occur when a piece of good code is patched up with some additional nested **if** tests, disturbing the previous indentations or block markers.

Another common and frustrating error is putting a spurious semicolon after the condition-expression.

```
if (x == 1); y = 2*x;     /* T is now the empty statement */
                          /* y = 2*x becomes the TF-statement */
```

The syntax is impeccable, but the results may not be as intended.

► The else if Format ►

The **else if** is really a combination already covered by the foregoing syntax. In this case the F-statement happens to start with an **if** that may sprout further **else**s and **if**s!

Because this is a common construction, though, it deserves a special note. You often need a series of **if...else if** to cover a multichoice situation:

```
int x;
...
if
    (x == 1) puts("x = 1");
else if
    (x == 2) puts("x = 2");
else if
    (x == 3) puts("x = 3");
else if
    (x == 4) puts("x = 4");
else
    puts("x is none of the above!");
/* resume here for all cases */
```

Note the optional final **else** that traps any value of **x** not already matched by the chain of tests. Also observe that the layout clearly reveals the program's intention. Unless you had multiple T-statements, spurious braces would simply obscure matters.

► ANALYSIS OF CHKIP.C WITH EXPERIMENTS ►

Program 4.1, CHKIP.C, will give you some practice with **if** and **else**, as well as introducing you to **getche( )**, a standard library I/O routine declared in CONIO.H. The program also illustrates the use of a type cast in a typical situation. Figure 4.1 shows the screen output from a typical session with CHKIP.

► Type Casting ►

In the statement

```
ratio = (float) I / J;
```

```
/* chkip.c - simple conditional flow control */
#include <stdio.h>
#include <ctype.h>
#include <conio.h>
/* conio.h defines getche() */

main()
{
    int i = 0, j = 0;
    double ratio = 0.0;
    char ch, *cp;
/* we could also use int ch, see text */

    printf("\tEnter two smallish numbers: ");
    scanf("%d %d", &i ,&j);
    if (j != 0) {
        ratio = (float) i / j;
/* force conversion of int i to float before division */
/* further silent conversions occur - see text        */
        printf("%d / %d equals %f\n", i, j, ratio);
    } /* end if (j != 0) */
    else printf("%d / %d is undefined\n", i, j);

    if (i == j)
        puts("Your two numbers are equal");
    else if (i > j)
        puts("First number is larger");
    else
        puts("Second number is larger");

    printf("\tEnter a character: ");
    ch = getche();

/* getche() is "get char with echo"                   */
/* It waits for a keystroke, echoes it and returns its */
/* char value, which is then assigned to ch            */
/* No <enter> is needed with getche()                  */

 cp = &ch; /* assign the pointer &ch to cp
                which is a char pointer */

/* *cp now is the same as ch - so the maneuver serves only
   to illustrate pointer manipulation. You could replace
   *cp with ch in each of the following statements       */

        printf("\nYou entered \"%c\"\n",*cp);
    if (isalpha(*cp))
        printf("'%c' is alpha\n",*cp);
    else if (isdigit(*cp))
        printf("'%c' is a digit\n",*cp);
    else if (ispunct(*cp))
        printf("'%c' is punctuation\n",*cp);

    if (isalnum(*cp) && !isdigit(*cp) && !islower(*cp))
        printf("'%c' is uppercase letter\n",*cp);
    if (isgraph(*cp) || *cp == 040)
        printf("'%c' is printable or space\n",*cp);
}
```

► *Program 4.1:* CHKIP.C

```
          Enter two smallish numbers: 2 Ø
2 / Ø is undefined
First number is larger
          Enter a character: $
You entered "$"
'$' is punctuation
'$' is printable or space






Press any key to return to Turbo C . . .■
```

► **Figure 4.1:** *CHKIP screen output*

we force (or *coerce*) the compiler to *cast* or convert (internally and tempo-rarily) the **int i** to type **float** before the division by **int j** is attempted. Type cast-ing allows you to do this conversion trick between variables of *most* data types by using the target type specifier in parentheses followed by the vari-able to be converted.

   (*type specifier T*) *var*;

will internally and temporarily convert ***var*** to data type ***T***.

The type specifier, considered as an operator, is in precedence category 2, so it has higher precedence than *****, **/**, and **%**, which are in category 3. This explains why **(float) i /j** is interpreted as **((float) i)/j** rather than **(float) (i/j)**.

Casting can be used to influence the result of an arithmetic expression or to avoid type-mismatching errors, when passing arguments to functions, for example.

The following is a mixed bag of examples that are mostly legal but are not all equally useful:

```
int i, *int_ptr;
char c; *char_ptr;
```

```
    unsigned long ul;
    double d;
    float f;

    c = (char) i;                    /* cast int to char */

/*  (char) i = c; NO, NO — (char) i is not an lvalue */

    i = (int) *char_ptr              /* cast char to int */
/* assuming char_ptr points somewhere */

    int_ptr = (int *) char_ptr;
    char_ptr = (char *) int_ptr;
/* convert a char pointer to an int pointer and vice versa */
/* note the syntax */

    i = (int) f + (int) c;           /* cast float,char to int */
    i = (int) (f + c);               /* cast the float sum to int */
    f = (float) d;                   /* cast double to float */
    d = (double) i;                  /* cast int to double */
    ul = (unsigned long) i;          /* cast int to unsigned long */
    (void) func( );                  /* the value returned by
                                        func( ) is discarded */
```

The data type **void** was introduced in ANSI C to remove some potential trouble spots in K&R. The default return value of a function is **int** even if the definition does not explicitly return a value. Further, all functions, technically speaking, do return values of some kind whether you use them or not. **void** allows you and the complier to distinguish between a declaration such as *func( )*; [which is the lazy way or writing **int** *func( )*] and **void** *func( )*;. The latter says "discard the returned value of *func( )*." Objects of type **void** do not have values like the other types (even NULL is excluded as a value). A similar problem in K&R is distinguishing between functions taking arguments and those taking no arguments. A K&R declaration such as **char** *func( )*; can be legally followed by definitions such as **char** *func( )* or **char** *func(arg1,arg2)*. The ANSI C prototype declaration format removes this ambiguity by allowing **char** *func(void)*; when declaring a function with no arguments or **char** *func(type1 arg1,type2 arg2)*; when declaring a function with two arguments. The complier can now check that the function definitions and calls match the declarations.

Now some of the above examples of type casting are wasteful insofar as C already implicitly performs certain internal conversions (promotions and truncations) when evaluating expressions and making assignments.

For example, **c = i;** will truncate the **int i** from 16 to 8 bits in order to make the assignment to **char c**. The type cast **c = (char) i** simply makes this conversion explicit without altering the net result. So when are type casts essential?

Try omitting the **(float)** coercion in CHKIP.C. C will first perform the integer division **i/j** and then internally convert the integer quotient to **double** in order to make the assignment **ratio = i/j**. The result will be *nnnn*.000000, correct only to the nearest whole number. With **(float) i** you get a dramatic change. **int i** is converted to **float** and immediately promoted to **double** (since all FP calculations in C are performed with double precision). Next, **int j** is automatically promoted to **double** to match the data type of the dividend. The quotient is therefore a **double** before the assignment to **ratio**. **printf( )** will therefore show the answer correct to 6 decimal places (the default precision of **%f**).

Now try replacing **(float) i/j** with **(double) i/j**. If you have followed the previous discussion, you will realize that this will not alter the actual result; in fact, using **(double) i** is more logical and slightly faster. I had you use **(float) i** to illustrate the underlying theory.

Note carefully the difference between

```
i = (int) f + (int) c;                /* cast float,char to int */
```

and

```
i = (int) (f + c);                    /* cast the FP sum to int */
```

The answers might be different. In the second line, **char c** and **float f** will each be converted to **double** before the addition, then the sum will be rounded and truncated to **int**. The first line converts each to **int** and then performs an integer addition.

► DETOUR TO FORMAL CONVERSION RULES ►

It is time to list C's conversion policy during arithmetic evaluation a little more formally. There are rules for *unary* conversion (in which just a single operand is involved) and rules for *binary* conversion (in which two operands need to conform before the operation is carried out). We can combine these rules as follows:

1. Any operands of type **short** or **char** are converted to **int**.

2. Any operands of **unsigned char** or **unsigned short** are converted to **unsigned int**.

3. All **float**s are promoted to **double**s.

4. Types "array of T" are converted to types "pointer to T."

5. If either operand is **double**, the other is converted to **double**, giving a **double** result.

6. Else if either operand is **unsigned long [int]**, the other is converted to **unsigned long [int]**, giving an **unsigned long [int]** result.

7. Else if one operand is **long [int]** and the other is **unsigned [int]**, they are both converted to **unsigned long [int]**, giving an **unsigned long [int]** result.

8. Else if either operand is **long [int]**, the other (which must by now be an **int**) is converted to **long [int]**, giving a **long [int]** result.

9. Else if either operand is **unsigned [int]** the other is converted to **unsigned [int]**, giving an **unsigned [int]** result.

10. Else both operands must be **int**, and the result is **int**.

This seems a formidable list to remember, but most of the conversions are logical when you consider the internal representations of each data type.

With a complex right-expression made up of mixed data types, variables, or constants, you can picture the above rules being applied successively to pairs of operands according to the precedence and associativity rules. It is quite easy to simulate the compiler with pencil and paper, and often there is one dominating type, such as **double**, that simplifies the process of deciding the type of the final result.

► *Assignment Conversions* ►

For assignment conversions the rules are much simpler. If the lvalue has the same type as the evaluated right-expression, the assignment is trivial.

If the types differ, C attempts to convert the type of the right-expression to match that of the lvalue. With arithmetic types, this can always be done either by extension, as in **int** to **long** (safe), or by truncation, as in **double** to **long** (probably dangerous). Later you'll meet more complex data types that just refuse to be mixed or assigned. Following are examples of conversion of arithmetic types:

```
char c; unsigned char uc;
short s; unsigned short us;
int i; unsigned u;
long l; unsigned long ul;
float f; double d;
...

d = (c + ul)*(c – s + f)/(uc + l);
/* using a shorthand notation:
   Conversion rules for right-hand expression:

   rules 1 and 2: c and s –> int; uc –> ui
      d = (i + ul)*(i – i + f)/(ui + l)

   rule 3: f –> d
      d = (i + ul)*(i – i + d)/(ul + l)

   rule 5: d and x –> d
      d = (i + ul)*(d)/(ui + l)

   rule 6: ul and x –> ul
      d = (ul)*(d)/(ui + l)

   rule 7: l and ui –> ul
      d = (ul)*(d)/(ul)

   rule 5: d and x –> d
      d = (d)*(d)/(d)

   Assignment is double to double, no conversion */


/* Note: the order of evaluation is compiler dependent */

      i = d;              /* truncation */
      d = i;              /* int converted to double – safe */
      d = f;              /* float converted to double – safe */
      f = d;              /* f converted to double, double
                             assigned to double, then double
                             truncated to float */
```

► *BACK TO CHKIP.C—*
PROTOTYPES AND getche( ) ►

Rather than use **scanf( )** with a **%c** conversion string, CHKIP.C (Program 4.1) uses a useful standard library facility, **getche( )**. This is declared in CONIO.H as

> int getche(void);

This form of declaration is known as a *function prototype*—it provides both the user and the compiler with a clear indication of what arguments (if any) are legal and what value is returned (if any).

The prototype concept is one of the many important additions made to C as a result of the new ANSI standards. It allows the compiler writer greater scope to check that function calls are made with the correct number and types of arguments. There are special prototype formats to indicate when a variable number of arguments is allowed. For example,

> int printf(char *format,...);

in STDIO.H shows that **printf( )** has one string argument (pointer to **char**). The comma and three periods indicate that any number of arguments (including none) can follow.

The traditional (classic) pre-ANSI method of declaring and defining functions will still work, but it offers less protection. Pre-ANSI declarations of **printf( )** and **getche( )** might have looked thus:

> printf( );   /* returns int by default */
> getche( );   /* returns int by default */

giving no indication that their argument requirements were widely different.

Turbo C, of course, allows both approaches, and I used the classic style in earlier chapters to avoid digressions. There may be some temporary portability problems with non-ANSI systems, so you need to know both styles. You will still encounter the classic style in much of the literature and published C source code.

You are free (and encouraged) to browse around the *.H files to see the prototypes of the various functions together with macro definitions and conditional compilation directives. The definition and working code for

getche( ), however, is buried within the Turbo C libraries—out of sight, out of mind, and beyond tamperage!

The **int getche(void)** prototype tells you that it takes no arguments and returns an **int** value. You might have expected a **char** value, since the role of **getche( )** is to capture and display a keyboard character. Even though **getche( )** cannot return the **EOF** (– 1) that we discussed in Chapter 3, nevertheless it does return an **int**. In CHKIP.C, it is quite safe to assign

```
ch = getche( );
```

where **ch** is type **char**, in view of the assignment rules just covered. The zero upper byte of the **int** is discarded in any case—so it's no big loss.

CONIO.H, derived from the DOS abbreviation **CON** (for console), contains several related routines for console I/O. They overlap the I/O routines in STDIO.H to some extent, reflecting the separate historical strands of UNIX and MS-DOS. For now, notice that many of the **get** variants work with input from files or streams, of which **stdin** (your keyboard) is just one particular example. This will become clearer when we tackle file I/O in Chapter 8.

Try replacing **getche( )** in CHKIP.C with **getch( )**. The only difference is that **getch( )** does not echo your keystroke on the screen. This is useful in many situations, such as selecting from a menu—you want to capture the chosen key without disturbing the menu layout.

It is instructive to add the following line after **getche( )**:

```
printf("The ASCII value is %d\n",ch);
```

Now try keying some control-key combinations and see if you understand the results. Ctrl-R will display **18** (i.e., 82 – 64) confirming that pressing Ctrl subtracts 64 from the corresponding letter code. You will also see some of the IBM extended ASCII symbols. Ctrl-C, by the way, will interrupt your program prematurely. The Alt-key combinations will give bizarre results since they emit special scan codes giving pairs of characters.

► *CONDITIONAL EXPRESSIONS— SHORTHAND USING ? AND :* ►

Ever searching for compact notation, C offers the *conditional expression* as a shorthand way of writing the commonly occurring if (*X*) {*Y*} else {*Z*} type of statement. It is well worth mastering its peculiar syntax since it can simplify your source code in many situations. In

    max = (x > y) ? x : y;

the right side of the assignment is a conditional expression, signaled by the *conditional operator* symbols **?** and **:**. The complete statement is equivalent to

    if (x > y)
        max = x;
    else
        max = y;

which results in **max** being set to the larger of **x** and **y** (or to **y** if they are the same). The conditional expression consists of three expressions separated by **?** and **:** (plus optional white space).

  test-expression **?** *T-expression* **:** *F-expression;*

This ternary (three-part) form is evaluated as follows:

1. If the test-expression evaluates to nonzero (true), the T-expression is evaluated, and this becomes the value of the conditional expression.

2. If the test-expression evaluates to zero (false), the F-expression is evaluated, and this becomes the value of the conditional expression.

Since the whole conditional expression ends up with a value, it can be used just like any other non-lvalue C expression. You can use it as the right-expression in an assignment as we did with **max**, or it can be part of a compound expression as in

    i = ((x > y) ? x : y)*(j >= 0 ? j : −j)/3;

This highlights the advantage of the conditional expression. The above line would take two **if**s, two **else**s, four assignments, and possibly additional temporary variables. Do you lose too much in legibility? This is a subjective issue. Once the conditional expression is familiar to you, you quickly spot that the expression

j >= 0 ? j : −j

evaluates to the absolute value of j since it evaluates to −j only if j is negative.

A few details need attention. The precedence of **?** and **:** is very low (category 13), just above the assignment operators (category 14), and well below the relational operators (categories 6 and 7). This means that parentheses are not strictly needed in

max = (x > y) ? x : y;

as they would be in

if (x > y) {...}

You should go with what the bible says: "...they [parentheses] are advisable anyway, however, since they make the condition part of the expression easier to see." (*The C Programming Language*, page 48).

Since the conditional expression is a single entity, C performs the usual conversions and promotions during evaluation, taking note of both the T-expression and the F-expression. There is a potential pitfall here. Take the following snippet:

```
int i;
double d;
...
i = (i > 0) ? i : d;
```

You might expect that if i were greater than zero, the right-expression would evaluate to type **int** with value i, which could then be assigned to the **int** lvalue without conversion. In fact, the presence of the **double d**, even when it is not directly involved in the i-positive case, forces the right-expression to **double** under all conditions. In this example, of course, the assignment immediately triggers a conversion back from **double** to **int**, so error-prone truncation only occurs in the i < 0 case. You can see that care is needed if conditional expressions are embedded in more complex code—remember to watch the data types of all three components.

Here are a few more examples of **?**...**:** in action.

```
#define MAX(x,y)     ( (x) > (y) ? (x) : (y) )
#define MIN(x,y)     ( (x) > (y) ? (y) : (x) )
#define MY_DIV(x,y)  ( (y) ? ((x)/(y)) : BIG_QUO)
```

The compactness of the conditional expression is especially useful in *parametrized macro* definitions, as shown above. The parenthetical profusion is absolutely essential, allowing the macros to be called with complex arguments as in

d = MAX(a + 2*b, (n − m)/(k + MIN(4*p,q(r − 1))));

Here the *formal parameters* **x** and **y** in **MIN(x,y)** would be replaced in situ by the *actual parameters* as follows:

((4*p) > (q(r − 1)) ? (q(r − 1)) : (4*p))

This is known as *token replacement*. In many cases, the parentheses may prove to be redundant, but it is better to use them since we have no advance knowledge of the relative precedences of the operators used in the actual parameters and the macro definition. Omitting the parentheses in a macro is extremely hazardous—bugs can lie dormant for years.

Macros are often used in libraries as alternatives to functions. They avoid the overhead of function calls but are less flexible since you cannot take the address of a macro. Pointers to functions, on the other hand, allow you to pass functions as arguments to other functions.

► *THE while LOOP* ►

Like **if**, **while** corresponds to normal English usage. You can repeatedly execute a statement or block of statements while a certain condition is true:

```
while (condition-expression)
    T-statement
TF-statement
```

First of all, *condition-expression* is evaluated. If it is zero (false) control passes immediately to *TF-statement*. If *condition-expression* is nonzero (true), *T-statement*, consisting of one or more possibly empty statements, is executed.

If a **break** statement is executed during the T-statement, control immediately passes to the TF-statement, and you *exit* the loop.

If a **continue** statement is executed during the T-statement, control moves back to the **while** condition, which is retested to determine whether the loop will repeat (if true) or terminate (if false).

If neither **break** nor **continue** are encountered, the T sequence is completed normally, and the **while** condition-expression is reevaluated. Again depending on this test, you either reexecute the T sequence or drop through to the TF-statement.

In less fancy verbiage, we say that T is looped until the **while** condition is false or a **break** is made.

Note that there is one exceptional situation in which looping ends regardless of condition tests: within a function definition the **return** statement always terminates execution and returns control to the calling routine. I will exclude this possibility for the moment to simplify the exposition.

If there is no **break** and the condition remains true forever, the loop is *endless*—your needle is stuck in the groove until you interrupt manually, reboot, or lose power.

Normally, though, some action within the loop or within the condition itself is geared to render the condition false or induce a **break** sooner or later. When that occurs, you exit the loop and resume normal, sequential execution. Take the following simple case:

```
int count = 10;

while (count >= 0) {
    printf("Countdown is %d\n",count);
    count = count − 1;
}
puts("BLAST OFF!");
```

As you saw with **if**, a compound T-statement requires block markers. The above snippet will display

```
Countdown is 10
Countdown is 9
...
Countdown is 0
BLAST OFF!
```

Within the T-statement, we are reducing the value of **count**, ensuring that when **count** reaches −1 the **while** condition will fail. Let's make this program more like real C.

```
int count = 10;

while (count >= 0)
    printf("Countdown is %d\n",count −−);
puts("BLAST OFF!");
```

The postdecrement saves a line, saves a pair of braces, and incidentally saves a little time since **count −−** translates into a faster machine code instruction than **count = count − 1** or **count −= 1**. Consider also the following:

```
int count = 11;

while (−−count + 1)
    printf("Countdown is %d\n",count);
puts("BLAST OFF!");
```

Here the countdown loop will end when **−−count + 1** reaches 0 (false), i.e., after **Countdown is 0** has been displayed.

An artificial variant to show how **break** works might be

```
int count = 10;

while (count >= 0)
    if (count = 3) {
        puts("ABORT!");
        break;
    }
    printf("Countdown is %d\n",count −−);
puts("BLAST OFF!");
```

The loop exits when **count** reaches 3. Usually, though, **break** is used to exit upon some abnormal or error condition not immediately involved in the **while** condition being tested.

Often you will find deliberate endless loops that rely on internal tests or events to exit or abort. Rather than construct a complex **while** condition, some loops start with **while(1)** or **while(true)**, which clearly mean loop forever. Within such loops you are bound to find some terminating mechanism! In addition to the built-in **break** and **return** statements, the C library offers the **exit( )** and **abort( )** facilities in PROCESS.H. These are machine-dependent functions or macros that terminate not only the loop but the whole program. **exit( )** is the more graceful termination—it will close files, flush buffers, and perform similar *housekeeping* chores. **exit( )** takes an integer argument that indicates the status of the exit as in

    if (*calamity*) exit (*n*);
    ...

The status number, *n*, is transmitted to DOS as the reason for program termination. A status of 0 indicates normal termination. A variant of **exit( )**, written **_exit( )**, exits without any prior housekeeping. The **abort( )** facility also terminates without housekeeping but writes an error message to a designated device called **stderr** (usually your screen) before calling **_exit( )** to perform the emergency termination.

    exit( ), unlike **abort( )**, allows you to invoke your own *exit functions.* You set up a pointer to the first exit function using **atexit( )** in STDLIB.H. Each call to an exit function can chain to another up to a total of thirty-two functions. These allow you to perform your own "cleaning up" operations before the standard ones are invoked by **exit( )**.

    These program termination facilities are essential in the real world, where a disk-full or printer-not-ready condition can occur at precisely the wrong time.

    Since **while** loops can be nested, you have to watch your indents, braces, and the scope of any **break** statements. Just like the nested **if...else** situation outlined earlier, **break** will terminate the innermost, enclosing **while**. KEYCNT.C (Program 4.2) offers a simple test bed to try out nested **while**s.

► *ANALYSIS OF KEYCNT.C* ►

    The outer loop can be invoked only four times since **count** decrements from 3 to − 1 before the outer **while** condition becomes zero. The inner loop cycles until either a *q* or *x* is keyed. Avoiding these two characters keeps you forever in the inner loop. So, to exit the outer loop and thence the program, you need to type four *q*s or *x*s in any combination (e.g., three *q*s and one *x*). You might find this useful one day!

    KEYCNT.C illustrates again the power of C's expressions. The function **getch( )** is invoked, converted to **char**, assigned to **ch**, and compared with

```
/* keycnt.c -- test nested while loops */
#include <stdio.h>
#include <conio.h>

main ()
{
     int count = 3;
     char ch = '\0';

     while (count---- >= 0) {
          while ((ch = (char) getch()) != 'q') {
               printf("ch = %c\n",ch);
               if (ch == 'x') break;
          }
          puts("Inner loop ends!");
     }
     puts("Outer loop ends!");
}
```

► *Program 4.2:* KEYCNT.C

'q' all within the **while** condition. Try replacing the **printf( )** line with

    printf("ch = %c\n",ch = (char) getch( ));

and remove the **getch( )** from the **while** condition expression to get

    while (ch != 'q')

The second argument in **printf( )** is an assignment expression and function call neatly rolled into one.

► *The Busy while* ►

Since you can pack a lot of action inside the **while** condition-expression, you often see examples of code where the **while** T-statement is empty:

    while ((ch = getche( )) == SPACE);

will simply ignore any keystrokes giving **ch** equal to **SPACE** (a predefined value). Notice that one ; after the) is all you need to indicate an empty statement. Beginners are sometimes tempted to write

    while ((ch = getche( )) == SPACE);;   /* surplus ; */

This is legal but wasteful since it gives you two empty statements, one within the **while** loop and one outside it.

Another instructive example is

```
int count;
char *ch_ptr;                    /* pointer to char */
char name[ ] = "Borland";        /* initialize array of char */
ch_ptr = &name[0];               /* or ch_ptr = name;! */
...
count = 0;
while (*ch_ptr++)
    count++;
/* advance pointer to end of string, count the number of chars
    excluding final NUL */
```

The intriguing condition-expression (*ch_ptr++) will evaluate to false only when the final ASCII NUL is reached in the string "Borland\0". Or will it? Astute readers may notice that the operators * (indirection) and ++ (postincrement) have equal precedence (both in category 2—see Appendix E). So do we take

(*ch_ptr)++

to mean "add 1 to the **char** at address **ch_ptr**" or do we interpret it as

*(ch_ptr++)

meaning "take the **char** at the pointer given by **ch_ptr++**"? Clearly, it makes a difference, and we need to be told!

The answer lies in the associativity rules for category 2 operators like * and ++. They associate from right to left, so *(ch_ptr++) is the correct interpretation. But does the indirection occur before or after the pointer is incremented? You need to note very carefully how the postdecrement works. Although ++ increments **ch_ptr** as a side effect, the expression **ch_ptr++** returns the old, non-incremented value. So the sequence of events for *(ch_ptr++) is as follows:

1. **ch_ptr++** is evaluated first, returning old value of **ch_ptr**.

2. The variable **ch_ptr** is incremented.

3. The * operator "grabs" the **char** at old **ch_ptr**.

I spell out this example in detail because it is the source of much confusion. The convolutions are not yet over. What increment does **ch_ptr ++** actually achieve? Pointers in C have their own special arithmetical rules.

► POINTER ARITHMETIC AND THE sizeof OPERATOR ►

When we write **ch_ptr ++** or **−− ch_ptr** or **ch_ptr + 3**, we are certainly changing the value of the pointer variable **ch_ptr**. C helpfully (some say unhelpfully) takes into account the size of what the pointer is pointing at before doing the arithmetic.

Each data type and variable in C has an associated size, expressed as a number of basic storage units. This basic unit is machine dependent, but in most systems, including IBM PC Turbo C, data-type size is measured in bytes. Thus **char** is of size 1, **int** and **short** are size 2, **float** is size 4, and so on.

Furthermore, larger objects like arrays (and structures and unions to be seen later) have sizes that depend on their particular declarations and assignments. Remember, too, that all these sizes may differ between different C implementations. We therefore need some mechanism to ease the writing of portable code.

The solution is the operator **sizeof** that determines the size of any data type or object:

```
int i, size, *int_ptr, table[10];
char ch, *chr_ptr, name[30];
double d, grid[20];
...
size = sizeof(int);        /* size now = 2 */
size = sizeof(ch);         /* size now = 1 */
size = sizeof(size);       /* size now = 2 since size is int */
size = sizeof(ch_ptr);     /* size = 2 or 4 depending on memory
                               model */
size = sizeof(float);      /* size now = 4 (32 bits) */
size = sizeof(d);          /* size now = 8 (64 bits) */

size = sizeof(name);       /* size now = 30 */
/* NOTE: sizeof treats name as a 30-byte array NOT as the pointer
         to an array */
size = sizeof(&name[0]);   /* size = 2 or 4 depending on memory
                               model */
```

```
/* above gets the pointer size */

    size = sizeof(table);        /* size now = 10*2 = 20 */
    size = sizeof(grid);         /* size now = 20*8 = 160 */
```

► *Portability and sizeof* ►

You are sometimes tempted to use the "fact" that **int** is 16 bits. For example, the function **malloc(N)** in ALLOC.H allocates **N** bytes of memory (the details are not important), so to allocate enough memory for 12 integers you could write **malloc(24);**. This works fine with Turbo C, but you have unnecessarily constrained your program. By writing **malloc(12*sizeof(int));** you achieve portability to systems that may have 32-bit **ints**.

► *Pointer Sums with sizeof* ►

When you add 1 to a pointer, you are really adding **(sizeof)** storage units, so the actual increment depends on the size of the object being pointed at. The same logic applies to subtraction.

```
i = *int_ptr++;        /* int_ptr incremented by sizeof(int) = 2 */
ch = *--chr_ptr;       /* chr_ptr decremented by sizeof(char) = 1 */
j = *(int_ptr+2);      /* int_ptr incremented by 2*2 = 4 */
```

The general idea behind pointer arithmetic can be summarized in the following manner: for

```
T *ptr_to_T;           /* T is a type specifier. Declare a pointer to T */
```

(ptr_to_T + i) evaluates as (ptr_to_T + i*(sizeof(T))

(ptr_to_T++) evaluates to (ptr_to_T + sizeof(T))

(ptr_to_T--) evaluates to (ptr_to_T - sizeof(T))

► *PHILOSOPHICAL INTERLUDE* ►

Some people complain that C encourages opaque code, while others praise the language for offering compact notation. The truth is that C's powerful expression/statement approach can be misused. Theoretically, you might be able to cram most of your program into one C statement, but there is a commonsense limit beyond which your intentions become clouded and your code becomes not just illegible but also impossible to alter without painful side effects. C's philosophy is to break problems down into a large number of simple, easy-to-analyze functions. Within each function, your statements should also be kept as simple and clear as possible.

Meanwhile, back in the loop....

► THE do...while LOOP ►

A normal **while** loop is only entered if the leading condition turns out to be true. It is useful to have another construct, called **REPEAT...UNTIL** in other languages, in which the loop condition is tested at the end of the loop. This approach ensures that the loop is always performed at least once. The C syntax is

```
do
    loop-statement
while (loop-condition)
```

A loop-statement can be empty, single, or multiple with braces. It is always executed before the **while** loop-condition is evaluated. Remember that parentheses are mandatory around the loop-condition. If this is zero (false) the loop is over, otherwise control returns to the keyword **do**, and we loop again.

If a **break** statement is executed during a **do...while** loop, a premature exit occurs, and control passes to the statement beyond the matching **while**.

A **continue** statement will send control forward to retest the condition.

Although less common than the normal **while** loop, the **do...while** is convenient when some input or event must be established at least once and then possibly repeated. For example

```
int choice;
...
do {
    puts("Enter Menu item# 1 – 8 (9 to exit): ");
    scanf("%d",&choice);
    if (choice == 9) break;
```

```
   if (choice == 1) {
     /* process choice 1 */
     ...
     break;
   }
   /* handle other valid choices */
   ...
   ...
   } while (choice < 1 || choice > 9);
```

Here the menu prompt always appears at least once and keeps appearing if an invalid choice is made. Within the loop we can **break** as soon as a good choice has been processed.

The above sequence of **if**s to process choices is effective enough, but is considered somewhat inelegant in C, which provides a specific **switch...case...break...default** construct for multiway branches.

► *THE switch STATEMENT* ►

Before discussing the formal syntax of the **switch** statement, let's revamp the above menu example.

```
     int choice;
     ...
     do {
         puts("Enter Menu item# 1 – 8 (9 to exit): ");
         scanf("%d",&choice);
         switch (choice) {
             case 9: break;
/* choice 9 will exit switch – no action */
             case 1: func_1( );
                     break;
/* choice 1 will invoke func_1( ) then exit */
             case 2: func_2( );
                     break;
             case 3: func_3( );
             case 4: func_4( );
                     break;
/* choice 3 will invoke func_3( ) followed by func_4( ) */
/* choice 4 will invoke just func_4( ) */
             case 5:
             case 6:
```

```
                case 7:
                case 8: func_x( );
                        break;
      /* choices 5 − 8 will invoke func_x( ) */
                default: puts("Bad choice!);
                        break;
            } /* end of switch */
         } while (choice < 1 || choice > 9);
      /* repeat menu display for bad choices */

      /* reach here after a good choice 1 − 9 has been processed */
```

There are several new keywords at work here.

First, the **switch (choice)** statement establishes the integer variable **choice** as the *control* expression for the following multiway choices. C evaluates the current value of **choice** and searches sequentially for a match in the list of **case** *n*: labels.

Each **case** *n*: line acts like the named label you saw in the **goto** syntax at the beginning of this chapter. You can picture the machine performing a **goto** label **case** *n*: whenever **choice** equals the integer value *n*. The statement or statements following the **case** *n*: label will be executed until a **break** is encountered or until we reach the end of the whole **switch** sequence, signaled by the final matching, enclosing }.

Note that there is no need to list the **case n**: labels in any particular order apart from grouping common-action cases like 5–8. Each **case** *n:* will be found no matter where it is positioned. On the other hand, you must avoid **case** label duplications within the same **switch** sequence.

If **choice** is 9, a match is made at the line **case 9:**, and execution of the **break** statement occurs—leading to an instant exit from the **switch** sequence down to the **while** statement. The **while** condition is false, so we also exit the **do...while** loop. Note carefully that **break** is now terminating the **switch**, not the **do...while** as in the previous menu example.

Suppose you entered **choice** as 1. It would then match the **case 1:** label and obey whatever statements are found there, namely a call to **func_1( )** (assumed to be declared and defined elsewhere) followed by a switch-break and thence a **do** loop exit as with the **case 9:**.

The choice 3 is especially instructive. After the **case 3:** label we find **func_3( );**, so this function will be called. Since there is no **break** statement following, the program carries on and obeys the statements for **case 4:**. As in BASIC, control passes by intervening labels, picking up all instructions in its path. So, a choice of 3 will perform **func_3( )** followed by **func_4( )** and then meet a **break** to exit. Choice 4, of course, invokes only **func_4( )**.

I cannot overstress the action of choice 3—it is the source of many bugs. Unless you want a choice to trigger the work for other, later choices, you must put in **break**s to prevent the code from *running on*.

Now look at at choices 5–8. Here we have the situation where the same action, **func_x( )**, is needed for different choices. Hence the labels **case 5:** to **case 7:** are empty. Control will end up at **case 8:** for all choices in the range 5–8.

The special label **default:** is optional. If it is used, it will attract the attention of any case not covered by specific **case n:** labels. In my example, any integer entered as **choice** outside the range 1 <= **choice** <= 9 will be trapped by **default:**, giving a warning display. When control exits to the **while** condition test, the **do** loop will be reinvoked, and the menu prompt will reappear.

In the absence of a **default:** label, any unmatched cases will simply filter down to the final } of the **switch** sequence with no particular action being triggered.

The final **break** after the **puts("Bad choice!)"** is not actually needed—the end has been reached already! However, it is considered good style: if you ever go back and enlarge the **switch** choices, that final **break** serves as a *sentinel*.

After that informal breeze through a fairly complex construction, let's recap **switch**, giving the syntax with more precise notation.

```
switch (control-expression) {
    case constant-expression-1:
        statement-sequence-1;
        [break];

    case constant-expression-2:
        statement-sequence-2;
        [break];

    ...
    ...

    [default:]
        default-statement-sequence;
        [break];
    }
```

The value of the control-expression must be integer compatible, i.e., of type **int**, **char**, or any of the **int** variants (**short**, **long**, **signed**, or **unsigned**).

Later you will meet a data type called **enum** that is also integer compatible. **float** and **double** are absolutely verboten.

The control-expression itself can be any constant (not too useful!), variable, or function returning an **int**-like value.

The case labels, though, must be constants or *constant-expressions*. **case 'A':** and **case (1 + 4):** are valid, but **case choice:** and **case (2*i):** are not. The colon is C's standard way of indicating a label as you saw earlier.

► *switch Caveats* ►

Note that **continue**, unlike **break**, has no impact on the **switch** sequence. If you have a **switch** embedded in some other control loop, however, a rashly used **continue** might cause strange aberrations. It will affect only the nearest enclosing control loop, not the **switch**.

Because **switch** is really a multiple **goto**, it is possible to write code that violates the structured rules presented earlier in the section on **goto**. The **case n:** labels can be legally positioned alongside any statement in the **switch** body just as **goto** labels can go anywhere within a function. If your **case n:** labels are badly placed, they can result in initialization code being bypassed or branches into or out of nested control loops.

I have saved the best control loop to the end. The **for** loop, well known to BASIC and Pascal users, provides a powerful and concise method of loop iteration under a wide variety of conditions.

► *THE for LOOP* ►

Let's start with a simple example before the laying on of the syntax.

```
int count;
...
for (count = 0; count <= 10; count++)
    printf("Countup is %d\n",count);      /* body of loop */

puts("That's all!");                       /* first statement after loop */
```

This will display the fascinating sequence

```
Countup is 0
Countup is 1
```

Countup is 2
...
Countup is 10
That's all!

After the keyword **for** there are always three expression statements within the parentheses (some or all of which may be empty), representing in order of appearance:

1. The **for** loop counter initialization (**count = 0** in the above example). You can also have multiple initialization expressions separated by commas as in

   for (count = 0, i = 100; count <= 10; count++)

   (See section on *comma expressions* below.)

2. The **for** loop test condition (**count <= 10**). Unlike **while (count <= 10)** the parentheses are optional.

3. The **for** loop modifier (**count++**) sometimes called the *reinitializer*. This may also contain multiple expressions separated by commas as in

   for (count = 0, i = 100; count <= 10; count++, i--)

   Following the **for** line is the body of the loop, which comprises a single- or multiple-statement block (possibly empty). In the above example the body consists of the single statement,

   printf("Countup is %d\n",count);   /* body of loop */

   so no curly braces are required.

► *The for Loop—Step by Step* ►

When the **for** in my example is encountered, the following sequence of events occurs:

1. The initialization statement is executed (**count** is initialized to zero). This step occurs only once.

2.   The loop condition (**count** < = 10) is evaluated.

If loop condition is zero (false),

exit the **for** loop and resume control after the last statement in the loop, displaying **That's all!**.

If loop condition is nonzero (true),

the body of the **for** loop is executed, displaying the current value of **count**. Then execute the loop modifier, expression statement 3, to reinitialize the loop. **count** is postincremented by 1. The loop now repeats from step 2 and the test condition is re-evaluated.

If you trace this sequence in the example, it is clear that **count** < = 10 is true until **count** has been incremented from 0 to 11. After 11 iterations of the **for** loop body, the condition test gives false, and the looping ends. Hence you get a simple counted loop, just one of the many applications of the **for** loop. The **for** loop flow can always be simulated with a longwinded **while**.

```
int count;
...
count = 0;                           /* initialize */
while (count < = 10) {               /* loop condition */
    printf("Countup is %d\n",count); /* body of loop */
count + + ;                          /* loop modifier */
}
puts("That's all!");                 /* first statement after loop */
```

Note carefully the position of the loop-modifer statement—it follows the loop body.

► *The Endless Loop Revisited* ►

As with **while** loops, the **break** and **continue** statements can be used to exit a **for** loop or force an early reevaluation of the **for** loop-modify expression. Recall, too, that within a function definition, a **return** always preempts a loop of any kind, sending control back to the statement after the function call. The dreaded **goto** may also be used to exit the loop.

In the absence of such abnormal exits, it is important that the loop condition contains variables that are altered either in the modifier statement, in the loop body, or both. Iterations that do not somehow *converge* to a false loop condition will loop forever.

```
for( i = 0; i <= 20; j++)          /* ??? */
    puts("This show will run and run!");
```

Since i remains at 0, the test i <= 20 is forever true.

The body of the loop often provides the loop modifier and/or the exit condition. In fact, you can have a **for** with one or more empty statements. Here are three examples:

```
int j = 0;
...
for (;j <= 3;)                     /* no init, no modifier */
    printf("j = %d\n",j++);

int j;
for (j = 0;;j++)                   /* no condition means true */
    if (j <= 3) printf("j = %d\n",j);
    else break;

int j = 0;
for (;;)                           /* no init, no condition, no modifier */
    printf("j = %d\n",j++);
    if (j >= 3) break;
```

An empty loop condition is taken as being always true. The last snippet is similar to the deliberate **while (1)** you saw earlier. It deliberately sets up an endless loop condition and relies (hopefully) on a **break** or **return** to terminate. In fact, a common macro in the C world is #define **forever for (;;)**.

► *Nested for Loops* ►

By now you will be unsurprised to learn that **for** loops can be, and often are, nested.

```
int i, j;
for (i = 0; i <= 10; i++)
    for (j = 0; j <= 10, j++)
        printf("i = %d, j = %d\n",i,j);
puts("All done!");
```

will display the following 121 lines:

```
i = 0, j = 0
i = 0, j = 1
...
i = 1, j = 0
i = 1, j = 1
...
...
i = 10, j = 0
i = 10, j = 1
...
i = 10, j = 10
```

It is easy to add unwanted semicolons after the **for(...)**. If you write

```
int i, j;
for (i = 0; i <= 10; i++);            /* ????? semicolon ????? */
    for (j = 0; j <= 10, j++)
        printf("i = %d, j = %d\n",i,j);
puts("All done!");
```

the syntax is good, but the first **for** loop body is now an empty statement that will be pointlessly "obeyed" 11 times. The **printf( )** will be invoked only 11 times, not 11×11 as intended.

An interesting point arises: what will be the value of **i** when the first loop ends? In Modula-2 there is no guarantee that **FOR** loop counters preserve useful values outside the loop. C, on the other hand, imposes no such limitations, so **i** has the usable value 11 when the loops ends.

► COMMA EXPRESSIONS ►

I mentioned earlier that a **for** loop could start with multiple expressions in the initializer and modifier (reinitializer) sections.

```
for (count = 0, i = 100; count <= 10; count++, i−)
```

would initialize **count** and **i** as shown, and each iteration would increment **count** and decrement **i**. These are particular cases of a construct called the *comma expression*. Generally, you can have any number of expressions separated by commas as in

```
exp1, exp2, exp3,...expn
```

C always evaluates these one by one, from left to right, but only the data type and value of the final, rightmost evaluation are preserved and returned as the type and value of the whole comma expression. The comma in this context has the *lowest* precedence of all the C operators (see group 15 in Appendix E), so parentheses are only rarely needed to avoid ambiguity with function-argument commas. For example,

```
k = j++, i-=;
```

would increment **j**, decrement **i**, and then assign the old value of **i** to **k**. In the above **for** loop, the two comma expressions are used purely for their side effects—their resulting values are discarded. This is a common situation in C. Unless the resulting value of an expression evaluation is assigned to an lvalue, it simply disappears. **i++** certainly increments the variable **i**, but the value of the comma expression, namely the value of **i++**, is discarded.

► *ANALYSIS OF REVSTR.C* ►

The comma expression can pack a lot of punch into a **for** loop. You can often avoid nested loops by processing several indices together. Try REVSTR.C (Program 4.3) as an exercise in using **for** to reverse the characters in a string. The **for** loop here is typical of many array manipulating loops. In this particular case, the array is a character string.

► *A Peep at STRING.H* ►

The library function **strlen( )** is introduced in REVSTR.C to obtain the length of the string **name**. **strlen( )** is one of 30 or so string handling functions defined in STRING.H. You should locate this in \turboc\include and print out the prototype declarations. Most of these functions take arguments

```
/* revstr.c - reverse a string using for loop */

#include <stdio.h>
#include <string.h>
/* get prototype declaration of strlen() */

main () {

    unsigned i, j;
    int ch;
    char name[] = "aibohphobia"; /* the fear of palindromes */

    for (i = 0, j = strlen(name)-1; i < j; i++, j- {
/* i selects chars from start to middle, j selects them from end
   to middle. Loop stops when i >= j */
        ch = name[i];
        name[i] = name[j];
        name[j] = ch;
    }
    printf("\'aibohphobia\' spelled backwards is %s\n",name);
}
```

► *Program 4.3:* REVSTR.C

of type pointer to **char**, e.g.,

> unsigned strlen(char *str);
> /* returns length of string as unsigned int excluding the final NUL */

> char * strcpy(char *destin, char *source);
> /* copies source string to destination string. Returns a pointer
>   value = destin */

> int strcmp(char *str1, char *str2);
> /* compare the two strings str1 and str2 */
> /* returns an int < 0 if str1 < str2
>   = 0 if str1 = str2
>   > 0 if str1 > str2
> where the comparison is made lexicographically as in a
> dictionary sequence */

As you can see the returned values vary according to function.

C does not have a data type **string** per se, like BASIC, but when you get acquainted with the STRING library, you'll find that you can do anything with strings just as easily as in BASIC. You can't copy strings with **A$ = B$** as in BASIC, but you simply write **strcpy(*a,b*)** where *a* and *b* are array names or pointers to **char**.

For the moment we'll need only **strlen( )**, which returns an **unsigned int**, namely the length of the string excluding the final NUL. Because I set j to strlen(name) − 1 in the **for** loop initialization expression, j indexes the *last* character in **name**. **ch** is used as a temporary variable while **name[i]** and **name[j]** are swapped.

The chief lesson of REVSTR.C is the use of i ++ and j −− in the **for** loop— they allow a single loop to pick out characters from either end of the string.

Once you have mastered the logic of REVSTR.C, enter and run PALIN.C (Program 4.4). It defines a function, **rev( )**, based on the **for** loop in REVSTR.C. You can use this to experiment further with reversing strings and finding palindromes (words or phrases that read the same in both directions). With **rev( )** you should be able to modify the program so that any string entered via the keyboard using **scanf( )** can be displayed in both directions. Then you could use **strcmp( )** to compare the two.

Note that the definition of **rev( )** uses the ANSI prototype style, with the formal argument declared within the parentheses. The logic of PALIN.C should be plain sailing, apart (possibly) from the use of global variables. In Chapter 7 we'll be looking at these and other storage classes in more detail.

```c
/* palin.c  - reverse a string */
#include <stdio.h>
#include <string.h>
/* get prototype declaration of strlen() */

#define MAXLEN 80

void rev(char *str);
/* function declaration */

    char name[] = "able was i ere i saw elba";
    char copy[MAXLEN];
/* these are global variables declared outside main() */

main () {

    strcpy(copy,name);
    rev(copy);
    printf("\'%s\' spelled backwards is \'%s\'\n",name,copy);
}

void rev(char *str)
{
    unsigned i, j;
    int ch;

    for (i = 0, j = strlen(str) - 1; i < j; i++, j-) {
/* i selects chars from start to middle, j selects them from end
   to middle. Loop stops when i >= j */
        ch = str[i];
        str[i] = str[j];
        str[j] = ch;
        }
}
```

► *Program 4.4:* PALIN.C

► *SUMMARY OF CHAPTER 4* ►

Summing up, the key point of Chapter 4 is how to control the flow of program execution while maintaining legible, structured source code. The **goto** with named labels (**label_name:**) should be used with care to avoid the traditional problems of unstructured programs.

◄► You met the conditional tests of **if** and **else**, which select alternative blocks of statements depending on C's purely arithmetic evaluation of Boolean expressions (true is nonzero, false is zero or NULL). Nested **if** and **else** clauses demand clear logic and matching indentations to avoid the dangling-**else** pitfall. The **else if** form allows a legible sequence of multichoice selections.

◄► Two of the basic library I/O routines from CONIO.H, **getche( )** and **getch( )**, were introduced as alternatives to **scanf( )** when you want to grab a single **char** from the keyboard. A detour on type casting showed how you can coerce variables from one data type to another, overriding C's standard rules for internal arithmetical and assignment conversion. The latter were listed and their dangers analyzed.

◄► The new **void** data type lets you override the normal **int** default return value of a function. **void** also distinguished functions declared with *no* arguments, e.g., *func(void);*, from K&R functions with *unspecified* arguments, e.g., *func( );*.

◄► The rationale and syntax of function prototyping was illustrated with **int getch(void)** and **int printf(char *format,...)**, and I stressed the importance of studying the prototypes in the various header files supplied with Turbo C.

◄► The ternary conditional expression, *lval = X ? Y ; Z;*, offers a compact alternative to **if** (*X*) (*lval = Y;*) **else** (*lval = Z;*).

◄► Parametrized macros behave rather like functions without the calling overheads, but, unlike functions, macros cannot be passed via pointer as arguments to other, generic functions. The formal arguments in macros are replaced in situ, token by token, with the corresponding real arguments, so protecting parentheses are *de riguer* to avoid diabolical bugs.

◄► **while** (*condition*){*loop*} loops until (*condition*) becomes false or until some abnormal exit statement, such as **break**, **goto**, **exit( )**, **abort( )**, or

return is encountered. **continue** forces a premature reevaluation of (*condition*). **while(1)** is used to generate an endless loop that relies on abnormal termination, **while** loops can be nested, and the (*condition*) often packs in many expression statements for their side effects.

◄► C interprets ***ptr++** as ***(ptr++)** because of the right-to-left associativity of the equal-precedence operators, ***** and **++**.

◄► Pointer arithmetic is based on the size of the pointee. Expressions like **ptr++** and **ptr − 3** can only be understood if you know how many bytes are used to store ***ptr**. **sizeof( )** ensures portability. **ptr + N** evaluates to **ptr + N*sizeof(T)** where ***ptr** is of type *T*.

◄► **do** {*loop*} **while** (*condition*); is a variant of **while** that guarantees at least one attempt to execute {*loop*} before (*condition*) is tested. Premature termination is possible as with the **while** loop.

◄► The **switch** (*n*) statement offers a concise, legible multiway choice mechanism, using **case** *n:* labels. *n* is restricted to integral values. **break** must be used to prevent unwanted running-on from a matching label to the next label. **default:** is used to trap any unmatched switches.

◄► The **for** loop offers flexible "counted" loops sensitive to many different termination criteria. The generic form is **for** (*init*; *condition*; *reinit*) {loop_body}. Theoretically, a C program can be packed into a **for** loop with an empty body since each of the three expression statements can be as complex as you wish, using comma expressions with side effects.

◄► Comma expressions are evaluated left to right and evaluate to their rightmost expression.

◄► All the control flow structures can be inter-nested to any depth. Nested **for** loops are common for scanning multidimensional arrays.

◄► C does not have a specific string data type like BASIC's. Strings are realized as arrays of **char**, and a suite of library functions declared in STRING.H allows all the usual string and substring manipulations found in other languages.

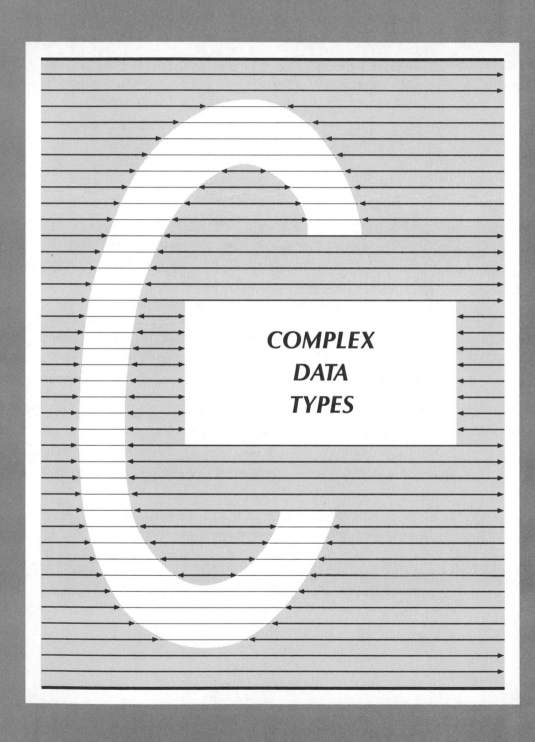

COMPLEX
DATA
TYPES

► *CHAPTER 5* ►
TAPPING THE POWER OF C

The data types used so far have been either simple, atomic types like **int**, **float**, and **char**, or pointers to them. You also met the one-dimensional array based on these types. C allows more complex data types based on arbitrary combinations of the basic types, and you can even define your own personal data types using the keyword **typedef**.

In this chapter you'll meet *multidimensional* arrays, *enumerated* types, **typedefs**, and conditional directives.

Before I discuss higher-dimensional arrays, there are some new facts about the relationship between arrays and pointers to be mastered.

► *ARRAYS AND POINTERS—A FRESH LOOK* ►

The one-dimensional array *x*[*n*] defined in Chapter 4 lets you reference a series of *n* variables *x*[0] to *x*[*n*-1] (all of the same data type) by means of a single integer-type index or subscript.

```
    int vec[100], i, sum;
    ...
/* here you set values in vec */
    ...
    for ( i = 0, sum = 0; i < 100; i++)
        sum += vec[i];
/* total the elements vec[0] to vec[99] */
```

Whenever C encounters the identifier **vec** without a subscript, it is interpreted as a pointer to **int** (as a pointer to the first **int** of the array **vec[100]**, in particular).

The major advantage of treating arrays as pointers shows up when you want to pass an array as an argument to a function. By passing a pointer to the first array element rather than passing the whole array, the function can be written without prior knowledge of the size of the array. In the program

VECSUM.C (Program 5.1), I establish a function **intvecsum(n,array)** that will sum the first *n* elements of any integer array.

► *Analysis of VECSUM.C* ►

The function **intvecsum( )** has **int_array[ ]** as its second dummy argument, and there is no specific reference to the array dimension. The empty brackets indicate an *open* array—the number of elements is left open, as it were.

```
/* VECSUM.C - calling a function with an array argument */
/* Program 5.1 */

long intvecsum(unsigned long n, int int_array[]);
/* use modern style function declaration */

/* declaration needed because function is encountered (in main)
   before its definition _and_ it returns a non-int */   .

   int vec[8] = {0, 1, 2, 3, 4, 5, 6, 7};
   int arr[6] = {23, 27, 24, 0, 8, 123};
/* define/declare and initialize two external arrays */

void main()
{
    long vecsum;
    unsigned long siz;
    printf("\n\tSize of vec array is %u bytes",sizeof(vec));
    siz = sizeof(vec)/sizeof(int);
    printf("\tNumber of elements in vec = %u\n",siz);
    vecsum = intvecsum(siz, vec);
    printf("\n\tThe vec elements total = %ld\n", vecsum);
    printf("\n\tFirst 3 arr elements total = %ld\n",intvecsum(3,arr));
}

/* define intvecsum() */

long intvecsum(unsigned long n, int int_array[])
/* use modern style function definition format */

/* intvecsum() takes two args:
            number of elements to be summed
            an 'open' array of int
   intvecsum() returns a long int value */
{
    long sum = 0;
    unsigned long i;
/* vars local to function */

    for (i = 0; i < n; i++)
        sum += int_array[i];
/* total the elements int_array[0] to int_array[n-1] */
    return sum;
}
```

► *Program 5.1: VECSUM.C*

The **array[ ]** form is allowed when declaring formal arguments and also when a declaration is immediately followed by an initializer. The compiler can fill in the array size from the number of elements in the initializer.

As you can see, the function has been invoked with **vec** (an 8-element array) and **arr** (a 6-element array), proving that **intvecsum( )** will work with variable-length arrays. You may wish to test this for yourself by setting up other arrays.

What really gets passed to **intvecsum( )** is a pointer value, namely a *copy* of **vec** (**&vec[0]**) or **arr** (**&arr[0]**). The function then blindly sums a certain number of elements, counting up from this base. Try invoking **intvecsum(10,arr)**. You will probably get a spurious answer with no warning that **arr** only has 6 elements. You will be adding to the true sum of **arr[6]** whatever lies in memory at the addresses (**arr + 6**), (**arr + 7**),....,(**arr + 9**).

Keep in mind that by receiving a copy of the constant pointer **vec** as an argument, the function has direct access to the array elements. **intvecsum( )** simply reads the array elements, but there is nothing to stop you from changing the function so that it writes new values into any part of the array. Such side effects can be exploited or they can be a nuisance. Passing pointers, then, is a mixed blessing. It allows you to handle open arrays, but it exposes the array to side effects. Since C always passes arguments by value, you have to pass a copy of a pointer if you want to simulate passing by *reference* in order to change the real argument.

The **sizeof( )** operator is used to derive the actual number of elements in an array. The general strategy for any type *T* is

```
number_of_array_elements = sizeof(array_of_T)/sizeof(T);
```

Using **unsigned long** for these variables is a possible overkill! I used it as a reminder that arrays *can* exceed 65,535 elements.

sizeof(array_of_T), you should notice, provides a quirky exception to the rule that array names are interpreted as pointers. When used with **sizeof( )**, an array argument is taken as the whole array, not as the pointer. Otherwise **sizeof(array_name)** would be interpreted as **sizeof(&array_name[0])**, which would always return the size of a pointer (2 or 4 bytes)!

In VECSUM.C, try replacing **int int_array[ ]** with **int *int_array** in both the declaration and definition of **intvecsum( )**. You will find no difference in operation, providing another illustration that **intvecsum( )** is actually treating the argument as a pointer.

► *Arrays and Pointers—The Differences* ►

In spite of the intimate relation between pointers and arrays, there are subtle differences that can undoubtedly be a source of confusion. At the risk of boring the cognoscenti, let's delve deeper into this subject. Take the following declarations:

```
int vec[100], *ip, **ih;
/* an array of ints, a pointer to an int, and a pointer to a pointer to an int */
    double table[50], *dp, **dh;
/* an array of doubles, a pointer to a double, and a pointer to a pointer
to a double */
```

Both **vec** and **ip** are pointers to **int**. However, **vec[100]** has 200 bytes of contiguous storage allocated at a memory location that is fixed at run time, so during execution **vec** is effectively a pointer constant, namely the fixed address **&vec[0]**. In spite of appearances, **vec** is not an lvalue; it cannot be changed or assigned to. Each of the **vec[i]** *are* **int** lvalues, though—otherwise the array would hardly be useful! When you initialize **vec[100]** you are setting values in each **vec[i]**, but the pointer **vec** is unchanged. Keep in mind that whether you initialize **vec[100]** or not, **vec** receives a real pointer value as a result of the declaration, and 200 bytes are definitely allocated.

The pointer **ip**, on the other hand, is a variable awaiting some assignment before it becomes useful. Potentially, **ip** can address any byte in the system (subject only to the pointer constraints of the memory model in force). But immediately after the declaration, **ip** is not pointing anywhere in particular—it may contain some (possibly legal) old garbage, or it may have a 0 (NULL) value, which is C's way of saying that **ip** is definitely not pointing at anything.

If C meets the expression ***ip**, it tries to access the **int** at address **ip**. This attempt will be illegal if **ip** is NULL or outside the legal addressing range, and you will get a run-time error message. If **ip** holds residual rubbish, so will ***ip**, and you may not get any warning. A very high proportion of programming errors turn out to be due to misdirected pointers, and they are often quite difficult to trace. The lesson is clear: avoid using ***ip** until **ip** is assigned a valid address. How to do this will now be considered.

► *Setting Pointers* ►

There are two common ways of setting a useful address in a virgin pointer: dynamic memory allocation and assignment from an existing address. Let's look at each in turn.

► *Dynamic Memory Allocation*

You can dynamically allocate some contiguous memory, using **calloc( )** or **malloc( )**. These library functions in ALLOC.H or STDLIB.H grab and clear (set to 0) the number of bytes requested, provided there is sufficient free memory in the *heap*.

The heap is a section of RAM set aside for such allocations. In fact, the heap is what's left of your 640K when all the other memory demands, such as the OS, TSR (terminate and stay resident) programs and data, and the current program code, data, and stack have been met.

During execution there may be many **malloc( )** and **calloc( )** calls requesting memory for a variety of reasons. Allocations are made in multiples of 16-byte paragraphs. They can sometimes fail because of *fragmentation* even if the total of free memory in the heap exceeds your request, so you should always check for success after each call.

The key to **malloc( )** and **calloc( )** is that they return a *generic* pointer value that represents either the address of the first byte of the region allocated or NULL if the heap cannot meet the demand. By casting this returned value to type pointer to **int**, say, then testing for NULL and assigning it to **ip**, you have a definite target to point at—just as if you had declared an array of **int**, in fact.

Using expressions such as **ip[*N*]** or ***(ip + *N*)**, you can write and read the (*N* + 1)th integer in the allocated memory. Dare I stress that if you make *N* too large (plus or minus), you can recklessly intrude outside the allocated region with bizarre results?

To free a **malloc( )** or **calloc( )** memory allocation and return it to the heap, you call the **free( )** function using the original pointer as the argument: **free(ip);**. This ability to grab and return blocks of RAM of variable sizes during a program explains the term *dynamic* memory allocation (in contrast to *static* memory allocations determined by the compiler/linker and maintained until the program exits).

An example of **malloc( )** in action follows:

```
#include <stdio.h>
#include <alloc.h>
#include <stdlib.h>
/* exit( ) and malloc( ) are in STDLIB.H.  malloc( ) is also in ALLOC.H.
   calloc( ) is in ALLOC.H.  puts( ) is in STDIO.H */
    ...
    int *ip, ints_req = 100;
    ...
    ip = (int *) malloc(ints_req*sizeof(int));
```

```
/* try to allocate 100*2 bytes in memory heap. A NULL (zero) pointer is
   returned if allocation fails, else a pointer to the allocated
   memory is returned */

/* malloc returns a generic 'pointer to void' so the (int *) is an essential
   type cast forcing malloc's pointer to be a 'pointer to int' before the
   assignment to ip */

        if (ip == NULL) {
            puts("Insufficient memory for allocation!");
            exit (1);
/* exit (n) terminates the program, telling DOS the reason, e.g. exit (0) for
   normal termination, exit (1) for error type 1. */
        }

/* The same effect with calloc( ) would require:

        ip = (int *) calloc(ints_req,sizeof(int));
*/
        ...
/* now you can use ip as a valid pointer to a 100 int block */
/* Note that all 200 bytes are cleared to 0 */
```

This example introduces two new constructs briefly explained in the comments: type casting of pointers, and the **exit( )** function. For the moment, just note the general concepts and syntax—they will be covered in more detail later.

The prototype declarations for **malloc( )** and **calloc( )** follow, together with those of two related memory-management functions:

```
        void *malloc(unsigned memsiz_chars);
/* malloc returns a 'pointer to void' value. You have to type cast this to
   'pointer to T' before assignment, where T is the data type of the
   target block contents. Pre-ANSI systems use char *malloc( ), so
   watch for possible portability snags */

        void *calloc(unsigned number_elements,
                                unsigned element_size);
/* as for malloc, except that two args are required. Their product gives the
   memory size allocated in bytes */

        void free(void *original_ptr);
/* return the original malloc or calloc allocation to the heap */

        unsigned coreleft(void);                    /* or unsigned long */
```

```
/* returns the number of unused memory units in the heap.
   Results and usage depend on the memory model in force */

      void *realloc(void *original_ptr, unsigned newsize);
/* used after malloc or calloc, realloc expands or shrinks the original
   block, copying the previous contents if possible. Returns a
   pointer to new block — this may be a different value from
   the original allocation*/
/* There are far versions: farmalloc( ), farcalloc( ), farfree( ),
   farcoreleft( ) and farrealloc( ) for handling allocations
   over 64KB in the larger memory models with 32 – bit far
   pointers and a far heap. */
```

Now you can look at the second, more direct method of setting pointer values.

► *Direct Pointer Assignment*

You can simply assign an existing, initialized, valid pointer to **ip** during or after its declaration as in

```
      int vec[100], *ip = vec;              /* equivalent to ip = &vec[0] */
/* *ip and vec[0] now represent the same integer */
```

The assignment ***ip = vec;** can be rather puzzling at first sight. If this was a normal assignment statement rather than part of a declaration initializer, you would appear to be trying to assign a pointer value to the ***ip** (an **int**)! What, in fact, is happening is

```
int vec[100];
int *ip = vec;
```

Written this way, you can take the second line to be equivalent to **(int *)ip = vec**, where **(int *)** plays the role of the type specifier, pointer to **int**. The assignment is now seen in its true light: **ip = vec**—you *are* assigning pointer to pointer. I'll have more to say on C's declaration syntax quite soon.

► *Type Casting with Pointers*

The idea of **(int *)** as a type specifier has already cropped up as the type cast applied to the pointer **(void *)** returned by **malloc( )**.

Generally speaking, Turbo C will warn you without aborting if you try to assign **ptr_to_T1** to **ptr_to_T2** where *T1* and *T2* are incompatible types. The onus is on the programmer to heed or ignore the warnings. The problems can be quite subtle, depending on the legal address boundaries for different data types. For example, **ptr_to_char** can legally take any odd or even number within the memory model limits, but more complex types may be constrained to byte addresses that are multiples of 2, 4, or 8. The safest course is to type cast the right-hand pointer.

```
int *ip;
char *cp;
...
ip = (int *)cp;
cp = (char *)ip;
```

The **malloc( )** and **calloc( )** pointers to **void** must always be type cast before assignment as shown in the earlier examples. Similarly, when passing pointer arguments to a function, you must ensure that they match the pointer types in the function prototype.

► *The Pointer Having Been Set...* ►

Once you have assigned an address to **ip**, ***ip** will be interpreted as an **int** even if **ip** has been wrongly made to point at a **float** or **double**. Also, arithmetic on **ip** will be automatically based on **sizeof(int)** = 2, so **(ip + 1)** will advance the pointer by 2 bytes to point to the next integer (or whatever lies ahead!). Similarly, with pointer to **double**, once **dp** is given an address ***dp** will be taken as the 8 bytes at address **dp**, with bizarre results if these are not in fact in double-precision FP format. Also, **−−dp** will predecrement **dp** by the **sizeof(double)**, namely 8. All of which underlines the importance of getting the pointer type correct.

► *Handles or Pointers to Pointers* ►

The declaration **int **ih;** means

```
(int *) *ih;
```

so ***ih** is a pointer to **int**. Therefore, **ih** is a pointer to a pointer to an **int**.

****ih** represents an **int**, but before using it as such you now have to check that both **ih** and ***ih** are non-NULL.

Multiple indirection like this can be extended to any depth (until RAM or paper or reason runneth out).

It is often useful to have a *master* pointer or *handle* pointing to a table of pointers that, in turn, point to objects of interest. As the objects move about in memory, the table of pointers is updated, but access is guaranteed via the fixed handle. (The word *handle* has acquired other meanings in the computer world, so take care. Some handles are simply integers or channel numbers, not pointers to pointers.)

You'll shortly meet another application for ****ih** as I pursue the relationship between pointers and arrays.

► *The Pointer as an Array* ►

Now that you've seen the array as a pointer, you are ready for the obverse of the coin—the concept of the pointer as an array. Consider again the familiar snippet

```
        char ch, *cp, name[30] = "Borland";
   /* a char, a pointer to char and an array of char */

        cp = name;          /* same as cp = &name[0] */
        ch = name[4];       /* ch now = 'a' */
```

When you write **ch** = **name[4]**, some internal pointer arithmetic is generated to evaluate the right-expression:

name[4] → *(name + 4*sizeof(char)) → *(name + 4) → 'a'→ ch

where **name** is the pointer **&name[0]** and → indicates the direction of the evaluation. The **name** pointer is advanced 4 bytes, then dereferenced to give the fifth character of "**Borland**". This process is a simple example of the *storage mapping function* that C uses to evaluate all array subscripts. Now the same result arises if you write

```
    ch = *(cp + 4*sizeof(char));     /* ch now = 'a' */
```

since you have assigned **cp** = **name**.

As you may guess from this, C allows you to treat the pointer **cp** as an array identifier and write

```
        ch = cp[4];                    /* ch again = 'a' */
    /* if you think this should be ch = *cp[4], reread the previous
        paragraph. Note that x[4] implies indirection on x after
        the pointer addition */
```

In other words, the notation $x[i]$, whether x is considered an array of T or a pointer to T, really means $*(x + i*sizeof(T))$. As always, the onus is on you, the programmer, to ensure that x and i are meaningfully defined. In the above example, **name[31]** and **cp[69]** may well return rubbish without complaint from memory locations beyond the region allocated to **name**.

► *More Pointer Arithmetic* ►

You've seen that

```
    ptr2_to_T = (ptr1_to_T + int_value);
```

and

```
    ptr2_to_T = (ptr1_to_T – int_value);
```

give new pointer values depending on the size of the underlying type, **T**. You may correctly guess from this that it is also legal and useful to subtract pointer values if they share the same underlying type.

```
        int_lvalue = ptr2_to_T – ptr1_to_T;
    /* assuming ptr2_to_T >= ptr1_to_T */
        int_lvalue = ptr1_to_T – ptr2_to_T;
    /* assuming ptr1_to_T >= ptr2_to_T */
```

Provided that the noted inequalities hold, the difference between two compatible pointers represents the number of *elements* of type **T** (each of **sizeof(T)**) that lie between the pointers. Watch out for this potential stumbling block: If you picture the two pointers merely as byte addresses, you can be deceived into thinking that their "numeric" difference represents the number of bytes between them. Nothing could be further from the truth unless **sizeof(T)** is 1 byte!

Adding and multiplying two pointers is not a fruitful exercise, so avoid it.

► *Pointers to Functions* ►

The pointer arithmetic covered so far does not apply to all pointer types. For example, C allows pointers to functions but these are excluded from the pointer arithmetic you've seen with arrays. A pointer to a function is best viewed as the address in memory where control jumps to when the function is called. Clearly, it makes no sense to add or subtract integers to such addresses, and, incidentally, it is illegal to apply **sizeof( )** to a function. The main application of pointers to functions arises when you want to pass a function as an argument to another function—as with arrays, C achieves this with a pointer argument.

► *Pointers—Near and Far* ►

Pointer arithmetic with **far** pointers has some quirks that I'll cover in the next few sections. (You may wish to skip these first time round and proceed to the section entitled Arrays of Pointers and Pointers to Arrays.)

Turbo C offers three classes of pointers to cope with the vagaries of the 8088/6 segmented addressing scheme. These are **near** (16-bit), **far** (32-bit), and **huge** (also 32-bit).

The default classes of pointer you get when you write **T *ptr_to_T**, (declare a pointer to data type **T**) depend on the prevailing memory model, which is *tiny, small, medium, compact, large,* or *huge.* These are selected from the Options/Compiler/Model subsubmenu in the IDE main menu.

The default model is small, which automatically provides **near** pointers stored in 16 bits (sufficient to address 64KB of code and 64KB of data without overlap). All the example programs so far have assumed this small model default, so your pointer declarations were **near** by default. You could have used the addressing modifier **near** as follows:

```
    int near *ip;
    char near *ch_ptr;
/* explicitly declare near pointers */
```

without affecting the pointers generated.

Regardless of the memory model in force, you are allowed (with due care) to override the default pointer class by using the modifiers **near**, **far**, or **huge** in the pointer declaration (and in certain function declarations also). The reason you need to know something about these different pointer classes is that the pointer manipulations I have been discussing are radically affected.

Appendix F gives a brief technical summary of the 8088/6 registers and explains why these three pointer variants and six memory models are needed.

► *The Four Segments*

The key point is that the 8088/6 uses four 16-bit registers, known as *segment* registers: CS (code segment), DS (data segment), SS (stack segment), and ES (extra segment). These registers hold the base addresses of their respective segments. Without further support, a 16-bit segment register could only access a 64KB address space, but the IBM PC can actually address 1 megabyte via a 20-bit address bus.

The trick works like this. Imagine the segment register shifted left by 4, giving a 20-bit value. The "shifted" register can be envisaged as addressing 64KB distinct *paragraphs* of 16 bytes each. If the contents of a 16-bit *offset* register are added to the 20-bit segment address, the 8088/6 can now access any byte in the full 1-megabyte address space. (The address calculation, by the way, is done internally by the chip.) We often refer to the address *segment:offset* as a shorthand for the byte address *(segment*16) + offset*.

You are actually using 32 bits to obtain a 20-bit addressing space; the extra addressing capacity is lost because many different segment:offset pairs can represent the same byte address. For example, Table 5.1 shows seventeen valid representations of the same byte address. Obviously, before you start using conditionals like **(ptr1 == ptr2)** or **(ptr1 >= ptr2)** you need to know exactly how your pointers relate to segment:offset pairs. Similarly, adding integers to pointers can become problematical near segment boundaries. Turbo C's memory models and pointer classes offer the most reasonable solution short of switching to the linear addressing mode of the 80386 (protected mode) or any of the Motorola M68000 family!

► *Small and Tiny Models*

The four segment registers can keep track of four (possibly overlapping) 64KB segments, each of which must start on a paragraph (16-byte) boundary. With the 16-bit **near** pointer you can consider, say, the DS register fixed

Segment:Offset	Real Address
0000:0100	0100
0001:00F0	0100
0002:00E0	0100
...	...
0010:0000	0100

► **Table 5.1:** *Hex representations of a single byte address*

while the pointer supplies the offset, giving a 64KB upper limit to the program's data. You can see that pointer arithmetic and comparisons are simplified with this arrangement: you manipulate only the 16-bit offset from 0000 to FFFF (just like an **unsigned int**), and all is well provided you don't overflow. (Overflow will not affect the segment.)

Likewise, if the CS register is fixed, a **near** pointer can cope with programs not exceeding 64KB of code. In fact, by restricting both code and data to 64KB each (without overlap), the default small memory model can operate with **near** pointers throughout. With the small model, three of the segment registers—DS, SS, and ES—all start at the same address, while the CS is set so that the code segment cannot clash with the common data/stack/extra segment.

The tiny model also uses **near** pointers, but all four segment registers are given the same starting address—meaning that both code and data together cannot exceed 64KB. Programs within the tiny model limit have the advantage that the .EXE code produced can be converted to the economical .COM version using the DOS utility EXE2BIN.

► The Larger Memory Models

The other models vary in having **far** pointers for some or all of their segments, allowing either data or code, or both, to beat the 64KB barrier—but the pointer arithmetic required is more complex.

The **far** pointer is the default for all pointers in the large and huge models. In the intermediate models, you get the following mixed defaults: medium gives **far** for code, **near** for data; compact gives **near** for code, **far** for data. Table 5.2 summarizes the model-pointer defaults.

| Model | Data Segments | | Code Segment | |
	pointer	size	pointer	size
Tiny	near		near	64KB (code and data)
Small	near	64KB	near	64KB
Medium	far	1MB	near	64KB
Compact	near	64KB	far	1MB
Large	far	1MB	far	1MB
Huge	far	1MB	far	1MB

► *Table 5.2:* *Memory models and default pointer classes*

► *The far Pointer*

The 32-bit **far** pointer contains both the segment:offset values, but because of the address ambiguities mentioned above, the test **if (far_ptr1 == far_ptr2)** may fail even when the same effective address is being compared, e.g., 0000:0100 does not equal 0001:00F0, although both represent address 0100.

The **==** and **!==** operators are applied to the 32-bit segment:offset as though it were an **unsigned long**. The reason for testing all 32 bits for equality and inequality stems from the essential need to correctly compare pointers with NULL, the pointer represented as 0000:0000. As you have seen, non-NULL addresses may well have their offsets zero.

On the other hand, **far**-pointer arithmetic and the comparisons $>$, $>=$, $<$, and $<=$ are applied only to the offsets. If you add or subtract too much to a **far** pointer, then, you simply overflow the offset without affecting the segment: (0000:FFFF + 2) will give you 0000:0001 with possibly unfortunate results and no forewarning!

► *The huge Pointer*

The **huge** pointer comes to the rescue! Although stored as segment:offset in 32-bits like **far**, the **huge** pointers are automatically *normalized* to allow safe comparisons and arithmetic. The secret is to convert each segment:offset in such a way that the offset lies in the range 0 to F (hex, of course). If you followed the derivation of a real address from a segment:offset pair, you will see that for each real address there can be only one normalized segment:offset. For example, real address 100 is uniquely normalized as 0100:0000 because none of the other pairs has an offset between 0 and F.

When you increment a **huge** pointer offset past a 16-byte paragraph, it is automatically renormalized, updating the segment part. You can now safely move your pointers around data structures exceeding 64KB. Likewise, comparisons are applied to the full 32-bits, giving a true test of equality, inequality, and relative size.

I leave you to verify that arithmetic on **huge** pointers is well behaved. You can safely compare **if (huge_ptr1 >= huge_ptr2)** and so on, without worrying about segments and offsets. But as you can imagine, the price paid for this ease of pointer manipulation is some CPU overhead for the normalizations.

Note the default pointer is **far** even in the **huge** model, so you always have to ask for huge pointers if you want them as in

```
int huge *ip;                          /* ip is a huge pointer to int */
```

► Modules and the 64KB Limit

You should keep in mind that the larger memory models can only beat the 64KB *total* code and data limits when you break your programs into suitable *modules* or source files. Regardless of memory model, each compilable module is limited to one code segment and one data segment. By definition, these are each limited to 64KB. However, if you divide a big program into smaller source files, compile them separately, and then link them, you can have many distinct segments. What the larger models with 32-bit pointers allow is the resetting of CS and DS so that these separate 64KB segments can be accessed from anywhere in the program.

I now return to the pleasant world of small models and nice, normal, **near** pointers.

► ARRAYS OF POINTERS AND POINTERS TO ARRAYS ►

The base type of an array can be any type, excluding **void** and functions. When the base type is a pointer, some interesting situations arise. An *array of pointers* is declared as follows:

```
char *ptr[30];                    /* ptr[0]...ptr[29] are pointers to char */
```

The C syntax for such declarations is rather opaque compared with, say, Modula-2's

```
    ptr: ARRAY[0..29] OF POINTER TO CHAR;
(* or more legibly, with intermediate types:
    PointerToChar = POINTER TO CHAR;
    ArrayOfPointers = ARRAY[0..29] OF PointerToChar;
    ptr: ArrayOfPointers; *)
```

In C, the type of **ptr** is indicated "indirectly" by a *declarator* showing *how* **ptr** is used preceded by a type specifier showing the data type being pointed at. As you saw earlier with **int *ip**, you can look on **char *ptr[30]** as **(char *)ptr[30]**, which stresses the fact that **ptr[30]** is an array with base type **(char *)**, namely pointer to **char**. To get a better feel for C declarators, compare the following declarations:

```
    int x;        /* x is an int */

    int *x;       /* x is pointer to int – *x indicates usage */

    int x[20];    /* x is an array of 20 ints */
    int x[ ];     /* x is an open array of ints */
/* the number of elements is left 'open' – used in prototype declarations
    of formal arguments */

    int *x[ ];      /* x is an array of pointers to ints */
/* above could be written int *(x[ ]) but [ ] is higher precedence
    than '*' so parentheses are optional */

    int (*x)[ ];    /* x is a pointer to an array of ints */
/* these parentheses are essential – see next paragraph */

    int x( );     /* x is a function returning an int */

    int *x( );      /* x is a function returning a pointer to an int */
/* above could be written (int *)(x( )), but the function call ( ) is
    higher precedence than '*' so extra parentheses are optional */

    int (*x)( );    /* x is a pointer to a function returning an int */
/* The parentheses (*x) are essential here */

    int (*x[ ])( );   /* x is an array of pointers to functions returning ints */
```

Not all of these declarations will be of immediate significance; they are listed together to indicate the variety of declarators allowed in C. The two declarations I will concentrate on are those for *arrays of pointers* and *pointers to arrays*.

Returning to the declaration

```
char *ptr[30];                    /* ptr[0]...ptr[29] are pointers to char */
```

note first that the precedence of the array brackets is higher (category 1) than that of the indirection operator (category 2), so **char *ptr[30]** is taken as **(char *)(ptr[30])**, whence **ptr** is an array of pointers to **char**.

Each variable **ptr[i]** is a pointer to **char**, but remember that the declaration simply allocates space for 30 pointers—they cannot be used until useful addresses have been assigned to them.

```
        char name[25] = "Borland";
        char *ptr[30];              /* array of pointers to char */
        ptr[3] = name;             /* or = &name[0] */
/* ptr[3] can now be used – the other ptr[i] not yet defined */

/* or using malloc: */
        for (i = 0; i < 30; i++) {
            ptr[i] = (char *) malloc(25*sizeof(char));
            if (ptr[i] == NULL) exit (1);
        }
/* give each ptr[i] 25 chars (bytes) to point at */
```

A common use for arrays of pointers is storing a set of variable-length messages. Rather than waste space using fixed-length arrays of characters to match the longest string, the array of pointers approach allows each string to be just as long as needed. The following snippet illustrates this:

```
        char *err_ptr[ ] = {
/* 0 */        "All's Well!",
/* 1 */        "Insufficient Memory",
/* 2 */        "Drive A not Fitted" ,
/* 3 */        "Power Off",
/* 4 */        "Wrong Version",
/* 5 */        "Read the Manual" };

/* the declaration could have been written char *err_ptr[6], but
    the [ ] notation is sufficient, and allows future addition
```

of more error messages. The array will be set to [n] if
you supply n string constant initializers. */

```
        int err_code = 0;
        ...
/* some event here may set err_code */
        if (err_code < 0 || err_code > 5) {
            puts("\n\tUnknown Error Code\n");
            exit(9); }
else { puts(err_ptr[err_code]);
        exit(err_code); }
```

Each **err_ptr[i]** receives the address of the start of a particular string constant, and this is exactly the type of argument that **puts( )** expects. The final ASCII NUL for each string is quietly supplied by the compiler when the string constants are stored. To perform more complex operations that depend on the value of **err_code**, the **case...switch** construct would be a natural choice. For simple string selection, as illustrated above, the array of pointers to **char** is ideal.

► *Pointers to Arrays* ►

Next, contrast **char *(ptr[30])**, an array of pointers, with

```
char (*ptr_a)[30]; /* pointer to array of char */
```

The parentheses here dictate that **ptr_a** is a *pointer to an array* of 30 **char**s, not *ever* to be confused with an array of 30 pointers to **char**!

Once **ptr_a** has been properly initialized, you can dereference it with (***ptr_a**) to give you an array of 30 characters. Then you can access individual **char**s with (***ptr_a)[0]**, (***ptr_a)[1]**, and so on. Since the array is really a pointer to **char**, the real nature of **ptr_a** is "pointer to pointer to **char**." This explains the assignment **ptr_a = &name** in the following snippet illustrating the differences between arrays of pointers and pointers to arrays:

```
        char name[30] = "Borland";        /* initialize an array of 30 chars */
/* name[0] = 'B'; name[1] = 'o',..., name[7] = '\0' final NUL */
/* The identifier name is interpreted as &name[0], a pointer */
/* to the first char of name[ ] */
```

```
char *ptr_c;                    /* pointer to a char */
char *(a_ptr[30]);              /* array of 30 pointers */
char (*ptr_a)[30];              /* pointer to array of 30 chars */
char **cpp;                     /* pointer to pointer of char */

ptr_c = name;                   /* set pointer to start of name[30] */
a_ptr[0] = ptr_c;               /* set first pointer of array */
cpp = &ptr_c;                   /* both sides are 'ptr to ptr to char' */
ptr_a = &name;                  /* both sides are 'ptr to array' */
/* NOT ptr_a = &name[0] since right-hand is only 'ptr to char' */

ch = (*ptr_a)[0];               /* ch now = "B" */
/* since name is array of 30 char, &name is ptr to array of 30 char, just like
    ptr_a. (*ptr_a)[0] is same as name[0] */

puts(name);
puts(ptr_c);
puts(a_ptr[0]);
puts(*ptr_a);
puts(*cpp);

/* all five statements will display Borland */

ptr_c++;                        /* advance ptr_c by 1 byte */
cpp++;                          /* advance cpp by 2 or 4 bytes
                                    depending on pointer size */
ptr_a++;                        /* advance ptr_a by 30 bytes! */
/* Note that ptr_T++ increments ptr_T by sizeof(T) */
```

Until you hit the last three statements and comments, you may have been lulled into thinking that **ptr_c**, **cpp**, and **ptr_a** were pretty much the same kind of beast! They do happen to get you to the "**Borland**" string in their own fashion, but their underlying data types are different.

ptr_c is a pointer to **char**, **sizeof(*ptr_c)** = 1
cpp is a pointer to (**char ***), **sizeof(*cpp)** = 2 or 4
ptr_a is a pointer to array of **char**, **sizeof(*ptr_a)** = 30

The implications should be digested before proceeding.

► *MULTIDIMENSIONAL ARRAYS* ►

You have seen the array base type as simple (**char**, **int**, and so on) and as "pointer to simple." The next step is to see that the base type of an array can itself be an array. The *array of arrays* provides the basic mechanism for handling multidimensional data. For example, you can declare a two-dimensional *matrix* by writing

```
int mat[4][3];                        /* mat is a 4 x 3 matrix of integers */
```

Each of the twelve elements of **mat[4][3]** can be referenced via the **int** variables **mat[i][j]** where the *row* subscript i ranges from 0 to 3, and the *column* subscript j ranges from 0 to 2.

► *Matrices in Action* ►

Nested **for** loops are commonly used for processes that need to access all the elements of a matrix, for example

```
int max, row, col, sum, mat[4][3];
    ...
/* program here sets the values for mat[i][j] */
    ...
max = mat[0][0];
for (row = 0, sum = 0; row < 4; row++)
    for (col = 0; col < 3; col++) {
        if (mat[row][col] > max) max = mat[row][col];
        sum += mat(row,col);
    }
/* find max element and get total of all 12 elements */
```

Exactly how the elements of **mat[4][3]** are stored in RAM is rarely of interest to the programmer—you just set up the subscripts and use **mat[i][j]** like any other **int** variable. In fact, C stores multidimensional arrays in *row-column* sequence as follows, with **mat[0][0]** at the lowest memory location:

```
mat[0][0], mat [0][1], mat [0][2], mat[0][3]
mat[1][0], mat [1][1], mat [1][2], mat[1][3]
mat[2][0], mat [2][1], mat [2][2], mat[2][3]
```

Occasionally, you can make use of this fact, by treating **mat[4][3]** as a linear array of 12 elements.

```
      int mat[4][3], *pm, i;
      pm = &mat[0][0];          /* point to first row, first col */
      pm[1] = 0;                /* mat[0][1] now zero */
      i = pm[2];                /* i now = mat[0][2] */
/* You can now use a single, faster 'for' loop to initialize the elements
   of mat[4][3] */
      for (i = 0; i < 12, i++)
         pm[i] = 0;
```

You can also initialize a matrix during its declaration as in:

```
      int mat[4][3] = { {11, 10, 9},
                        { 8,  7, 6},
                        { 5,  4, 3},
                        { 2,  1, 0} };
```

This sets **mat[0][0]** to 11, **mat[0][1]** to 10, and so on. If you omit the **[4][3]** ranges by writing **[ ][ ]**, C will set the ranges for you according to the initializer list.

As with single array initialization, the number of initializers may be less than the stated number of elements—if so, the unassigned elements are set to 0. Having too many initializers will trigger an error message. Note how the curly braces are used to group the rows and columns of the initializer matrix.

► *Dimensions Unlimited* ►

Higher dimensional arrays are defined by a simple extension of the above scheme.

```
      float galactic_temp[100][100][100];
/* the temperature measured at each of the 1,000,000 cartesian test
   points (x,y,z) in the galaxy */

      unsigned int hits[10][24][30][24][100];
/* the number of hits in season 0 – 9, for club 0 – 23, by player 0 – 29,
   at stadium 0 – 23, against pitcher 0 – 99 */
```

Before declaring such arrays, you should make sure that you have enough RAM (for example, 34MB for the baseball database!). In fact, when you study disk file I/O in Chapter 8, you'll see that there are more practical ways of handling large amounts of data.

► *Multidimensional Arrays as Function Arguments* ►

As with simple arrays, you can pass multidimensional array arguments to functions by passing a base pointer to the first element. However, to permit the compiler to compute element addresses, you must supply additional information in the formal argument definition. In VECSUM.C, **intvecsum( )** was declared as

```
long intvecsum(unsigned long n, int int_array[ ]);
```

which allowed any size of array to be passed. But if you want a function to operate on matrices, you cannot get away with

```
long intmatsum(unsigned long n, int int_mat[ ][ ]);                    /* NO */
```

It is necessary to specify the second dimension range, for example,

```
long int3matsum(unsigned long n, int int_mat[ ][3]);                   /* OK */
```

This would allow you to pass any **[x][3]** matrix to a suitably coded function. Similarly, for a 3-dimensional array, you need to spell out the second and third dimension bounds, for example, **[ ][4][5]**. The first dimension range can vary in the actual array argument, but subsequent dimension ranges must be fixed and matched in both actual and formal arguments. There are several ways around this restriction—using **int *ptr** arguments for the start of the array and passing the array bounds as separate arguments. I will not pursue them here. Rather, I want to quickly cover enumerations, one of the remaining data types that C offers. I'll give you the flavor with some example programs and defer the formal definition until later.

► *ENUMERATIONS* ►

The basic idea behind enumerations is to increase source code legibility by providing mnemonic identifiers for small classes of related objects, for example,

```
enum days { mon, tue, wed, thu, fri, sat, sun }
            today, holiday;
```

/* declare a new enumeration type: 'enum days' and also declare two
variables of type 'enum days' viz. today and holiday */

```
enum days workday;
```
/* later, declare another variable, workday, as type 'enum days' */

You can now assign any of the enumerated *values*, **mon**, **tue**, and so on, to variables of **enum** type **days**.

```
today = tue;
holiday = sun;
```

You can now test and compare values and/or variables in many obvious ways.

```
if (holiday == wed)
    puts("Wednesday is a holiday");
if (sun > sat)
    puts("Sunday follows Saturday");
```

Notice first that the values **mon**, **tue**,..., **sun** resulting from the above declaration are treated internally as **int** constants 0 to 6, the values being assigned in the sequence entered. You are allowed to vary this natural assignment at the time of declaration, but the values are fixed thereafter.

```
enum days {mon = 1, tue = 2, wed = 3, thu = 4, fri = 5, sat = 6,
            sun = 0} deadline, freeday;
```

Once they are declared and given integer values, the enumerated value identifiers are not lvalues, so you cannot assign values to them later in the program. The variables of **enum** type **days** can be also be considered as internally taking any of the declared **int** values, so with the previous declaration you could write either **deadline = 1** or **deadline = mon** with the same result. However, the whole point of enumeration types is to increase legibility.

```
long total_expenses = 0, expenses[7];
enum days { mon, tue, wed, thu, fri, sat, sun }
            today, special;
special = sun;
...
```
/* set the expenses here for each day */

```
    ...
/* now total them for whole week */
    for (today = mon; today <= sun; today++) {
        if (today == special)
            expenses[today] *= 2;          /* up a notch! */
        total_expenses += expenses[today];
    }
    printf("\n\tTotal expenses for week =
                    %ld\n",total_expenses);
```

Other popular enumerations are the names of months, the graphics modes and colors of your monitor, file error states, and so on. The original K&R C did not offer enumeration types—they were added later to "keep up with the Wirths." You still find C programs that use the **#define** method of creating mnemonics, i.e.,

```
#define MON 1
#define TUE 2
...
```

where an enumeration would offer more flexibility. The above **#define** does not create a data type, which would allow dedicated **days** type variables, but simply replaces occurrences of **MON** with the constant 1. Without **enum**, your day variables would be **int** or perhaps **unsigned char**. It is largely a matter of personal taste and style.

▸ *Enumeration Tags* ▸

In the declaration

```
enum days { mon, tue, wed, thu, fri, sat, sun } today, holiday;
```

the identifier **days** is known as the enumeration *tag*—a word that will crop up again when you meet structures and unions. The tag turns out to be optional. If **today** and **holiday** are the only **enum** variables you'll ever need to declare, there is no strict need to declare a tag.

```
enum { mon, tue, wed, thu, fri, sat, sun }
            today, holiday;
/* no tag, so all vars must be listed here */
```

In this case, you could not declare further variables later in the program because **enum** *tag var1*, *var2* is required. Tag names and enumeration value identifiers follow the same rules as normal variable identifiers regarding duplications. They need only be unique within their scope.

► *TYPE DEFINITION AND CONDITIONAL COMPILATION* ►

I'll conclude this chapter with a brief look at two related topics: **typedef**, the useful *type definition* facility for creating your own names for data types, and *conditional compilation* operators. Both facilities can increase the portability of your programs.

► *The typedef Mechanism* ►

Consider the declarations

```
unsigned char ch;            /* ch is a variable */
typedef  unsigned char BYTE;  /* BYTE is a data type */
```

The presence of the keyword **typedef** alters the interpretation of the following declaration. The identifier **BYTE** is not a variable like **ch**, but rather a synonym for the type specifier **unsigned char**. In subsequent lines you can write, for example,

```
BYTE flag, marker;          /* declare two vars of type BYTE */
BYTE *byte_ptr;             /* declare a pointer to BYTE */
byte_ptr = (BYTE *)malloc(n*sizeof(BYTE));
/* type cast (void *) to pointer to BYTE */
```

with exactly the same effect as writing

```
unsigned char flag, marker;
unsigned char *byte_ptr;
byte_ptr =
    (unsigned char *)malloc(n*sizeof(unsigned char));
```

The use of uppercase letters for the data-type synonym is not mandatory, but it does improve legibility.

Note that **typedef** cannot create new data types; it simply adds new names as aliases for existing types. With the simple examples shown so far, I could have used the **#define** directive as in

```
#define   BYTE unsigned char
```

which, you'll recall from Chapter 1, causes the preprocessor to replace all occurrences of **BYTE** with **unsigned char**. **typedef**, on the other hand, is a compile-time construct, so **BYTE** actually joins the "list" of data types. This difference shows up when you use **typedef** with more complex declarations beyond the scope of simple textual substitutions.

```
typedef   char *STRING;
typedef   double (*PTR_FUNC_D)( );
```

Here we have created a mnemonic synonym, **STRING**, for the type pointer to **char**. The second line gives us the single data type name **PTR_FUNC_D** for the type "pointer to function returning **double**." The new names greatly simplify declarations. Rather than write

```
char *menu_heading, *buffer;
double (*func_p1)(char *), (*func_p2)(unsigned char), (*array_fp[10])( );
```

you can use the more intuitive declarations

```
STRING menu_heading, buffer;
PTR_FUNC_D func_p1(STRING), func_p2(BYTE), array_fp[10];
```

Here, **func_p1** is a pointer to a function taking a "pointer to **char**" as an argument and returning a **double**. **func_p2** is a pointer to a function taking an **unsigned char** as an argument and returning a **double**. In the final example, you have an array of ten pointers to functions (with unspecified arguments), each returning a **double**. The **typedef** version eases the undoubted pain of deciphering complicated declarators like **(*array_fp[10])( )**—and you can readily concoct even worse cases. If the data type calls for additional modifiers such as **far**, the source text clutter can be reduced even more.

► *Portability and typedef*

In addition to simplifying complex declarations, **typedef** is a wonderful aid in improving portability. Suppose you have a Motorola M68000-based C program using many 32-bit **int** variables. (Recall that C mandates only the relative sizes of **short**, **int**, and **long**.) Moving this program unchanged to Turbo C, where **int** is 16-bit, could prove hazardous. You might be reduced to replacing several hundred **int** declarations with **long** to preserve the program's precision and prevent overflow. It is therefore common practice to start programs with some **typedef**s (or tuck them in a header file). In a program with

```
typdef int M_INT;
typedef long M_LONG;
typedef short M_SHORT;
```

all **int**s would be declared as **M_INT i, j, k;**, while pointers to **int** would be: **M_INT *ip, *iq;**, and so on. Porting is now simplified by changing some or all of these three type definitions to match the target system:

```
typedef long M_INT;
```

All the **M_INT** declarations would be magically transformed from **int** to **long**, as would any type casts you may have used.

```
M_INT *ip;
char *cp;
ip = (M_INT *)cp;
/* cast cp from "pointer to char" to "pointer M_INT" */
```

Of course, there may be other tweaks required. Each C implementation has its private quirks, pace the ANSI committees. Even within a complex package like Turbo C, there are options that might require subtle changes in the source code. For example, running a program in a different memory model might call for different pointer declarations. C offers a flexible mechanism called *conditional compilation* that allows you to write one version of your source code that can respond to different situations.

► *Conditional Compilation Commands* ►

C offers several *preprocessor conditional commands* that can help to auto-mate the changes mentioned in the previous section. The compiler can be made to conditionally bypass any portion of the source code by using **#if, #else, #elif, #endif, #ifdef,** or **#ifndef.**

These directives work rather like the familiar **if...else if...else** conditional statements, but there are important differences. In the following schema, the *process-sections* can represent any sequence of source code, including other preprocessor lines. They need not be statements or blocks as with **if...else if...else** (although they usually are).

```
#if constant-expression-1
      process-section-1
[#elif constant-expression-2
      process-section-2]
[#elif ...
      ...]
[#else
      process-section-n]
#endif
      normal-compilation-section
```

As might be obvious from the layout, you are telling the preprocessor to bypass ***process-section-1*** if ***constant-expression-1*** evaluates to zero (false)—in which case, each optional **#elif** (note the spelling) is evaluated in turn until a nonzero (true) expression is encountered or the optional **#else** is reached. Once a "true" section is processed, "control" passes to the **#endif** line and normal preprocessing resumes. The net result is that only one of the sections will be processed and the rest will be ignored. The impact of all this is that the preprocessor passes on to the compiler only those sections of your source code that meet your various **#if...#elif...#else** conditions. You can spread these tests all over your source text, and they can be nested just like normal program conditionals. When nesting, you need a matching **#endif** for each **#if** loop. Since the process-sections are quite arbitrary (not neces-sarily block structured with { }), the **#endif** is an essential sign to the prepro-cessor that the matching **#if** condition is ended.

```
#if x
      section – x – true
#if y
      section – x – true – y – true
```

```
#else
     section – x – true – y – false
#endif
/* ends if y */
#else
     section – x – false
#endif
/* ends if x */
```

The **#if...#endif** sequence cannot straddle different files. You cannot, for instance, pull in parts of the sequence from **#include** files.

► *The #if...#elif Constant Expression*

The various *constant expressions* shown in the **#if...#elif** tests must obviously consist of constants or calculable combinations of constants that evaluate to zero or nonzero integer-compatible values. To form such expressions, you can use any or all of the following binary operators:

   * / % + – << >> == != < <= > >= & ^ | && ||

together with the unary operators

   – ~ !

and the ternary, conditional operator

   x ? y : z

Turbo C also allows the use of **sizeof( )**, although this is not required by the ANSI C standards and risks portability.

```
#if (sizeof(int) == 4)
     typedef int M_INT;
/* any other 32-bit int code here */
#elif (sizeof(int) == 2 && sizeof(long) == 4)
     typedef long M_INT;
/* any other 16-bit int code here */
#else
     call – for – help – here!
#endif
```

► *The #ifdef and #ifndef Directives*

The ifdef (if defined) and ifndef (if not defined) test whether an identifier has been previously defined as a preprocessor macro name. **#ifdef name** is exactly the same as **#if 1** (true) provided that **name** is already known to the preprocessor from some earlier, current **#define name** *xxxx* directive. If **name** is not currently defined then **#ifdef name** is treated exactly like **#if 0** (false). Because of this translation, **#ifdef** can be used with **#elif** and **#else**, and it must be terminated with a matching **#endif**.

#ifndef works the other way round: If **name** is currently undefined then **#ifndef name** behaves like **#if 1** (true). If **name** is defined then **#ifndef name** is the same as **#if 0** (false).

► *The defined Operator*

You can also use the new ANSI C keyword **defined** as follows:

```
#if defined name
    compile – if – name – defined
#else
    compile – if – name – undefined
#endif
```

where **defined name** evaluates to 1 (true) if **name** is currently defined, otherwise it evaluates to 0 (false).

At first sight, **if defined** seems to be a superfluous duplication of the **#ifdef** directive. However, you can combine Boolean expressions with **defined name** in ways not possile with **#ifdef** and **#ifndef**.

```
#if defined name ¦¦ defined(tag) ¦¦ defined title
    section – if – either – name – or – tag – or – title – defined
#elif defined unix && defined !msdos
    section – if – unix – defined – AND – msdos – NOT – defined
#endif
```

The optional parentheses shown around **tag** are for legibility only—they are not part of the macro name. You can mix **defined name** with other Boolean expressions as in

```
#if defined(tag) && (sizeof(int) == 4))
    compile – this – section
#endif
```

► *The #undef Directive* ►

To add to the merriment, you can *undefine* any macro (whether previously defined or not) by using the directive **undef name**. You are free to *redefine* **name** later if you so desire. Undefining an undefined **name**, by the by, is pointless but legal.

You must distinguish carefully between an undefined macro name and an empty macro name. For example,

```
#define name xxxx
#undef name
#ifdef name
    this – section – bypassed
#endif
#ifndef name
    this – section – compiled
#endif
#define name
#ifdef name
    this – section – is – processed
#endif
#ifndef name
    this – section – bypassed
#endif
```

At this point, **name** is defined but empty (not to be confused with ASCII NUL or pointer NULL). Any subsequent occurrence of **name** will be ignored (replaced by nothing at all):

```
#define name "Stan"
    puts(name);                 /* display "Stan" and new line */
#undefine name
    puts(name);                 /* error – undefined identifier */
#define name
    puts(name);                 /* puts( ) will display a new line */
```

► *Conditional Compilation in Action* ►

You may be wondering what you can do with all this defining, undefining, and testing for defined macros. Here are some practical examples.

▸ *Default Macro Values*

When you have a large collection of .H include files together with **#define**s scattered around your program files (modules), which macro names are defined or what values have been assigned to them often may be uncertain. The actual order in which include files are **#include**'d can clearly be significant. Some discipline is called for. A typical plan may use a special include file called LOCAL.H or DEFAULT.H with lines, such as

```
#ifndef BUFF_SIZE
#define BUFF_SIZE 512
#endif
```

The idea here is that if no earlier .H file has defined **BUFF_SIZE** then the default value of 512 is supplied. If any earlier definition is current the above **#define** is safely ignored. This widely used example illustrates the important point that conditional compilation should more correctly be called "conditional preprocessing and/or conditional compilation." If you browse around the Turbo C .H files, you will meet many instructive applications of the conditional directives.

▸ *Commenting Out the Comments*

Another simple application is to "comment out" a whole section of source code that may already include comments. Since you cannot normally nest comments in C, you cannot simply surround arbitrary sections of code with /* and */. (Turbo C offers a nested-comment option but this is not portable.) The following snippet illustrates the problem in trying to comment-out two lines that include a comment:

```
/*
/* messages.c */
    printf("hello, world!\n"); */
    printf("how are you?\n");
```

The first */ pair terminates the attempt prematurely. Now look at this solution:

```
#if 0
/* messages.c */
    printf("hello, world!\n");
#endif
    printf("how are you?\n");
```

I deliberately entered a false expression so that everything between **#if 0** and **#endif** will be ignored by the compiler.

► *Optional Debugging Aids*

A similar ploy can be used when you have optional sections of code to display debugging data during program development. Once the program is running well, you want to suspend these displays but keep the debugging code around just in case!

```
#define DEBUG 1
/* change this to 0 to suspend debugging code */
    ...
#if DEBUG
    printf("ptr1 = %p, name = %s\n",ptr1,name);
#endif
    ...
```

► *Setting Macros Externally*

In fact, you could switch debugging on and off without touching the source code. Both TC.EXE (the integrated development compiler) and TCC.EXE (the command-line compiler) allow you to define macro names and optionally pass their values to your program at compile time. With TC.EXE you select **D**efines in the **O**ptions menu and type

```
DEBUG = 1
```

or

```
DEBUG = 0
```

With this strategy, your program would not need a **#define DEBUG** directive—you would just retain the **if DEBUG** test.

Multiple defines are separated with semicolons, and equated values are optional.

```
DEBUG = 1; STAN_TEST; VERSION = 1.5
```

Here, **#ifdef STAN_TEST** would return true even though no value has been assigned.

With TCC.EXE you can include a – Dname or – Dname = value switch to the command line that invokes the compiler:

```
tcc  – DDEBUG = 1 myprog
```

► *Selecting Pascal and C Function Declarations*

For a more exciting application of conditional compilation, here is an extract from the Turbo C header file, ALLOC.H.

```
#ifdef _ _STDC_ _
#define _Cdecl
#else
#define _Cdecl cdecl

void *Cdecl calloc(unsigned nitems, unsigned size);

#if defined(_ _COMPACT) || defined(_ _LARGE) || defined(_ _HUGE_ _)
unsigned long _Cdecl coreleft(void);
#else
unsigned _Cdecl coreleft(void);
#endif
```

To understand what is going on here, you need to know that Turbo C allows you to compile and run C programs in Pascal mode and that you can link in program modules written in Pascal. Pascal functions pass their arguments in a manner diametrically opposite to C's argument-passing convention. When you invoke Pascal mode (via the Code Generation submenu of the Options menu or the – p switch with TCC.EXE), the Pascal conventions will apply to all functions unless you explicitly override with the **cdecl** modifier. The declarations

```
int cdecl func1(arg1,arg2);
void func2(arg3,arg4);
```

tell Turbo C that **func1( )** must be treated as a C function, regardless of Pascal mode, whereas **func2( )** can be treated as Pascal or C depending on the mode in force.

There are other differences between C and Pascal, such as the naming and case-sensitivity of variables, which need not detain us here. Suffice it to know that variables can be declared with the modifiers **pascal** or **cdecl** to warn the compiler of your intentions. If you are wondering why anyone would want to run in Pascal mode, it turns out that in some situations Pascal functions run faster (though they are restricted to a fixed number of arguments as a result of the left-to-right passing convention).

Most of the standard library functions need the **cdecl** modifier so that they can link with your program correctly in Pascal mode. With this background, look again at the ALLOC.H extract.

```
#ifdef _ _STDC_ _
#define _Cdecl
#else
#define _Cdecl cdecl
```

When you are running in normal, standard C mode (the default), the macro name _ _**STDC**_ _ is defined to the compiler, so the macro name _**Cdecl** is defined as empty.

In Pascal mode, _**Cdecl** is defined as the modifier **cdecl**. You can now see that two different declarations of **calloc( )** are generated depending on the mode selected.

```
void * calloc(unsigned nitems, unsigned size);
/* standard C mode */

void *cdecl calloc(unsigned nitems, unsigned size);
/* Pascal mode */
```

In the declaration of **coreleft( )**, a further consideration arises. Depending on the memory model in force, we want **coreleft( )** to return either an **unsigned int** or an **unsigned long int**. A Boolean expression using #if **defined** does this selection automatically.

```
#if defined(_ _COMPACT_ _) || defined(_ _LARGE_ _) ||
                              defined(_ _HUGE_ _)
unsigned long _Cdecl coreleft(void);
#else
unsigned _Cdecl coreleft(void);
#endif
```

The macro name _ _**COMPACT**_ _, for example, is defined automatically by the compiler only if the compact model is selected. Note also that _**Cdecl** is still there to protect you in Pascal mode.

► *SUMMARY OF CHAPTER 5* ►

Here are the key points covered in Chapter 5.

◄► The array **int vec[10]** consists of ten **int** elements **vec[0]** to **vec[9]**. The identifier **vec** is the base pointer **&vec[0]**.

◄► A function can take an open array, **vec[ ]**, as a dummy argument without prior knowledge of the size of the real array argument used in the function call. Arrays are passed to functions via their base pointers.

◄► **sizeof(array_T)** gives the total number of bytes in the array, while **(sizeof(array_T)/sizeof(T))** gives the total number of elements of type *T* in **array_T**.

◄► The declarations **int vec[10];** and **int *ip;** both create integer pointers, **vec** and **ip**. However, the constant pointer **vec** points to a definite, fixed memory location, whereas the variable pointer **ip** points "nowhere," and ***ip** cannot be used until **ip** is initialized.

◄► You can initialize a pointer using the dynamic memory allocation functions **malloc(mem_size)** and **calloc(elem_number, elem_size)**. Before assignment, you must type cast the generic **(void *)** pointers returned by **malloc( )** and **calloc( )**: ip = (int *)malloc (mem_size), then test **(ip == NULL)**.

◄► Pointer assignments such as **ip = vec;** require that the pointer types are compatible, otherwise you get a "**Doubtful pointer conversions in function...**" warning. Type casting allows incompatible pointer assignments: **ptr_T1 = (T1 *)ptr_T2**.

◄► **int **ih;** declares a pointer to a pointer to integer, sometimes called a handle.

◄► A pointer can be indexed like an array: t = **ptr_T[i];**, which is the same as t = *(ptr_T + i*sizeof(T)).

◄► All sums on pointers depend on the size of the pointer type. Pointers of the same type can be subtracted but cannot be usefully added: **num_elems_ptr2_ptr1 = (ptr1_T − ptr2_T);**

◄► The declaration **int *x( );** declares a function, **x( )**, returning a pointer to integer. By contrast, the declaration **int (*x)( );** declares that **x** is a pointer to a function returning an integer. Functions can be passed as arguments to functions by means of pointers (rather like passing arrays to functions).

◄► Turbo C pointers come in three flavors: **near**, **far**, and **huge**. Unless explicitly specified, the pointer class is defaulted according to the memory model set up by menu options or TCC.EXE switches. The six models are tiny, small, medium, compact, large, and huge. They determine the sizes of the code and data segments available.

◄► **near** pointers are 16-bit offsets with fixed segments. **far** and **huge** pointers are 32-bit with variable segment:offset values. **huge** pointers have normalized offsets, allowing safer pointer arithmetic.

◄► **int *ip[10];** declares an array of ten pointers to **int**, while **int (*ip)[10];** is a pointer to an array of 10 **int**s.

◄► Multidimensional arrays are declared **int mat[3][4], hype[3][4][5];**.

◄► Pass multidimensional array arguments to functions via base pointer. You need to specify every dimension except the first.

◄► Enumerations are declared by **enum [tag] {*e1*, *e2*, *e3*} *x1*, *x2*;**. The listed identifiers, *e1*, *e2*,... behave like integers, 0, 1,.... The enum variables *x1*, *x2*,... can be assigned any of the *e1*, *e2*,... values. Enum variables can also be declared by **enum *tag v1*, *v2*;**.

◄► **typedef** gives you synonyms for any existing data type:

```
typedef char *STRING;
typedef int *PTR_FUNC_INT( );
```

◄► Conditional compilation is controlled by the directives **#if**, **#elif**, **#else**, **#endif**, **#ifdef**, **#ifndef**, **#if defined** *xxx* in conjunction with **#define** *xxxx*, **#undef** *xxxx*, and constant-expressions. External macro names can be defined and assigned values via the TC.EXE menu or the TCC.EXE command line.

◄► The **cdecl** modifier with variables or functions overrides the Pascal conversion and argument-passing conventions when running in Pascal mode.

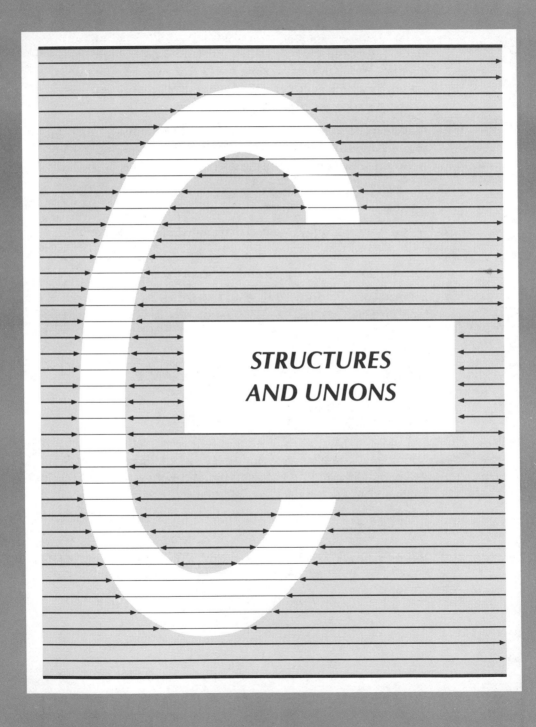

STRUCTURES
AND UNIONS

► *CHAPTER 6* ►
ADAPTING DATA TYPES TO YOUR APPLICATIONS

C's most versatile data type is the *structure*. It allows you to create and manipulate sets of objects of mixed types, including other structures and pointers of any kind. If you have used the *records* of Pascal or Modula-2, you will already be familiar with the general concept, although the details differ.

As you grapple with the syntax for declaring and manipulating structures, keep in mind that *data structures* form one of the two basic abstract elements of contemporary computer science. As Niklaus Wirth puts it, "Programs = Algorithms + Data Structures." In C language terms, this could be restated as, "Programs ― Functions + Pointers to Structures." Being able to assign single identifiers to complex collections of data and then compose functions that operate on them was a major step forward in software engineering. Learning which data structures to employ is as least as important as knowing which algorithms to use. In fact, the two often appear as inextricably bound together as the chicken and the egg.

► *THE STRUCTURE DECLARED* ►

Until now your arrays have been restricted to holding elements of any one base type: integers, characters, pointers, and other arrays of a fixed base type. The structure lifts this restriction. You declare a structure using the keyword **struct** followed by a list declaring each of the *components* (also known as *members* or *fields*) required in the structure.

The layout of the declaration aims at legibility. For smaller structures, you often find the following one-line format:

```
    struct employer { char name[MAXN]; int id, ext; } emp;
/* structure has 3 fields: one array, two ints */
/* one variable, emp, declared */
```

For larger structures use the following layout:

```
#define NAME_SIZE 30

    struct player {                          /* optional tag */
       char name[NAME_SIZE];                 /* field 1 */
       unsigned char player_number;          /* field 2 */
       float batting_average;                /* field 3 */
       BOOL active;                          /* field 4 */
    } pl1, pl2;                              /* struct vars */
/* pl1 and pl2 are two variables of type 'struct player' */
```

The components listed between the curly braces can be as numerous as you like and of any data type except **void** and function. The component types can be the basic ones like **char** and **float**, user-named types from earlier **typedef**s, pointers to any of these, or arrays of any of these. The type **BOOL**, for example, comes from an earlier **typedef unsigned char BOOL**, as explained in Chapter 5.

The variables **pl1** and **pl2**, once initialized, can be envisaged as each holding values for each of the four component variables. Before I explain how these four members are set up and accessed, let's explore the implications of the **struct** declaration.

The user-supplied *tag* **player**, appearing after **struct**, can be used later in your program to declare more variables of type **struct player**:

```
    struct player pl3, pinch_hitter;
/* declare two more player structures */
```

In other words, **struct player** represents a type specifier that acts just like **int** or **unsigned long** when declaring variables of the type specified.

As with **enum**, the tag can be omitted when you want to declare all your structure variables in one fell swoop:

```
#define NAME_SIZE 30

    struct {
       char name[NAME_SIZE];
       unsigned char player_number;
       float batting_average;
       BOOL active;
    } pl1, pl2, pl3, pinch_hitter;
/* four variables of this 'struct' type — no more needed */
```

The above declaration is effectively the same as the two previous declarations combined, but you won't be able to declare more variables with this structure type because you don't have a type specifier called **struct player**. You could, of course, edit your program to add some variables after pinch_hitter.

Even when you have no more structure variables in mind, though, a mnemonic tag identifier such as **player** is often useful as an aid to documentation and discussion.

Another common alternative is to use **typedef** to create a synonym for **struct player**. Consider the following snippet:

```
typedef struct {
    char name[NAME_SIZE];
    unsigned char player_number;
    float batting_average;
    BOOL active;
} PLAYER_REC;
/* no memory allocated yet! */

/* now we can declare structure variables */
    PLAYER_REC pl1, pl2, outfielder;
/* memory now reserved */

/* or declare pointers to structure variables */
    PLAYER_REC *player_ptr;
/* no structure memory allocated here */

/* and arrays of pointers to player structures */
#define TEAM_SIZE 45

    PLAYER_REC *team[TEAM_SIZE];
/* TEAM_SIZE pointers only - no structures created.
    Each team[i], i = 0 to i = 44, is a pointer to a PLAYER_REC */

/* and arrays of player structures */
    PLAYER_REC squad[TEAM_SIZE];
/* each squad[i], i = 0 to i = 44, represents a player structure */

/* perhaps arrays of arrays of PLAYER_REC structures */
#define LEAGUE_SIZE 28

    PLAYER_REC league[LEAGUE_SIZE][TEAM_SIZE];
/* declares LEAGUE_SIZE x TEAM_SIZE separate players */
```

A tag such as **player** can still be inserted after **typedef struct**, but is now less useful since **PLAYER_REC** plays the role of **struct player**. If you do use a tag, you simply have two equivalent ways of declaring further variables.

```
typedef struct player {
    char name[NAME_SIZE];
    unsigned char player_number;
    float batting_average;
    BOOL active;
} PLAYER_REC;

struct player pl1;
/* same as PLAYER_REC pl1; */
struct player *player_ptr;
/* same as PLAYER_REC *player_ptr */
```

In the early days of C, before **typedef** was introduced, the structure tag played a more important role. Nowadays, as you can guess, it is often omitted in favor of the more economical and legible **typedef**s.

Confusing tags with **typedef** names is a common source of bugs, so make sure you understand the examples. I have used the uppercase convention for my **typedef** name, but you'll encounter code in which tags and type names look very similar.

I have introduced pointers to structures and some more exotic variants to whet your appetite. You'll see them in action shortly.

► THE STRUCTURE ANALYZED ►

Let's see what the various **struct player** and **PLAYER_REC** declarations have achieved. First of all, for each variable of this structure type, C reserves enough memory to hold the listed components. (The actual timing of this memory allocation need not concern you for the moment.) How much memory is enough? Well, you can simply add up the bytes for each component, or you can use **sizeof(struct player)** to determine the total allocation more accurately.

► Effects of Word and Byte Alignment ►

The theoretical and actual memory sizes of structures can differ between the various C implementations and between different options within the same implementation. This is because of possible byte-alignment restrictions of certain **struct** components. For example, some C's would quietly add a dummy byte to place the **float** on an even address.

With Turbo C, you have an Alignment option in the Options/Compiler/Code Generation menu. This toggles you between *word* alignment, whereby non-**char** variables are always placed on even-byte boundaries, and *byte* alignment, whereby all variables are placed at odd- or even-byte addresses according to the next space available. Byte alignment packs the components one after the other, and this is the normal default when you first invoke TC. Word alignment may take up a little more memory, but the 16-bit data transfers of the 8086/80286 will work faster. With word alignment, the **PLAYER_REC** structure would have a dummy byte before the **float** and a dummy byte after the **BOOL** to ensure an even total size, namely 38 bytes. With the command-line compiler (TCC.EXE), use the − **a** switch to get word alignment and the switch − **a** − (default setting) to get byte alignment. Table 6.1 should clarify the situation.

So far you have seen how to declare structures and how to determine their size. It is time to examine the vital process of accessing the member variables within the structure.

Component	Range	Size
char name[30]		30 bytes
unsigned char player_number	0–255	1 byte
float batting_average	fp number	4 bytes
BOOL active	1 = active 0 = inactive	1 byte
		Total (theoretical) 36 bytes
sizeof(struct player) (with byte-alignment option)		**Total (actual)** 36 bytes
sizeof(struct player) (with word-alignment option)		38 bytes

► *Table 6.1: Using sizeof( ) to determine memory allocation*

► ACCESSING THE STRUCTURE COMPONENTS ►

The variable **pl1** of type **PLAYER_REC** (or equivalently, of type **struct player**) represents a set of four variables of the types declared in the **struct** list. You can access these individually using the *member*, or *selection*, operator (a period) as follows:

```
    pl1.player_number = 29;
    pl1.batting_average = 0.335;
    pl1.active = TRUE;
/* TRUE is #defined earlier as 1 */

    strcpy(pl1.name,"Clark");
/* remember that pl1.name is an array – name, i.e. a constant pointer. So
    pl1.name = "Clark" is illegal; you must use the string copy function */
```

The general format is ***struct_var.member_var***. You use this joint identifier just as if it were a variable of the type of ***member_var*** as declared in the structure's member list, and you can therefore do anything that's legal for that type. Here are a few examples.

```
    strcpy(pinch_hitter.name,pl1.name);
/* copy pl1.name to pinch_hitter.name */

    pl2.batting_average += 0.001;
/* notch up pl2's average */
    fptr = &pl1.batting_average
/* get a pointer to a component */
    pl2.player_number = pl3.player_number++;
/* assign pl3's old number to pl2, then increment */

    pinch_hitter.active = FALSE;
/* deactivate the PH */

    pl2.active = !date_sick;
/* right – hand evaluates to TRUE if date_sick is 0 */

    printf("Player #%d is hitting %f\n",
        pl1.player_number,pl1.batting_average);
    if (pl2.active) printf("Player %s is active\n",
                        pl2.name);
```

(Pascal and Modula-2 programmers should note the absence of a **with** construct in C. You must write out the ***struct_var.member_var*** in full each time.)

► STRUCTURE ASSIGNMENTS ►

A major convenience for the programmer is the ability to assign all the component values of one structure variable to those of another structure variable of the same type. For example,

```
pinch_hitter = pl1;
```

will move the four component values sitting in **pl1** over to the corresponding four members of **pinch_hitter**. This single structure assignment is the equivalent of the four separate assignments

```
    strcpy(pinch_hitter.name,pl1.name);
/* this is effectively an assignment of one array to another */
    pinch_hitter.player_number = pl1.player_number;
    pinch_hitter.batting_average = pl1.batting_average;
    pinch_hitter.active = pl1.active;
```

Observe that this structure assignment has achieved the "assignment" of one array to another—a feat that cannot be accomplished outside of a structure without the **strcpy( )** function (or some equivalent character-copying code).

This economical structure-assignment maneuver is only possible if the left and right structures are declared as the same type. If you declare two structures with exactly the same size and format but different types, you lose structure assignment compatibility.

```
struct giant {
    char g_name[NAME_SIZE];
    unsigned char g_player_number;
    float g_batting_average;
    BOOL g_active;
} g_pl1, g_pl2, g_pl3, g_pinch_hitter;
...
...
g_pinch_hitter = g_pl3;        /* OK – same struct types */
pl1 = g_pl2;                   /* ILLEGAL – different struct types */
pl1.active = g_pl2.active      /* OK – members are compatible */
```

As this example shows, however, the individual components of different structures can be assigned just like any other compatible variables. To achieve **pl1 = g_pl2;**, therefore, you would need to make four separate assignments. Better still, ask yourself if you really need a separate **struct giant**. Since the data formats are identical, you could save time and trouble by declaring

    PLAYER_REC g_pl1, g_pl2, g_pl3, g_pinch_hitter;

Before we relinquish **struct giant**, there is a useful observation to make. Within **struct giant** I went to the trouble of naming each component differently from **PLAYER_REC**. In fact, component names need only be unique within a structure. It is legal to have

```
struct player {
    char name[30];
    unsigned char player_number;
    float batting_average;
    BOOL active;
} pl1, pl2, pl3, pinch_hitter;

struct giant {
    BOOL active;
    unsigned char player_number;
    float batting_average;
    char name[30];
} g_pl1, g_pl2, g_pl3, g_pinch_hitter;
```

At first sight it would appear unseemly to have two variables called **name**, two named **active**, and so on, in adjacent declarations. Indeed, the K&R 1978 C specification expressly forbade the above kind of component-name duplications. (This restriction was relaxed, though, if the components had the same types and relative positions within the two structures.) Nowadays it is legal to duplicate component names in different structures since the *struct_var.member_var* format ensures uniqueness.

► STRUCTURE INITIALIZERS ►

As with arrays, you can initialize structure variables during their declaration:

    PLAYER_REC mays { "Willie Mays", 45, 0.333, FALSE };

(Some compilers are less tolerant than Turbo C and will not initialize automatic arrays or structures.) The now-familiar rules for initializers apply. Each constant expression within the curly braces is assigned in turn to each component of the structure. If there are too many initializers, or if they are not assignment-compatible, you get an error. If there are insufficient initializers, the unmatched components are cleared to zero. (I use the word *zero* to cover all the possible internal forms that C can generate to clear different component data types, including **int 0**, **char '\x0'**, **long int 0L**, **double 0.0**, and pointer **NULL**.)

► *NESTING STRUCTURES* ►

Once a structure is declared, variables of that type can be used within another structure. Take the following simple example:

```
typedef struct {                 /* no tag */
   unsigned char month, day;    /* fields 1 & 2 */
   unsigned int year;           /* field 3 */
} DATE;                         /* structure type name */

DATE signing_date = { 9, 15, 1929 };
                                 /* declare & initialize a DATE variable */
/* sizeof(DATE) is 4 */

typedef struct {
   char name[NAME_SIZE];
   unsigned char player_number;
   float batting_average;
   BOOL active;
   DATE date_joined;            /* new field 5 is a struct */
} PLAYER_REC;
/* sizeof(PLAYER_REC) now = 40 (byte aligned) or 42 (word aligned) */

PLAYER_REC pl1, pinch_hitter;
/* pl1 and pinch_hitter are two PLAYER_REC variables */
```

First I **typedef**ed a simple structure type called **DATE**. Then I declared and initialized a variable, **signing_date**. Next I added a new variable of type **DATE**, **date_joined**, to the player record. Within **date_joined** the components are referenced via the variable names **date_joined.month**, **date_joined.day**, and

date_joined.year. Within **pl1**, the new components must now be accessed using

```
pl1.date_joined.month
pl1.date_joined.day
pl1.date_joined.year
```

Note the positions of the two member operators. This format arises quite naturally whenever the *struct1_member* in *struct1_var.struct1_member* is itself of the form *struct2_var.struct2_member*. Substituting the latter value gives

struct1_var.struct2_var.struct2_member

This nesting of structures can be continued to any depth, and the rules for accessing the lower level components are obvious extensions of our two-level example. You can end up with as many member operators as the nesting depth as in

struct1_var.struct2_var.struct3_var.struct3_member

In spite of the length and complexity of such constructs, the simple fact to remember is that the the whole expression behaves exactly like a variable of the type of the last named member. Using our new **PLAYER_REC**, here are some valid statements.

```
pl1.date_joined.month = 3;
pl1.date_joined.day = 25;
if (pl1.date_joined.year <= 1950 && pl1.active) {
    pl1.active = FALSE;
    ...
}
pinch_hitter.date_joined.month += 2;
signing_date.year = pl1.date_joined.year;
...
switch (pl1.date_joined.month) {
    case 1: puts("January"); break;
    case 2: puts("February"); break;
    ...
    default:
        puts("Month error");
        exit(1);
}
```

Nested structures can be initialized using nested initializers! If we add

```
PLAYER_REC ruth = {"Babe Ruth", 1, 0.389, FALSE,
                   { 10, 18, 1925 } };
```

the three fields of the **date_joined** structure are initialized with the nested expression, **{ 10, 18, 1925 }**. Having too many initializers at any level will give you an error signal. Having too few initializers results in the surplus members being cleared to zero.

► *Restrictions on Nested Structures* ►

There is one important restriction on nested structures: you cannot include a structure variable within its own structure. For example,

```
/* ILLEGAL declaration */
    struct bad {
        int a;
        struct bad no_no; /* NOT ALLOWED */
        double c;
    } none_such;
```

is illegal because it could lead to an infinite sequence of memory allocations! If this limitation depresses you, you will be pleased to hear that C does allow a structure to hold a pointer to variables of its own type:

```
/* This declaration is LEGAL */
    struct good {
        int a;
        struct good *yes_yes; /* pointer to struct is ALLOWED */
        double c;
    } any_such;
```

The compiler can make sense of this. The component **yes_yes** is a fixed-length pointer (16 or 32 bits depending on the memory model) of type pointer to **struct good**. The memory allocation is therefore predetermined.

It turns out that many important abstract data structures can be realized in C using this mechanism. *Linked lists* and *trees*, for example, require structure elements to contain one or more pointers to other structure elements of the same type.

► *A SIMPLE LINKED LIST* ►

To give you the flavor of this approach, let's revamp the **PLAYER_REC** structure as follows:

```
typedef struct player {
    char name[NAME_SIZE];
    unsigned char player_number;
    float batting_average;
    BOOL active;
    DATE date_joined;
    struct player *next;          /* new field 6 is pointer to next record */
} PLAYER_REC;

PLAYER_REC clark, ruth, mays;
```

The new field **next** is of type pointer to **struct player**. By setting various addresses in this field for different **PLAYER_REC** variables, we can create a linked list of player records. I'll fill in the details later, but for now assume that the variable **mays** has been initialized with appropriate values for **mays.name**, **mays.player_number**, and so on. We set **mays.next** to **NULL** to indicate that this record does not point anywhere. This is the normal convention for indicating that there is no **next**, in other words, **mays** is the last player in the linked list. We now enter Babe Ruth's data into the structure variable **ruth**, ending with the assignment

```
ruth.next = &mays;
```

Informally, you can say that **ruth** points to **mays**. Using the **next** field as a pointer or *link* explains the term *linked list*. To complete our list, we put Jack Clark's data into **clark** and set

```
clark.next = &ruth;
```

What we now have is a very simple linked list of three players. Starting with **clark**, we can scan the list by picking up pointers to the next player record until a **NULL** pointer is reached. For example, from **clark.next** we can access **ruth** as ***clark.next** provided that **clark.next** is not **NULL**. You can even access **mays** directly using the construct ***(*clark.next).next** since this is equivalent to ***ruth.next** (we know that **ruth.next** isn't **NULL**).

► *THE STRUCTURE POINTER MEMBER OPERATOR (– >)* ►

Note that the member operator (.) has higher precedence (category 1) than the indirection operator, (*, category 2). (See Appendix E for complete listing.) Therefore, *clark.next is treated as *(clark.next), which is precisely what we seek, i.e., the structure being pointed at by clark.next. In the case of *(*clark.next).next, the parentheses are needed. The member operators associate left to right, while direction operators associate right to left. To make the code even more legible, you may want to write

```
*(*(clark.next).next)
```

which highlights the sequence of events.

Now suppose you have a pointer to **PLAYER_REC** called **player_ptr**. To access the components of *player_ptr, the structure being pointed at, you would need expressions like

```
(*player_ptr).name
(*player_ptr).player_number
(*player_ptr).batting_average
```

and so on. The parentheses here are essential in view of the previous remarks about precedence. Because this method of component access is so common in C, K&R wisely provided a special operator called *structure pointer member*, or *right arrow*, to simplify your typing. The two symbols – (minus) and > (greater than) are combined (with no white space) to give the operator –>. This has the same category 1 precedence as the normal member operator. The previous three expressions can be written more concisely as

```
player_ptr –>name             (*player_pointer).name
player_ptr –>player_number    (*player_pointer).player_number
player_ptr –>batting_average  (*player_pointer).batting_average
```

Parentheses are not required with –> since the compiler dereferences **player_ptr** first as part of the –> operation. When you mix –> with more complex expressions, of course, parentheses may be needed.

Using our linked-list declarations, here are some examples of –> in action.

```
        (clark.next) –>batting_average = 0.450;

   /* since "clark.next = &ruth" and "*clark.next = ruth"
      the above is the same as (&ruth) –>batting_average = 0.450;
      which is the same as ruth.batting_average = 0.450; */

          ((clark.next –>next) –>active = FALSE;

   /* since "(*clark.next).next = ruth.next = &mays"
      the above is the same as
          ((*clark.next).next) –>active = FALSE;
      which is the same as
          (*(*clark.next).next).active = FALSE;
      which is the same as
          mays.active = FALSE */

   /* since "." and " –>" are equal precedence and associate left to
      right, you can also write:
          clark.next –>next –>active = FALSE;
      with no parentheses! */
```

► *ADVANTAGES OF LINKED LISTS* ►

The neat thing about this type of data structure is that you can easily insert and delete records. Changing **clark.next** to **&mays**, for example, effectively strikes out **ruth**! Changing **ruth.next** to **&aaron** and then setting **aaron.next** to **&mays** adds **aaron** to the list.

For more complex manipulations such as forward and reverse scanning of a list, the *double-linked list* is often used. This adds another pointer to point to the previous record.

```
typedef struct player {
    char name[NAME_SIZE];
    unsigned char player_number;
    float batting_average;
    BOOL active;
    DATE date_joined;
    struct player *next;          /* field 6 is pointer to next record */
    struct player *prev;          /* new field 7 is pointer to previous
                                     record */
} PLAYER_REC;

PLAYER_REC clark, ruth, mays;
```

Under this dispensation **clark.prev** would be **NULL**, indicating that this is the first record in the list, while **mays.prev** would be set to **&ruth**.

My examples are hardly realistic, of course. Since the three player records have known identifiers, we can access them directly without scanning the linked list. I've used these examples to establish the general technique and terminology that we'll use later with more realistic applications employing arrays of pointers to structures.

► *POINTERS TO STRUCTURES* ►

Pointers, as you can see, play a central role in C. This role is underlined when you consider pointers to structures and pointers to functions. The previous section showed how structure elements can be linked together in various ways by means of pointers embedded in the structure itself. A further use of pointers arises because structures are usually passed to functions *indirectly as pointers* just as you saw with array and function arguments to functions. At one time, in fact, structures could only be passed to functions as pointers, but this restriction is now lifted. Although you can have a **func(PLAYER_REC pl)** in Turbo C taking a structure argument, only a copy of the structure is passed (C always passes by value), so **func( )** cannot change the actual argument. Also, it can put a strain on available memory if the structure is a large one.

Similarly, although a function defined as **PLAYER_REC func( )** can return a structure value directly, it is more common to return a pointer to a structure as with **PLAYER_REC *func( )**.

You will recall that an array identifier like **name** is actually a pointer to the first element of the array **name[ ]**. In the same way, a function identifier **func** used without the **( )** is taken as a pointer to **func( )**. This is not the case with structure variables. The variable **pl1**, declared to be of type **PLAYER_REC**, is *not* a pointer to anything. You must apply the address operator to get **&pl1**, the address of **pl1**, as with simple variables. You can also declare variables of type pointer to structure X as well as arrays of structures and arrays of pointers to structures. A few examples will help clarify these distinct objects.

```
typedef struct player {
    char name[NAME_SIZE];
    unsigned char player_number;
```

```
        float batting_average;
        BOOL active;
        DATE date_joined;
        PLAYER_REC *next;
    } PLAYER_REC;
/* PLAYER_REC is type 'struct player' */

/* sizeof(PLAYER_REC) is now 42 (byte alignment) */

    PLAYER_REC pl1, pl2, outfielder;

    PLAYER_REC *player_ptr;
/* declare a pointer to struct player */

    player_ptr = &pl1;
    pl2.next = player_ptr;
/* assign pointer values */
    player_ptr -> active = TRUE;
/* assign a component value */
    PLAYER_REC *team[TEAM_SIZE];
/* declare an array of 'pointers to struct player'*/

    if (&out_fielder) team[0] = &out_fielder;
/* the first pointer of this array now points to the struct
   variable outfielder - if not-NULL */
    team[0] -> player_number = 39;
/* assign a component value */
    PLAYER_REC squad[TEAM_SIZE];
/* declare an 'array of type struct player' */

    squad[2] = pl2;
/* the third element of squad is now pl2
   complete assignment of all fields */

    PLAYER_REC *trade(PLAYER_REC *pl_ptr);
/* declare a function, trade, that takes as argument a 'pointer
   to struct player' and returns a value 'pointer to struct player'*/
```

► ALLOCATING DYNAMIC MEMORY FOR STRUCTURES ►

When I declared **pl1**, C established a fixed amount of RAM to hold the member variables of **PLAYER_REC**. Declaring a pointer to a structure, however, does not allocate any memory for that structure, nor is the pointer set to point at anything in particular! As you saw in Chapter 5, pointers need to be initialized in some way before they are usable. In my previous examples, I did this with assignments of known addresses of existing structure variables such as **&ruth**.

Using **malloc( )** is another way of creating real space for a structure and at the same time establishing a pointer to that space.

When allocating dynamic memory for structures with **malloc( )**, using **sizeof( )** is always safer, easier, and more portable than "manually" counting bytes. Writing **malloc(42)** to get one **PLAYER_REC** allocation is clearly dangerous in view of my earlier comments on alignment boundaries.

The argument for **sizeof( )** should be the data type **struct player**, or its **typedef** synonym **PLAYER_REC**, or another variable of that type. So **sizeof(PLAYER_REC)** or **sizeof(pinch_hitter)** will each give you the right structure size, but **sizeof(player)** is illegal since **player** is a tag not a type or variable. Examine the following snippet:

```
PLAYER_REC *player_ptr;            /* declare a pointer to struct player */
    ...
    if ((player_ptr = (PLAYER_REC *)malloc(sizeof(PLAYER_REC)))
                                == NULL) {
        puts("\n\tInsufficient memory for player allocation\n");
        exit(1);
    }
/* here we have player_ptr pointing to first byte of allocated
    memory – all ready to 'take in' player values */
    ...
```

Here we have a typically "busy" piece of C code. The **if** statement first invokes **malloc( )**, then type casts its **(void *)** returned value to type pointer to **PLAYER_REC**, assigns that pointer to **player_ptr**, and finally tests for NULL! Remember that the value being tested is the value of the assignment statement, namely the lvalue resulting from the assignment.

You should now read through PLAYER.C (Program 6.1). It's a somewhat longer example than usual, so don't expect to digest it all at once. A detailed analysis appears in Chapter 7 since PLAYER.C relies on the **static** storage specifier to control scope and visibility.

```
Program 6.1

/* PLAYER.C - a simple, volatile player database */
/* Program 6.1 */
/* overall strategy due to N. Gehani, AT&T Bell Labs */

#include <stdio.h>
#include <alloc.h>
#include <ctype.h>
#include <string.h>

#define FOUND 1
#define MISSING 0

#define PL_MAX 2         /* max number of player */
#define NAME_MAX 25      /* max name + 1 null */
#define HDG "Pl# Name                    Posn  RBI ERA    DATE Active"

        typedef struct {
                unsigned char month, day;
                unsigned int year;
        } DATE;

        typedef unsigned char BOOL;

        typedef enum {
           X, P, C, I, S, O, D
         } POSITION;

         typedef struct player {

                char name[NAME_MAX];
                unsigned char player_number;
                POSITION player_position;
                unsigned int rbi;
                double era;
                DATE date_joined;
                BOOL active;
         } PLAYER_REC;


        static PLAYER_REC *pptr[PL_MAX];
/* global to all functions in this file,
   but not accessible elsewhere.
   Declares an array of 'pointers to PLAYER_REC structure' */

        static int pind;
/* player index used with pptr[] */

        static int db_size;
/* number of players in database */
/*----------------------------------------*/
/* INIT_PLAY - set up player database     */
/* data in memory only - until Chapter 8! */
/*----------------------------------------*/

void init_play(void)
{
    int dbind;     /* local var - scans the database */
    char pos;      /* ASCII player position */

    if (coreleft() < sizeof(PLAYER_REC)*(PL_MAX+8)) {
        puts("\n\tInsufficient Memory for Player DB");
        exit(1);
    }
```

► *Program 6.1:* PLAYER.C

```
    for (dbind = 0; dbind < PL_MAX; dbind++) {
        if ((pptr[dbind]=(PLAYER_REC *)malloc(sizeof(PLAYER_REC)))
                                    ==NULL) {
            puts("Memory Allocation Failure");
            exit(1);
        }

/* here pptr[dbind] points to an allocated record awaiting input */

        printf("\n#%3d Enter Player Number <99=exit>: ",dbind);
        scanf( "%d",&(pptr[dbind]->player_number) );

        if (pptr[dbind]->player_number == 99) break;

        printf("\n    Enter Player Name: ");
        scanf( "%s",pptr[dbind]->name );
/* Next item could be entered with getch() but I want to */
/* show scanf() with %s                                  */
        printf("\n    Enter Player Position: ");
        scanf("%s",&pos);
        pos = toupper(pos);
        switch (pos) {
            case 'P': pptr[dbind]->player_position = P; break;
            case 'C': pptr[dbind]->player_position = C; break;
            case 'I': pptr[dbind]->player_position = I; break;
            case 'S': pptr[dbind]->player_position = S; break;
            case 'O': pptr[dbind]->player_position = O; break;
            case 'D': pptr[dbind]->player_position = D; break;
            default:  pptr[dbind]->player_position = X;
        }
        if (pptr[dbind]->player_position != P) {
            pptr[dbind]->era = 0.0;
            printf("\n    Enter Runs Batted In: ");
            scanf( "%d",&(pptr[dbind]->rbi) );
        }
        else {
            pptr[dbind]->rbi = 0;
            printf("\n    Enter Earned Run Average: ");
            scanf( "%lf",&(pptr[dbind]->era) );
        }
        printf("\n    Enter Date Joined (mm/dd/yyyy): ");
        scanf( "%2d/%2d/%4d", &((pptr[dbind]->date_joined).month),
                              &((pptr[dbind]->date_joined).day),
                              &((pptr[dbind]->date_joined).year) );

        printf("\n    Active=Y or N? :");
        scanf( "%s",&pos);
        pptr[dbind]->active = ('Y' == toupper(pos));
    } /* end for loop */
    db_size = dbind;           /* set current size of database */
}
/*--------------end init_player--------------------*/


/*------------------------------------------*/
/* ASC_POS() converts position code to ASCII */
/*------------------------------------------*/

char *asc_pos(POSITION x)
{
    switch (x) {
        case P: return "P";
        case C: return "C";
        case I: return "I";
```

► *Program 6.1:* PLAYER.C (continued)

```
                case S: return "S";
                case O: return "O";
                case D: return "D";
                default:  return "X";
        }
}
/*------------------end asc_pos--------------*/


/*-------------------------------*/
/* LIST_PLAYER - lists the database */
/*-------------------------------*/

void list_play(int start)
{
 int dbind;
puts  (HDG);
    for (dbind = (start>=0 ? start : 0);
         dbind < db_size;
         dbind++) {
      printf
      ("\n%3d %-26s %1s       %3d      %7.3f  %2d/%2d/%4d %s\n",
       pptr[dbind]->player_number, pptr[dbind]->name,
       asc_pos(pptr[dbind]->player_position), pptr[dbind]->rbi,
       pptr[dbind]->era, pptr[dbind]->date_joined.month,
       pptr[dbind]->date_joined.day, pptr[dbind]->date_joined.year,
       (pptr[dbind]->active) ? "Y":"N");
    }
}
/*------------------end list_player-------------*/


/*----------------------------------------------*/
/* GET_STR returns a pointer to a copy of arg string */
/*----------------------------------------------*/

char *get_str(char str[])
{
        char *ptr;

        if ((ptr = (char *)malloc(strlen(str)+1)) == NULL) {
            puts("Insufficient Memory for get_str");
            exit(1);
        }
        else
           strcpy(ptr, str);
        return ptr;
}
/*-------------------- end get_str -------------------*/


/*-----------------------------------------------------*/
/* GET_NAME() sets global index pind to pptr[] array   */
/* such that pptr[pind] points at record with target name */
/* Returns FOUND or MISSING                            */
/*-----------------------------------------------------*/

static int get_name(char target_name[])
{
        if (strcmp(target_name, pptr[pind]->name) == 0)
           return FOUND;
/* first test if previous find is still useful */

        for (pind = 0; pind < db_size; pind++)
           if (strcmp(target_name, pptr[pind]->name) == 0)
```

► *Program 6.1:* PLAYER.C (continued)

```
                return FOUND;
        pind = 0;
        return MISSING;
}
/*--------------------end get_name------------------------*/


/*------------------------------------------------------*/
/* GET_NUMBER() sets global index pind to pptr[] array  */
/* such that pptr[pind] points at record with target number */
/* Returns FOUND with good pind or MISSING with pind=0  */
/*------------------------------------------------------*/

static int get_number(unsigned char target_number)
{
        if (target_number == pptr[pind]->player_number)
            return FOUND;
/* first test if previous find is still useful */

        for (pind = 0; pind < db_size; pind++)
        if (target_number == pptr[pind]->player_number)
            return FOUND;
        pind = 0;
        return MISSING;
}
/*--------------------end get_number----------------------*/

/* ---------------*/
/* NUMBER_TO_NAME */
/*----------------*/
char *number_to_name(unsigned char tn)
{
        return get_number(tn) ? get_str(pptr[pind]->name) : NULL;
}
/*----------------*/
/* NAME_TO_NUMBER */
/*----------------*/
unsigned char name_to_number(char tname[])
{
        return get_name(tname) ? pptr[pind]->player_number : MISSING;
}

void main()
{
    char *tname = "S";
    unsigned char tnumber = 0;
    while (tnumber != 99) {
        printf("\nEnter Target Number <99=Exit>: ");
        scanf("%d",&tnumber);
        if (tnumber == 99) break;
        if ((tname = number_to_name(tnumber)) != NULL)
            printf("\tName is %s\n",tname);
        else puts("\tNo such Player Number");
    }
    while (strcmp(tname,"X") != 0) {
        printf("\nEnter Target Name: ");
        scanf("%s",tname);
        if (strcmp(tname,"X") == 0) exit (0);
        if ((tnumber = name_to_number(tname)) != NULL)
            printf("\tNumber is %d\n",tnumber);
        else puts("\tNo such Player Name");
    }
}
```

► *Program 6.1: PLAYER.C (continued)*

► UNIONS ►

A *union* in C corresponds to the *variant record* of Pascal and Modula-2. The basic idea is to create a structurelike object in which only one set of components is active at any particular moment. Unions are declared using the keyword **union** with a similar syntax to **struct**:

```
union stats {
    unsigned int rbi;            /* runs batted in */
    float era;                   /* earned-run average */
} player_stats;
/* declare player_stats a variable of type 'union stats.' */
```

The first point to realize is that the variable **player_stats** does not occupy 6 bytes (2 for **unsigned int** and 4 for **float**). Unlike a structure, a **union** allocates only enough memory for the largest component—in this case 4 bytes for the **float era**. The **union** variable **player_stats** can hold either **rbi** or **era** but not both simultaneously. If you assign, say, **player_stats.rbi = 120;**, only two of the four bytes will be occupied, so, if you tried to display the variable **player_stats.era** before some other assignment came along, you would get bizarre results. Similarly, after **player_stats.era = 4.70;**, accessing **player_stats.rbi** would give you nonsense. The moral is to use only the active variable of the two.

There are two main reasons for using unions. First, you can save memory since two (or more) fields are effectly overlaid. If the program is such that only one component is active at any given time, the system does not have to allocate space for each individual component. The **player_rec** example hardly justifies a union on this basis, but consider

```
union results {
    int grid[2000];
    double test[500];
} lab_test;
```

If **lab_test.grid** and **lab_test.test** results are never processed at the same time, you save 4KB.

► Unions in Action ►

The second reason for unions is that they allow you to change the interpretation of a group of bits, rather like a supercharged type-casting operation.

A major application for this is writing portable libraries. If you have a union such as

```
union x {
     type1 a;
     type2 b;
} combo;
```

you can load **combo.a** with a value and then read it as **combo.b**. Depending on the particular types of **type1** and **type2**, you can perform many advanced tricks such as fooling functions as to the real nature of your arguments. Remember that unions are manipulated like structures, so you can use pointers to unions for argument passing, arrays of pointers, and so on. The −> operator works in the same way. Look at the following snippet:

```
     type1 rval;
     type2 lval;
/* type1 and type2 are previously defined types */
     typedef union x {
         type1 a;
         type2 b;
     } COMBO;

     COMBO *combo_ptr;
/* declare a 'pointer to type union x' */
     combo_ptr −>a = rval;
     lval = combo_ptr −>b;
```

Without worrying about the deep meaning of this, observe the use of −> and how the bit-patterns for **rval** have been coerced into an entirely different format. The types involved will often be structures. A good example of this appears in DOS.H in the Turbo C \include subdirectory.

```
/* Copyright (c) Borland International Inc., 1987
     All Rights Reserved
*/
struct WORDREGS
     {
     unsigned int ax, bx, cx, dx, si, di, cflag, flags;
     };
struct BYTEREGS
     {
```

```
        unsigned char al, ah, bl, bh, cl, ch, dl, dh;
        };
    union REGS {
        struct WORDREGS x;
        struct BYTEREGS h;
        };
```

(Appendix F outlines the 8088/86 register model, but to follow this next section you need some technical DOS background.)

You can declare variables of type **union REGS** and then set values in either the 16-bit registers (AX, BX,...) or in their upper or lower halves (AH, AL,...).

Turbo C offers several functions for direct access to DOS. For example, **intdos( )** can call any of about 80 DOS "universal" functions using interrupt 33 (0x21). You set a function number in register AH, set various values in other registers, and call **intdos( )**. After the particular action is invoked, which can range from setting the time to creating a file, back comes a set of register values as a result of the call. The **union REGS** allows considerable flexibility in handling the many function-call variations. The simplified **intdos( )** prototype

```
    int intdos(union REGS *inregs, union REGS *outregs);
```

indicates that you send **intdos( )** a pointer to union argument, **inregs**, and get one (**outregs**) back. The **outregs** set of values includes the carry flag **cflag** that you can test for errors. In addition, the **int** returned by **intdos( )** is the value DOS puts in register AX (usually an error number). MYTAB.C (Program 6.2) offers a brief example as a test bed for further experiments with other DOS functions. It would not normally be necessary to check the carry flag after such a simple call—I do so merely to show how **union REGS** is used.

► *Analysis of MYTAB.C* ►

DOS function 2 of interrupt 0x21 will display whatever single ASCII character is placed in DL before the call. Since **regs** is the union of two structures, you need two member operators, **regs.h.ah**, to access the **ah** component of the **h** structure. You pass a pointer to union, **&regs**, as the **inregs** argument. The **outregs** argument is passed via the same pointer—although you could have declared a separate **union REGS** variable for this.

```
Program 6.2

/* MYTAB.C - using DOS 0x21 interrupts */

#include <dos.h>
#include <stdio.h>

#define FAIL 0
#define OK 1

/* mytab() displays one tab on screen; returns nonzero for
   success */

int mytab()
{
    union REGS regs;

    regs.h.ah = 0x02;      /* DOS function 2 is display a char */
    regs.h.dl = '\t';      /* set DL to Horizontal Tab */
    intdos(&regs, &regs);  /* call the function */
    return(regs.x.cflag ? FAIL : OK);
}

void main()
{
    puts("It's mytab, I believe!");
    mytab() ? puts("Waiter!") : puts("Error!");
}
```

► *Program 6.2:* MYTAB.C

In this trivial example, once the **inregs** registers are set using the **regs.h** member of the union, you have no further use for them. Remember that **&regs** is essential for **outregs** because the function actually alters **regs** (C simulates "passing by reference" by using "passing by pointer value").

Note especially that **outregs** uses the **x** structure of the union from which we pick up **cflag**. The value returned by **mytab( )** is either **FAIL** or **OK** depending on **regs.x.cflag**:

    return(regs.x.cflag ? FAIL : OK);

This is a good illustration of the economical *a ? b : c* operator. Achieving this returned value using **if (regs.x.cflag == 0) {...} else {...}** would be awkward and not in the best C traditions!

Similarly,

    mytab( ) ? puts("Waiter!") : puts("Error!");

relies on the fact that **mytab( )** not only invokes the function but also returns **FAIL** (0) or **OK** (1).

► *Caveats about Unions* ►

Unlike the variant records of Pascal and Modula-2, the unions in C do not have a **CASE tag** mechanism for distinguishing the components. In C, therefore, you must take care that any writing or reading of union variables is done using the appropriate component variants—unless, of course, you are deliberately coercing the two fields. In other words, you must remember which component is currently active. If I revamp **PLAYER_REC** to be

```
typedef struct player {
    char name[30];
    unsigned char player_number;
    union {
        unsigned int rbi;
        float era; } stats;
    BOOL active;
} PLAYER_REC;

PLAYER_REC pitcher, dh, player;
```

the intent is to store either **era** (earned-run average) for pitchers or **rbi** (runs batted in) for dh's (designated hitters). You've already seen structures inside unions. Here you have unions inside structures! Assuming that a given player (in the American League, presumably) never needs both statistics, the above structure simplifies the creation of a player database. C will allocate memory for the worst case, namely 4 bytes for a pitcher's **era** variant. For dh's, only 2 of these bytes will be occupied. You can write and read values as follows:

```
pitcher.stats.era = 5.21;
dh.stats.rbi = 56;
tot_rbi += dh.stats.rbi;
team_era = (pitcher.stats.era * inns + x)/tot_inns;
```

without danger. If you have a general variable such as **player**, however, you may have no a priori knowledge of which component is active. One obvious answer to this is to add a player-position field to **RECORD_PLAYER**. One way of doing this uses an enumeration type.

```
typedef enum {
    X, P, C, B1, B2, B3, SS, LF, CF, RF, DH } POSITION;
```

```
typedef struct player {
    char name[30];
    unsigned char player_number;
    POSITION player_position;
    union {
        unsigned int rbi;
        float era; } stats;
    DATE date_joined;
    BOOL active;
} PLAYER_REC;

PLAYER_REC pitcher, dh, player;
...
if (player.player_position == P) {
    /* use the era field here */
}
else if (player.player_position == DH) {
    /* use the rbi field here */
}
...
```

Before leaving unions, I should mention that they share most of the syntactical rules of structures. You can omit the tag identifier, you can use **typedef**, you can pass unions or pointers to unions as function parameters, and functions can return unions or pointers to unions.

► GOING DOWN TO THE BIT LEVEL ►

Since C is a systems programming language it has features for manipulating at the bit level not usually found in high-level languages. In applications programs you are primarily concerned with bytes (characters) or groups of bytes (strings, integers, floating point numbers, pointers, or addresses). You are seldom interested in the individual bits that make up these variables.

When you tackle the problems of writing compilers, operating systems, communications packages, or device drivers (to name but a few possibilities), the need to set, clear, or test a particular bit within a field or register arises in many contexts. To give two concrete examples, a stored sequence of 0's and 1's, called a *bit map*, is often used to represent the state of a disk. Each free sector is mapped to a 0 in the bit map, while an occupied sector is signaled by a 1. The operating system must constantly monitor and update the bit map as files are created and deleted. A simpler example is the use of a byte as a status flag, where groups of bits indicate some property, for example, bit 7 ON equals "read-only"; bit 6 ON equals "busy"; bits 0–2 equal "interrupt level 0–7," and so on. C has a set of *bitwise* operators and a means of defining *bit fields*.

► *Bitwise Operators* ►

The bitwise operators work only on integerlike objects such as **int** and **char**. Table 6.2 lists their names, symbols and operation. What is probably the most common mistake in using these operators stems from a confusion between the bitwise operators **&** and ¦ and their *logical* operator twins **&&** and ¦¦. Also, ˜ is often confused with ! (logical negation). A few examples are worth pages of exposition. I'll use 8-bit **char** variables for simplicity—the 16- and 32-bit extensions follow naturally. Table 6.3 shows examples based on **a** and **b** with the following bit patterns:

a = 00010110 = 18 decimal
b = 10011010 = 158 decimal

Symbol	Name	Operation
&	Bitwise AND	$c = a$ & b. Each bit in c is the bitwise AND of the corresponding bits in a and b.
¦	Bitwise OR	$c = a$ ¦ b. Each bit in c is the bitwise OR of the corresponding bits in a and b.
^	Bitwise XOR	$c = a$ ^ b. Each bit in c is the bitwise XOR of the corresponding bits in a and b.
~	Bitwise Negate	$c = $ ~ a. Each bit in c is the bitwise negation of the corresponding bit in a.
>>	Bit Right Shift	$c >> n$. The bit pattern in c is shifted to the right by n places.
<<	Bit Left Shift	$c << n$. The bit pattern in c is shifted to the left by n places.

► **Table 6.2:** *Bitwise operators*

	a & b = 00010010	
	a ¦ b = 10011110	
	a ^ b = 10001100	
	˜a = 11101001	
	˜b = 01100101	
Left shift	a << 1 = 00101100	(0 pushed in at right)
	a << 2 = 01011000	
	a << 3 = 10110000	
	a << 4 = 01100000	(1 overspill discarded on left)
Right shift	a >> 1 = 00001011	
	a >> 2 = 00000101	(1 overspill discarded on right)
	a >> 3 = 00000010	
If b is unsigned	b >> 1 = 01001101	(0 pushed in at left)
If b is signed	b >> 1 = 11001101	(sign bit ‒ I pushed in at left)

► a = 00010110, b = 10011010

► **Table 6.3:** *Illustrations of bitwise operations*

The rules for each bit-by-bit composition are shown in Table 6.4.

Right shifts vary with signed and unsigned variables. To maintain the correct sign when shifting signed values, the sign bit is pushed in from the left as the bits are shifted right. In all cases, any bits that spill out from either end during a shift are discarded and lost.

Now look at **a** and **b** as decimal values (18 and 158, respectively) rather than as bit patterns. The logical, non-bitwise operators give the following results:

(a && b) is equivalent to 1 (true) since **a** is true (nonzero) AND **b** is true (nonzero).
(a ¦¦ b) is also 1 (true) while !a = !b = 0 (false).

The logical parallel to the bitwise XOR is != , since (a != b) evaluates to 1 if either **a** is zero and **b** is nonzero or **a** is nonzero and **b** is zero but evaluates to 0 if both **a** and **b** are zero or if both are nonzero.

AND (&)	0 & 0 = 0; 1 & 0 = 0; 0 & 1 = 0; 1 & 1 = 1; (i.e., both must be 1 to give a 1)
OR (¦)	0¦0 = 0; 1¦0 = 1; 0¦1 = 1; 1¦1 = 1; (i.e., either or both must be 1 to give a 1)
XOR (^)	0 ^ 0 = 0; 1 ^ 1 = 0; 1 ^ 0 = 1; 0 ^ 1 = 1; (i.e., either but not both must be 1 to give 1, hence the name eXclusive OR)
NEGATE (~)	~0 = 1; ~1 = 0 (i.e., reverse or invert each bit)

► **Table 6.4:** *Rules for bit-by-bit composition*

► *Bitwise Applications* ►

The bitwise operators are often used to clear, set, or invert individual bits within a flag or bit map. The idea here is to create a certain constant bit pattern called a *mask* and then perform operations such as (*a* = *a* & mask), (*a* = *a* ¦ mask), or (*a* = *a* ^ mask) in order to update the bit pattern in *a*. These manipulations are so commonplace that the shorthand *op* = , as you saw with + = , is available:

a &= mask; a ¦= mask; a ^= mask;

The choice of masks requires some practice, but once you are familiar with the following rules, things are quite logical:

1. Use **&** with mask-bit = 0 to clear a bit to 0.

2. Use **&** with mask-bit = 1 to leave a bit unchanged.

3. Use ¦ with mask-bit = 1 to set a bit to 1.

4. Use ¦ with mask-bit = 0 to leave a bit unchanged.

5. Use ^ with mask-bit = 1 to invert a bit.

6. Use ^ with mask-bit = 0 to leave a bit unchanged.

Suppose the **char status** has the bit flags defined as shown in Table 6.5.

Bit Number	Meaning
0	0 = file closed; 1 = file open
1	0 = read-only; 1 = read/write
2	0 = random; 1 = sequential
3	0 = private; 1 = public
4	reserved
5	reserved
6	reserved
7	0 = floppy; 1 = hard disk

► **Table 6.5:** *Sample status byte*

To create legible masks, you can start with some **#define**s.

```
#define OPEN_CLOSED      1
#define READ_WRITE      (1 << 1)
#define RAND_SEQ        (1 << 2)
#define PRIV_PUB        (1 << 3)
#define FLOP_HARD       (1 << 7)
/* these give you a 1 in each bit position.
    You can build masks from them as follows */

    status |= (RAND_SEQ | PRIV_PUB);
/* set bits 2 and 3, leaving the others unchanged */
    status &= (OPEN_CLOSED);
/* clear bit-0, leaving others unchanged */
    status ^= (FLOP_HARD | OPEN_CLOSED);
/* reverse bits 0 and 7, leaving others unchanged */
    if (status & OPEN_CLOSED)   { /* do something if bit-0 set */ }
}
```

► *Shifts in Action* ►

The shifts offer a faster alternative to multiplication and division by powers of 2. For example, $a << 2$ is equivalent to $a*4$, while $a >> 3$ gives the same result as $a/8$. The same care over truncation and overflow is needed, and you should note that >> and << have lower precedence (category 5) than + and − (category 4). Shifts associate from left to right, so you sometimes find strange expressions like

```
int i;
i << 4 >> 8;
```

used to extract the middle 8 bits from a 16-bit integer. Note also that a = a << 2 can be shortened to a << = 2, and so on.

► *BIT FIELDS* ►

The bit field facility allows you to name structure components as individual groups of bits within a 16-bit field (maximum). As with the status byte listed above, bit fields allow you to pack a lot of information in a small space. The syntax is as follows:

```
struct status {
    unsigned open            :1; /* width of bit field */
    unsigned read            :2;
    unsigned random          :1;
    int permit               :4; /* int is allowed */
    unsigned                 :3; /* unused − so no name */
    unsigned pointer         :5;
} freg, greg, *reg_ptr;
```

The above 16-bit structure allocates six groups of bits and names five of them. Apart from the bit width specifier (:n) the usual rules for structure declaration apply. There are a few minor quirks, as you'll see soon. The member selection operators are used to access structure components.

The component **freg.open** would occupy bit 0, the first, low-memory bit of the structure. The **reg_ptr −>read** component would be 2 bits in bit positions 1–2, and so on. The :*n*; after each declaration indicates the width of that field. A zero bit width, (:0), is legal—it tells C to align the next field on an even address (padding, if necessary). Identifiers are optional, as shown in the fifth, unused field above.

Although bit fields can occupy odd or even bit positions within a structure, they cannot straddle integer boundaries. You can form arrays of structures containing bit fields, but arrays of bit-field variables are not allowed. It is also illegal to form the address of a bit-field variable with **&** since there is no guarantee that it has a byte address.

Only **signed** and **unsigned int**s are allowed, but note carefully that the actual valid range of each identifier is dictated by its bit width. One consequence of this is that a bit field of width 1 must be declared as **unsigned** since it can never hold a negative value! When you extract and manipulate a bit-field component, it will be treated as declared (**signed** or **unsigned int**) in the obvious way. For example, a bit field of width 2 holding the binary value 11 would be taken as 3 if **unsigned** but as − 1 if **signed**. The sign bit is always taken as the leftmost bit of the field. Bizarre results can occur if you overflow the real bit-field range:

```
        greg.read = 3;
        greg.read *= 2;
 /* the 2-bit field now holds 4 (binary 10), not 6 */
```

Bit fields are commonly used to match the peculiar storage layouts of hardware devices—a communications interface, for instance, may provide signals and data via groups of bits within a 16-bit register. With memory-mapped I/O, such registers are actual memory locations. Rather than use bitwise operators to extract these values, bit fields can be used for elegance and legibility.

Portability of such code may be a problem, though, mainly because different systems have different conventions with respect to how bytes are stored within words in memory. The "low-byte/low-address" scheme, favored by DEC and National Semiconductor, contrasts with the "high-byte/low-address" convention of Intel and Motorola. (The fierce proponents of each approach have been labeled "little endians" and "big endians" in honor of Swift's *Gulliver's Travels*.) The following program by Samuel P. Harbison and Guy L. Steele Jr. in *C: A Reference Manual* (Englewood Cliffs, New Jersey: Prentice-Hall Inc., 1987) is worth knowing if you plan to port your code to alien machines. It also provides an excellent insight into unions.

```
#include <stdio.h>

union { long Long; char Char[sizeof(long)]; } u;
/* u can be viewed as a long or as a sequence of byte */

int main( )
{
```

```
      u.Long = 1;                    /* low-order byte of long set to 1 */
      if (u.Char[0] == 1)            /* check which char has the 1 */
          puts("Addressing is right – to – left (little – endian)");
      else if (u.Char[sizeof(long) – 1]) == 1)
          puts("Addressing is left – to – right (big – endian)");
      else puts("Addressing is strange");
      return (0);
  }
```

The byte order will affect how bit fields exceeding 8 bits are organized. Another machine-dependent factor can be the maximum bit fields allowed—this is normally dictated by the word size of the CPU.

Finally, it is perfectly legal to mix bit fields with normal variables within a structure or union. If file size was a critical factor, for example, you could pack three fields into one byte of the **PLAYER_REC** structure.

```
typedef struct player {
    char name[29];
    unsigned char player_number;
    unsigned position            :4; /* 16 positions 0-15 */
    unsigned doctor              :3; /* 8 doctor codes 0-7 */
    unsigned active              :1; /* 0 = inactive 1 = active */
    union {
        unsigned int rbi;
        float era; } stats;
    DATE date_joined;
} PLAYER_REC;
```

▸ *SUMMARY OF CHAPTER 6* ▸

◂▸ A structure is a record containing a list of arbitrary variables. The declaration syntax is

```
struct [tag] {
    type1 var1;
    type2 var2;
    ...
    typen varn;
} [struct_var1, struct_var2,...];
```

This allows you to declare structure variables immediately as above or later with

struct tag struct_var3, struct_var4,...;

if a tag has been named.

◄► Components are referenced as *struct_var.member_var*. If *struct_ptr* is a pointer to a structure, the components can be referenced as

(*struct_ptr).member_var)

or more economically as

struct_ptr –>member_var

◄► Structures of the same type can be assigned:

struct_var1 = struct_var2;

This transfers all components, including any arrays within the structure.

◄► Structures cannot contain themselves as a member, but they can contain nested structures and pointers to themselves. This opens the door to interlinked data structures of all kinds.

```
struct node {
    type1 data;
    struct facts {
        type2 data2;
        type3 data3;
    }
    struct node *next;
    struct node *previous;
} list1, list2,...;

struct tree {
    type1 data;
    struct tree *left;
    struct tree *right;
} tree1, *tree_ptr1,...;
```

◄► C allows certain forward references to "pointers to structures" before the structure has been declared:

```
         struct s1 { type1 data1; struct s2 *s2_ptr;} struct_s1;
/* forward reference to (struct2 *) - struct2 not yet declared */
         struct s2 { type2 data2; struct s1 *s1_ptr;} struct_s2;
```

◄► The size of a structure can depend on the word- or byte-alignment option chosen. Dynamic memory for structures can be allocated using **struct_ptr = (struct *)malloc(sizeof(struct))**.

◄► Unions are a special form of structure. (They are similar to the variant records of Pascal.) The two components of a union "share" the same memory allocation, but only one of them can be accessed at any moment. Unions are declared and accessed using the same syntax as for structures:

```
union [tag] {
      type1 member_var1;
      type1 member_var2;
} [union_var1, union_var2, *union_ptr1,...];

union tag another_one;              /* if tag available */

union_var1.member_var1 = x;
union_var2.member_var2 = union_var1.member_var1;
union_ptr ->member_var1 = y;
```

sizeof(union *tag*) is the maximum of **sizeof(*type1*)** and **sizeof(*type2*)**. Unions can be nested in structures and vice versa.

◄► Bitwise operators perform bit-by-bit, Boolean operations on integer types. The bitwise AND (**&**) must not be confused with the logical AND (**&&**). Likewise, bitwise OR (¦) is not the same as logical OR (¦¦). The bitwise XOR does not have a logical ^^ sibling (you use **!=** for logical XOR). The two shift operators, **<<** and **>>**, can be used to multiply, divide, and extract bit patterns.

◄► Bit fields are special structure components that allow you to have **int** variables of specified bit width (0–16). They enable you to access device-dependent bit positions within bytes or words; they can also reduce record sizes by using bits as flags or small numeric fields.

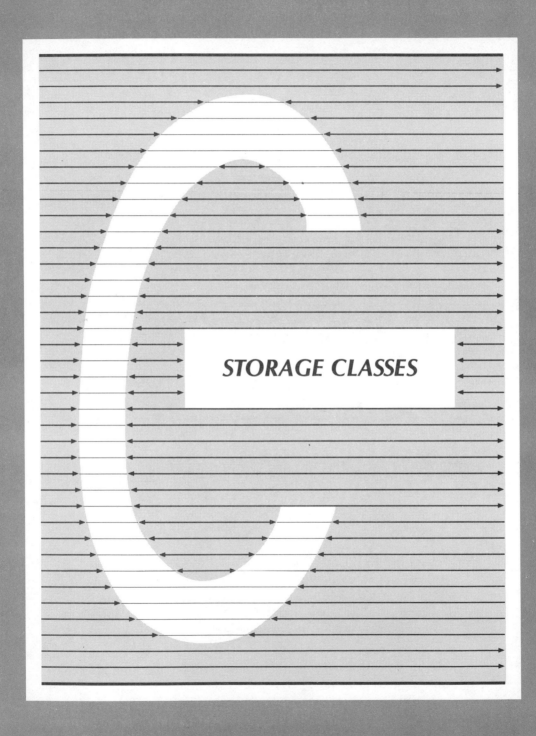

STORAGE CLASSES

► *CHAPTER 7* ►

I have touched on the subject of storage classes several times, hinting that they govern the accessibility and life span of the objects you declare and define in C. In this short chapter, I will knit together the various strands of this important subject and introduce some new storage classes. I will then analyze PLAYER.C (from Chapter 6), in which storage classes play a leading role.

Before attempting to establish a formal terminology and syntax, I will show you some of the storage classes in action. Be aware of the fact that prior to ANSI C there were several ambiguities in this area, and different implementors still use different interpretations of K&R. The use of terms such as *scope*, *external*, and *extent* is also inconsistent in the C literature. I plan to converge to the truth by a series of approximations!

Every variable and function in C has an associated type and storage class. You have already seen how the type of an object establishes its memory requirements and its range of legal operations. The storage class determines other essential properties of the object such as *scope* (where is its declaration active?), *visibility* (from which parts of the program is it accessible?), and *extent* (when is it created, initialized, and destroyed?). In addition, the storage class can indicate whether selected integral variables should be stored in registers (if any are available) to improve execution speed. As you'll see, these properties are not exclusive—they overlap in various ways.

► *STORAGE CLASS SPECIFIERS* ►

A single storage class specifier can be used when you declare or define an object in order to establish (or request) certain storage class properties for that object. In most cases these properties have defaults that depend on whether the object is a variable or function and on where the declaration or definition is made. Explicit storage class specifiers are relatively rare, but don't be fooled! Storage classes, whether specified up front or not, are always assigned and always play a vital role in how your program behaves.

For those important occasions when you do need to alter the defaults, the storage class specifier goes in front of the data type specifier and modifier(s), if any. Here are some typical declarations/definitions that use the four basic storage class specifiers, **auto**, **static**, **extern**, and **register**. The comments will be expanded as I proceed.

```
{
auto long sum  =  3;
...
}
/* sum is defined long int, storage class automatic.
   sum will be created and reinitialized each time this
   block is executed.  sum disappears outside the block.
   The specifier auto is the default and can be omitted
   in this context */

...
static char ch  =  '\0';
/* ch is defined/initialized as a char with static extent.
   ch is 'private' to a block, function or file */

...
static int func(void);
/* func( ) declared: it returns an int and will be defined
   as static later in this file  -- see below */

...
static int func(void)
{ /* function body */ }
/* func( ) defined, but will not be exported to linker.
   func( ) is therefore 'private' to this file */

...
extern int count;
/* count is declared int, storage class external.
   No storage allocated  -- count will be
   defined in another file */

...
extern void func2(double d);
/* func2( ) is declared external; its returned value is discarded;
   its name will be passed to the linker.  func2( ) is
   accessible from other files */

/* NOTE: extern is always assumed with function declarations
   in the absence of the static specifier */

...
{
register unsigned i;
...
}
```

```
/* i is unsigned int; same as auto except that if possible
   i will be stored in a register rather than RAM */
   ...
```

(This selection should be considered as isolated examples rather than as a contiguous sequence you might expect to find in a legal program. It is intended to illustrate the variety of combinations available.)

Technically speaking, the keyword **typedef** is also a storage class specifier, but I will confine my discussion to the four classes listed above for the time being.

The word *default* in relation to storage classes must be treated with caution. With type specifiers it makes no difference whether you write **unsigned** or **unsigned int** since **int** is the true default. But you'll meet situations in which a variable "defaults" to external because of the placement of its declaration, and yet the apparently innocent, superfluous use of the **extern** specifier materially affects the situation! In other words, there are occasions when you must omit the default storage specifier. I'll point out these quirks as we continue.

To appreciate the differences between the four storage classes, you need to carefully distinguish the related concepts of scope, visibility, and extent.

► *SCOPE* ►

The declaration of an identifier is *active* over a certain region of the source code text, known as its scope. With one major and two minor exceptions, an identifier cannot be legally referenced outside its scope. These exceptions allow what are known as *forward references*.

The two minor anomalies are

1. **goto label** is valid before the **label:** is encountered.

2. **struct**, **union**, and **enum** tags can be forward referenced under some circumstances (see Chapter 6).

The major exception is that the C compiler will supply the *implicit declaration* **int func( );** if you call **func( )** before its explicit declaration. The use of prototype declarations, encouraged under ANSI C and Turbo C, can eliminate this potentially dangerous situation.

So, in the majority of cases, the scope starts with the declaration. Where the scope ends depends on where the declaration is made in relation to the source text, i.e., outside or inside a function definition.

► *Scope of Top-Level Declarations* ►

Declarations made at the head of a program file, before any of the function definitions, are called *top-level* declarations. The scope of these is from the point of declaration until the end of the source file. This is often called *global* scope (but there are some caveats about this description that I'll explain later).

► *Scope of Declarations within Functions* ►

Declarations made within a function definition fall into two categories. They can occur as *formal parameter declarations*, in which case their scope is from the point of declaration to the end of the function definition, or they can occur at the start (or head) of any block within a function definition. A *head-of-block* declaration has a scope from the point of declaration to the end of that block.

Both formal parameters and head-of-block variables are said to have *local* scope. The scope of a formal parameter is local to the function, while the scope of a head-of-block variable is local to its block. (Be careful not to misuse the term *local*—it has different meanings when applied to scope and extent. You will see later that a variable with local scope need not have local extent. Unless the context is absolutely clear, avoid statements such as "*x* is local." The correct usage is, "*x* has local scope," or, "*x* has local extent.")

Program 7.1 is a generic C source file to illustrate how scope is affected by the location of the declaration.

Note the absence of storage class specifiers! In GENERIC.C the scope has been determined completely by the placement of the declarations. The variables **global_int** and **global_ch_ptr** can be used freely within **main( )** and any of the functions.

► *VISIBILITY* ►

Normally an identifier is *visible* throughout its scope, that is, references to that identifier will be related by the compiler to the original declaration in

```
/* GENERIC.C */

/* top--level ---- outside any function definitions */

/*-------------------------------------------*/
/* include header files */
/*-------------------------------------------*/

#include <any.h>
/* any declarations pulled in here are top--level with scope
   extending to the end of the file GENERIC.C */

/*----------------*/
/* macros */
/*----------------*/

#define X Y
/* any macro names here have scope until end of file or until an
   #undef undefines them */

/* #includes and #defines can be placed anywhere, but they are
   usually safer as shown to give maximum scoping */

/*-----------------------------------------------------*/
/* func2 prototype declaration */
/*-----------------------------------------------------*/
     void func2(int a, char *b);      /* note the ; for a func
                                         declaration */

/* vars a and b are not formally declared here -- they provide a
   'template' so that calls to func2() made before its definition
   can be checked for valid arg types and numbers */

/* you are still at top--level! */

     int global_int;       /* two top--level declarations */
     char *global_ch_ptr;  /* scope is the whole source file */

/*-------------------------------------*/
/* func1() definition */
/*-------------------------------------*/

int func1(a,b,c)              /* no ; after a func definition */
/* now inside func1() definition */
/* formal parameters classic style declarations */
     int a,b,c;
/* scope of a,b,c is local ---- from here until the end of the
   function definition */
/* a and b have no connection with the prototype args of
   func2() */
{
/* head--of--block A */
     int local_int_A;        /* scope is block A */
     ...
     {
     /* head--of--inner--block B */
     int local_int_B;        /* scope is block B */
     ...
/* scopes of local_int_A and local_int_B overlap here */

     ...
     } /* end block B */
     ...
} /* end block A, also end func1() definition
```

► *Program 7.1:* GENERIC.C

```
/*-------------------------------end of func1() definition--------------------
-----------*/

/*-------------------------------------*/
/* main() starts here */
/*-------------------------------------*/

void main (void)
{
/* head--of--block */
     int local_int_main;       /* 2 local--scope vars */
     char *local_ch_ptr_main; /* scope is main() */
     ...
     func2(local_int_main, local_ch_ptr_main); /* call func2() */
     func2(global_var, global_ch_ptr);         /* call func2() */
/* both calls valid, since actual args are assignment compatible with those of the
   prototype; also, the actual args are used within scope */
     ...
     int_local_main = func3(local_int_main);
/* call to an undeclared function, func3()!
   The compiler will make an implicit declaration:
   extern int func(); hoping that func3 will be defined eventually ---- see note on
   implicit declarations above.
   If func3() is not defined elsewhere, a link--time error occurs.  If func3() is
   defined as returning a non--int results may be bizarre */
     ...
}
/*-------------------------------------end of main()---------------------------
-----------------*/

/*-------------------------------------*/
/* func2()  definition */
/*-------------------------------------*/

void func2(int a, char *b) /* modern style formal parameter declaration */
/* scope of a and b is whole of func2() body ---- unrelated to earlier a's and b's */
{
...
/* global_int and global_ch_ptr could be used here, as well as a
and b */
...
}
/*---------------------------end of func2() definition---------------------------
*/

/*********************/
/* end of source file */
/*********************/
```

► **Program 7.1:** *GENERIC.C (continued)*

order to determine data type and current value. The annoying exceptions occur when the same name is legally used to declare a new identifier within the scope of the original identifier. If duplicate identifier names were ruthlessly banned, scope and visibility would coincide!

Visibility therefore relates to the region of a source text in which an identifier reference refers to the object as originally declared or defined. An identifier is never visible outside its scope, but it may become invisible during its scope!

As you read through a source text, you will see identifiers coming in and out of scope according to the scoping rules outlined above. If all the identifiers are uniquely named, then scope and visibility coincide throughout. When identifier names in the same *name space* are duplicated, however, one declaration may *hide* a previously declared identifier.

ANSI C specifies five name spaces: macros, labels, tags (for **struct**, **union**, and **enum**), components (of **struct** and **union**), and all others (variables, functions, **typedef** names, and **enum** constants). Name spaces are also called *overloading classes*. C keeps a separate table of names for each of these, so the five objects called **same** in the following bizarre snippet are all distinct and can share the same scope level without clashing.

```
#define same  ==                    /* macro name */
   if (x same y) {...}
...
#undef same
...
int same;                          /* variable name */
struct same {                      /* tag */
   int same;                       /* component */
} Same;                            /* 'same' here would be illegal */
same:                              /* label */
Same.same = same;                  /* ! */
```

Pre-ANSI C compilers may have different name spaces, so for maximum portability (and common sense) you should avoid excessive duplications regardless of class.

An illegal duplication occurs if you try to redeclare an identifier belonging to the same name space while still at the same scope level as the original identifier. Replacing **Same** with **same** in the previous snippet would result in an error since the **int** variable **same** is still in scope and **struct** variables share the same name space as other variables.

Once you move into a distinct scoping level, though, the same identifier can be legally redeclared. The original identifier is hidden until the new declaration's scope ends. Rather than attempting a rigorous definition of scope levels, I offer an example that should clarify the situation.

```
    int i = 9;                     /* top – level */

main( )
{
```

```
        float i;
        char ch;
        i = 3.141;              /* i is a float throughout main( ) */
        ...                     /* int i is now hidden but still in
                                   scope with value 9 */
}
void func1(void)
{
        i = 3;                  /* i reverts to int */
        ...                     /* float i is out – of – scope and
                                   therefore invisible */
        ch = 'A';               /* ILLEGAL reference! ch not visible */
}
void func2(void)
{
        char i;                 /* i is a char throughout func2( ) */
        ...                     /* int i is hidden again but still in
                                   scope with value 3 */
}
/* char i is now out – of – scope and therefore inaccessible */
/* More on this when extent of variables is dicussed */
/* i reverts to int here if any further references */
```

Since Turbo C supports identifiers that comprise as many as thirty-two characters (allowing more choices than there are atoms in the solar system) you may wonder why programmers cannot avoid such confusing duplications. I wonder too. It may be that certain small "temporary" identifiers such as i, sum, and count are irresistible. It is also the case that individual functions are often developed in isolation, so hiding does serve as a useful protection against unplanned duplications.

The key point is that a reference to an identifier must be interpreted as applying to the currently visible declaration.

► *EXTENT* ►

The extent of an object refers to the period of time during which the object is allocated storage. Extent is therefore a run-time property. As with scope, though, your source code controls extent by means of storage classes and the placement of declarations and definitions. Extent applies only to variables and functions since other objects, like data types and **typedef** names, are not run-time entities.

There are three classes of extent:

1. *Static* extent applies to those objects that are allocated fixed memory locations when the program executes and retain those allocations until the program ends. All functions have static extent, as do variables declared at the top level. Variables declared elsewhere are not normally of static extent, but some can be made so with the **static** and **extern** storage class specifiers. A static-extent variable is initialized only when it is first created. If no explicit initializer accompanies its declaration/definition, a static-extent variable is cleared to zero.

    The two key properties of static-extent variables are that they endure throughout the program and they retain their values between function calls regardless of their scope and visibility. (In addition to this correlation between **static** and the property of "permanence" you'll meet in C a less obvious connotation, namely "private." This will be clarified when I explain the **static** storage class.)

2. *Local* or *automatic* extent applies only to variables, never to functions. Local-extent variables are allocated memory (and given values, if initialized) as their local function or block is executed. At the end of this execution, local-extent variables are destroyed, their memory is deallocated, and their values are lost. If the function or block is reexecuted, local-extent variables are automatically re-created at the point of declaration and any initializers are reapplied. This explains the term automatic extent. In the absence of explicit initializers, automatic variables will contain garbage when created. Contrast this with static-extent variables, which are always initialized either to zero or to your specific instructions.

    Formal parameters are always of local extent, but other variables can have either static or local extent depending on the declaration format and placement. The general rule is that top-level variables have static extent and head-of-block variables have local extent. You can vary these defaults only by using storage class specifiers.

3. *Dynamic* extent applies only to temporary, user-generated objects allocated with **malloc( )** (or a similar dynamic memory-allocation library function) and deallocated using **free( )**. The dynamic classification is not strictly a part of C's scoping or extent rules. Keep in mind that although **malloc**ed objects are created and destroyed at arbitrary moments in your program, the pointers you use to access them are represented by variables subject to the scoping and extent rules under discussion.

► *Extent and the Memory Map* ►

From a RAM point of view, it is useful to picture three areas of user memory defined at run time: the *text* or *code* area holding the .EXE file (machine instructions), the *data* area storing all the static objects, and the *dynamic* area holding the automatic and dynamic variables.

The layout of the text and data areas depends on the memory model. The small model limits you to two 64KB segments, one for text and one for static data. With the larger memory models the text and data areas may each occupy several distinct 64KB segments.

The dynamic area contains both the stack and the heap. The stack is a constantly changing LIFO (Last In First Out) data structure in which automatic variables (including any local parameters being passed to functions) are temporarily created, accessed, and discarded. The heap is the area from which **malloc( )** grabs its memory allocations. Its size will vary with memory model, the amount of user RAM, and the size of your program and data areas.

You should now have a feel for scope, visibility, and extent. Their properties are as summarized in Table 7.1.

► *SCOPE AND EXTENT RELATIONSHIPS* ►

Now I come to the tricky parts: how do these properties affect programming strategies, and how do you establish each property for any given object in a C program?

Though extent and scope are closely related, they are distinct properties. C allows you to have objects with static extent that are not accessible from all parts of the program. In other words, although scope cannot "exceed" extent (there's nothing there to access), extent can "exceed" scope (it's there but you can't access it). To explain the implications of this, I need to discuss how C programs are constructed from several files.

Declaration Point	Scope/Visibility* (from declaration to end of...)	Extent
Outside Function (top-level)	File	Static
Inside Function		
Formal parameter	Function	Local
Head-of-block	Block	Local or Static**

> * *Scope equals visibility unless hidden by duplicate name.*
> ** *All functions have static extent. Extent of variables depends on storage class specifier.*

► *Table 7.1:* Scope, visibility, and extent

► *Scope and Separately Compilable Files* ►

I mentioned earlier that top-level and inside-function scopes are often called *global* and *local* scopes respectively. As in Pascal, top-level declarations extend to the end of the file, while the inside-function declarations are confined to their local function or block.

In C, however, the word *global* has somewhat different connotations than in Pascal. As in Pascal, a global C identifier is certainly "available" to all following sections of its file, but, unlike standard Pascal, a C program may consist of several separately compilable files (often referred to as modules). Indeed, unless you want to forgo the assistance of the C library functions, your final programs will definitely contain code pulled in from many files.

Apart from the fact that you supply a unique file holding the function **main( )**, all the component files are technically equal—there is no built-in priority scheme for modules.

main( ) always starts the ball rolling. It can process any visible data and call any accessible function. A called function in turn can process its own visible data and call any of its accessible functions. The process continues until the final statement, which is usually back in **main( )**, is reached.

Four types of data are available to a function: local parameters (copies of actual arguments passed to the function); local "working" variables declared within the function; dynamic variables created with **malloc( )**; and, finally, any visible global variables. The latter may be top-level-declared/defined objects global to a particular file, or they may be set up to be global to several files. Some authors use the term *semiglobal* for identifiers limited to a particular file, reserving *global* for identifiers that can straddle several files.

How do scope and extent fit into this grand plan? The answer lies with the interaction between storage classes and the linking process.

► *The Role of the Linker* ►

The linker combines the various .OBJ files (some of which may be embedded in standard or user-supplied libraries) to produce the final executable .EXE file.

You can see immediately that this complicates the simple division of identifiers into local and global scopes. Some objects may be global for a particular file, and others may need to be accessed from several files. You may also wish to hide the details of a data structure but allow its manipulation via certain functions. (This is known as *data abstraction* and has the further merit that the data can be restructured without the user being bothered.) Conversely, selected functions within the same module may need to be hidden while some variables are freely exported. (These problems do not arise with standard Pascals, which do not support separate compilability, but Modula-2 and Ada programmers will recognize the situation.)

For these and other reasons, C lets you vary the accessibility of objects with the **extern** and **static** storage class specifiers. During separate compilations you'll want to suspend the **identifier unknown** message by explicitly or implicitly tagging certain objects as *external*, thereby exporting their names to the linker.

► *EXTERNAL IDENTIFIERS* ►

C uses the physical file as a basic mechanism to establish the scoping of objects, but objects within any file can be made external (explicitly or by default). Now automatic variables come and go with no fixed abode, so we certainly exclude these from being external. Only static-extent objects can be sensibly passed to the linker, thereby allowing other files to access them.

Remember that all functions have static extent (you cannot alter this property), so they are obvious candidates for exporting to the linker. In fact, unless you take special action, a function defaults to external, meaning that functions in any file are usually callable from any file linked to it. As you'll see, you can select which static-extent identifiers, functions, or variables, are exported, but there are complications if the same object is declared in several files.

Summing up, whatever scope an object may enjoy within its own file, it can only be referenced by other files if it has static extent and if its identifier is known to the linker. The function of the **extern** storage class specifier (whether explicit or implied) is to give a variable static extent and to export its identifier to the linker. By contrast, the **static** specifier (which must always be stated explicitly) conveys static extent but witholds the identifier from the linker, thereby reducing its accessibility to a particular file, function, or block (depending on the scope). This is the "private" connotation of **static** that I mentioned earlier.

(This terminology, already suffering from two connotations for the word *static*, has become further confused because some books refer to top-level **static** declarations as *external* or *external static*, [meaning that they are external to the functions in a file] as opposed to *internal static*, [which would mean **static** declarations made at head-of-block within a function]. I will reserve the designation *external* for those **extern**ed objects available to several files.)

The same external object can be declared (no storage allocated) in several files but must be defined (storage allocated) in only one of the .OBJ files presented to the linker. The linker first has to check for consistency among these independent declarations of the object and its unique definition and then make sure that all references in the component .OBJ files are made to the defined object (the "real" one, i.e., the one with memory allocated at a known run-time location).

Even with our simple HELLO.C, these machinations have been involved behind the scenes! The **#include** directive in HELLO.C brought into your source code various function and variable declarations. The compiler passed the external function name **printf** to HELLO.OBJ, and the linker checked it against the appropriate precompiled definition in one of the .LIB collections of .OBJ files.

► *Referencing and Defining Declarations* ►

It will become increasingly important to keep in mind the fundamental difference between *referencing declarations* and *defining declarations* of identifiers.

With functions it is easy to spot the difference. Function definitions have bodies containing the necessary code, whereas function declarations have no bodies. Functions can be declared at the top level or at head-of-block within another function's definition, but it is illegal to define a function within a function definition. (Pascal users may consider this a strange limitation since Pascal allows the nesting of procedure definitions.) Remember, though, that a function can be called recursively from within its own defining body. This is a direct result of the scoping rules stated earlier—the scope of a function stretches from its definition or declaration point to the end of its containing file.

► EXTERNAL FUNCTIONS ►

All C functions are external by default no matter where they are declared or defined. The storage class specifier **extern** is assumed unless you use **static**, which is the only other legal specifier for a function. When you declare an external function, you are telling the compiler/linker that somewhere, in this file or in another to be linked, this external function will be defined just once. A function is made external simply by omitting the storage class specifier. You are allowed to add a redundant **extern** to a declaration or definition of an external function.

By passing all the external function names (including possible duplicate declarations) to the linker, you ensure that all calls to *func*( ) will be associated with the unique definition of *func*( ). This simply means that the externally defined *func*( ) becomes freely accessible by linking its .OBJ file with your own .OBJ files. By *accessible,* of course, I mean callable—the source code for *func*( ) may well be under lock and key beyond your reach, and you may just have the minimum written explanation of what the function does and how to call it.

► STATIC FUNCTIONS ►

What the **static** specifier does with functions is to limit this accessibility by withholding the function name from the linker. If you create the file MYPROG.C as follows:

```
/* MYPROG.C */
...
```

```
static int secret(char ch)          /* function defined as static */
/* ch is local scope, local extent */
{ /* body of secret( ) */
    int i = 0;
    ...
    return i;
}

int public(char ch)                 /* function defined as external */
/* extern storage class specifier by default */
/* ch is local scope, local extent */
{ /* body of public( ) */
    ...
    return 2*secret(char ch);
/* Legal call to secret( ) since scope of secret( ) is from definition point
   to end of MYPROG.C */
}
/* end of file MYPROG.C */
```

you can compile it to MYPROG.OBJ and let other programmers link it to their .OBJ files. You offer them MYPROG.H, which contains the prototype declaration **int public(char ch);** with some comments on how to call it and what it does. The **secret( )** function cannot be called directly by other users even if they know of its existence. When they write THEIRPRG.C, compile it to THEIRPRG.OBJ, and then link it with MYPROG.OBJ to get THEIRPRG.EXE, any attempted calls on **secret( )** other than the ones made within MYPROG.OBJ would result in a link-time error. The **static** specifier has prevented the export of the name **secret** to the linker. The function **public( )** was declared as external (by default) in MYPROG.H and defined as external in MYPROG.C with matching arguments and returned values. The compilation of THEIRPRG.C would "warn" the linker that an externally defined function called **public( )** is expected somewhere, and this expectation would be eventually fulfilled.

The following snippet recaps the syntax of **extern** and **static** with function declarations and definitions:

```
[extern] [type] func1([arglist]);
/* the declared function is known to the linker — it will be
   defined as external elsewhere */

/* WARNING: you cannot omit both extern and type */
/* [type] will default to int and storage class will default to
   extern — BUT you cannot omit BOTH lest the resulting
   declaration looks like the func1 call: func1( ); ! */
```

```
static [type] func2([arglist]);
/* the declared function will be defined later in this file with
    storage class static and matching type and arglist */
[extern] [type] func1([arglist])
        [parameter declarations]
{ function_body
  [return var;]
}
/* define an external function – NO storage class specifier
    implies extern; other files can reference this function */

/* [type] defaults to int */
/* NOTE: extern and type can BOTH be omitted in a definition –
    there is no possible confusion with a call to func1( ); */

static [type] func2([arglist])
        [parameter declarations]
{ function_body
  [return var;]
}
/* define a static function – explicit storage class specifier
    is required; this function can be referenced within current
    file only – name not exported to linker */
/* [type] defaults to int safely, because the storage class is explicit. */
```

The first example above carries a warning. Consider the following variants:

```
/* classical declarations */
    extern int myfunc( );
    extern myfunc( );          /* [type] defaults to int OK */
    int myfunc( );             /* defaults to extern OK */

    myfunc( );                 /* NOT a declaration but a CALL */
```

In other words, you cannot default both the storage class and the returned type. I recommend that you always supply both storage class and type to provide increased legibility and peace of mind.

As I mentioned earlier, the keyword **static** is often a source of confusion. All defined functions, whether **extern** or **static**, have static extent. Both **func1( )** and **func2( )** (above) are assigned storage throughout the run life of the linked program, and the defining names **func1** and **func2** are pointer constants that hold the addresses of their respective implementation codes. Their scopes differ as stated, however. **func2( )** can only be called from within its own file, and **func1( )** can be called from any file that declares **func1( )** consistently and is linked to the defining file.

► *EXTERNAL VARIABLES* ►

As with functions, you can control whether variable identifiers names are passed to the linker or not. The basic principle is the same: If a variable is to be accessible from other files, it must have static extent. It must also be declared external in each client file and defined as external somewhere just once. Unlike functions, variables only default to external when declared/defined at the top level, outside the functions. Elsewhere, the explicit specifier **extern** is needed with the declaration to request linkage with the variable's definition in some other file.

The definition of the external variable is distinguished from any of its declarations by the *absence* of the specifier **extern**! Also, to avoid chaos, only the defining declaration can have an optional initializer attached. When you think about it, initialization only makes sense for a static-extent variable at the time it is created, that is, at run time when the definition is encountered. Keep in mind that static-extent variables are initialized only once, either to zero in the absence of an explicit initializer or to the constants of the evaluated initializer.

Before ANSI C clarified the distinction between external-variable referencing declarations (no storage allocated, no initializer) and defining declarations (storage allocated, optional initializer), different compilers used different strategies. Fortunately, Turbo C follows the ANSI C proposal that external variables be declared and defined as follows:

```
/* start of file A */
    ...
    extern int x;                  /* this is a referencing declaration */
/* compiler knows that x is an external int to be defined
   elsewhere. No memory yet, so no initializer */
/* location of this declaration will determine its scope in file
   A. Regardless of scope, x will have static extent */
    ...
    x++;                           /* reference to x is OK if visible in A */
    ...
/* end of file A */
/***************/

/* start of file B */

/* top – level only */
    int x = 3;                     /* this is the defining declaration */
/* Note absence of extern. Note optional initializer */
/* Scope of x is whole of file B */
    ...
```

```
/* end of file B */
/*****************/
```

The variable **x** defined in file B is truly global in the sense that any function in any file like A that declares **extern int x;** can access **x** within that declaration's scope. As with external functions, the linker must check that any external variable declarations encountered are consistent with the unique variable definition. Such global variables are clearly exposed to inadvertent changes in unexpected places that can make debugging even more painful.

► STATIC VARIABLES ►

You can protect a variable from abuse by using the **static** specifier, just as you saw with functions. **static int x;** tells the compiler not to pass the name **x** to the linker. **static** also performs the important task of giving **x** static extent, no matter whether the declaration occurs at the top level or head-of-block. Note that formal parameters cannot be declared as **static** since they exist only for argument passing and must clearly be of local scope and extent.

The presence of **static** in a declaration also indicates that it is a defining declaration, so memory is allocated. Any explicit initialization is performed just once—when the declaration is encountered. In the absence of an explicit initializer, **static** variables are cleared to zero. It is important to note that static variables can only be initialized with constants or constant expressions, whereas **auto** variables can be initialized using constants or other previously declared variables.

The once-only **static** initialization must be understood—it contrasts fundamentally with the reinitializations that occur each time an **auto** (or local-extent) declaration is executed. Consider the following snippet:

```
{ int i = 1;                    /* auto implied */
  static int j = 6;
  ...
  i++; j++;
  printf("i = %d, j = %d\n", i, j);
}
```

If the above block were executed three times in succession, the resulting display would be

```
i = 2,  j = 7
i = 2,  j = 8
i = 2,  j = 9
```

You can see that i is set to one each time round, while j retains its previous value once it has been initialized.

► *Static Variables in Action* ►

This example highlights a common application for **static** variables: Often you simply want to preserve a value between function calls or block executions, and the other implications of **static** (nonexport and privacy) are incidental. An oft-used illustration is that of calculating a seed for a random-number generator. Each call calculates a new seed based on the previous value, so either a global variable or an internal static variable must be used. The latter is safer, as explained earlier.

Although Turbo C contains the library functions **rand( )** and **srand( )** in STDLIB.H, it is instructive to write your own pseudorandom-number generator. LOTTERY.C (Program 7.2) keeps picking three lucky numbers until you enter a Q to quit.

```
/* lottery.c - picks three lucky numbers */

#include <stdio.h>
#include <stdlib.h>
#include <time.h>

#define FIRST_SEED 17
#define MULTIPLIER 5
#define INCREMENT 1
#define MODULUS 4096

int randy(void);
void show3rand(void);

void main(void)
{
    do {
      show3rand();
      printf("\nHit a key for more - Q to Quit: ");
    }
    while (getche() != 'Q');
}

int randy(void)
{
    static int seed = FIRST_SEED;
    seed = (seed*MULTIPLIER + INCREMENT) % MODULUS;
    return seed;
}

void show3rand(void)
{
    printf("\n\tLucky Numbers are %d,%d,%d\n",randy(),randy(),randy());
}
```

► *Program 7.2: LOTTERY.C*

► *Analysis of LOTTERY.C*

I refer you to Donald Knuth's definitive text on random number generators, *The Art of Computer Programming* (*Volume 2: Seminumerical Algorithms*. 2d ed. Reading, Mass.: Addison-Wesley, 1981). My extremely naive example is a linear congruential formula explained on page 170 of that book. The key point is that the first time **randy( )** is called, **seed** is initialized with the constant **FIRST_SEED**. Subsequent calls bypass the initializer, and **seed** retains the same value it had when **randy( )** was last exited.

Because **randy( )** itself is **extern** by default, other files could access it by declaring **int randy(void);**. On the other hand, the variable **seed** cannot be accessed or altered except via calls to **randy( )**. Even **main( )** and **show3rand( )** cannot access **seed** directly even though they are in the same file as **randy( )**. By defining **randy( )** as **static**, you could block access to **seed** from any function outside LOTTERY.C.

► *SUMMARY—* *THE IMPORTANCE OF SCOPE AND EXTENT* ►

The key to program security and robustness is local and global scope. Local variables are protected from deliberate or accidental change by functions or blocks of code outside their own bailiwick. Global variables are more at risk in that they can be legally changed by any statement in any function within their scope. Globals must therefore be used sparingly and only where functions need to share and modify the same variables.

I have some bad news and some less bad news on how a function can access a global variable. First, the bad news: the global variable might appear in the body of the function. If so, it is possible for the function to modify the variable quite independently of the normal argument passing mechanism. This reduces the modularity of the program and should be avoided.

The less bad news is that you can pass a global variable as an argument to the function. In this case, remember that the formal parameters of a function have local scope so that the function acts on a local copy of the real argument. Any side effects are therefore confined to the called function, but you may be able to make use of the returned value back in the calling function. The only other way to directly change a global is to pass a pointer as argument. This has its dangers, but at least the format of the function indicates what is going on. The following snippet shows the three possibilities:

```
/* how functions can attack a global variable */
    ...
        int i = 0;                  /* top – level global */
void inci(void);
int inc1(int i);
void inc2(int *i);

void main( )
{
        inci( );
        printf("\ni = %d",i);   /* i now = 1 */
        i = inc1(i);
        printf("\ni = %d",i);   /* i now = 2 */
        inc2(&i);
        printf("\ni = %d",i);   /* i now = 3 */
}

void inci(void)                 /* increments i in body – not a good idea */
{
        ++i;
}

int inc1(int j)                 /* increments a copy of i & returns value */
{
        return ++j;
}

void inc2(int *j)               /* takes &i as arg and increments i */
{
        ++(*j);
}
```

► *THE register STORAGE CLASS* ►

The final storage class specifier to consider is **register**. It is applicable only to automatic variables (both head-of-block and formal parameters) of integer type, such as **int**, **unsigned**, **short**, **char**, and 16-bit pointers. Unlike the other specifiers I have discussed, **register** is entirely a suggestion to the compiler. The suggestion in

```
{ register int i;                    /* set to auto if no register free */
      for (i = 0; i < 10000; i + + )
      { ... }
}                                    /* i no longer exists here */
```

is that since i is heavily used it should be allocated to a register, if possible, rather than to the usual RAM of the stack. If there is no spare register the declaration is taken as **auto int i;**.

All data movements and arithmetical operations are much faster with data in registers than when memory has to be accessed. Using registers, then, is a good thing, and the more frequently a candidate variable is accessed during its lifetime the more the savings will show.

On the other hand, the 8088/86 family is not excessively endowed with registers! Because of all the other jobs that registers have to do during execution (holding temporary values, keeping track of segments and stacks, and so on) SI and DI are usually the only ones available for holding **register** variables. Recall that SI and DI are each 16-bit, which explains the restriction to integer and near-pointer data types. These two registers will be assigned on a first-come, first-served basis, so you should position your **register** declarations accordingly.

The scope of a register variable is exactly the same as that of the corresponding **auto** variable. In the above example, i ceases to be a **register** variable as soon as the **for** loop ends. The register, if one was assigned, is then free for any subsequent **register** requests.

Under some unusual circumstances it is possible that the same **register** declaration could be encountered a second time with a different register allocation prevailing, so your variable could be **register** on one occasion and **auto** on another.

One important limitation applies to **register** variables. You cannot apply the address operator (&) since a register variable does not have a memory address. Even if a register is not found, Turbo C would signal an error after processing the following snippet:

```
int *kp;
register int k;
kp = &k;                             /* ILLEGAL even if k is non-register */
```

This makes sense portability-wise in view of the fact that you can never be certain whether a register would be found for k on any particular system or invocation.

► *Register Variables and Optimization* ►

Using registers for automatic variables, including formal parameters with functions, is a common ploy undertaken by *optimizing* compilers. Uncontrolled optimization can have some bizarre, self-defeating effects, so sensible compilers like Turbo C allow you to select from various optimizing strategies or to disable optimization completely. Since one of these options affects the **register** specifier, this is a good opportunity to review the optimization aspects of Turbo C.

If you browse through the IDE Options/Compiler menu, you'll find the Optimization submenu with the following selections:

► *Optimize for:*   Toggles between **Size** and **Speed**. Compiler will choose either the smallest or the fastest code sequence. The equivalent TCC.EXE command-line options are − G for **Speed** and − G − for **Size**.

► *Use register variables:*   Toggles between on and off. When on, the compiler will try to use **register** for **auto** variables; when off, the **register** specifier is ignored (except that **&** is still illegal with a **register** variable). Apart from timing exercises and interfacing with certain assembly-language routines, this option is better left on (the default). The TCC.EXE equivalents are − r (on) and − r − (off).

► *Register optimization:*   Toggles between on and off. Do not confuse this with the previous option. Register optimization, when on, attempts to save unnecessary data movements between RAM and registers. If a compiler has already assigned a certain value to a register, and a subsequent expression that needs this value is encountered, a less clever compiler would waste some CPU cycles by generating an unnecessary fetch from memory. An optimizing compiler can often recognize this situation and go straight to the appropriate register, thereby suppressing redundant load instructions. This feature must be used with care because a variable can be changed via a pointer without updating the register holding the original value. The TCC.EXE switches for register optimization are − Z (on) and − Z − (off).

► *Jump optimization:*   This also toggles on and off. When on, the compiler will try to reduce code size by eliminating redundant branch operations, tightening up loops and **switch...case** statements. The TCC.EXE equivalents are − O (on) and − O − (off).

► Optimization Problems and the volatile Modifier ►

An example of inappropriate optimization is revealed in benchmark results issued in regard to another well-known C compiler. A certain LOOP benchmark took 11.0 seconds on the nonoptimized version and 0.0** seconds (** time was negligible) on the optimized version. Assuming the LOOP tested was something like

```
int i;                    /* or register int i; */
for (i = 0; i < BIG_LIMIT; i++);    /* empty loop body */
```

which simply loops BIG_LIMIT times without doing anything, the optimized version clearly detected that i was not gainfully employed and replaced the statement with what Thomas R. Clune has called the "moral equivalent," e.g.,

```
i = BIG_LIMIT;
```

The time to execute this is proudly announced as negligible! Now if the loop was used in a real, nonbenchmark program to create a deliberate pause (there is hardly another possible reason) the optimization would be a nuisance, to say the least. On the other hand, you may well want all the optimizing tricks to be available elsewhere in the program. ANSI C comes to the rescue with the **volatile** data type modifier. It is also available on Turbo C, (but it is not implemented semantically on the LOOP benchmarked compiler). You declare a **volatile** variable in the obvious way, i.e.,

```
volatile int i;
```

volatile contrasts with the **const** (constant) modifier. It warns the compiler that i may be subject to unexpected changes from outside the immediate program, perhaps by an interrupt routine or by accessing an I/O port. This warning will prevent an optimizing compiler from assigning i to a register, and it will inhibit other types of register and loop optimizations. Using **volatile int i** in the pause loop, for example, would prevent the unwanted optimization.

I should also mention the **interrupt** function modifier, a non-ANSI C feature of Turbo C that is often used in conjunction with **volatile**. When you want to write special functions called *interrupt handlers* to create a memory-resident program that responds to some outside event, for example, you declare such functions with

```
return_type interrupt inthandler(reg_list);
```

This simplifies life by making the compiler take care of many of the house-keeping chores, such as saving and restoring registers as you enter and exit from the interrupt.

► ANALYSIS OF PLAYER.C ►

Now that you have a better understanding of storage classes, you can look at PLAYER.C in Chapter 6 with more comprehension. Note first that the **main( )** function is set up simply to test the basic functions.

init_play( ) enters the player data.
list_play( ) lists the database.
number_to_name( ) finds the name of a given player's number.
name_to_number( ) finds the number of a given player's name.

These and several other functions are all **extern** by default, so you can envisage them being collected together, compiled, and set up as a library to be incorporated into applications programs.

Other variables and functions, including the database array of pointers to the PLAYER_REC structure, have been declared as **static**:

```
        static PLAYER_REC *pptr[PL_MAX];
/* global to all functions in this file,
    but not accessible elsewhere.
    Declares an array of 'pointers to PLAYER_REC structure' */

        static int pind;
/* player index used with pptr[ ] */

        static int db_size;
/* number of players in database */

static int get_name(char target_name[ ])
        { /* body */}
```

```
static int get_number(unsigned char target_number)
    { /* body */ }
```

This division between external and static objects is a simple example of data abstraction. You provide a set of primitive functions to initialize, access, list, and maintain the database. Other programmers can build up applications programs based on these primitives without any knowledge of how the database is implemented. One obvious advantage is that the applications programmer cannot accidentally or maliciously violate the abstract data structure's integrity; less obvious is the flexibility you enjoy in changing the structure. If the function names are unaltered, the application programs can run with minimum disturbance. (Often relinking is all that's needed.)

The global variable **pind** is directly changed in the bodies of **get_number( )** and **get_name( )**, apparently disregarding my earlier warnings. However, **pind** and these two functions are **static**, which confines the danger. **pind** also plays an important role in reducing the amount of searching required. Assuming that successive inquiries often apply to the same player, I preserve that last found index, and check a match there before embarking on the admittedly inelegant **for**-loop search. A larger database, of course, would call for either a binary search on a sorted array or some form of indexing. Remember that the data abstraction approach allows such enhancements without affecting the applications software.

► *Miscellaneous Notes on PLAYER.C* ►

- ► The function **toupper(pos)** declared in CTYPE.H returns the uppercase of **pos** if **pos** is a lowercase ASCII letter, otherwise it returns the argument unchanged. There is a slightly faster macro version, **_toupper( )**, which works correctly only when the argument is a lowercase letter. In the present context, the function is safer—I trap nonmatching entries as position *X*. Note that CTYPE.H also contains **tolower( )**, **_tolower( )**, and **toascii( )**. The latter simply clears all but the bottom 7 bits from an integer argument to guarantee that you have a valid ASCII code, 0–127.

- ► The machinations between the **enum** values **P**, **C**, etc., and the ASCII symbols ''P'', ''C'', etc., should drive home the point that enumerations are simply synonyms for integers. Displaying **P** directly would give a misleading **0**.

► The format **scanf("%2d/%2d/%4d", ...);** is best understood by reading Appendix C, but I'll cover it briefly here. The characters "**/**" in the format string are set to match the same character in the input date. The **%2d** indicates that a *maximum* of two digits is expected. A proper program would test for sensible date input. Here is an official MS-DOS **date** structure defined in DOS.H,

```
struct date {
int da_year;
char da_day;
char da_mon;
};
```

with many functions for capturing and converting the current time and date to strings and UNIX formats (see Appendix G).

► The expression **(pptr[dbind] – >active) ? "Y" : "N"** as an argument in **printf( )** is another illustration of C's compact notation.

► **get_str( )** is another security mechanism. Database queries are given pointers to a copy of the answer string, rather than as pointers into the database itself. Corruption of the database is made more difficult.

► BASIC users need to get used to **strcmp( )** and **strcpy( )** for comparing and copying strings!

► The fact that a function like **number_to_name( )** is defined in one line as in

```
char *number_to_name(unsigned char tn)
{
        return get_number(tn) ? get_str(pptr[pind] – >name) : NULL;
}
```

highlights the general principle that C favors a large number of simple functions rather than a small number of complex functions. There are no magic rules for the ideal division of a program into functions, but one clue here is that **number_to_name( )** is **extern**, while **get_number( )** is **static**.

► SUMMARY OF CHAPTER 7 ►

◄► The most succinct summary of Chapter 7 is Table 7.1 coupled with Table 7.2, below. Together they provide an overall picture of C's scoping, visibility, and extent rules and how they are related to the storage class specifiers.

◄► You also saw how **static** and **extern** were used to control the modularity of programs in conjunction with separately compilable source files and the linkage operation.

◄► The difference between **static** and **auto** variables can be summed up as follows:

Static-extent variables, scalar or array, can only be initialized during declaration/definition with constants or constant expressions. In the absence of explicit initializers, static variables are cleared to

Storage Class	Where	What	Default	Action
auto	head block	vars	yes	defining; local extent
[auto]	formal-parms	vars	[omit]	defining; local extent
extern	top-level, head-block	vars funcs	no yes	declaring; static extent, export to linker
[extern]	top-level, head-block	vars funcs	[omit] [omit]	defining; static extent, export to linker
static	top-level, head-block	vars funcs	no no	defining; static extent, no export to linker
register	func parms, head-block	vars	no	defining; local extent, register if possible, else auto

► **Table 7.2:** *Storage class specifier summary*

zero. Such initializations are applied *only once*, prior to program execution. A static variable retains its value between function calls.

Automatic scalar variables must be initialized explicitly, using any assignment-compatible expression, constant, or variable. Automatic arrays cannot be initialized. These initializations will be applied each time the automatic variable is created. An automatic variable loses it value between function calls.

FILE I/O

► CHAPTER 8 ►
FULL STEAM AHEAD

So far you have been communicating with the computer via the screen and keyboard. Both your input data and the output results of your programs have disappeared after each session. No great loss, to be sure, with the possible exception of the PLAYER.C database!

Turbo C, of course, has been busy saving your programs in permanent disk files, and it's time to show you how you can do the same for your data. I was tempted to do this earlier, but until I had covered structures and storage classes I felt that a reasonable exposition of C's file input/output (I/O) operations would leave too much unexplained and "on trust."

► C, ANSI C, AND I/O ►

Languages such as BASIC and Pascal provide predefined, built-in I/O operations invoked with **SAVE**, **PRINT**, and **WRITELN**, for example. The C language proper has no such keywords, but ANSI C has specified a complete set of standard library routines that all conforming implementations must offer.

In the K&R bible similar libraries were implied, mainly based on the UNIX concepts of device files and hierarchical directories, but they were never, strictly speaking, an integral part of the language definition. Over the years, library routines have tended to diverge in name, number, and functionality in spite of efforts by various groups to standardize. (This has been especially true of I/O routines.) The ANSI C committee has decreed a set of library functions, weeding out some of the less portable UNIX-only routines.

The names of these functions and macros (and to a large extent, the names of the libraries themselves) are reserved in principle. Further, ANSI C allows any library function to be additionally implemented as a "safe" macro (one that evaluates each argument just once), possibly allowing the direct generation of assembly-language code by the compiler. This approach removes the function-calling overhead and further blurs the distinction between built-in and library routines.

So, one could say that C is as at least as well endowed with I/O and similar operations as any other language. Whether **getche( )** or some equivalent is "inside" C or in an approved linkable library might be counted as irrelevant from a practical point of view as long as the function performs efficiently and as specified. It is source-code portability that matters—no one expects object code to run unchanged on disparate systems!

Implementors can add to the library to their heart's content, but **printf( )**, **getche( )** and all the old favorites must be available and perform according to the book in order to qualify as ANSI C conformists. Programs using only the standard library routines are as portable as anyone can expect in this mad, mad world. The ANSI C standard is not yet engraved in stone, but Borland has both taken great pains to provide routines that conform to the latest draft and retained some of the older functions that may be useful during the interregnum.

This chapter will concentrate on the most useful, MS-DOS oriented I/O functions found in Turbo C's STDIO.H, but first I'll briefly review the basic vocabulary.

► *WHEN IS A FILE NOT A FILE?* ►

What is a file? As with most questions in computerdom, there is no single answer for all seasons. At the average end-user level, a computer file is the electronic version of the eponymous manila folders that refuse to go away. Files are simply collections of data given a unique name by which the data can be referenced and updated. Files are usually stored on disks or tapes from which particular characters, blocks, or records can be transferred temporarily to RAM for display, updates, and subsequent rewrites to permanent mass storage.

The type of access available is often used to characterize a file or the file storage medium. *Sequential* files require byte-by-byte scanning to reach any given record, while *random* files allow some mechanism for moving directly to the target. Disks can handle both sequential and random files, but tapes are by nature confined to sequential access.

► *THE LOGICAL AND THE PHYSICAL* ►

Users are not usually concerned with a file's physical disposition, i.e., how the data is encoded (ASCII or EBCDIC), the sectors and tracks allocated, and so on. The task of translating from the "logical" (file name) to the "physical" (a set of bytes residing on some mysterious surfaces) is given to the operating system. (I will use the terms *file name* or *file specification* to indicate the drive, path, name, and extension, unless any of these are specifically excluded.)

This translation process is extremely machine- and OS-dependent, not to mention OS-version dependent! (Although I will not get too involved with MS-DOS technicalities, I will assume that you are working with MS-DOS/PC-DOS version 2.00 or later since this version marked a significant turning point in MS-DOS file organization.)

DOS has to locate a directory entry that matches the file name, check its file size and attributes (read-only, hidden, etc.), and find the starting cluster number from the FAT (file allocation table). Then it has to allocate a *file handle*, which is a pointer to an FCB (file control block). From this point onward, the operating system can perform most of the basic operations (such as reading and writing) in terms of the file handle.

► *UNIX and Device Files* ►

The UNIX operating system, developed with, by, and for C, extended the traditional concept of a file to almost anything that can be treated as a data source (input) and/or as a data sink (output or destination). From this philosophy emerged the idea of device files, which allow programmers to treat devices such as keyboards and screens as though they were files. Files and devices are effectively treated as abstract *streams* or unstructured sequences of bytes, regardless of contents, origin, or destination.

► *Illegitimate Son of UNIX?* ►

MS-DOS gradually adopted the file-directory structure, the device file, and the stream from UNIX. They allow a wide range of generalized stream

I/O commands that work if the data is being input from keyboards, joysticks, communications ports, or conventional disk files, or if it's being output to screens, printers, modems, or disk files. You can even fool the system into thinking that a designated region of RAM is a disk with directories and files.

Clearly, all these "files" have their individual physical quirks and buffering requirements, but the beauty of the device-file concept is that both UNIX and MS-DOS let you write code that is largely device independent, leaving the user to *redirect* and *pipeline* input and output as required.

For example, A>DIR *.C will display the directory listing by sending data to the standard output "file" (the screen), while

A>DIR *.C > FILENAME.EXT

redirects the data to the disk file called FILENAME.EXT. Similarly, you can send the output of one command to the input of another using the pipe operator ¦, as in A>DIR *.C¦SORT > DIRECT.LST. Here, the output of DIR is sent to SORT, and the sorted output written to the disk. Pipes can be chained as in

A>TYPE FILENAME.EXT¦SCRUB¦NOPARITY > PRN.

Programs in these chains are often called *filters* for obvious reasons. The multitasking UNIX and singletasking MS-DOS pipeline mechanisms differ considerably, but the overall effects are the same.

► *Text and Binary Files* ►

In one important respect, MS-DOS deviates from UNIX in its treatment of files. UNIX takes the view that the content and format of a file is not the concern of the operating system but should be entirely determined by the individual programs using the file. The files created by UNIX utilities are "flat" sequences of bytes that start at the beginning and end at the end! There is no special byte placed at the end of a file as a flag since this would violate the notion that all 0–255 byte values are democratically equal.

A UNIX programmer is free to create formatted files using special byte values as delimiters, fixed fields, or whatever—this is a private matter between the programmer and the file. The UNIX kernel keeps track of each file's length, so as you read these bytes it can signal when there are no more left. This signal is the EOF discussed in Chapter 3. EOF must be a value impossible to find by reading any byte. The value is defined in STDIO.H:

```
#define EOF ( – 1)                                /* end of file indicator */
```

MS-DOS, on the other hand, uses Ctrl-Z (decimal 26) as a unique text-file terminator, and this raises the problem of how to handle binary files (such as object-code files) that may contain this value at any point. The net result is that, unlike UNIX, MS-DOS has to make a distinction between binary files (anything goes) and text files (ASCII plus terminator). This and other differences led to various extensions to the C file I/O library routines. I'll point these out as we proceed.

The difference between DOS text and binary files shows up in the treatment of newline characters. In text mode the CR/LF pair, generated by many devices when Enter is keyed, is internally translated into a single LF or newline character '\n' (octal 012) with a converse translation in the other direction. With binary files, no such translation is made—you have a simple one-to-one transmission of each byte.

► *Buffering* ►

When you have streams of data moving to and from diverse devices in a system, matching speeds becomes a major headache. As a naive example, it would not be sensible to transfer to a disk file each of my keystrokes one by one as I peck at the keyboard. An area of memory called a *buffer* is used, and my typed characters rest there until a suitable moment when they can be economically transferred to disk.

The optimum size of a buffer depends on the relative speeds of the two devices and how they respond to each other. You don't want the buffer filling up too often, forcing frequent writes, nor should it be so large that a power failure wipes out eight hours of work. *Flushing* a buffer, by the way, is the essential final operation that you use to write out what's left before moving on to other things, possibly reassigning the buffer to some other purpose.

A similar situation occurs when you're reading from a disk. You could certainly display a text file by grabbing one byte at a time from the disk and sending it to the screen, but it is more rational to fill a buffer (typically by reading a disk sector) and then pull from the buffer as required. Note that in multiuser systems great care is needed since your buffer data will be out of date if the disk file is changed by some other action. Note also that the same buffer can often be used for transfers in either direction, depending on the nature of the two devices. Further, there are many situations where a hierarchy of buffers is needed. For example, you might need to have a disk buffer feeding a printer buffer.

You'll also meet different buffering strategies. Should you flush a buffer only when full, after each newline character, or on demand? The C libraries provide the tools for setting buffer behavior if the default strategies are unacceptable.

Throughout an I/O system there are a myriad of buffering needs, the exact forms of which will vary with the source and destination. You need to have a general feel for what a buffer is (a first-in-first-out queue), but the C functions covered in this chapter, with help from DOS, usually take care of the details.

When you write something to a file, you can safely picture it as going straight there. In the current jargon we say that the buffering is *transparent*. For advanced programming, you can dig down nearer to the operating system and forgo the luxury of the power tools provided.

► STREAMS ►

I defined a stream as a potentially endless sequence of bytes that you can associate with a particular physical device or file. Once a stream is established, you interface with it in a uniform way whether it represents a disk file or some I/O device. For your added convenience, as they say, all streams can be treated identically even though the associated device might vary from a keyboard to a plotter not yet invented.

I can now show you the C code needed to create streams, attach them to a device file, and perform I/O.

► *File Pointers and the FILE Structure* ►

In C a stream is represented by a *file pointer* of type **FILE** * where **FILE** is a structure defined in STDIO.H. **FILE** defines nine fields that represent the current status of a stream.

```
/* Copyright (c) Borland International 1987
   All Rights Reserved
```

Extract from STDIO.H Turbo C version 1.5

```
*/
#include <stdio.h>
        ...
typedef struct {
        short           level;          /* fill/empty level of buffer */
        unsigned        flags;          /* File status flags */
        char            fd;             /* File descriptor */
        unsigned char   hold;           /* Ungetc char if no buffer */
        short           bsize;          /* Buffer size */
        unsigned char   *buffer;        /* Data transfer buffer */
        unsigned char   *curp;          /* Current active pointer */
        unsigned        istemp;         /* Temporary file indicator */
        short           token;          /* Used for validity checking */
}       FILE;                           /* This is the FILE object */
        ...
```

The significance of each component will emerge as I proceed. For now it is sufficient to get a feel for how streams are set up.

► *Opening and Closing Streams* ►

A variable of type **FILE** is established by *opening* a stream. The usual method uses **fopen( )** from STDIO.H. This associates a stream with a named file by initializing a variable of type **FILE** and returns a pointer to it (known as a *file pointer*). Nearly all of C's standard I/O is performed with file pointers. **fopen( )** takes two arguments, a file name and a stream type, as follows:

```
        char *filename;                 /* string representing full file name */
        char *type;                     /* string controls type of stream */
        FILE *fp;                       /* declare a pointer to FILE structure */

/* set up filename and type here before calling fopen( ) */

        fp = fopen(filename, type);
/* open filename according to value of type and return fp.
        type can be "r" (read – only), "w" (write – only), "a" (append),
        – see Table 8.1 for full list */
        ...
        fclose(fp);
/* close filename – see text */
        ...
```

```
        fp = fopen("hello,c","r");
    /* open hello.c for reading only (input) */
            ...
        fclose(fp);
    /* close hello.c */
```

Once a stream is attached to a real file, it becomes a little pedantic to distinguish the two, so you can talk about reading a file or reading a stream interchangeably.

► *fopen( ) Failures*

If the **fopen( )** call is unsuccessful, a NULL pointer will be returned, and an error code is placed in the global variable **errno**. The following snippet will crop up frequently in various guises and is definitely worth remembering:

```
    if ((fp = fopen(filename, type)) == NULL) {
        printf("/nCannot open %s/n",filename);
    /* or use perror(errmsg); to get a more specific error message
    based on value of errno */
            exit (1);
        }
```

Apart from when it encounters illegal file names, inactive drives, and missing files, **fopen( )** can also fail because MS-DOS sets an upper limit on the number of streams that can be open at any given moment. The CONFIG.SYS file determines this upper limit with **FILES** = *<number>*, where *<number>* defaults to 8 and must not exceed **OPEN_MAX** in STDIO.H (usually 20).

► *fclose( ) and fcloseall( )*

Because of the limit on the number of streams that can be open simultaneously, it is important to *close* streams when you've finished with them. This frees up various system resources and reduces the risk of exceeding the limit. Closing a stream also flushes out any associated buffers, an important operation that prevents loss of data when writing to a disk. You close a stream as follows:

```
    fclose(fp);                              /* close the stream with file pointer fp */
```

fclose( ) returns an **int** value; 0 for successful closure, EOF if the closure failed for any reason. The function **fcloseall( )** is worth knowing when you want to exit a program with many open streams.

```
int i;
...
i = fcloseall( );
/* flush and close all open streams except stdin, stdout.
   Return the number of streams closed */
printf("\nWe had %d files open\n",i);
```

Note that **fcloseall( )** is a Turbo C extension to ANSI C.

► *Stream Types* ►

The **type** variable or constant in **fopen( )** can be any of eighteen strings. These strings determine the mode and type of stream you want, as shown in Table 8.1. Cutting through the morass, you can see that there are really three basic stream types, "r" (read), "w" (write), and "a" (append). The variants are formed by tagging on " + ", "t", or "b".

Since text mode is the default, the most common types you'll encounter are the following:

"r"— Open an existing text file for reading only. Signals an error if the file doesn't exist.

"w"—Erase file if existing one found; create and open a file for writing only.

"a"— Open a text file for appending (write at the end) or create a new file if one with the given name does not exist.

The dangers of "w" should be familiar to you BASIC users—**OPEN #3 FILENAME, OUTPUT** will erase an existing file with the name **FILENAME** before creating a new, empty file of that name.

The **filename** in **fopen( )** can be any string constant or variable that evaluates to a legal DOS file specification. The pleasant news is that once you have your file pointer from **fopen( )**, the file name is no longer needed for subsequent I/O.

► *fflush( ) and flushall( )*

You saw that **fclose( )** and **fcloseall( )** performed any necessary buffer flushing. There are two functions that will flush without closing the stream— **fflush( )** and **flushall( )**. The action of flushing depends on the file type—a file

Text or Binary Files

Type	Stream
"r"	Read only (input)—existing file
"w"	Write only (output)—create new file
"a"	Append mode (output)—write at end of existing file or create new file
"r + "	Update. Read/Write (input/output)—existing file.
"w + "	Update. Read/Write (input/output)—create new file.
"a + "	Update. Append mode (input/output)—update at end of existing file or create new file.

► *Where x represents one of the types above,* **"x"**

  defaults to **"xt"** *(text file) if* **_fmode** *equals* **O_TEXT**.
  defaults to **"xb"** *(binary file) if* **_fmode** *equals* **O_BINARY**.

► **_fmode** *is the file-translation global variable, normally set to* **O_TEXT**.
► **O_TEXT** *and* **O_BINARY** *are defined in FCNTL.H.*

Text Only Files

Type	Stream
"rt"	Read only (input)—existing file
"wt"	Write only (output)—create new file
"at"	Append mode (output)—write at end of existing file or create new file
"r + t"	Update. Read/Write (input/output)—existing file.
"w + t"	Update. Read/Write (input/output)—create new file.
"a + t"	Update. Append mode (input/output)—update at end of existing file or create new file.

► *The* **"xt"** *forms give text file modes regardless of* **_fmode** *settings.*

► *Table 8.1: Stream types in* **fopen( )**

Binary Only Files

Type	Stream
"rb"	Read only (input)—existing file
"wb"	Write only (output)—create new file
"ab"	Append mode (output)—write at end of existing file or create new file
"r + b"	Update. Read/Write (input/output)—existing file
"w + b"	Update. Read/Write (input/output)—create new file
"a + b"	Update. Append mode (input/output)—update at end of existing file or create new file

► The **"xb"** forms give binary file modes regardless of **_fmode** settings.

► **Table 8.1:** Stream types in **fopen( )** (continued)

open for reading will have its input buffer cleared, while a file open for writing gets its output buffer written out to the file.

```
        fflush(fp);                    /* flush buffer but leave stream open */
  /* returns int = 0 for success, EOF for failure */
        flushall( );                   /* flush all buffers of all open files but
                                          leave them open */
  /* returns int = number of buffers flushed */
```

Note that **flushall( )**, like **fcloseall( )**, is a Turbo C extension to ANSI C. The following simplified extract from STDIO.H will remind you of the importance of conditional directives in achieving portability:

```
#if !__STDC__                   /* defined = 1 for ANSI C conformists */
      int       fcloseall(void);
      int       flushall (void);
#endif
```

► The Standard Streams ►

There are five special streams that you never have to open or close since the system does it for you. Looking again at STDIO.H, observe the identifiers **stdin**, **stdout**, and **stderr** (ignore **stdaux** and **stdprn** for now).

```
extern FILE          _streams[ ];       /* external array of FILE structs */

#define stdin        (&_streams[0])
#define stdout       (&_streams[1])
#define stderr       (&_streams[2])
#define stdaux       (&_streams[3])
#define stdprn       (&_streams[4])
```

They are defined as fixed pointers of type **FILE** *, so they certainly fit the bill as far as defining streams are concerned. Whenever a Turbo C program runs, these three pointers are internally initialized so that **stdin** is associated with your standard input device (the keyboard), and **stdout** and **stderr** are both associated with the standard output device (your screen). Not only can you use these identifiers wherever a file pointer is legal (and sensible, of course—you can't write a file to your keyboard), but these pointers can also be effectively transferred to other streams or device files whenever redirection or piping is invoked (typically from a DOS command). And that, briefly, is how redirection is achieved.

The reason for **stderr** (standard error output) is that you normally want error messages from functions such as **perror( )** to appear on your screen. If such messages were sent out on **stdout** they would run the risk of being redirected to a disk file. Of course, there are situations where you may want error messages in a file—if so, you can always redirect **stderr** to another stream.

► *Console and Stream I/O Functions* ►

Although any stream I/O can be directed to the three standard streams, the C libraries contain a mix of functions. Some of these are general stream I/O functions (for files or the console) and others are dedicated to console I/O. Recognizing this fact can simplify your mastery of the somewhat daunting list of I/O routines. For example,

printf( ) sends formatted output to **stdout** (wherever that is pointing).
cprintf( ) always sends formatted output to the console (screen).
fprintf( ) sends formatted output to any stream.
vprintf( ) works like **printf( )** with a variable argument list.
vfprintf( ) works like **fprint( )** with a variable argument list.

The **scanf( )** family that gets formatted input from a keyboard or file shows a similar pattern.

scanf( ) gets formatted data from **stdin** (wherever that is).
cscanf( ) always gets formatted data from the console (keyboard).
fscanf( ) gets formatted data from any stream.
vscanf( ) works like **scanf( )** with a variable argument list.
vfscanf( ) works like **fscanf( )** with a variable argument list.

The **f** suffix in many I/O functions indicates that you will find a file-pointer argument in addition to the normal arguments. Here is an example.

```
int   fprintf  (FILE *fp, const char *format, ...);
int   printf   ( const char *format, ...);
```

Once you have mastered **printf( )** and **scanf( )**, the other variants follow quite readily.

To get some useful work out of this preamble, I will introduce two simple buffered I/O routines, **getc( )** and **putc( )**. These handle only one byte at a time, but you can do a lot of fruitful work despite that limitation.

► *The getc( ) Routine* ►

Given the declarations

```
#include <stdio.h>              /* essential for macros */

     int ch;                    /* treated as a char but allow for EOF */
     FILE *fp;                  /* file pointer */
```

the statement

```
ch = getc(fp);                 /* read a byte and return it as int */
```

simply reads a byte from the stream given by the file pointer **fp**, assuming that the stream is open for reading or update. The word *simply* is perhaps an exaggeration! There are a number of subtleties in getting a single byte from a stream. There may not be such a byte, or there could be a byte in the stream that for some reason is reluctant to be read. So let's discuss EOF conditions (no more bytes to read) and real error conditions (the byte cannot be read).

► *Testing for EOF and File Errors* ►

As explained in Chapter 3, I declare **ch** as an **int** because if **getc( )** tries to read beyond the last byte in the stream it will return the special value EOF, defined as (– 1) in STDIO.H. Normally, **getc( )** returns a byte representing the character read (whether the stream is text or binary) into the lower byte of the **int ch** with no sign extension.

Declaring **ch** as a **char** is fairly safe with text files but dangerous with binary files. Meeting the byte 0xFF, which is quite legal and not unusual in a binary file, would signal a spurious EOF.

You need a useful macro called **feof( )**, which can be used under any conditions to test if a true end-of-file condition occurred on the last input operation. The **unsigned int flags** component in the **FILE** structure holds the following status flags, defined mnemonically in STDIO.H:

```
#define _F_RDWR      0x0003          /* Read/write flag */
#define _F_READ      0x0001          /* Read only file */
#define _F_WRIT      0x0002          /* Write only file */
#define _F_BUF       0x0004          /* Malloc'ed Buffer data */
#define _F_LBUF      0x0008          /* line – buffered file */
#define _F_ERR       0x0010          /* Error indicator */
#define _F_EOF       0x0020          /* EOF indicator */
#define _F_BIN       0x0040          /* Binary file indicator */
#define _F_IN        0x0080          /* Data is incoming */
#define _F_OUT       0x0100          /* Data is outgoing */
#define _F_TERM      0x0200          /* File is a terminal */
```

These flags are best left for the I/O functions to manipulate. I show them to indicate the range of data stored in the **FILE** structure and to explain the EOF and file-error macros.

The **flags** bits of each active stream are being constantly monitored using expressions such as

```
        if (fp –>flags & _F_OUT) {...}
/* test outgoing flag with bitwise AND */
        ...
        (fp –>flags) |= _F_TERM;
/* set terminal flag with bitwise OR */
```

The **feof( )** macro is defined as

```
#define feof(f)                 ((f) –>flags & _F_EOF)
```

so if the **_F_EOF** flag (bit 5) is set (indicating a genuine end-of-file situation) **feof( )** returns 1 (True). The following snippet shows **feof( )** in action:

```
/* assume fp open stream for input */
     ch = getc(fp);                  /* grab a char – int */
     if (feof(fp)) {
/* macro expands to If (((fp) –>flags & _F_EOF)) */
          puts("No more! Fini!");
          fcloseall( );
          exit (1);
     }
/* returns TRUE if non-spurious end-of-file was
   detected on the last input from stream fp */
```

Note that the **_F_EOF** flag remains set until the stream is closed or rewound (I'll explain **rewind( )** in a minute), so further attempts with **getc( )** are blocked.

The macro **ferror( )** works similarly but tests the **_F_ERR** flag, which gets set for a host of hardware- and software-related reasons.

```
#define ferror(f)                   ((f) –>flags & _F_ERR)
```

I strongly urge you to test **ferror(fp)** after each stream I/O operation, but, to be honest, it is a "custom more honored in the breach...."

```
/* after each read or write: */
     if (ferror(fp)) {
         puts("File read or write error!");
         fcloseall( );
         exit (1);
     }
```

The **_F_ERR** flag remains set until **clearerr( )** or **rewind( )** is called or the stream closed. If you want to program repeats after a file error, you should call **clearerr(fp);** first.

► *The Current Pointer Moves...* ►

Each call to **getc( )** advances a pointer in the *fp* **FILE** structure called **curp**, the *current active pointer*. You can picture **curp** as tracking progress in the stream—the next I/O operation will usually take place at the current active pointer.

Most I/O functions refer to **curp** for some reason or other, and many update it after reading or writing to the stream. In terms of the given file pointer, **fp**, the I/O routine accesses **fp −>curp**. You should never idly fool around with this member!

The simple function **ftell( )** will return the **long int** value of **curp** as follows:

```
long file_pos = 0L;
file_pos = ftell(fp);            /* where are we in stream fp? */
/* if ftell fails it returns − 1L and sets errno */
```

If you have awfully long streams, you get **curp** mod 2^{32}!

There are two functions that allow you to alter **curp** without you having to access **fp −>curp**. You can use them to get random access to certain streams (usually binary and on disk) provided that you know how they are formatted. I am more concerned now with sequential streams, in which **curp** soldiers on from byte to byte, but let me show you briefly how **curp** can be made to point at arbitrary bytes in a stream.

▸ *Setting the Current Active Position*

Immediately after opening a stream, the current active pointer is zero and points to the first byte of the stream. **rewind(fp)** winds **curp** back to the start of the stream, returning an **int** value of 0 if successful and a nonzero value if unsuccessful. This unnatural reversal of "false equals success" and "true equals failure" should be noted—it is quite common in I/O functions. **rewind( )** also clears the **_F_EOF** and **_F_ERR** flags, as noted in the **feof( )** discourse.

For more exotic changes, you use **fseek( )** on an opened stream as shown in the following snippet:

```
#include <stdio.h>
/* defines SEEK_SET = 0; SEEK_CUR = 1; SEEK_END = 3
   as possible values for 'fromwhere' */

        long recsiz = 0L, offset = 0L;
        int fromwhere, seek_fail; /* 0 = success */
        FILE *fp;
        ...
```

```
/* open the stream here */
    ...
        offset = recsiz;
        fromwhere = SEEK_CUR;
        seek_fail = fseek(fp, offset, fromwhere);
/* move curp offset bytes from current position */
        if (seek_fail) {
                puts("\nSeek Failure!");
                fcloseall( );
                exit (1)
        }
    ...
```

fseek( ) repositions **curp** by **offset** bytes from either the start, the current position, or the end of the stream, depending on the value of **fromwhere** (0, 1, or 3, respectively). You can use the mnemonics defined in STDIO.H as shown. Note that **rewind(fp)** has the same effect as **fseek(fp, 0L, SEEK_SET)**.

► *The putc( ) Routine* ►

The call

```
putc(ch, fp);                   /* write the lower byte of ch to stream */
```

will output **ch** to the stream at the current position with the same declarations I used for **getc( )**,

```
#include <stdio.h>             /* essential for macros */

    int ch;                    /* treated as a char but allow for EOF */
    FILE *fp;                  /* file pointer */
```

but with the stream opened for write, append, or update modes. **putc( )** also returns an **int** value—either the byte just written (top byte cleared) if the write was successful or an EOF if an error occurred. Writing to an output stream cannot cause a normal end-of-file error since sequential files usually just grow on you. However, many possible hazards such as device-full, write-protect, and parity-fail problems can interfere with progress. The **ferror( )** macro can be usefully called, or you can test the value of **putc( )** after each call.

► *Variants fgetc( ) and fputc( )*

Note that STDIO.H also defines **fgetc( )** and **fputc( )**. These are operationally equivalent to **getc( )** and **putc( )** but are true functions not macros. The difference is only important if you ever want to pass these as arguments to another function. Remember that the identifier **fgetc**, unlike **getc**, is a pointer to a function type and can be used as an argument.

► *STREAMS IN ACTION* ►

Here is KOPY.C (Program 8.1), a simple program that will copy the file HELLO.C to HELLO.CBK. Later on this will be generalized to allow each file name to be entered on the command line from the DOS prompt.

```
/* kopy.c -- simple file copy program Program 8.1 */
#include <stdio.h>

void main(void)
{
    FILE *infile, *outfile; /* two stream pointers */
    int ch = 0, bytes = 0;  /* count the bytes copied */

/* try to open HELLO.C for read--only, binary file */

    if ((infile = fopen("hello.c","rb")) == NULL) {
        perror("Sorry about HELLO.C");
        exit (1);
    }

/* try to create/open HELLO.CBK for write--only, binary file.
   If file exists, delete old one first */

    if ((outfile = fopen("hello.cbk","wb")) == NULL) {
        perror("Sorry about HELLO.CBK");
        exit (1);
    }

/* both files open, so copy infile to outfile until EOF */
    while ((ch = getc(infile)) != EOF) {
        putc(ch, outfile);
        ++bytes;
    }
/* close both to flush stream */

    fclose(infile);
    fclose(outfile);

/* report completion and stats */

    printf("\nTotal of %d bytes KOPY'd",bytes);

}
```

► *Program 8.1:* KOPY.C

► *Analysis of KOPY.C* ►

I declare two file pointers with the suggestive names **infile** and **outfile**. The **fopen( )**s are combined with the test for success. Note the literal strings for the file names and modes. HELLO.C is opened for "r" (read-only), while HELLO.CBK is opened for "w" (write-only). If a file called HELLO.CBK is found in the current directory, KOPY.C will erase it. If HELLO.C is not found, **perror("Sorry about HELLO.C");** will display

    Sorry about HELLO.C : No such file or directory

The second part of the above message is triggered by the value set in the global variable called **errno**. A colon is displayed after your optional message string argument to **perror( )**. Using **perror( )** is a neat way of letting Turbo C do the error analysis.

Both files are opened as binary to solve the problem of copying the end-of-file (Ctrl-Z) code. Try changing the modes to "r" and "w" (or whatever) to check this out.

The actual copying is done with

```
while ((ch = getc(infile)) != EOF) {
    putc(ch, outfile);
    ++bytes;
}
```

There are more concise ways of doing this without using the **ch**, but my version is legible. Try **putc(getc(infile), outfile)** for fun—but you must watch the parentheses.

I did not use the file name HELLO.BAK since this extension is used by DOS and Turbo C—it would be impolite to erase a possibly useful file. Nor did I call the program COPY.C for obvious reasons!

When you have KOPY.EXE working, rename your HELLO.C and test the error message. You can try opening HELLO.CBK in mode "ab". If the file already exists, you will copy (append) HELLO.C to the end of HELLO.CBK.

Next I'll show you how to make KOPY.C a tad more flexible. The new version is VKOPY.C (Program 8.2). The **argc** and **argv** indentifiers are explained in the following section.

Do not run VKOPY from within the IDE menu. Compile and Link to VKOPY.EXE and exit to DOS. Read the next section before running VKOPY from the DOS prompt.

```
/* vkopy.c -- improved file copy program Prog8.2 */
#include <stdio.h>

void main(int argc, char *argv[]) /* new! args for main() */
{
    FILE *infile, *outfile;
    int ch = 0, bytes = 0;

    if (argc != 3) {
        puts("\nUsage is VKOPY filename1 filename2\n");
        exit (1);
    }

    if ((infile = fopen(argv[1],"rb")) == NULL) {
        printf("\nSorry %s",argv[1]);
        perror("");
        exit (1);
    }

    if ((outfile = fopen(argv[2],"wb")) == NULL) {
        printf("\nSorry %s",argv[2]);
        perror("");
        exit (1);
    }

    while ((ch = getc(infile)) != EOF) {
        putc(ch, outfile);
        ++bytes;
    }

    fclose(infile);
    fclose(outfile);

    printf("\nTotal of %d bytes VKOPY'd",bytes);
}
```

► *Program 8.2:* VKOPY.C

► *Using main( ) with Command-Line Arguments* ►

C has an indispensible mechanism through which **main( )** can obtain parameters entered at the DOS command level. If I type VKOPY *file1 file2* at the DOS prompt, it would be nice to pass the two file names to VKOPY.EXE, making it more flexible and more like the official DOS command COPY. Any data entered after the command or program name can be considered as a command-line argument, but some conventions must be agreed on in order to cope with the variety of formats encountered. DOS and C consider each string, including the command name itself, to be a distinct argument. Obviously, strings are separated by spaces or tabs.

Two special identifiers, **argc** and **argv**, are used to pass to **main( )** the number of command-line arguments and pointers to each argument. You have to set up **main( )** as follows:

```
main(int argc, char *argv[ ])
{ ... }
```

argc will then provide the number of command-line arguments, including the command itself—so **argc** is never less than 1. The **argv[ ]** is our old friend from Chapter 5, an array of pointers to **char**, or, equivalently, an array of strings. Each of **argv[0]**, **argv[1]**,... up to **argv[argc – 1]** is a pointer to a command-line argument, namely a NUL-terminated string. The pointer **argv[argc]** is set to NULL to mark the end of the array.

You may now execute VCOPY by typing **VKOPY HELLO.C HELLO.CBK** on the command line (or you can choose two files of your own). **main( )** will access the following values:

argc = 3 (command plus 2 arguments).

argv[0] points to empty string "" (DOS 2.x or earlier).
argv[0] points to "C:\VKOPY\0" (DOS 3.0 or later. Note that drive and directory have been added).

argv[1] points to "HELLO.C\0".
argv[2] points to "HELLO.CBK\0".
argv[3] is NULL.

VKOPY will also work with full-file path specifications, but, unlike the DOS COPY command, it will not default the output file name and path or handle wild cards.

Using an array of strings (or an array of pointer to **char**) solves the problem of variable-length arguments. You will sometimes see **argv** declared as **char ∗∗argv**, which is also an array of strings (see Chapter 5).

It is important to know that all the **argv[ ]** arguments are passed as strings, so a command line such as **C>SEND 12 350.45** will not get you an integer and a floating-point number. You would have to convert "**12**" and "**350.45**" from ASCII to numeric using **atoi( )** (ASCII to integer) and **atof( )** (ASCII to FP double).

The white space between arguments is essential: the familiar commas used in C functions will not delimit command-line arguments. Quotation marks can be used to produce a single argument from entries containing white space. The following line has three arguments including SEND:

C>SEND "nice day" fish,chips

► *The env Argument* ►

main( ) will not accept any old arguments. Apart from **argc** and **argv**, the only other legal argument allowed is **env**, from which you can find out the DOS environment parameters (established with the DOS SET command). You can define **main( )** as follows:

```
main(int argc, char *argv[ ], char *env[ ])
{ ... }
```

Each **env[i]** returns a string of the form

```
"environment_var = environment_val"
```

until you reach a NULL pointer, which means that no more environment values have been SET.

You can also use **getenv( )** and **putenv( )** within a program to access, change, or delete an environment value. They are declared like this:

```
        char *getenv(char *environment_var);
/* if arg is "PATH" for example, getenv returns the string found
    in the environment, eg "C:\;C:\TURBOC" or 0 if PATH not SET */
        int putenv(char *environment_string);
/* the arg string eg "PATH = B:\" will be added to the environment,
    or will overwrite an existing PATH setting. "PATH =" will
    clear any existing setting */
```

When you spawn *child processes* using the **exec...( )** family of functions to load and run other programs, you can also pass new environment values.

► *Your Environment Revealed* ►

Here is SHOALL.C (Program 8.3), which displays all the arguments mentioned. This can be run from the IDE, but run it from the DOS prompt with some dummy arguments to test the command-line display. MS-DOS 3.0 and later versions will produce different displays than previous versions.

Figure 8.1 shows the screen display I get from SHOALL. The PROMPT shown has become very popular—it displays the date, time, and directory in reverse video at the top of the screen.

I now return to the standard I/O library routines.

```
/* shoall.c -- display command line & environment Prog8.3 */
#include <stdio.h>

void main(int argc, char *argv[], char *env[])
{
    int i;

    if (argc == 1)
        puts("\nSHOALL has no arguments");
    else {
        puts("\nSHOALL has following arguments:");
        for ( i=0; i<argc; i++)
            printf("%d:\t%s\n",i,argv[i]);
    }

    puts("\nDOS Environment Values:");
        for ( i=0; env[i] != NULL; i++)
            printf("%d:\t%s\n",i,env[i]);
}
```

► **Program 8.3:** *SHOALL.C*

```
 Mon  1-11-1988 / 20:25:18.48 : C:\TB

C>shoall jim joe stan

SHOALL has following arguments:
0:
1:      jim
2:      joe
3:      stan

DOS Environment Values:
0:      COMSPEC=A:\COMMAND.COM
1:      PATH=C:\;C:\TURBOC;C:\TB;A:\
2:      PROMPT=$e[s$e[1;1H$e[0m$e[K$e[7m $d / $t : $p $e[0m$e[u$n$g

C>^_
```

► **Figure 8.1:** *SHOALL screen output*

► *THE get...( ) AND put...( ) FAMILIES* ►

There are several variants on **getc( )** and **putc( )**, some of which you have already encountered. I list them all here with their revealing prototypes or macros and brief notes.

► *fgetc( )*

int fgetc(FILE *fp); is a real function version of the **getc( )** macro.

► *fgetchar( )*

int fgetchar(void); is not in ANSI C and is the same as **fgetc(stdin)**. It grabs a byte from the standard input, which is usually the keyboard unless redirection is in force.

► *getchar( )*

getchar( ) is a simple macro defined as

#define getchar( ) getc(stdin)

so it takes no argument but simply returns a character as in **int** (or EOF on a failure) from **stdin**. This is an excellent illustration of the use of the special predefined file pointer **stdin**—this stream and its pointer are already **fopen**ed for you and do not have to be **fclosed**! getchar( ) is a holdover from the old line-buffered UNIX terminal days. getch( ) and getche( ) are more convenient for the PC console input.

► *getch( )*

int getch(void); also returns a single integer-character (or EOF) from the keyboard, regardless of where **stdin** is pointing. The character does not echo to the screen.

► *getche( )*

int getche(void); works exactly like **getch( )** except that the keyed character echoes to the screen.

► *ungetc( )*

int ungetc(char ch, FILE *fp); "undoes" a **getc( )** by pushing the **char ch** back on the argument stream, **fp**. **ungetc( )** is useful in many "look ahead" situations—you can grab a byte, test it, and reject it or push it back for the next **getc( )**. Without **ungetc( )** many scanning loops prove quite tricky to implement. **ungetc( )** always returns the integer-character you have pushed. Ungetting an EOF (but who would want to?) does not affect the stream and returns an EOF. If you **ungetc( )** twice without a **getc( )** in between you effectively remove the first ungetted character from the stream. Several operations, like **fseek( )** and **rewind( )**, also remove the effect of an **ungetc( )**.

► *ungetch( )*

int ungetch(int ch); is the console-only version of **ungetc( )**. Redirection is ignored.

► *getw( )*

int getw(FILE *fp); is not in ANSI C and works like **getc( )** but reads a 2-byte integer from the stream. You must be careful with **getw( )** for two reasons. First, the function will not worry about byte boundaries—you get the two bytes as found whether they represent a genuine **int** or not. Second, although **getw( )** returns EOF at the end of a stream, just testing for EOF is insufficient since − 1 is a legitimate **int** value. You must use **feof( )** or **ferror( )** as discussed in the **getc( )** section.

► *gets( )*

char *gets(char *str); reads a string into **str** from **stdin** until a newline character is received. The newline is replaced by a NUL in the returned string. A NULL pointer is returned on errors.

► *cgets( )*

You must place the maximum string length needed in **str[0]** before calling **cgets( )**, which is defined as

```
char *cgets(char *str);
```

cgets( ) always reads from the console (keyboard) and plays some tricks by returning the length of the input string into **str[1]**. The string type goes into **str[2]**, **str[3]**,.... If the maximum is reached before a newline character, input stops. A newline is converted to a NUL. The final string is always at least **str[0]** + 2 bytes long. The function returns **&str[2]**—there is no error signal.

► *fgets( )*

char *fgets(char *str, int n, FILE *fp); is a stream version of **cgets( )** that will read at most **n** − **1** bytes from the stream into **str**. An earlier newline character will terminate but goes into the string. A NUL is always added at the end of **str**. A NULL pointer is returned on errors.

Before leaving all these **get...( )**s, take a quick look at the definition of **getc( )**, the one I started out with.

► *The Macro getc( )* ►

```
#define getc(f ) \
( ( ( − − ( (f ) −>level ) >= 0 ) \
? (unsigned char)( ++ (f ) −>curp)[ − 1] : _fgetc (f ))
```

You may have forgotten the \ symbol. It acts as a line break for long macro lines, since a newline character is syntactically significant in a **#define** sequence. The **level** component of **FILE** is a **short int** marking the buffer-refill level. Each call on **getc( )** predecrements the level; while it is non-negative, the first part of the **?:** clause is invoked. This advances **curp**, the stream active position pointer, and grabs the previous (i.e., current) byte by using the array trick **[− 1]**. The byte is type cast to **unsigned char**. If the level goes negative, an internal function **_fgetc( )** is invoked to fill the buffer.

See if you can decipher the **putc( )** macro.

```
#define putc(c,f ) \
(( ++ ((f ) −>level) < 0) \
? (unsigned char)(( ++ (f ) −>curp)[ − 1] = (c)) : \
_fputc ((c),f ))
```

I now give you all the **put...( )** variants with few comments since they follow, mutatis mutandis, the **get...( )** routines.

► *putchar( )*

This macro is defined in STDIO.H as

```
#define putchar(c) putc((c), stdout)
```

meaning that **putchar( )** will place a byte argument on the standard output. Note the essential parentheses in **(c)**. EOF is returned on errors.

► *fputc( )*

int fputc(int ch, FILE *fp); is the function version of the macro **putc( )**. EOF is returned on errors.

► *fputchar( )*

int fputchar(int ch); /*non – ANSI C*/ is the same as **fputc(int ch,stdout)**. EOF is returned on errors.

► *putch( )*

int putch(int ch) is the console version of **putc( )**. No errors are signaled.

► *putw( )*

int putw(int w, FILE *fp); is not in ANSI C and writes **w** as two bytes into the stream, ignoring any alignment problems. EOF is returned on errors, but **ferror( )** should be used since EOF is a valid **int**.

► *puts( )*

int puts(char *str); is an old friend from Chapter 1. It displays the string plus a new line on the active **stdout**. On success, it returns the last character displayed; on failure you get an EOF.

► *cputs( )*

void cputs(char *str); works only on the console (screen) and with NUL terminated strings. No newline character is appended and no value is returned whether it's successful or not.

► *fputs( )*

Like **cputs( )**, **fputs( )** writes the NUL-terminated string with no newline character, but it writes to the designated stream. It's defined as

int fputs(char *str, FILE *fp);

Like **puts( )** it signals success by returning the last character, with EOF being returned on failures.

► *MORE ON BUFFERING* ►

In the **FILE** structure you will see the fields

```
short      bsize;          /* buffer size */
/* short is same as int in Turbo C – used here to increase portability */

       unsigned char *buffer;
/* data transfer buffer */
/* buffer points to first byte of buffer! */
```

Each open (active) stream has a pointer, **file_var.buffer**, to access its private buffer of size **file_var.bsize**, where **file_var** is of type **FILE**. Since **file_var** is usually referenced via a file pointer (for example, **fp** of type **FILE ***) you would be more likely to see expressions such as **fp –>buffer**, or **fp –>bsize**.

As you've seen, the standard I/O functions set up and control the members of ***fp** for you, so you rarely need direct access to the buffers. The STDIO.H functions therefore offer what is known as *buffered I/O*. You should, however, be aware of the fact that there are many *low-level* I/O routines available in Turbo C that offer only the basic read/write tools for file access, leaving you to set up your own buffering strategy and attend to most of the housekeeping chores.

Some confusion arises when these latter routines are called *unbuffered* since, at some level or other, all I/O is buffered with either software or hardware—even a single-byte buffer is a buffer! Low-level I/O functions, as opposed to standard I/O functions, are declared in IO.H.

For advanced work, **setbuf( )** and **setvbuf( )** allow you to set up your own buffers and buffering strategy.

► *NON-ANSI C ROUTINES* ►

The following are non-ANSI C routines provided by Borland to maintain continuity in areas where many I/O versions prevail or because they are useful on the PC.

int	fcloseall	(void);
FILE	*fdopen	(int handle, char *type);
int	fgetchar	(void);
int	flushall	(void);
int	fputchar	(int c);
int	getw	(FILE *fp);
int	putw	(int w, FILE *fp);
char	*strerror	(const char *string);
int	unlink	(const char *filename);
#define	fileno (f)	((f) ->fd)
#define	remove (filename)	unlink(filename)

► *BLOCK I/O* ►

There are two important stream routines still to cover. They allow you to read and write whole blocks of data with one deft function call. They are declared in STDIO.H as follows:

```
size_t fread (void *ptr, size_t size, size_t n, FILE *fp);
size_t fwrite (const void *ptr, size_t size, size_t n, FILE *fp);
```

The data type **size_t** is an ANSI C addition to improve portability. It is predefined as an integer type large enough to hold **sizeof( )** results. For most systems it can be taken as **int**.

The **fread( )** is given the usual stream argument, assumed to be open for reading or updating. In addition you tell it to read **n** items of data each of **size** bytes. The destination for all **n*size** bytes is the area pointed at by the generic **ptr**. You may recall that **void *ptr** allows **ptr** to be type cast to a pointer to any data type.

So, there are four arguments:

1. The source of the transfer is a stream opened for input equals **fp**.

2. The number of chunks equals **n**.

3. The size of each chunk equals **size**.

4. The receiving area (a pointer to memory) equals **ptr**.

Items 3 and 4 are closely related. If you are sending **int**s, then **ptr** must be of type pointer to **int**, so **size** must be **sizeof (*ptr)**, namely 2 bytes for Turbo C.

It is your responsibility to ensure that the destination can hold the total number of bytes being sent, namely (**n** * **sizeof(** * **ptr))**.

The returned value of **fread( )** is the number of items sent, not the number of bytes.

fwrite( ) works similarly but in the opposite direction; *from* **ptr** as the source *to* the stream opened for output. The number and size of the elements being written are defined in exactly the same way.

A small difference you may have spotted in the declaration is that **ptr** is declared as **const**. The idea is that the source pointer is not changeable. This is not the same as saying that the objects being pointed at are invariant!

Block I/O gets exciting when you consider that the **n** items to be transferred from, say, memory to disk or disk to screen, can be records defined as arrays, structures, or unions of any complexity. A lot can be done with a single **fread** and **fwrite**. Indeed, I will conclude this chapter with SPLAYER.C (Program 8.4), a partial version of PLAYER.C that saves the player database to disk. The functions not reprinted here are exactly as found in PLAYER.C. The function **save_play( )** has been added, and **init_play** has been modified to call **save_play** after each record is entered.

```
/* SLAYER.C - a simple, disk version of PLAYER.C database */
/* Program 8.4 -- requires functions and main() from Program 6.1 */
/* overall strategy due to N. Gehani, AT&T Bell Labs */

#include <stdio.h>
#include <malloc.h>
#include <ctype.h>
#include <string.h>

#define FOUND 1
#define MISSING 0

#define PL_MAX 2        /* max number of player - vary for tests */
#define NAME_MAX 25     /* max name + 1 null */
#define HDG "Pl# Name            Posn RBI ERA    DATE Active"

        typedef struct {
                unsigned char month, day;
                unsigned int year;
        } DATE;

        typedef unsigned char BOOL;

        typedef enum {
            X, P, C, I, S, O, D
          } POSITION;
```

► *Program 8.4: SPLAYER.C*

```
        typedef struct player {

                char name[NAME_MAX];
                unsigned char player_number;
                POSITION player_position;
                unsigned int rbi;
                double era;
                DATE date_joined;
                BOOL active;
            } PLAYER_REC;


        static PLAYER_REC *pptr[PL_MAX];
/* global to all functions in this file,
   but not accessible elsewhere.
   Declares an array of 'pointers to PLAYER_REC structure' */

        static int pind;
/* player index used with pptr[] */

        static int db_size;
/* number of players in database */

/*--------------------------------------------------*/
/* SAVE_PLAY - write n player records to PLAYER.DAT */
/*--------------------------------------------------*/

int save_play(PLAYER_REC *play_ptr, int n)
{
    FILE *play_fp;
    int saved;

    play_fp = fopen("PLAYER.DAT","ab");
/* open binary file for append - each player is added at end */
    if (play_fp == NULL) {
        perror("PLAYER.DAT");
        exit(1);
    }
    saved = fwrite(play_ptr, sizeof(PLAYER_REC), n, play_fp);
/* number of player recs actually saved - n were requested */
/* return 0 if error */
    fclose(play_fp);
    if (saved == n)
        return saved;
    else
        return 0;
}

/*----------------------------------------*/
/* INIT_PLAY - set up player database     */
/* data in memory only                    */
/*----------------------------------------*/
void init_play(void)
{
    int dbind;      /* local var - scans the database */
    char pos;       /* ASCII player position */

    if (coreleft() < sizeof(PLAYER_REC)*(PL_MAX+8)) {
        puts("\n\tInsufficient Memory for Player DB");
        exit(1);
    }
 for (dbind = 0; dbind < PL_MAX; dbind++) {
    if ((pptr[dbind]=(PLAYER_REC *)malloc(sizeof(PLAYER_REC)))
                                ==NULL) {
        puts("Memory Allocation Failure");
        exit(1);
    }
```

► **Program 8.4:** *SPLAYER.C (continued)*

```
    /* here pptr[dbind] points to an allocated record awaiting input */
          printf("\n#%3d Enter Player Number <99=exit>: ",dbind);
          scanf( "%d",&(pptr[dbind]->player_number) );

          if (pptr[dbind]->player_number == 99) break;

          printf("\n    Enter Player Name: ");
          scanf( "%s",pptr[dbind]->name );
    /* Next item could be entered with getch() but I want to */
    /* show scanf() with %s                                  */
          printf("\n    Enter Player Position: ");
          scanf("%s",&pos);

          pos = toupper(pos);
          switch (pos) {
              case 'P': pptr[dbind]->player_position = P; break;
              case 'C': pptr[dbind]->player_position = C; break;
              case 'I': pptr[dbind]->player_position = I; break;
              case 'S': pptr[dbind]->player_position = S; break;
              case 'O': pptr[dbind]->player_position = O; break;
              case 'D': pptr[dbind]->player_position = D; break;
              default:  pptr[dbind]->player_position = X;
          }
          if (pptr[dbind]->player_position != P) {
              pptr[dbind]->era = 0.0;
              printf("\n    Enter Runs Batted In: ");
              scanf( "%d",&(pptr[dbind]->rbi) );
          }
          else {
              pptr[dbind]->rbi = 0;
              printf("\n    Enter Earned Run Average: ");
              scanf( "%lf",&(pptr[dbind]->era) );
          }
          printf("\n    Enter Date Joined (mm/dd/yyyy): ");
          scanf( "%2d/%2d/%4d", &((pptr[dbind]->date_joined).month),
                              &((pptr[dbind]->date_joined) /day
                              &((pptr[dbind]->date_joined).year));
          printf("\n    Active=Y or N? :");
          scanf( "%s",&pos);
          pptr[dbind]->active = ('Y' == toupper(pos));
    /* save one player rec in PLAYER.DAT */
    /* save_play allows future enhancement - save several records */
          if (save_play(pptr[dbind],1))
              puts("\nSaved in PLAYER.DAT");
          else
              puts("\nRecord not saved??");

          } /* end for loop */
          db_size = dbind;        /* set current size of database */

}
/*--------------end init_player--------------------*/
```

► **Program 8.4:** *SPLAYER.C (continued)*

► *SUMMARY OF CHAPTER 8* ►

◄► Files and devices come in all shapes and sizes, but C and DOS allow you to control them via a uniform logical concept called the stream.

◄► Input and output between different elements require buffering—much of which is done behind the scenes.

◄► Streams can be redirected and piped by attaching them to files and devices. Many I/O functions can operate on streams with no prior knowledge of the physical devices or applications.

◄► C offers a rich array of I/O routines, both buffered and unbuffered, formatted and unformatted.

◄► Text and binary streams require different treatment for EOF detection and CR/LF to new-line translation.

◄► **getc( )** and **putc( )** are single-byte I/O routines, but from these over 30 variations can be understood.

◄► Random access is obtained by setting a pointer to scan the stream. **fseek( )** and simple calculations can direct the pointer to any given record.

◄► Block I/O is accomplished via **fread( )** and **fwrite( )**.

THE GRAPHICS
TOOLBOX
OPENED WIDE

► *CHAPTER 9* ►

At the end of 1987, Borland released Version 1.5 of Turbo C. For most users, the most exciting addition of Version 1.5 is a graphics library, so this chapter is devoted to graphics programming. I will cover other additions of the new version in Chapter 10.

I recall reading a magazine article complaining of the lack of graphics tools in Turbo C on the very day my copy of Version 1.5 arrived, just a few weeks before the official launch. In the relatively brief reign of Version 1.00 several outside vendors released graphics "enhancer" packages for Turbo C (see Appendix H). Some of these may still be useful, but on the whole Version 1.5 is remarkably complete and economical. I will cover a selection of the Turbo C functions to give you a feel for what is available. More complete specifications and examples can be found in Appendix G.

I'll give you enough geometrical and PC video-hardware knowledge to master the Turbo C graphics routines, but don't expect any more here than the basics. The jungle starts when you try listing all the different adapters and monitors. This is an area, the cynics say, where there are so many standards you are bound to find one you like. If you find references to objects irrelevant to your own installation, please be patient.

The Turbo C graphics tools are broadly similar to those provided with Turbo Pascal and will therefore be familiar to many readers. For those new to the graphics world, I provide a few basic notes.

► *THE DISPLAY ADAPTER* ►

Every PC has a special *display adapter* circuit board containing some *display memory* (or *video memory*) that is physically distinct from your main RAM but nevertheless part of the address space of the CPU. The starting and ending absolute addresses of the display memory vary with model and are usually of no direct interest to the user—the system knows where to find the video memory, and with some boards the programmer is actively discouraged from peeking and poking.

The size of the display memory, though, and its logical division into *pages* (or *planes*) is of importance since these dictate the sort of graphics tricks you can accomplish. The simplest adapters provide 4KB, with more expensive models offering 16KB, 64KB, 1MB, and ever upward.

The cathode ray tube (CRT) display unit (or *monitor*), is fed from the display memory via a programmable black box called the CRT controller chip. You can imagine one of the pages of the display memory being transformed in various ways to generate signals for your particular CRT screen. This page is called the *visual page*.

When you have more than one page of display memory available, you can independently load data into another page, the *active* page, which is ready to display almost instantly as required. Note that "active" refers to the invisible page, which is being replenished by the program, not the visual page, which is generating the display. The visual page must be not be written to during the display cycle. Animation effects depend on flipping between active and visual pages.

► RASTER SCAN ►

The transfer from memory to screen, in the form of a raster scan, is repeated 60 times per second (or 50 in some countries) giving the illusion of a steady display. Video memory is specially wired with multiple I/O ports to the CPU and the CRT controller. Simultaneous access by the CPU and CRT controller leads to a display aberration known as *snow*.

Between each refresh cycle an important event takes place: the electron beam painting the screen has to switch off and get from the bottom right corner back to the starting point at the top left corner (see Figure 9.1). This *vertical retrace* provides an important opportunity for the display memory to be updated by your program without causing snow. This is especially important if you have only one page of display memory. The key design elements relevant to all graphics applications are the vertical retrace period (typically a millisecond or so), the memory-to-memory transfer rate, and the number of pages.

► DISPLAY MEMORY MAPS ►

Groups of bits or groups of bytes in memory are *mapped* to positions and attributes on the screen. The mapping varies according to which *video mode* is operative. Display adapters and monitors vary in the number and types of modes they can support.

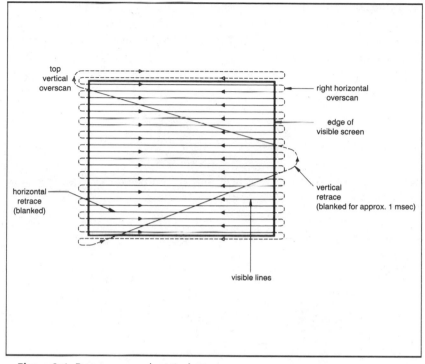

► **Figure 9.1:** *Raster scan and vertical retrace*

There are many different modes, but they can be classified into two distinct groups—*text* and *graphics*.

► *Text Mapping* ►

With text mapping, two adjacent bytes in display memory map to a region of the screen large enough to display a single character. One byte specifies the character, (you have 256 combinations with IBM Extended ASCII) and the other byte controls the character's attributes (intensity, underlining, reverse video, suppression, blinking, and, possibly, color). Each character is generated by hardware and takes up a fixed area of the screen. The usual maxima are 80 characters per line and 25 lines per screen, as shown in Figure 9.2. A simple calculation shows that for an 80 × 25 text display you need 2 × 80 × 25 = 4000 bytes per page.

► *Text Coordinate Systems*

Figure 9.2 also shows the *Cartesian* coordinate system used for text in Turbo C: X, the column position, runs from 1 through 80 from left to right on each line, and Y, the line or row position, runs from 1 through 25 from top to bottom. You refer to a screen position as (X,Y). The top left corner of the text screen is (1,1), and the bottom right corner is (80,25). (Note that Y runs in the opposite direction to conventional graphs.)

The relation between row, column, and character position in a page of display memory is

character_offset = (row × 80 × 2) + (column × 2)
attribute_offset = character_offset + 1

You will also encounter text formats with 40 characters per line. The mapping principle is the same with these.

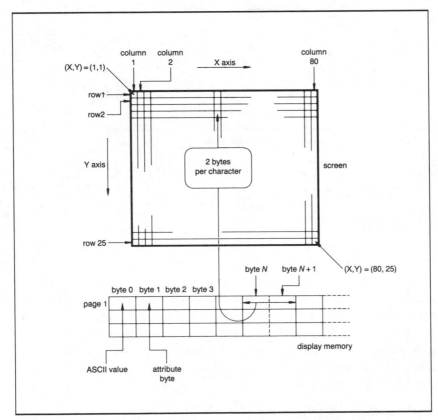

► *Figure 9.2:* Memory-mapped display for normal text

Pages usually start on even kilobyte boundaries, so there are often unused bytes between pages. Finding the address of a character in the second and subsequent pages must allow for these gaps.

Now that you know something of text mapping, I'll show you how Turbo C handles text windows.

► *Text Windows*

A text window is a mapping of display memory to a rectangular area of the screen. The minimum window is 1 row by 1 column, and the maximum is the whole screen, which is the default when your program starts. The **window( )** function specifies four coordinates, two for the top left corner and two for the bottom right corner.

```
        window(20, 10, 30, 15);
/* active text window has corners at (20, 10), (30, 10), (30, 15) and (20, 15)
    going in a clockwise direction. */
```

will create an active text window as shown in Figure 9.3. A call to **window( )** with illegal coordinates will be ignored, and no error message will be generated (**window( )** returns **void**). **window( )** does not create borders, so you have to draw your own (Program 9.1, will show you how). **window( )** simply alters the effect of certain CONIO.H console-display functions such as **cprintf( )** and **cputs( )** by sending output to the active window. The vital point to remember is that a window, once created, establishes a new set of local coordinates.

As with all coordinate systems in mathematics, there are *absolute* and *relative* addressing methods. **window( )** itself uses the absolute coordinates for the window corners, but many of Turbo C's window functions use coordinates relative to the top left corner of the window, taking this position as (1,1). You get from relative to absolute coordinates by adding a displacement to each coordinate. This translation is illustrated in Figure 9.3.

Turbo C allows you to save, restore, and move any rectangular areas of screen text with **gettext( )**, **puttext( )**, and **movetext( )** without regard to any windows you may have set up. Even if you have the MDA text-only adapter, the Turbo C window-management functions will allow to spice up your programs. With **gettext( )** and **puttext( )**, for example, you can save and restore arbitrary rectangular areas of the screen (including the whole screen).

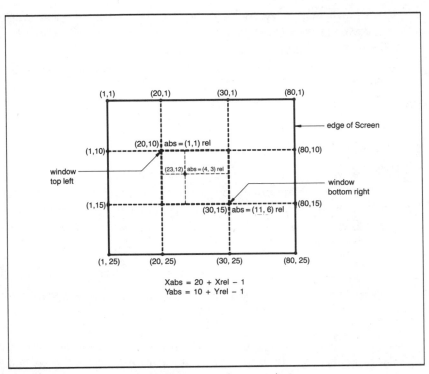

► **Figure 9.3:** *Absolute and relative text window coordinates*

► *Graphics Mapping* ►

The graphics memory map is fundamentally different from the text map. As shown in Figure 9.4, the screen in graphics mode is conceptually divided into a fine mesh of individual dots or *pixels* (picture elements). The dots are not, of course, Euclidean points, although it is often convenient to treat them as such.

Any particular pixel can be suppressed or illuminated, which is the whole foundation for creating graphical images. The *resolution* of the display is described in terms of the number of pixels per line and the number of pixels per column. A 640 × 200 display, for example, is considered *hi-res* (high resolution) and will allow more detailed images than a 160 × 200 *lo-res* (low-resolution) display. Some raster-scanning systems use interlacing whereby odd- and even-numbered lines are displayed on successive scans. The viewer is not aware of this trickery and the programmer is only involved if

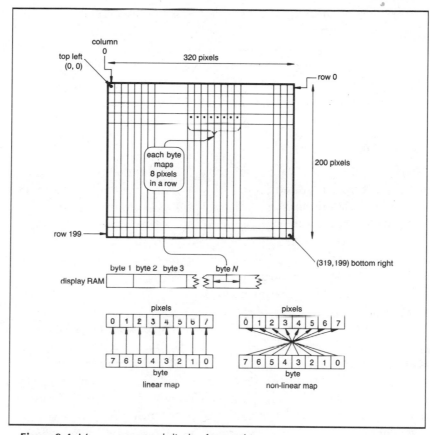

► *Figure 9.4:* Memory-mapped display for graphics

interlacing affects the memory mapping. Even then, the graphics functions often hide you from the underlying complexity.

► The Impact of Resolution

Resolution is important when you want smooth curves and diagonal lines. Also, since monitor screens are wider than their height (or vice versa) and/or have pixels that are not perfect squares, there exists the *aspect-ratio* problem. The pixels I am looking at now as I type have an aspect ratio of 4:3 (4 units high and 3 units wide). This is especially noticeable when I try to draw exact squares and pleasant circles. To reduce distortion, certain *scaling* corrections have to be made in one direction or another. Most drawing functions include some aspect-ratio scaling, but you can provide your own corrections as well.

All the popular graphics adapter/monitor combinations offer a choice of resolutions. Turbo C gives programmers functions such as **detectgraph( )**, **getgraphmode**, **setgraphmode( )**, and **restorecrtmode( )** to test which modes are available and to set, change, or restore the mode.

► *Pixel Encoding*

To represent a pixel state as "on" or "off" requires only 1 bit of display memory, but a pixel may take from 1 to 16 bits when you take into account the possible coding of the pixel attributes. The actual number of bits depends on the *palette*, that is to say, the range of colors available. The words attribute and color are often used loosely and interchangeably to include such factors as intensity or shades of gray. Do not worry if you see color-coding schemes used with "monochrome" adapters and displays.

The display-memory requirements for a 320×200 resolution 4-color system, taking 2 bits per pixel, would be $2 \times 320 \times 200 = 128,000$ bits $= 16$KB per page. The same resolution on a 16-color display with 4 bits per pixel would need 32KB per page. If you want more colors and more pages the memory requirements build up quite nicely, which explains the growth of EMS—the extended memory system devised by Intel, Lotus, and others to beat the PC's 1MB addressing-space limit. There are also special ways of addressing display memory that conserve the PC's own address space.

The different ways that the bits for each pixel can be stored in memory provide more complications. For some modes the mapping is linear, for others you find noncontiguous groups of bits representing banks of odd- and even-numbered lines. Tracking all these and masking off queer bits is a programmer's nightmare. Luckily, the Turbo C graphics functions do most of the hard work. You'll see that once you have passed certain parameters to the initialization function, **initgraph( )**, you work with the same set of high-level tools, however complex the pixel mapping happens to be.

► *Device Drivers*

The secret to interfacing software with so many different adapters and monitors is an intercessory program called the *graphics device driver*, written specially for each group of adapters. You are familiar with other device drivers such as disk and mouse drivers. They perform all the nasty little signal translations between logical and physical objects.

At this point, all you need to know about these esoteric driver programs is that you must have one (or more)! Turbo C supplies drivers for ten of the most popular graphics boards. They all have helpful file names with the extension .BGI. When your program is executed, the appropriate driver must be available for *dynamic loading* from disk or for incorporation into your .EXE file with the help of Turbo C's BGIOBJ.EXE utility (to be explained later in this chapter).

► *Graphics Coordinates*

As with text mappings, you refer to positions on the graphics screen in terms of (X,Y) coordinates. With text modes, there is a definite, hardware-generated cursor that reminds us of the current (X,Y) position. With graphics modes there is no preordained cursor, but we still refer to the next writing position on the screen as the CP, though in this case it stands for *current position* rather than *cursor position*. If you want a visible cursor on a graphics display, you have to generate one.

There are two other differences between graphics coordinates and text coordinates: in graphics, (X,Y) refers to a pixel "point" rather than to a character position, and the top left pixel is (0,0) not (1,1)—compare Figures 9.3 and 9.4.

The resolution of the mode you are in dictates the legal range of values for X and Y. For a 640 × 200 resolution, X ranges from 0–639 (left to right) and Y ranges from 0–199 (top to bottom). The functions **getmaxx( )** and **getmaxy( )** return these X and Y upper limits for the graphics mode in force. You'll meet many such **get...( )** routines that, like **sizeof( )**, simplify the writing of portable code.

► *Pixel Geometry*

All the drawing primitives rely ultimately on selecting pixels according to some relation derived from analytical geometry. $Y = aX + b$ ($a, b <> 0$), for instance, represents all the pixels on the unique straight line through the points $(0, b)$ and $(-b/a, 0)$. $Y = b$ represents a horizontal line through $(0, b)$, and $X = b$ is the vertical line through $(b, 0)$. Similarly, the equation $(X-a)^2 + (Y-b)^2 = R^2$ represents a circle of radius R centered at (a,b), and so on. Euclidean planes and points, of course, cannot be represented on a finite screen with discrete pixels, so you constantly have to decide whether images are to be scaled, clipped, wrapped around, scrolled, or made to reappear on the opposite edge.

Enormous effort has been expended by graphics programmers to devise plotting algorithms that work in fast integer arithmetic, avoiding slow floating-point sums.

► *Viewports*

In graphics modes, you can assign a rectangular area of pixels to a *virtual screen* called a *viewport* to distinguish it from a text window. In fact, the concepts and applications of windows and viewports are quite similar, and for example, you use four coordinates (top, left, bottom, right) when defining a viewpoint with **setviewport( )**, or when writing pixels within a viewport. The difference is that the coordinates are absolute with the former and relative with the latter. For each window function there is a comparable viewport function—you just have to learn which is which!

Viewports, however, offer more sophisticated features such as *clipping*, which allows you to cut drawings at viewport boundaries. (In text windows, characters usually wrap around and scroll as though they were in normal, but smaller, screens.) You can also produce special effects by applying bit-wise operations on sets of images. Neither viewports nor text windows come with visible surrounding rectangles, but in graphics mode you can draw pretty frames around a viewport simply by selecting a *line style* with **setlinestyle( )** and then calling **rectangle( )** as in

```
setlinestyle(line_type, line_pattern, line_thickness);
rectangle(top, left, right, bottom);
```

Unlike the text-mode user-supplied rectangle, which is limited to using the IBM extended ASCII line and corner symbols, the graphics frames can be Louvres or Guggenheim to taste.

As with text modes, you can move arbitrary rectangles of graphics data between screen and memory with functions such as **getimage( )** and **putimage( )**, regardless of any viewports you may have defined.

► TEXT-TEXT AND GRAPHICS-TEXT ►

Having seen a little of the theory behind text and graphics memory maps, let's return to the different adapter/monitor combinations available. They fall into two main groups—those capable of text mode only, such as the IBM MDA, and those that can handle both text and graphics modes, such as the Hercules DA, and the IBM CGA and EGA boards. The dual purpose models can be switched between several different modes, some of which use text mappings and others of which use graphics mappings with different resolutions.

The standard IBM PC range provides internal hardware and ROM BIOS support for five distinct text modes and seven graphics modes (I exclude three graphics modes assigned exclusively to the PCJr). Which of these you can access depends initially on the adapter fitted and the drivers available. If you have the proper adapter and drivers, exploitation of the features provided in each mode then rests with your monitor.

I have to choose my words carefully. All multimode systems are capable of displaying text in text mode (normal ASCII plus attribute mapping) as well as text in graphics mode (using pixels to create characters in various ways). I'll call the latter graphics-text to avoid confusion.

► *Graphics-Text* ►

There are two types of graphics-text: *bit-mapped fonts* and *stroked fonts*. A bit-mapped font defines a fixed pixel pattern for each text symbol within a small rectangle. Turbo C provides a predefined bit-mapped font with characters based on an 8 × 8-pixel grid. In theory this provides an astronomical 2^{64} distinct symbols, but in practice a working set of 128 or 256 is selected to match the keyboard. You can intermix these character bit patterns with normal graphics elements in display memory to provide legends for your graphs, pie-slices, and bar charts.

You can use software to do creative (not to mention hideously unattractive) things with a graphics-text that you can't do with text-mode text. Some examples are justification, rotation, inversion, magnification, Hebrew vowel pointing, and accenting. The bit-mapped approach has severe limitations, however, such as the well-known invasion of the "jaggies" when characters are enlarged beyond a certain size. Scaling up a bit-mapped character quickly reveals the rough edges.

The *stroked-font* approach reduces these problems. Each character in a stroked font is coded as a drawing, using line and curve segments, rather than as a small set of pixels. Deep down, of course, everything displayed is really a set of pixels, and ultimately the resolution of the monitor sets the limit. With advanced splining techniques, however, the typographic disasters of magnification can be reduced.

Turbo C provides four stroked fonts: Triplex, Small, Sans Serif, and Gothic, which are stored in the files TRIP.CHR, LITT.CHR, SANS.CHR, and

GOTH.CHR, respectively. As with .BGI driver files, you have to make them available to any program that calls on them. They can be dynamically loaded from disk as required or converted to .OBJ files with BGIOBJ.EXE and linked into your .EXE code. The trade-off, as with drivers, is program size versus execution speed. The built-in 8 × 8 bit-mapped font is always available at run time, so you don't have to worry about loading or linking it.

Specialist vendors provide more exotic fonts that include foreign-language character sets. (See Appendix H.) In addition, the technique of scanning and digitizing from artwork has simplified the problem of creating fonts (especially when compared with the old manual bit-picking methods).

► *Displaying Texts* ►

The special display functions **putch( )**, **cputs( )**, and **cprintf( )** in CONIO.H work only with text-text. Version 1.00 of Turbo C did not support text windows, so the CONIO.H routines have been modified in Version 1.5. to output to the active text window. If the latter is the whole screen (as it is by default when you fire up), then they work just like their cousins from STDIO.H. If you have a smaller text window active, then **putch( )**, **cputs( )**, and **cprintf( )** output is displayed differently—scrolling and word wrap occur within the confines of the window. Even **getche( )** has been modified because it echoes on the keyed character to the screen in window fashion.

If you use the STDIO.H display functions **printf( )** and **puts( )** (no leading **c** for console), windows are ignored—output just appears from wherever the CP is and plows on regardless.

Graphics-text, as you may guess, requires special treatment. The CONIO.H functions handle only text-mode ASCII strings. With graphics-text you need to allow for different style sizes, and both the height and length of the text become relevant.

The function **outtext( )** is the graphics-text equivalent of **cputs( )**—it sends a string of graphics-text to the active viewport. Its operation is subject to many parameters that set the font style and size, justification mode, and orientation. The latter allows you to display both horizontally (left to right) and vertically (bottom to top, with the characters rotated 90 degrees counterclockwise). **outtextxy( )** works in the same way as **outtext( )** but it first sets the CP to a given (X,Y).

These parameters are tested and changed with the functions **gettext settings( )**, **settextjustify( )**, and **settextstyle( )**. In the absence of a graphics-text equivalent to **cprintf( )**, you cannot immediately format numbers and strings on the screen in the traditional text-mode way. You can use **sprintf( )** to send formatted output to a string and then massage the string for **outtext( )**.

To summarize, with text-text you are relying on a hardware character generator that takes an ASCII byte plus an attribute byte and forms its own character image for the monitor. Most computer printers are set up to handle text-text with just minor tweaks for attribute changes (bold, italics, underlining, and so on).

The graphics mapped fonts do it all with software. They take extra memory and CPU cycles but offer much in return—scaling, sloping, style-changing, proportional-spacing, and WYSIWYG (what you see is what you get) displays for desktop publishing. Printing graphics fonts is more difficult since the mappings and resolutions of screen and printer seldom match.

The Turbo C tools reflect the dichotomy between graphics and text. Each function in the graphics library works only in one of the two modes.

► *SOME POPULAR DISPLAY ADAPTERS* ►

Adapters such as IBM's monochrome display adapter (MDA) work only with a single color in text mode. With the IBM extended ASCII code you do get several line-segment symbols from which you can build up simple rectangular shapes and bar charts that a lay onlooker might consider to be "graphical." Although the MDA can only handle ASCII text, it excels at this task with crisp, high-resolution characters ideal for the mainstream of office word processing. The MDA has been widely cloned and imitated.

The IBM Color/Graphics Adapter (CGA) can operate in seven modes, four for text and three for graphics. The IBM Enhanced Color Adapter (EGA) provides four more graphics modes.

The Hercules Display Adapter (DA) offers an excellent compromise, offering a monochrome version of the CGA for graphics and a text mode with the quality of the MDA.

It is quite feasible to have more than one adapter board fitted as long as each knows its place.

Table 9.1 lists the properties of each of the modes assigned in the *video byte* at address 0x40:0x49 of all true blue PC's. The mode numbers in Table 9.1 relate to the internal values of the IBM video byte—Turbo C uses a different convention, although the numbers do coincide for the text modes.

Since several adapters can share the same mode value, there is another byte at address 0x40:0x87, the *equipment byte*, which is used to encode, inter alia, the type of adapter. In theory, software can poll these bytes to discover what video boards are fitted. In practice, there are many clones and compatibles out there to muddy the waters.

► IBM COMPATIBILITY AND DIRECT VIDEO ►

The official IBM-recommended method of accessing the PC video facilities is via a set of ROM BIOS or DOS services (or with high-level language commands that call on these services). I gave you a glimpse of this approach by using **int86( )** and **intdos( )** in Chapter 6. For maximum speed and control,

Mode	Type	Resolution	Colors/Attributes	Adapters
0	Text	40 × 25	16 g	CGA, EGA
1	Text	40 × 25	16 f 8 b	CGA, EGA
2	Text	80 × 25	16 g	CGA, EGA, Compaq
3	Text	80 × 25	16 f 8 b	CGA, EGA
4	Graphics	320 × 200	4	CGA, EGA, Compaq
5	Graphics	320 × 200	4 g	CGA, EGA, Compaq
6	Graphics	640 × 200	2	CGA, EGA, Compaq
7	Text	80 × 25	mono	EGA, MDA, Hercules*
8	N/A (PCjr)			
9	N/A (PCjr)			
10	N/A (PCjr)			

► **Table 9.1:** *Standard IBM PC video modes*

Mode	Type	Resolution	Colors/Attributes	Adapters
11	Reserved			
12	Reserved			
13	Graphics	320 × 200	16	EGA
14	Graphics	640 × 200	16	EGA
15	Graphics	640 × 350	2	EGA
16	Graphics	640 × 350	4/16**	EGA

f   = *foreground color*

b   = *background color*

g   = *shades of gray in the color-suppressed modes on composite output.
However, the RGB output carries full-color signals.*

*   *also provides 720 × 348 monochrome graphics mode*

** *depends on video memory available*

► ***Table 9.1:*** *Standard IBM PC video modes (continued)*

though, many programs bypass these services and send data directly to display RAM.

The BIOS approach is safer since it improves portability across different PC models from IBM and other BIOS-compatible suppliers. Minor hardware deviations from the official IBM PC standard can vitiate the direct-video methods and force expensive recoding. Since the world is full of true and false PC clones and incompatible "compatibles," Borland offers you a simple solution. The global variable **directvideo** can be set to enlist the BIOS for console output services or it can be set to shun these services in favor of the direct memory approach:

```
directvideo = 0;              /* use the IBM BIOS calls */

directvideo = 1;              /* output directly to video RAM */
```

Only you can determine which setting is better for your equipment. My own Spartan XX clone works fine both ways with a Hercules DA clone! Once you determine your optimum setting, remember to include the statement near the start of each **main( )**. Note that it *is* a statement, not a declaration, so it must follow any top-level declarations in a function.

► *LINKING THE GRAPHICS LIBRARY* ►

Another chore to do before you start drawing pie charts all over the screen concerns GRAPHICS.LIB, the collection of over seventy compiled .OBJ graphics functions. There is only one GRAPHICS.LIB for all the memory models, unlike the case with the other main libraries, which exist in unique versions: CS.LIB (small model), CM.LIB (medium model), and so on. Turbo C links the appropriate C?.LIB library automatically, but you must tell the system if you need GRAPHICS.LIB.

To ensure that your graphics programs are linked correctly you *must* add GRAPHICS.LIB to each of your .PRJ project files. Even for single-file programs that do not usually have explicit .PRJ files, you must create one. For example, to compile and link TWINDOW.C (which you'll see shortly) under TC.EXE, a TWINDOW.PRJ file must exist with the entry

    twindow graphics.lib

With TC.EXE you would use the command line,

    C>TCC TWINDOW GRAPHICS.LIB.

Forgetting to add GRAPHICS.LIB is a real pain because the error messages may not show up until after a long compile-and-link session.

To work with all the memory models, the GRAPHICS.LIB functions are prototyped in GRAPHICS.H as **far** functions, and all pointer arguments are declared with **far** pointers. This, and the presence of many essential structure, enumeration, and mnemonic definitions, makes it vital to

    #include <graphics.h>

with all graphics programs. Similarly, CONIO.H must be **#include**d for all text-mode work.

► *SETTING THE TEXT MODES* ►

Summing up so far, your video board can work in two distinct modes—text mode and graphics mode. They are both supported by GRAPHICS.LIB (there is no separate TEXT.LIB). I'll concentrate on text modes for a while since they provide a painless (or less painful?) introduction to the Turbo C graphics toolbox.

You use the **textmode( )** function with a single mode argument to put you into one of the five text modes. CONIO.H declares an enumeration,

```
enum text_modes { LASTMODE = – 1, BW40 = 0, C40, BW80,
                  MONO = 7 };
/* recall that enumerations increment by 1 from 0 unless otherwise
   explicitly initialized. So C40 = 1, BW80 = 2 */
```

allowing you to write

```
#include <conio.h>          /* vital */
  ...
textmode(BW40);             /* same as textmode(0); */
textmode(BW80);             /* same as textmode(2); */
  ...
  ...                       /* assume you switch to graphics here */
  ...
textmode(LASTMODE);         /* or textmode( – 1) */
/* this will restore you to the previous text mode, namely BW80 */
```

textmode( ) does not return a value or signal an error. It does reset any text window, making the whole screen your current text window. It also clears any text attributes to normal, as though you had called **normvideo( )**.

The text-mode mnemonics are explained in Table 9.2. Once you are in text mode, you can check the status of various parameters with **gettextinfo( )**. This loads the following **text_info** structure with pertinent data:

```
struct text_info {
    unsigned char winleft          /* left window coordinate */
    unsigned char wintop           /* top window coordinate */
    unsigned char winright         /* right window coordinate */
    unsigned char winbottom        /* bottom window coordinate */
```

```
/* window corners are in absolute coordinates */
    unsigned char attribute        /* text attribute */
    unsigned char normattr         /* normal attribute */
    unsigned char currmode         /* current mode */
    unsigned char screenheight /* bottom – top */
    unsigned char screenwidth  /* right – left */
    unsigned char curx             /* X coord relative to window */
    unsigned char cury             /* Y coord relative to window */
};
```

The following snippet shows **gettextinfo( )** in action with some simple, miscellaneous text-mode functions that are self-explanatory:

```
    struct text_info my_text      /* declare a structure */
    ...
    textmode(BW80);               /* set text mode */

    window(10, 20, 29, 23);
/* reset window from 80 x 25 to 20 x 4 */

    gotoxy(1,1);
/* move CP to (1,1) relative to current window */

    gettextinfo(&my_text);
/* CP = (10,20) in absolute coordinates */

    cprintf("Cursor is at (%2d,%2d)",my_text.curx,my_text.cury);
/* but curx = 1 and cury = 1 */

    clrscr( );                    /* clear the active window */
```

Symbol	Enum Value	Text Mode
LASTMODE	–1	Restore previous
BW40	0	Black and White (16 gray). 40 × 25
C40	1	Color (16 f, 8 b). 40 × 25
BW80	2	Black and White (16 gray). 80 × 25
C80	3	Color (16 f, 8 b). 80 × 25
MONO	7	Monochrome. 80 × 25

▸ *Table 9.2:* Graphics-text modes

```
        cprintf("winleft is %2d,wintop is %2d",
                my_text.winleft,my_text.wintop);
/* displays 10,20 absolute */

        gotoxy(10,1);              /* move to (19,20) absolute */
        clreol( );                 /* and clear to end of line */

        delline( );                /* now clear the whole line that contains
                                      the CP */
        gotoxy(1,1);
        cputs("This is line 1 of   /* no newline with cputs( ) */
              window");
        insline( );
/* insert a blank line by pushing down the line with the CP.
   All lower lines are pushed down. The bottom line will scroll
   out of the window. Line 1 is now blank, line 2 is old line 1 */
        cprintf("I am now at (%2d,%2d)\n",wherex( ),wherey( ));
/* display the window relative coordinates */

        ...
        textmode(BW40);

        ...
        textmode(my_text.currmode);   /* restore to BW80 */
/* or use textmode(LAST_MODE) */
```

The above snippet shows the simple **gotoxy( )** call moving the cursor using window-relative coordinates. The **window( )** function effectively reduces the screen size as far as any CONIO.H output is concerned, so **cprintf( )** would display in a box 20-characters wide and 4-characters deep. A string exceeding 20 characters would spill over to the following line. Calls on **window( )** with inappropriate corners are ignored, and no warnings are generated.

clrscr( ) clears the area defined by the active window. The CP is moved to (1,1), the top left corner. The three editing functions, **clrol( )**, **delline( )**, and **insline( )** operate as is indicated in the comments.

wherex( ) and **wherey( )** return integer values telling you the current position relative to the active window. They duplicate the **curx** and **cury** members of the **text_info** structure, but they save you from calling the more complex **gettextinfo( )** just to find out where you are on a screen.

To understand the attribute field in **struct text_info**, you need to look at the colors available in text mode.

► *Text Color* ►

The text modes that offer color work as follows (provided you have a color monitor, of course). You will recall that a text character and its attribute are encoded in adjacent bytes. The screen cell displaying the character can have a selected *background* color upon which the character appears in a *foreground* color. The attribute byte encodes both these colors and a *blink-enable flag* as follows:

Bits	Meaning
0–3	4 bits = 16 foreground colors possible
4–6	3 bits = 8 background colors possible
7	1 bit = blink-enable flag (0 = off, 1 = on)

It is instructive to look a little deeper at the color-encoding bits:

Bit	Meaning
0	Blue foreground
1	Green foreground
2	Red foreground
3	Intensity bit (0 = off, 1 = on)
4	Blue background
5	Green background
6	Red background

Sir Isaac Newton showed that mixing the three primary colors, red, green, and blue, in different proportions could produce all the colors of the visible spectrum. With the aid of the single intensity bit, the eight simple mixes of the foreground primaries provide sixteen different colors, eight of which (low intensity) are also available as background colors. Clearly the same combination of low-intensity background and foreground colors is unacceptable—the character merges with its background! Even with a high-intensity foreground, some of the background colors do not work very well (brown behind yellow, for example). The default attribute-byte setting, by the way, is 0x7, which gives white on black.

The colors derived from these combinations are defined symbolically in CONIO.H, as shown in Table 9.3.

The richer sixty-four-color palettes available with the EGA boards arise from the addition of an intensity bit to each of the three primary colors. I will limit this discussion to the sixteen-color systems.

Value	Symbol	Foreground/Background?
0	BLACK	both
1	BLUE	both
2	GREEN	both
3	CYAN	both
4	RED	both
5	MAGENTA	both
6	BROWN	both
7	LIGHTGRAY	both (white on some monitors)
8	DARKGRAY	foreground only (or black)
9	LIGHTBLUE	foreground only
10	LIGHTGREEN	foreground only
11	LIGHTCYAN	foreground only
12	LIGHTRED	foreground only
13	LIGHTMAGENTA	foreground only
14	YELLOW	foreground only (or bright yellow)
15	WHITE	foreground only
128	BLINK	foreground only

► **Table 9.3:** *Color codes*

Three functions accept the symbols in Table 9.3 as arguments to set the color attributes for all characters subsequently displayed until the attribute is changed (or you exit text mode). They are declared as follows:

```
        void textbackgound(int color);
/* use only colors 0 – 7 for background */

        void textcolor(int color);
/* use any color 0 – 15 for foreground */

        void textattr(int attribute);
/* sets both background & foreground but needs care if you use  the color
  symbols – see example */
```

These functions are called as follows:

```
#include <conio.h>
/* to get the #defined color symbols */
    ...
    textmode(C80);                  /* set color text mode 80x25 */

    textbackground(RED);
/* set background color to red. Turbo C shifts color value left by 4 before
   updating attribute byte. No effect on current display, but subsequent
   cprintf( ), cputs( ) output to screen will reflect new color */

    textcolor(WHITE);
/* set foreground color to white */
    cputs("This is WHITE on RED");

    textattr(WHITE + (RED << 4));
/* same effect as the two previous calls combined. You have to  shift the
   background bit pattern yourself as shown */

    textbackground(RED + BLINK);
/* set background color to blinking red! */
```

► *The Intensity Bit Isolated* ►

You can independently control the intensity bit without affecting the foregound or background colors:

```
    lowvideo( );
/* reduce brightness only by turning off intensity bit */
    highvideo( );
/* increase brightness only by setting the intensity bit */
```

To restore the text attribute to its original state, you use **normvideo( )** as follows:

```
    normvideo( );
/* restore background and foregound to attribute in force when the program
   started */
```

► *Delayed Effects* ►

Note that changing attributes and modes seldom affects the current display—you are setting things up to change the text that you output subsequently. Plan ahead! (One rare exception is when you change a palette index on the EGA adapter. The colors are immediately changed on the existing display, providing an opportunity for psychedelic effects that some users, alas, find hard to resist.)

► *The Monochrome Attribute* ►

If you use these color-change calls on a monochrome adapter/monitor, the attribute bit pattern will be interpreted somewhat differently. The intensity and blinking bits work identically, but color bits allow only four distinct combinations:

- ► Normal "white-on-black" corresponds to attribute value 0x07, which means that you can usually use **normvideo( )** to restore monochrome displays to "normal." In Program 9.1 you'll see that **text color(WHITE);** and **textbackground(BLACK);** also work.

- ► Underline, obtained with attribute value 0x01, corresponds to **text color(BLUE);** and **textbackground(BLACK);**.

- ► Reverse video, obtained with attribute value 0x70, corresponds to **textcolor(BLACK);** and **textbackground(WHITE);**.

- ► Hidden, relates to attribute value 0x00, the same as **textcolor (BLACK);** and **background(BLACK);**. This can be useful for certain animated titling tricks.

On each of these you can superimpose high intensity and blinking, although it's hardly useful with hidden characters! You should experiment on your system to see the effect of combinations such as flashing reverse video, highlighted underlines, ad nauseam. The following all work as you might expect:

```
normvideo( );          /* set to normal */
lowvideo( );           /* set to low intensity */
highvideo( );          /* set to high intensity */
```

As with color, these functions set the attributes for all subsequent characters displayed with **cprintf( )** or whatever. When you see the TC menu letters highlighted, you know that someone has programmed a sequence such as

```
textmode(MONO);
highvideo( );
```

```
cputs("C");                  /* unlike puts( ) no newline with cputs( )! */
normvideo( );                /* or lowvideo( ) */
cputs("ompile");
```

If you are doing a lot of this, you could write a general function to display any string with the first letter highlighted.

► TEXT WINDOW MANAGEMENT ►

Even if you have a text-only monochrome adapter you can still have fun with the Turbo C window tools. TWINDOW.C (Program 9.1) lets you experiment with the basic text and window functions. It also introduces the functions that move whole regions of text around the screen.

► Analysis of TWINDOW.C ►

Did you remember to add GRAPHICS.LIB to the TWINDOW.PRJ file? The comments should explain most of the tricks. Once you have TWINDOW.C running, it's a good idea to create a header file, MYGRAPH.H, with your own defines and macros. You can put #include <conio.h> and #include <graphics> in MYGRAPH.H so that the one #include <mygraph.h> pulls in the lot.

I have used just some of the available IBM extended ASCII symbols to create two window-framing styles. Since I use **gotoxy( )** to draw borders, some care is needed when you define the rectangle corners within or without a window.

The only reason for linking GRAPHICS.LIB in TWINDOW.C was to allow the use of **detectgraph( )** and **getmoderange( )**. (All other functions used are text-mode functions from CONIO.H.) These functions reveal what adapters are fitted without actually moving into graphics mode. I'll defer a full discussion until the section on graphics modes.

► The gettext( ) and puttext( ) Functions

These functions are used to switch the contents of my two windows. The prototypes reveal their usage.

```
int gettext(int left, int top, int right, int bottom, void *destination);

int puttext(int left, int top, int right, int bottom, void *source);
```

You define a rectangle using absolute coordinates, and it may or may not coincide with an active window. For **gettext( )**, you name a pointer to

```
/* twindow.c -- test text window functions */

#include <conio.h>
#include <graphics.h>

#define H_LINE   '\xC4'     /* IBM Extended ASCII */
#define V_LINE   '\xB3'
#define DH_LINE  '\xCD'
#define DV_LINE  '\xBA'

#define TLC      '\xDA'     /* top left corner etc */
#define TRC      '\xBF'
#define BLC      '\xC0'
#define BRC      '\xD9'
#define DTLC     '\xC9'     /* double-edged borders */
#define DTRC     '\xBB'
#define DBLC     '\xC8'
#define DBRC     '\xBC'

#define SINGLE_BORDER 1
#define TWIN_BORDER   2
#define UNDERLINE       textcolor(BLUE); textbackground(BLACK);
/* alternative to underline() */

     struct text_info mytext;
/* global: gives status of window, attributes, etc. */


/* the following functions show how the text attributes interpret
 * those used for color selection
 */
void underline(void)
{
    textcolor(BLUE);
    textbackground(BLACK);
}

void reversevideo(void)
{
    textcolor(BLACK);
    textbackground(WHITE);
}

void hide(void)
{
    textcolor(BLACK);
    textbackground(BLACK);
}


/* TEXT MODES ONLY */
/* MY_HLINE() draws selected char from (startx,starty) to
 * (endx,starty) = horizontal line.  Returns number of chars
 * drawn.  startx may be greater than endx.  Cursor ends up
 * in position following last char displayed.
 * coordinates are relative to active window
 */
int my_hline(int startx, int starty, int endx, char line_char)
{
```

► *Program 9.1:* TWINDOW.C

```
        int i;
        gotoxy(startx, starty);
        if (startx == endx) return(0);
        if (startx < endx) {
           for ( i=startx; i <= endx; i++)
               putch(line_char);
           return (i-startx);
        }
        gotoxy(endx,starty);
        for ( i=endx; i <= startx; i++)   /* endx < startx */
           putch(line_char);
        return (i-endx);
}

/* TEXT MODES ONLY */
/* MY_VLINE() draws a vertical line from (startx,starty)
 * to  (startx,endy).   starty can be greater than endy.
 * line_char is selected line symbol
 *  coordinates are relative to active window
 */

int my_vline(int startx, int starty, int endy, char line_char)
{
        int i;
/* no gotoxy needed here */
        if (starty == endy) return(0);
        if (starty < endy) {
           for ( i=starty; i <=endy; i++) {
               gotoxy(startx,i);
               putch(line_char);
           }
           return (i-starty);
        }
        for ( i=endy; i <= starty; i++) {
           gotoxy(startx,i);
           putch(line_char);
        }
        return (endy - i);
}

/* TEXT MODES ONLY */
/* MY_RECT draws a rectangle for top--left = (tlx,tly)
 *bottom--right = (brx,bry).  style=1 gives single border
 * style=2 gives double border
 */
int my_rect(int tlx, int tly, int brx, int bry, int style)
{
        int w, h;
        char hline_ch, vline_ch, tlc, trc, brc, blc;
        switch(style) {
            case 1;
            case 0;
               hline_ch = H_LINE;
               vline_ch = V_LINE;

               tlc = TLC; trc = TRC;
               brc = BRC; blc = BLC;
               break;
            case 2:
               hline_ch = DH_LINE;
               vline_ch = DV_LINE;
               tlc = DTLC; trc = DTRC;
               brc = DBRC; blc = DBLC;
               break;
             default:
               return(0);
```

► **Program 9.1:** *TWINDOW.C (continued)*

```
        gotoxy(tlx,tly);
        putch(tlc);
        w = my_hline(tlx+1,tly,brx-1,hline_ch);
        putch(trc);
        h = my_vline(brx,tly+1,bry-1,vline_ch);
        gotoxy(brx,bry);
        putch(brc);
        my_hline(brx-1,bry,tlx+1,hline_ch);
        gotoxy(tlx,bry);
        putch(blc);
        my_vline(tlx,bry-1,tly+1,vline_ch);
        return(w*h);                        /* area enclosed */
}


void main(void)
{

        int graphmode;
        int graphdriver;
        int himode, lomode;
        char savewin1[300], savewin2[300];

        directvideo = 1;
/* = 0 means use ROM-BIOS calls; = 1 means use video RAM directly
  */

        detectgraph(&graphdriver, &graphmode);
/* check the video hardware -- find highest resolution mode */

        getmoderange(graphdriver, &lomode, &himode);
        textmode(MONO);
/* set to 80 x 25 monochrome -- normal text-only, non--graphics DA
 */

        gettextinfo(&mytext);
/* get current text mode and window position */

        my_rect(9, 7, 49, 20, SINGLE_BORDER);

        my_rect(10, 8, 48, 11, TWIN_BORDER);

        window( 11, 9, 47, 10);

        gotoxy(2, 1);      /* relative coordinates */
        reversevideo();
        cprintf("driver = %d, max mode = %d",graphdriver, graphmode);
        gettext(12, 9, 47, 9, savewin1);
/* save window text in array savewin1 */
        normvideo();
        window(1,1,80,25);
        my_rect(10,  14,   48,  17, TWIN_BORDER);
        window( 11,  15,   47,  16);

        gotoxy(2,1);          /* = 12,15 absolute */
/*      underline(); or try the macro */
        UNDERLINE
        cprintf("TxtMode = %d,Winleft = %d,Wintop = %d",
        mytext.currmode, mytext.winleft, mytext.wintop);
        gotoxy(2,2);          /* = 12,16 absolute */
        normvideo();
        cprintf("Lomode = %d, Himode = %d",lomode,himode);
        gettext(12, 15, 47, 16, savewin2);
/* save the given screen text area in array savewin2 */
        normvideo(); highvideo();
        cputs(" <CR>..");  getch();
```

► **Program 9.1:** *TWINDOW.C (continued)*

```
/* temp pause - hit any key */
    gotoxy(1,1);
    clrscr();               /* clear text window 2 */
    puttext(12, 15, 47, 15, savewin1);
/* switch window 1 to window 2 */
    window( 11, 9, 47, 10);
    gotoxy(1,1);
    clrscr();
    puttext(12, 9, 47, 10, savewin2);
/* switch window 2 to window 1 */
}
```

► *Program 9.1:* TWINDOW.C (continued)

receive a copy of the display RAM holding this text area. Be clear on the fact that this includes both ASCII and attribute bytes for each character. The destination must therefore be large enough, i.e., at least 2 × height × width of the text area.

puttext( ) reverses the process by sending the bytes starting at ***source** to the display RAM representing the rectangle. As you can see in TWIN-DOW.C, this allows text to be moved without losing its attributes. The source and destination memory can be arrays or **malloc**ed. **puttext( )** sends the text sequentially, so if you are sending text to an active window you may get scrolling and a different physical layout. Try changing the window sizes to see the impact of this.

The returned **int** value for both functions is 1 for success, 0 for failure. Failure usually indicates that illegal rectangles for the particular mode were specified. You can guess that programs meant to operate on many different video boards would have to check **text_info.screenheight** and the other parameters to avoid illegal coordinates.

There is a simpler function, **movetext( )**, which displays a copy of a rectangle of text in another region of the screen. **movetext( )** is really a copy-text function. It assumes that your destination area is the same size as the source, so you need to specify only the source rectangle and one corner of the destination rectangle. The source display is not affected unless the rectangles overlap. A typical call might be

```
    movetext(10, 1, 14, 3, 16, 12);
/* copy text in rectangle (10,1)/(14,3) to (16,12/(20,14) */
```

All coordinates are absolute. The last two give the destination top left position, so simple arithmetic supplies the other corners. If the destination rectangle is all or part of an active window you may get bizarre results. Because of scrolling, the copy text may not appear the same as the source.

► *SUMMARY OF TEXT-MODE FUNCTIONS* ►

I now list the prototypes and summarize each text function in related groups. (As an additional aid, Appendix G contains a description of each text and graphics function with cross references and brief examples of use when appropriate.)

► *Text Mode Control*

```
void textmode(int mode);
/* set text mode – set full screen window – set normvideo */
```

► *Text-Window Control*

```
void window(int abs_top_left_x, int abs_top_left_y,
            int abs_bottom_right_x, int abs_bottom_right_y);
/* define active window */
```

► *Text I/O*

```
int cprintf(const char *format_string[,args...]);
/* formatted output to active window – return number of bytes */

int cputs(const *string);
/* output string to active window – return last char */

int putch(char ch);
/* output char to active window – return same char */

int getche(void);
/* returns a keyboarded char with echo to active window */
```

► *Text Manipulation*

```
void gotoxy(int rel_x, int rel_y);
/* move cursor to window – relative cell if possible, else ignore */

void clrscr(void);
/* clear the active window – then gotoxy(1,1); /
```

```
     void clreol(void);
/* clear from CP to end of line in active window — CP unchanged */

     void delline(void);
/* delete whole line in active window containing CP — move up any  lower
   lines — CP unchanged */

     void insline(void);
/* generate blank line in active window at CP with current background color.
   Scroll down any lower text lines */

     int movetext(abs_top_left_x, abs_top_left_y,   abs_bottom_right_x,
                  abs_bottom_right_y,
                  abs_new_top_left_x, abs_new_top_y);
/* copy screen text from one rectangle to another of the same  size.
   Returns TRUE for success, FALSE for failure */
```

► *Text Screen-Memory Transfers*

```
     int gettext(abs_top_left_x, abs_top_left_y,   abs_bottom_right_x,
                 abs_bottom_right_y,
                 void *destination);
/* copy from screen rectangle to memory at destination pointer.  Two bytes
   transferred per cell, character and attribute, so  Height*width*2 bytes
   are transferred. Returns TRUE for  success, FALSE for failure */

     int puttext(abs_top_left_x, abs_top_left_y,   abs_bottom_right_x,
                 abs_bottom_right_y,
                 void *source);
/* copy from memory at source pointer to screen rectangle. Two bytes
   needed per cell, character and attribute. Height*width*2  bytes are
   transferred. Returns TRUE for success, FALSE for failure */
```

► *Text Attribute Controls*

```
     void textcolor(int color);
/* select cell foreground color 0 — 15 with optional BLINK */

     void textbackground(int color);
/* select cell background color 0 — 7 */

     void textattr(int attribute_byte);
/* set cell attributes, foreground and background with optional BLINK */
```

```
          void highvideo(void);
/* set high intensity bit of current foreground color */

          void lowvideo(void);
 /* clear high intensity bit of current foreground color */

          void normvideo(void);
/* restore background and foreground attributes to normal state */
```

► Text-Mode Status Queries

```
          void gettextinfo(struct text_info *info_ptr);
/* set the fields in the text_info structure pointed at by info_ptr. The fields
    give you winleft, wintop, winright,  winbottom, attribute, normattr,
    currmode, screenheight,  screenwidth, curx, and cury */

          int wherex(void);
/* returns window – relative column coordinate of CP */

          int wherey(void);
/* returns window – relative row coordinate of CP */
```

► GRAPHICS MODES ►

Getting into a graphics mode is slightly more difficult than getting into text modes because there are more choices. Corresponding to **textmode( )** is the function **initgraph( )**, which initializes the system for the graphics board and mode of your choice and loads the appropriate driver.

► The initgraph( ) Function ►

initgraph( ) needs three arguments:

► *int *graphdriver*   The graphics driver is given by an integer or enumeration mnemonic. This must be passed as a pointer to an **int** variable since **initgraph( )** can alter its value under certain circumstances. If you pass the special driver argument **DETECT**, or 0, **initgraph( )** *auto-detects* a driver to match your hardware and tells you which driver, if any, was loaded. I'll tell you more about this when I discuss the **detectgraph( )** function.

► *int *graphmode*   The graphics mode is also an integer or mnemonic passed as a pointer to int. This parameter can also be set automatically using the **DETECT** driver argument.

► *char *driver_path_string*   The path string indicates where the driver .BGI file can be found. If the driver file is not found in the indicated directory, a search is made in your current directory. If all your .BGI files are in the current directory, you can use the NULL string path, '''' (two double quotes). If you invoke any of the stroked graphics fonts this path will also be used to locate the .CHR files, so it's wise to keep all .BGI and .CHR files in the same directory (usually \turboc). Remember that the DOS path symbol \ must be written "\\" inside the driver path string. (The use of "\" as an escape character was explained in Chapter 1.)

The initgraph( ) prototype in GRAPHICS.H is

```
void far initgraph(int far *graphdriver, int far *graphmode,
                   char far *driver_path_string);
```

The **far** modifiers are needed because the one graphics library serves all Turbo C memory models.

The following snippet provides a useful template for simple graphics work. Two simple graphics functions, **graphresult( )** and **closegraph( )**, are introduced.

```
#include <stdio.h>
#include <graphics.h>
    ...
    int graphdriver;
    int graphmode;
    int graph_error;
    ...
    graphmode = CGAC0; graphdrive = CGA;
/* enumerated in graphics.h */
/* vary these settings to suit your hardware */

    initgraph(&graphdriver, &graphmode, "c:\\turboc\\");
/* initialize system for CGA graphics 320x200, palette C0.
    graphmode is set to -2 thru -5 to indicate errors.
    Or you can call graphresult( ) to test for success */

    graph_error = graphresult( );
/* sets graph_error to zero if initgraph was successful.
```

Negative results of − 2 thru − 15 indicate diverse errors.
graphresult( ) reports errors after any graphics operation */

```
        if (graph_error < 0) {
                puts( grapherrormsg(graph_error));
/* converts graph_error to proper error message string */
                exit(1);
        }
/* here you can do your graphics stuff */
        ...
        closegraph( );
/* free all graphics memory allocations and revert to previous
   (pre – initgraph) mode */
```

CGA and CGAC0 are driver and mode mnemonics as enumerated in GRAPHICS.H. Turbo C supplies ten graphics drivers supporting a wide range of modes, as shown in the description of initgraph( ) in Appendix G.

► *The Auto-Detect Feature* ►

It is not easy to write universal PC programs that will work without prior knowledge of the adapter or monitor fitted. About the only lowest common device you can rely upon is the text-only MDA.

Turbo C offers the detectgraph( ) to give you some help. It detects which graphics adapter is fitted (if any) and tells you the highest resolution mode on that adapter's driver. detectgraph( ) can be called directly or indirectly. The direct call is made as follows:

```
#include <stdio.h>
#include <graphics.h>
        ...
        int graphdriver;
        int graphmode;
        ...
        detectgraph(&graphdriver, &graphmode);
        if (graphdriver < 0) {
                puts("Cannot detect a graphics card!");
                exit(1);
        }
/* graphdriver and graphmode now set with highest resolution  mode on
   adapter fitted */
        printf("\nCard detected is #%d, Hi-res mode is #%d",
                                graphdriver,        graphmode);
/* BUT graphics mode not initialized until you call initigraph( )  */
```

The indirect call to **detectgraph( )** occurs as follows:

```
#include <stdio.h>
#include <graphics.h>
      ...
      int graphdriver;
      int graphmode;
      int graph_error;

      ...
      graphdriver = DETECT;

      initgraph(&graphdriver, &graphmode, " ");
/* initgraph( ) will call detectgraph( ) for you and initialize
   system for the autodetected adapter.  graphdriver is set to
   the selected driver and graphmode is set to mode with highest
   resolution for that driver */

/* BUT if no graphics card fitted, graphdriver set to −2. So  test here,
   either: if (graphdriver < 0) or use graphresult( ) */
      graph_error = graphresult( );
      if (graph_error < 0) {
            puts( graperrormsg(graph_error));
            exit(1);
      }

/* now you can do your graphics stuff */
      ...
      closegraph( );
```

When you call **initgraph( )** with **graphdriver** set to the value **DETECT**,
initgraph( ) calls **detectgraph( )** internally to determine the available adapter. If it finds one, **initgraph( )** goes ahead and initializes on that basis. The chosen driver and mode are returned in **graphdriver** and **graphmode**—which explains why you have to use **&graphdriver** and **&graphmode** as arguments.

In view of this inner call, you may well ask if a direct call to **detectgraph( )** is ever needed. The answer is that you may wish to determine which adapter is fitted but not select its highest resolution mode. Consider the following:

```
/* same declarations as previous snippet */
      detectgraph(&graphdriver, &graphmode);
      if (graphdriver < 0) {
            puts("Cannot detect a graphics card!");
            exit(1);
      }
```

```
/* graphdriver and graphmode now set with highest resolution mode on
        adapter fitted */
            printf("\nCard detected is #%d, Hi-res mode is #%d",
                                graphdriver,       graphmode);
        /* BUT graphics mode not yet initialized until you initigraph( ) */

    if (graphdriver == CGA && graphmode == CGAHI)
            graphmode = CGAC3;
        else if (graphdriver == EGA && graphmode == EGAHI)
            graphmode = EGALO;

    ...
    /* override the detectgraph selection */
        initgraph(&graphdriver, &graphmode, "");
```

► *The closegraph( ) Function* ►

The **closegraph( )** function simply terminates the graphics mode established by **initgraph( )**. The memory allocated to the driver, fonts, and buffers is deallocated, and the original video mode is restored.

► *Switching Modes* ►

To switch to another graphics mode for the same driver you do not have to **closegraph( )** and reinitialize. Three functions, **getgraphmode( )**, **setgraphmode( )**, and **restorecrtmode( )** give you flexible control when switching and restoring modes. Consider the following extract:

```
/* usual #includes */
    ...
    int curr_mode;
    int graphdriver = ATT400;
    int graphmode = ATT400C1;
    ...
/* program starts in text mode */
/* now initgraph with ATT400 driver */
    initigraph(&graphdriver, &graphmode, "");
    curr_mode = getgraphmode( );
/* save the current mode */
    ...
/* do something in ATT400C1 mode */
    restorecrtmode( );
/* temporary switch to text mode ruling before initgraph.
```

```
        Screen cleared */
            puts("Now in text mode!");
            ...
            setgraphmode(curr_mode);
    /* Screen is again cleared and mode restored to ATT400C1 */
            ...
            graphmode = ATT400C0;
            setgraphmode(graphmode);
    /* switch modes – provided graphmode is valid for current driver. Screen is
        cleared and all graphics parameters set to their defaults */
            ...
    /* do something in ATT400C0 mode... */
            setgraphmode(curr_mode);
    /* Screen is again cleared and all graphics parameters set to their defaults.
        Mode restored to ATT400C1 */
            ...
```

As you can see, it is possible to switch graphics modes and also slip back into text mode without the overhead of **initgraph( )**.

► Graphics-Mode Applications ►

Once you have successfully called **initgraph( )**, you have at your command all the spectacular display effects provided in the Turbo C toolbox: lines, arcs, polygons, bars in two and three dimensions, circles, ellipses, and any creative combinations possible. You can set colors (if you have them), line styles, and fill patterns from a given repertory or design your own. You can write text in any of the five fonts, horizontally or vertically, with various magnifications and justification formats.

As a starter, TFONT.C (Program 9.2) determines a few facts about the adapter you have, then explores the various fonts available.

TFONT.C reveals some new functions that require some explanation.

► The getmaxx( ) and getmaxy( ) Functions

getmaxx( ) and **getmaxy( )** return **int** values for the maximum X and Y coordinates for the current resolution. On my Hercules clone, **maxx** equals 719, and **maxy** equals 347 [remember the screen starts at (0,0)].

```
/* Program 9--2 */
/* tfont -- check your adapter & play with graphics fonts */

#include <conio.h>
#include <graphics.h>
#include <stdlib.h>

void main(void)
{

      int nexty = 0;

      int graphmode, graphdriver;
      int curr_mode;

      int font, direction, charsize = 0;

      int xasp, yasp, maxx, maxy;
/* aspect ratios and max coordinates */

      directvideo = 1;
/* try = 1 or 0 to see if you are fully IBM PC compatible */

      textmode(MONO);

/* see what cards you have in there */
      detectgraph(&graphdriver, &graphmode);
      clrscr();
      gotoxy(10,12);
      cprintf("\nMy driver = %d, Hires mode = %d\n",
                          graphdriver, graphmode);
/* above gets me 7 (hercmono) and 0 (720x348 2 color) */
      gotoxy(10,20);
      puts("Hit any key..."); getch();
/* pause to note values */
      clrscr();
      graphmode = HERCMONOHI;
      graphdriver = HERCMONO;
/* set your own here -- or leave detectgraph's settings */

      initgraph(&graphdriver, &graphmode, "c:\\turboc\\");
/* gotcher! the \ needs the \ escape char, so \\ for paths */

      curr_mode = graphmode;
/* save mode for later */

       maxx = getmaxx();    maxy = getmaxy();
/* find max values of x and y coordinates */
      getaspectratio(&xasp, &yasp);
/* get aspect ratio */
      restorecrtmode();
/* temp flip back to text mode */

      gotoxy(20,10);
      cprintf("\nMax coordinates: X = %d, Y = %d\n", maxx, maxy);
      cprintf("\nAspect ratio is %d:%d = %6.4f\n",
      yasp,xasp,(float)yasp/xasp);
/* to display values */

      gotoxy(12,23);
      puts("Hit any key..."); getch();

      setgraphmode(curr_mode);
/* back to previous graphics mode with clear screen */
```

► *Program 9.2: TFONT.C*

```
        font = DEFAULT_FONT;
        direction = HORIZ_DIR;
        charsize = 3;
/* magnifies only the bit-mapped font. For stroked fonts,
    charsize = 0 allows setusercharsize() to do fine
    width/height adjustments */

        moveto(50,1);
/* graphics modes do not use gotoxy! */
    for (font = DEFAULT_FONT; font <= GOTHIC_FONT; font++) {
        if (font > DEFAULT_FONT) {
            charsize = 0;
            setusercharsize(4, 3, 3, 2);
/* increase font height 4:3, increase width 3:2 */
            if (font == SMALL_FONT) setusercharsize (2, 1, 7, 5);
/* give the small font an extra boost */
        }
        settextstyle(font, direction, charsize);
/* set font, horizontal, size */
        outtext("Hello Graphics Font World!");
        nexty += textheight("H");
/* you have to create your own newlines according to font heights
*/

        moveto(50,nexty + 10);
    }
        moveto(50,300);
/* you are still in gothic_font here...*/
        outtext("Can you see this? Hit any key..");
        getche();
        cleardevice();
/* clear graphics screen -- ready for more fun? */
/* try the vertical direction display with various fonts */
/* Always end with...*/
        closegraph();

}
```

► **Program 9.2:** *TFONT.C (continued)*

► *The getaspectratio( ) Function*

getaspectratio(&xasp, &yasp); sets two integer values from which you can calculate the aspect ratio. The **yasp** value is normalized to 10,000. Most pixels are taller than they are wide, so **xasp** is usually less than 10,000. My value of **xasp** is 7,500, giving an aspect ratio of 1.3333. You have to multiply the width of a square by this number in order to draw a rectangle that really looks square! For example, the following snippet will display a rectangular square,

```
        int xasp, yasp;
        long width, side;
        ...
        getaspectratio(&xasp, &yasp);
        width = side * (long)yasp / long(xasp);
/* improve on int/int accuracy. Aliter: you could cast to float */
        rectangle(0, 0, (int)width, (int)side);
```

Note that you have to be in graphics mode to get aspect ratios, hence the flip back to text mode to use **cprintf( )** in TFONT.C.

► *The moveto( ) Function*

You must use **moveto( )** to change the CP in graphics modes (in contrast to **gotoxy( )** for text modes). **moveto( )** and **gotoxy** share an important property—their (X,Y) arguments are relative, not absolute. The **moveto( )** arguments operate relative to a viewport (the graphics equivalent to a text window). TFONT.C has not used an explicit **setviewport( )**, so it operates with the default viewport, namely the whole screen. **moverel(***dx, dy***)** is a related function that is CP-relative. It moves the CP *dx* pixels along the X axis and *dy* pixels along the Y axis.

setviewport( ) works much like its text cousin, **window( )**. You give it four coordinates for the top left and bottom right corners, but you also provide a clip flag that determines if drawings are clipped at the viewport boundaries (clip flag nonzero) or not (clip flag zero). To find out all about the currently active viewport you call **getviewsettings( )**, which fills up a structure defined as follows:

```
struct viewporttype {
int left, top, right, bottom;
int clipflag;
{
    ...
struct viewporttype my_view;
    ...
getviewsettings(&my_view);
/* now look at my_view.left etc. */
```

► *The settextstyle( ) and Allied Functions*

settextstyle( ) is best studied alongside the three related functions **gettextsettings( )**, **setusercharsize( )**, and **settextjustify( )**. Despite their names these are all graphics functions (graphics-text, not text-text). The prototypes are

```
void far gettextsettings
        (struct textsettingtype far *textinfo);

void far settextjustify(int horiz, int vert);

void far settextstyle(int font,
            int direction, int charsize);

void setusercharsize(int xmul, int xdiv,
                int ymul, int ydiv);
```

As a general rule, there is a **get...( )** for every **set...( )** (or group of **set...( )**s) in the graphics library. **get..( )**s serve two purposes—finding out what's been set and saving settings for a quick restoration later on. The structure **textset tingstype** is declared as follows:

```
struct textsettingstype {
        int font;
        int direction;
        int charsize;
        int horiz;
        int vert;
};
```

When you call **gettextsettings( )** with a pointer to a variable of this structure type, the member variables are set with the current values:

```
        struct textsettingstype my_text;
        ...
        gettextsettings(&my_text);
 /* now my_text.font, etc. gives the current settings */
```

The setting functions control how **outtext( )** and **outtextxy( )** display strings, in terms of size, direction, and placement relative to the CP.

GRAPHICS.H has several useful enumerations giving the mnemonics listed in Tables 9.4, 9.5, and 9.6.

Justification operates in conjunction with the direction setting. "Justification" in this context refers to how each character is positioned relative to the CP and must not be confused with the more common process of ensuring that a line of text is stretched to give a flush margin.

You call **settextjustify( )** with two **int** arguments indicating the horizontal and/or vertical justification required. If there is no such call, the system takes its defaults from the direction value used in **settextstyle( )**. In the absence of a **settextstyle( )** call, the system assumes **DEFAULT_FONT** with **HORIZ_DIR**. You should experiment with these values in TFONT.C to see their effects.

The **charsize** argument magnifies all fonts unless set to 0, when it affects only the stroked fonts. Setting **charsize** to 2, for example, will display the default font on a 16 × 16 grid. The maximum magification is 10. If **charsize** is 0, the stroked fonts only can be more finely tuned by applying fractional

Font Name	Value	Meaning
DEFAULT_FONT	0	8 × 8 bit-mapped font (default)
TRIPLEX_FONT	1	Stroked triple font
SMALL_FONT	2	Stroked small font
SANS_SERIF_FONT	3	Stroked sans-serif font
GOTHIC_FONT	4	Stroked gothic font

► **Table 9.4:** *Font names*

Direction Name	Value	Meaning
HORIZ_DIR	0	Display left to right
VERT_DIR	1	Display bottom to top

► **Table 9.5:** *Direction names*

Justification Name	Value	Meaning
LEFT_TEXT	0	Horizontal justification Default for **HORIZ_DIR**
CENTER_TEXT	1	Horizontal and vertical justification
RIGHT_TEXT	2	Horizontal justification
BOTTOM_TEXT	3	Vertical justification
TOP_TEXT	4	Vertical justification Default for **VERT_DIR**

► **Table 9.6:** *Justification names*

adjustments to either height or width, or both. TFONT.C shows how the function **setusercharsize( )** is called with four integers.

```
if (font > DEFAULT_FONT) {
      charsize = 0;
      setusercharsize(4, 3, 3, 2);
/* increase font height 4:3, increase width 3:2 */
         if (font == SMALL_FONT) setusercharsize (2, 1, 7, 5);
/* give the small font an extra boost */
}
```

The general format is

setusercharsize(xmul, xdiv, ymul, ydiv);

which applies the factor (**xmul/xdiv**) to the current character width and (**ymul/ydiv**) to the current character height. Make sure that **charsize** is 0 and that both **xdiv** and **ydiv** are nonzero!

► Keeping Track of the Old CP ►

Because of all these different character-size possibilities, you can have a hard time deciding where the CP is after an **outtext( )** display. The following functions help you keep track of the CP.

► The getx( ) and gety( ) Functions

getx( ) and **gety( )** return the viewport-relative pixel coordinates. They correspond to the **wherex( )** and **wherey( )** text functions.

► The textheight( ) and textwidth( ) Functions

textheight(*string*) and **textwidth(*string*)** return the number of pixels in the argument string in the Y and X directions, respectively. They look at the current font style and size and calculate the number of pixels in either direction.

When **outtext( )** displays a string in the horizontal direction with **LEFT_TEXT** justification, the X coordinate of the CP advances by **textwidth(*string*)**. In all other cases the CP is unchanged.

TFONT.C uses **textheight( )** to simulate a new line that depends on the font style used. Liberal use of **textheight( )** and **textwidth( )** is recommended to keep programs font independent.

► *Loading Fonts with BGIOBJ* ►

I mentioned earlier that the .BGI and .CHR files must be loaded dynamically from disk as the program calls on them. They must be either in the driver default path of **initgraphg( )** or in your current directory. To save time, you can use the BGIOBJ utility to convert any .BGI or .CHR file into an .OBJ file at the expense of larger .EXE files. You do this as follows:

C>BGIOBJ TRIP.CHR

which will create TRIP.OBJ from the triplex font file. To tell the linker that TRIP.OBJ must be linked to TFONT.OBJ, you can add TRIP.OBJ to GRAPHICS.LIB as follows:

TLIB GRAPHICS + TRIP

where the .OBJ extension of TRIP is implied by default. TLIB.EXE is the new library manager supplied with Version 1.5 of Turbo C. As shown above, one of its functions is to incorporate .OBJ files into an existing library. TLIB can also build new libraries and maintain them by adding and deleting .OBJ files as required. (I'll explain TLIB in greater detail in Chapter 10.)

Alternatively, you can add the name TRIP.OBJ to your .PRJ file. With the TCC.EXE command-line compiler you can add TRIP.OBJ on either the TCC or TLINK command. Exactly the same process is involved if you want to incorporate a driver file into a library.

One more task is needed to warn your program that TRIP.OBJ is available. You must *register* TRIP and any other font or driver modules involved by invoking the routine **registerbgifont( )** (for fonts) or **registerbgidriver( )** (for drivers) before calling **initgraph( )**. The single argument for the registering routines is one of the symbolic array names defined as follows:

Driver File (.BGI)	registerbgidriver( ) arg
CGA	CGA_driver
EGAVGA	EGAVGA_driver
HERC	Herc_driver
ATT	ATT_driver
IBM8514	IBM8514_driver
PC3270	PC3270_driver

Font File (.CHR)	registerbgifont( ) arg
TRIP	triplex_font
LITT	small_font
SANS	sansserif_font
GOTH	gothic_font

Note carefully that the lowercase spellings differ from the font and driver enumerations used in **initgraph( )** and **settextstyles( )**.

The registering routines return a negative number to signal an error (such as font not found). Otherwise they return a driver or font number, so you test for success as follows:

```
if(registerbgifont(triplex_font) != TRIPLEX_FONT) exit(1);
...
initgraph(&graphdriver, &graphmode, "" );
...
```

On the smaller memory models you may run into the 64KB barrier if you try linking too many fonts and drivers.

Once TRIP.OBJ and CGA.OBJ, say, are linked into TFONT.EXE, they are available without the disk-access overhead, and the program can run on systems that do not have the TRIP.CHR or CGA.BGI files available (providing added security, in fact).

► *More Queries on the Graphics Status* ►

Here are a few more simple functions that report on what you have, where you are, and so on.

Note first that the Turbo C mode values listed under **initgraph( )** in Appendix G do not correspond in every case with the IBM video-byte values given in Table 9.1. For each driver the Turbo C mode numbers range from **lomode** (lowest resolution, usually 0) to **himode** (highest resolution). Some boards, of course, offer only one resolution. These limits can be found using the function **getmoderange( )**, while **getgraphmode( )** tells you the mode you are in.

```
int graphmode, my_mode;
int graphdriver;
int himode, lomode;
```

```
        detectgraph(&graphdriver, &graphmode);
/* check the video hardware – find highest resolution mode */
        initgraph(&graphdriver, &graphmode, "");
/* go for it */
        getmoderange(graphdriver, &lomode, &himode);
/* gives 0 - 5 for ATT400; 0 – 0 for HERC; 0 – 4 for CGA etc */
        my_mode = getgraphmode( );
/* save it for later */
```

► *Drawing Lines and Filling Polygons* ►

The most pleasurable aspect of computer graphics is seeing pages of boring code spring to life on the screen. There's no way I can do justice to this vast subject, on which whole libraries and industries have been built. Once you see how the functions for each pictorial element are invoked, it is really up to your artistic imagination to take over. Let's start with a simple example, TGRAF.C (Program 9.3) which fills the screen with randomly shaded circles. It introduces many of the basic functions.

To understand the drawing functions, you must know how to set the style and thickness of the line elements.

```
    /* Program 9--3 */
    /* tgraf -- check your adapter & draw/fill concentric circles */

    #include <conio.h>
    #include <graphics.h>

    #include <time.h>
    /* needed for random() */

    #include <stdlib.h>

    void main(void)
    {
        int i;
        int cx, cy, cr, cf = 0, dr;
    /* parameters for the circles - center coordinates & radii */

        int max_try;
    /* number of iterations */

        int graphmode, graphdriver;
        int curr_mode;

        int xasp, yasp, maxx, maxy;

    /* aspect ratios and max coordinates */
        textmode(MONO);
        directvideo = 0;
    /* try = 1 or 0 to see if you are fully IDM PC compatible */
```

► *Program 9.3:* TGRAF.C

```
        if (registerbgidriver(Herc_driver) < 0) exit(1);
/* omit this line if you have not created HERC.OBJ with BGIOBJ
   Remember to name graphics.lib and herc.obj in your TGRAF.PRJ
   file -- or use TLIB to add herc.obj to graphics.lib */

        detectgraph(&graphdriver, &graphmode);
/* gets highest res mode for detected driver */

        graphmode = HERCMONOHI;
        graphdriver = HERCMONO;
/* set your own here -- or leave detectgraph's settings */

        initgraph(&graphdriver, &graphmode, "c:\\turboc\\");
/* gotcher! the \ needs the \ escape char, so \\ for paths */

#if 0
/* comment out trick! Code below may be useful for debugging */
        curr_mode = graphmode;
/* save mode for later */
        maxx = getmaxx();    maxy = getmaxy();
/* find max values of x and y coordinates */
        getaspectratio(&xasp, &yasp);
/* get aspect ratio */
#endif

        randomize();
        max_try = 37;
/* set number of circles to be drawn and filled */

    for (i=0; i<=max_try; i++) {

        cx = 40 + random(660);
        cy = 40 + random(280);
        cr = 20 + random(20);
        cf = 1 + random(10);
        dr = 5+random(20);
/* play with above numbers for different effects */
        circle(cx,cy,cr+dr);
/* outer circle radius cr+dr */
        circle(cx, cy, cr);
/* inner circle radius cr */
        setfillstyle(cf,WHITE);
/* random fill pattern 1 -- 10 */
        floodfill(cx,cy,WHITE);
/* floodfill inner circle */
        setfillstyle(1 + random(10),WHITE);
/* get another fill pattern */
        floodfill((cx+cr+2),cy,WHITE);
/* floodfill between the two circles. Any point in area will
   seed the flood */
    }

        moveto(50,300);
        outtext("Can you see this? Hit any key..");
/* this will display in default font */
        getche();
        cleardevice();
/* clear graphics screen -- ready for more fun */

        closegraph();
```

► **Program 9.3:** *TGRAF.C (continued)*

► *What's My Line?*

Before calling any drawing function such as **line( )** or **circle( )**, you have the option to set the line style, using the appositely named function **setlinestyle( )**. This lets you choose one of two line thicknesses and one of five preset line styles, or you can construct your own line texture from a 2-byte bit pattern. **setlinestyle( )** is called like this.

```
int linestyle, thickness;
unsigned upattern;
...
setlinestyle(linestyle, upattern, thickness);
```

The line style and line thickness can be set using the enumeration menomics listed in Tables 9.7 and 9.8.

When line style is set to **USERBIT_LINE** (4), the **upattern** variable must contain your choice of bits to define a line pattern. Bits set to 1 will show, and

Name	Value	Meaning
SOLID_LINE	0	Solid line (default)
DOTTED_LINE	1	Dotted line
CENTER_LINE	2	Centered line
DASHED_LINE	3	Dashed line
USERBIT_LINE	4	User-defined line style

► **Table 9.7:** *Line-style mnemonics*

Name	Value	Meaning
NORM_WIDTH	1	one pixel wide (default)
THICK_WIDTH	3	three pixels wide

► **Table 9.8:** *Line-thickness mnemonics*

bits set to 0 will be hidden as the **upattern** is repeated along the line or curve being drawn. The solid line corresponds to **upattern = 0xFFFF**, and a dashed line could be created with **upattern = 0x3333**. If you are using a precanned shape you must supply a dummy argument in **upattern**. Here are a few examples.

```
        setlinestyle(DOTTED_LINE, 0, THICK_WIDTH);
        rectangle(100,50, 200,100);
    /* draw thick, dotted rectangle */
        unsigned my_pattern = 0x0F03
        setlinestyle(USERBIT_LINE, my_pattern, NORM_WIDTH);
        circle(getmaxx( )/2, getmaxy( )/2, 50);
    /* draw special pattern circle, 1 pixel wide */
    /* Center of circle is center of screen; radius is 50 pixels */
```

Setting line styles does not affect the color attributes in any way. Remember that changing a line style does not affect the screen immediately—the impact is on lines still to be drawn.

The **get...( )** function corresponding to **setlinestyle( )** is called **getline settings( )**. It fills a structure defined in GRAPHICS.H as follows:

```
        struct linesettingstype {
                int linestyle;
                unsigned upattern;
                int thickness;
        }
        ...
        struct linesettingstype my_line
        ...
        getlinesettings(&my_line);
    /* my_line.linestyle, my_line.upattern, my_line_thickness now  give you
        current line settings. Useful for restoring values  later */
```

Passing illegal arguments in any of these functions will set the internal error flag, which you can test by calling **graphresult** as explained earlier.

► *Drawing the Line*

All the coordinates used in the drawing functions are specified relative to the current viewport, the top left corner of which is taken as (0,0). The three functions for drawing linear segments are

```
line(int start_x, start_y, end_x, end_y);
```
/* draws a line in current style/thickness/color from start point to end point
– the CP can be anywhere and it is unchanged */

```
lineto(int end_x, int end_y);
```
/* draw a line in current style/thickness/color from CP to endpoint specified
in window-relative coordinates. The CP moves to this endpoint */

```
linerel(int disp_x, int disp_y);
```
/* draw a line in current style/thickness/color from CP to a point displaced
disp_x pixels in the X direction and disp_y pixels in the Y direction. The
CP moves to this endpoint, given by the coordinates (CPx + disp_x,
CPy + disp_y) */

linerel( ) is easy to remember if you think of a line relative to the current CP. The arguments are not coordinates but relative displacements and are therefore independent of the viewport.

In this context you may remember **moverel(***dx, dy***)**, which moves the CP *dx* pixels along the X axis and *dy* pixels along the Y axis. Like the **linerel( )** function, it can be considered CP relative, rather than absolute or window relative.

► *Polygons*

You could concoct your own triangles and trapezia with the above line segment primitives—but Turbo C makes life easier with a general polygon function. **drawpoly( )** takes two arguments, the number of points to be joined and an array giving their viewport-relative coordinates. An example will explain.

```
int triangle[ ] = {55, 120, 90, 100, 140, 130, 55, 120};
int trapezium[ ] = {80, 100, 100, 100,
                    120, 150, 65, 150, 80, 100};
int open_thing[ ] = {20, 15, 50, 50, 30, 60, 30, 55};

drawpoly(sizeof(triangle)/(2*sizeof(int), triangle);
drawpoly(sizeof(trapezium)/(2*sizeof(int), trapezium);
drawpoly(sizeof(open_thing)/(2*sizeof(int), open_thing);
```

/* even in simple cases it's better to let the machine calculate the number
of points. Note: there are two args for each point */

The above shapes are drawn in the current line style and color, of course, and the coordinates are viewport relative. A closed *n*-sided polygon needs *n* + 1 points since you have to repeat the starting point's coordinates for the end point. In the third example the "polygon" is open, proving that **draw poly( )** simply joins up points in the sequence indicated and gives no thoughts to the geometry of the situation.

► *Circles, Arcs, and Ellipses*

You met the **circle( )** function in TRGRAF.C. It takes three **int** arguments— the center coordinates and the radius. In TGRAF.C I deliberately let some of the circles overflow the screen. By means of **getmaxx( )**, **getmaxy( )**, **getx( )**, and **gety( )** you can reject circles with **(cx + cr)** > **maxx** and **(cx − cr)** < 0, and so on. No harm is done if a drawing exceeds the borders of a viewport, whether it is the whole screen or part of the screen. (A full-screen viewport always clips no matter what the clip flag says!)

The **arc( )** function draws circular arcs, but by setting the parameters in a certain way you can achieve a closed circle. An arc needs five parameters as follows:

```
arc(int x, int y, int st_angle, int end_angle,
      int radius);
```

Figure 9.5 shows the significance of these numbers. **x**, **y**, and **radius** give the center and size of the circle of which the arc is a part. The starting and ending angles of the arc are measured in degrees, where 0 degrees is the west-east line and 90 degrees is the south-north direction. If **st_angle** is 0 and **end_angle** is 360, the arc forms a complete circle.

The **ellipse( )** function actually draws elliptical arcs, but by setting the parameters you can get a closed ellipse. An ellipse needs six parameters as follows:

```
ellipse(int x, int y, int st_angle, int end_angle,
      int xradius, int yradius);
```

(See Figure 9.5.) **x** and **y** give the center of the ellipse, and **xradius** and **yradius** are the horizontal and vertical axes. The starting and ending angles are measured in degrees in the same orientation as given for **arc( )**.

Yet another useful structure-filling and fact-finding **get...( )** routine is **getarccoords( )**. You set a pointer to the following structure:

```
struct arccoordstype {
      int x,y;
      int xstart, ystart, xend, yend;
}
```

and get details about the *last* call to **arc( )** as in

```
      struct arccoordstype noah;
      getarccoords(&noah);
/* noah.x, noah.y give you the center of the last arc drawn.  noah.xtart etc.
   tell you where the last arc started and ended */
```

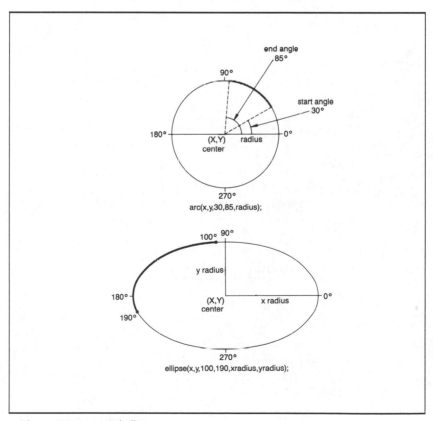

► *Figure 9.5:* Arcs and ellipses

Note carefully that the data obtained include translations of the arguments used in the previous call to **arc( )**—the angles have been converted to give you the window-relative coordinates of the arc's starting and ending points. This information is extremely useful when you are joining arc segments together or are joining them with line segments.

PGRAF.C (Program 9.4) shows you some of these functions in action. Adjust the parameters to suit your monitor and increase your understanding.

```c
/* Program 9--4 */
/* pgraf -- play with polygons */

#include <conio.h>
#include <graphics.h>

#include <time.h>
/* needed for random() */

#include <stdlib.h>

void main(void)
{
        int graphmode, graphdriver;
        int curr_mode;

        int triangle[] = {55, 20, 60, 200, 340, 30, 55, 20};
        int trapezium[] = {280, 100, 500, 100,
                           620, 250, 200, 250, 280, 100};
        int open_thing[] = {20, 15, 650, 150, 30, 260, 100, 55};

        struct arccoordstype noah;

        textmode(MONO);
        directvideo = 0;
/* try = 1 or 0 to see if you are fully IBM PC compatible */

        if (registerbgidriver(Herc_driver) < 0) exit(1);
/* omit this line if you have not created HERC.OBJ with BGIOBJ
   Remember to name graphics.lib and herc.obj in your PGRAF.PRJ
   file - or use TLIB to add herc.obj to graphics.lib */

        detectgraph(&graphdriver, &graphmode);
/* gets highest res mode for detected driver */

        graphmode = HERCMONOHI;
        graphdriver = HERCMONO;
/* set your own here -- or leave detectgraph's settings */

        initgraph(&graphdriver, &graphmode, "c:\\turboc\\");
/* gotcher! the \ needs the \ escape char, so \\ for paths */

        setlinestyle(DOTTED_LINE, 0, NORM_WIDTH);
        drawpoly(sizeof(triangle)/(2*sizeof(int)), triangle);
        moveto(50,300);
        outtext("Hit any key..");
        getche();
```

► *Program 9.4:* PGRAF.C

```
        cleardevice();
        setlinestyle(USERBIT_LINE, 0xFF3A, NORM_WIDTH);
        drawpoly(sizeof(trapezium)/(2*sizeof(int)), trapezium);
        outtext("Hit any key..");
        getche();

        cleardevice();
        circle(350,150,200);
        ellipse(350,150,135,275,200,100);
        arc(550,150,90,180,300);
        getarccoords(&noah);
        line(noah.xend,noah.yend,noah.xend+50,noah.yend);
        outtext("Hit any key..");
        getche();

        cleardevice();
        setlinestyle(DASHED_LINE, 0, THICK_WIDTH);
        drawpoly(sizeof(open_thing)/(2*sizeof(int)), open_thing);
        moveto(50,300);
        settextstyle(GOTHIC_FONT,HORIZ_DIR,4);
        outtext("Hit any key..");
        getche();
        cleardevice();
   /* clear graphics screen -- ready for more fun */

        closegraph();

   }
```

► **Program 9.4:** *PGRAF.C (continued)*

► *Filling In*

In TGRAF.C I filled in sections of each circle using the functions **setfillstyle( )** and **floodfill( )**. The prototypes are shown below. The section of **getfill settings( )** in Appendix G contains a table showing the mnemonics for the fill patterns that you can use.

```
        void setfillstyle(int fill_pattern, int fill_color);
   /* set the fill pattern and color.  fill_pattern can be a preset  or
      user – defined pattern */

        void far floodfill(int x, int y, int border_color);
   /* flood from (x,y) with curent fill pattern and color
      until a region with border_color is reached */
```

The principle is that when you move the CP to any point within a closed figure (known as the flood *seed*) and call **floodfill( )**, the interior of the figure is flooded with the prevailing pattern and color. These parameters are determined by calls to **setfillpattern( )** that use the pattern values shown under **getfillsettings( )** in Appendix G together with color values appropriate to your adapter and palette range (more on color graphics later).

If your CP is outside the closed figure, you get the disconcerting phenomenon known as *overfill*, in which all or part of the surrounding screen is flooded. This also happens if the figure is not strictly closed—the floodfill leaks out and invades more of the screen than you bargained for!

A strict topological definition of "closed" is beyond the scope of this book, but you can imagine that with complex figures made up of arc sequences, overlapping circles and rectangles, and so on, the flood radiates out in all directions until it meets pixels of the color specified by **border_color** or the edge of the current viewport, whichever is nearer. The limits usually coincide with lines and arcs you have previously drawn, but the extent of the floodfill is actually controlled by the enclosing color, not by shapes per se.

EMPTY_FILL can be used to "unfill" by flooding with the current background color.

In TGRAF.C I used **WHITE** as the floodfill border color for my monographics Hercules adapter since this is the "color" used to draw the circles. Similarly, I used **WHITE** as the fill color. The background color for mono displays is treated as **BLACK**, hence the confusing use of the term "2-color" for monochrome systems. The first fill pattern in TGRAF.C was a random number between 1 and 10, and I simply added 1 to this to get the second fill pattern between 2 and 11, thereby avoiding fill pattern 12. The latter is the **USER_FILL** pattern that, like the user-defined line style, has to be created with bit patterns of your own choosing.

To keep track of the current fill pattern and color you use the structure **fillsettingstype**, defined as follows:

```
struct fillsettingstype {
        int pattern;                    /* current fill pattern */
        int color;                      /* current fill color */
};
```

Calling **getfillsettings( )** will load this structure with the current values. This typical **get...( )** function is declared as

```
void getfillsettings(struct fillsettingstype far *fillinfo);
```

so a typical sequence might be

```
struct fillsettingstype curr_fill;
...
setfillstyle(XHATCH_FILL, RED);
```

```
                    /* fill something with heavy red cross hatch */
                        ...
                    getfillsettings(&curr_fill);
            /* saves curr_fill.pattern and curr_fill.color */
                    setfillstyle(LINE_FILL, BLUE);
                        ...
            /* fill something with blue lines */
                        ...
                    setfillstyle(curr_fill.pattern, curr_fill.color);
            /* restore previous fill pattern and color */
```

► *User-Defined Fill Patterns*

To establish and retrieve a personal fill pattern, you must use the functions **setfillpattern( )** and **getfillpattern( )**, which are declared as follows in GRAPHICS.H:

```
            void getfillpattern(char far *far upattern);
        /* copy your 8 – byte pattern to memory at pointer upattern */


            void far setfillpattern(char far *upattern, int color);
        /* upattern is an 8 – byte array defining your fill pattern */
```

The **upattern** is usually declared as an 8-byte array, in which you set bits to 1 for pixel-on positions, as in the following snippet,

```
                struct fillsettingstype curr_fill;

                char save_pattern[8];
                char my_pattern[8] = {
                    0xAA, 0x55, 0xAA, 0x55, 0xAA, 0x55, 0xAA, 0x55 };
        /* bit pattern is 10101010 01010101 repeated */
                    ...
                getfillsettings(&curr_fill);
        /* saves curr_fill.pattern and curr_fill.color */
                if (curr_fill.pattern == USER_FILL)
                getfillpattern(save_pattern);
        /* if current fill is user – defined you need this step to save
            the pattern */
                setfillpattern(my_pattern, YELLOW);
        /* fill something with my_pattern, yellow */
                    ...
                if (curr_fill.pattern == USER_FILL)
                    setfillpattern(save_pattern, curr_fill.color);
                else
```

```
                    setfillstyle(curr_fill.pattern,curr_fill.color);
    /* note different call needed to set a user pattern */
```

► *The fillpoly( ) Variant*

A simpler filling method is available for polygons. The **fillpoly( )** function draws a polygon just as **drawpoly( )** does and then proceeds to fill it using the current fill pattern and color. You do not have to position the CP within the closed figure, but the leak problem will emerge if your polygon is not closed.

fillpoly( ) is declared with the same arguments as **drawpoly( )**:

```
    void far fillpoly(int numpoints, int far *polypoints);
```

The border color does not have to be stated explicity since this is implied by the current drawing color (which is set via **setcolor( )** as you'll see shortly). Here is an example of **fillpoly( )** in action.

```
    /* fillpoly( ) */
        int trapezium[ ] = {280, 100, 500, 100,
                            620, 250, 200, 250, 280, 100};
        ...
        setcolor(BLUE);
    /* set drawing color to blue */
        setfillstyle(SOLID_FILL, RED);
        setlinestyle(SOLID_LINE, 0, NORM_WIDTH);
        fillpoly(sizeof(trapezium)/(2*sizeof(int)), trapezium);
    /* draw blue trapezium and fill with solid red */
```

► *The Bar-Chart and pieslice( ) Functions* ►

To add some graphical pizzazz to you statistical reports, Turbo C offers two bar-chart functions as follows:

```
    void far bar(int left, int top, int right, int bottom);
    /* draws and fills a rectangle with current fill pattern and  color, but without
        outline */

    void far bar3d(int left, int top, int right, int bottom, int depth, int topflag);
    /* draws a 3 – dimensional bar with outline given by current line  style
        setting and current drawing color. The depth is given  in pixels. The
        topflag is set non-zero if you want a top  drawn on your bar.  topflag = 0
```

```
/* Program 9--5 */
/* stats -- display bar charts and pieslices */
/* must LINK graphics.lib */
#include <conio.h>
#include <graphics.h>
#include <stdlib.h>


/* scale() */
/* calculate bar length for given screen  */

int scale(value, factor)
int value, factor;
{
     int maxx;
     maxx = getmaxx();
     return (int)((float)(value)*factor/maxx);
}

void main(void)
{

     int graphmode, graphdriver, cenx, ceny;
     int curr_mode;
     int salesx, i=0;        /* index sales */
     int sales[] = {100, 680, 345};
/* set up a test array of 3 sales values */
     int stangle[2], endangle[2], salestot;
     double anglefactor;
/* for pieslice calculations */
     int fillpattern;
     textmode(MONO);
     directvideo = 1;
/* try = 1 or 0 to see if you are fully IBM PC compatible */

     if (registerbgidriver(Herc_driver) < 0) exit(1);
/* omit this line if you have not created HERC.OBJ with BGIOBJ
   Remember to name graphics.lib and herc.obj in your PGRAF.PRJ
   file - or use TLIB to add herc.obj to graphics.lib */

     detectgraph(&graphdriver, &graphmode);
/* gets highest res mode for detected driver */

     graphmode = HERCMONOHI;
     graphdriver = HERCMONO;
/* set your own here -- or leave detectgraph's settings */

     initgraph(&graphdriver, &graphmode, "c:\\turboc\\");
/* setcolor(); here as required for drawing color */
     cleardevice();
     setlinestyle(SOLID_LINE, 0, NORM_WIDTH);
     setfillstyle(CLOSE_DOT_FILL, WHITE);
/* vary fill color to suit your palette! */
     for (i=0; i<=2; ++i) {
        salesx = scale(sales[i],400);
        bar(0, 10+i*25, salesx, (i+1)*25);
     }
     outtextxy(50, 300, "Hit any key..");
     getche();

     cleardevice();

     for (i=0; i<=2; ++i) {
        salesx = scale(sales[i],400);
        bar3d(0, 10+i*25, salesx, (i+1)*25, 4  ,1);
                                  /*  depth cap */
```

► *Program 9.5:* STATS.C

```
      }
      outtextxy(50, 300, "Hit any key..");
      getche();
      cleardevice();
      cenx = getmaxx()/2; ceny = getmaxy()/2;
      salestot = sales[0] + sales[1] + sales[2];
      anglefactor = (double)360/salestot;
   stangle[0] = 0; endangle[0] = 0 + (int)(sales[0]*anglefactor);
   stangle[1] = endangle[0]; endangle[1] =
                              stangle [1]+ (int)(sales[1]*anglefactor)
   stangle[2] = endangle[1]; endangle[2] = 360;
      fillpattern = LINE_FILL;
      for (i=0; i <= 2; ++i) {
           setfillstyle(++fillpattern, WHITE);
           pieslice(cenx,ceny,stangle[i],endangle[i],200);
      }
      outtextxy(50, 300, "Hit any key..");
      getche();
      cleardevice();

       closegraph();

   }
```

▸ **Program 9.5:** *STATS.C (continued)*

> suppresses the top. The 3d bar is also filled with the current fill pattern
> and color */

You can play some pretty tricks with these routines. If you want a two-dimensional bar with its outline drawn, simply use the three-dimensional version with a zero depth. The bars can be made horizontal or vertical, of course, by setting the appropriate corner coordinates.

The **pieslice( )** function is an extension of **arc( )** and takes the same arguments—the center of a circle, the start and end angles, and the radius in pixels. It draws the specified arc together with the two radii forming the slice. **pieslice( )** also fills automatically using the current fill pattern and color (just like **fillpoly( )** does).

> void far pieslice(int x, int y, int stangle, int endangle, int radius);
> /* draw an arc with center (x,y), viewport relative, join the end radii to form
>   a slice, then floodfill */

STATS.C (Program 9.5) shows how some simple sales figures can be translated into bar charts and pie slices.

Now that you've seen most of the drawing and filling functions, I want to move on to the important task of saving and moving graphics images.

► *SAVING BIT IMAGES* ►

Corresponding to the text-moving functions used earlier in TWINDOW.C are similar but more complex routines available in graphics mode. If you understood the basic ideas behind pixel mapping, you will appreciate that moving parts of a graphics screen to memory and back again is not as simple as handling a predictable number of ASCII and attribute bytes. The basic functions **getimage( )** and **putimage( )** correspond to **gettext( )** and **puttext( )** and work in a very similar manner, but you need another function, **imagesize( )**, to help you with the counting of bits.

```
        void far getimage(int left, int top, int right, int bottom,
                        void far *bitmap);
/* save the image in given rectangle (absolute coordinates) into  the
    memory area pointed at by bitmap */
        unsigned far imagesize(int left, int top,
                                int right, int bottom);
/* return the number of bytes needed to store the given rectangle. If more
    than 64KB needed, return − 1 */

        void far putimage(int left, int top,
                        void far *bitmap, int putimage_op);
/* send the bit image stored at bitmap to the screen starting at top,
    left − putimage_op determines how the screen image and new image
    combine bitwise − logically */
```

As you can see, when you move a bit image from memory to screen you have a choice as to how the newly arriving pixels combine with the corresponding pixels already on the screen. **putimage_op** is an integer parameter that controls this interaction. GRAPHICS.H defines the possibilities with the mnemonic enumerations listed under **putimage( )** in Appendix G.

The visual result of all these bit confrontations is hardware dependent and is especially so with complex color graphics adapters and monitors. The following snippet will help you experiment on your own machine.

```
#include <graphics.h>
/* lest you forget − also remember graphic.lib in
    your .PRJ file */

    int graphdriver = DETECT;  /* pass the buck */
    int graphmode
```

```
        void *buffer;                   /* for malloc( ) */
        int image_size;

        initgraph(&graphdriver, &graphmode, "c:\\turboc\\");
/* detectgraph( ) will be called internally to find hires mode
   for your driver */
        ...
/* create some screen images here */

        image_size = imagesize(10, 20, 30, 40);
/* get number of bytes in the screen rectangle image */
        if (image_size == -1) {
                outtext("Image > 64Kb");
                exit(1);
        }
        buffer = malloc(image_size);
        getimage(10, 20, 30, 40, buffer);
/* buffer gets image_size bytes */
        cleardevice( );
        ...
/* do some more creative screen play */
        putimage(10, 20, buffer, XOR_PUT);
/* send original bit image to screen and XOR with current image.
   Coinciding bits will cancel out (0 xor 0 = 1 xor 1 = 0), other positions
   will be set (0 xor 1 = 1 xor 0 = 1) */
/* try the other putimage_op values */
        ...
        free(buffer);                   /* deallocate */
        closegraph( );                  /* close down graphics */
```

► *The Active and Visual Pages* ►

Check the listing under **initgraph( )** in Appendix G to see if you are lucky enough to have more than one page of video RAM. The number of pages potentially available depends on the total video RAM assigned and on the mode selected. The general formula is

$$\text{bytes per screen} = (\text{number of bits per pixel}) \times (\text{number of pixels per screen}) \times 8$$

$$\text{number of pages} = (\text{total bytes video RAM}) / (\text{bytes per screen})$$

with suitable rounding to the lowest integer.

The mode dictates both the number of bits per pixel (palette size) and the number of pixels per screen (resolution). For example, a simple four-color palette uses only 2 bits per pixel, allowing more pages than a sixteen-color palette. Similarly, a 640 × 200 resolution allows more pages than a 640 × 480 resolution. Some adapters use the video-RAM allocation by offering increased resolution modes rather than extra pages.

The standard CGA board has only one 16KB page for all its modes. Depending on the amount of video RAM and the selected mode, the EGA boards can have from one to four pages, and the VGA board can have one or two pages. The Hercules adapter provides two 32KB pages. There are now hundreds of special graphics boards available with every conceivable combination.

If your adapter supports pages, there are two important functions in the Turbo C toolbox to examine. Look at the following declarations from GRAPHICS.H:

```
        void far setactivepage(int pagenum);
    /* make pagenum the active page - send all graphics output to this section
       of video RAM. Pages are numbered from 0 to  maxpage − 1 */

        void far setvisualpage(int pagenum);
    /* make pagenum the visual page − screen displays come from the this
       section of video RAM */
```

I explained the basic principles of video pages earlier in this chapter. To recap, all graphics output is directed to the active page, and all screen displays come from the visual page. When you first fire up in graphics mode, the default active and visual pages are both the same, usually 0. Unless you change this state of affairs, the various drawing routines will display their images immediately.

When you call **setactivepage(***N***)**;, the active page is switched to page *N* if you have one, otherwise the call is ignored, and no error message is generated. Subsequent calls to any graphics output functions will not affect the screen, but the images build up in page *N* behind the scenes. If you now call **setvisualpage(***N***)**;, the contents of page *N* immediately appear, replacing the original display. If you time these calls properly, you can create many special effects, including primitive animation. As a simple test bed here is PAGE.C (Program 9.6).

▸ *GRAPHICS COLOR* ▸

Even if your hardware is strictly monochromatic, it is well worth reading the following sections to get a general grasp of the subject—it may tempt you

```
/* Program 9--6 */
/* page -- switching active & visual pages  */

#include <conio.h>
#include <graphics.h>
#include <stdlib.h>

void main(void)
{
      int i,j;
      int graphmode, graphdriver;
      int curr_mode;

      int triangle1[] = {55, 20, 100, 200, 340, 100, 55,  20};
      int triangle2[] = {55,100, 340,  30, 100, 200, 55, 100};
/* both images contained in rectangle 55,20 340,200 */

/*      void *buffer;
      int image_size; */

      textmode(MONO);
      directvideo = 1;
/* try = 1 or 0 to see if you are fully IBM PC compatible */

      if (registerbgidriver(Herc_driver) < 0) exit(1);
/* omit this line if you have not created HERC.OBJ with BGIOBJ
   Remember to name graphics.lib and herc.obj in your PGRAF.PRJ
   file -- or use TLIB to add herc.obj to graphics.lib */

      detectgraph(&graphdriver, &graphmode);
/* gets highest res mode for detected driver */

      graphmode = HERCMONOHI;
      graphdriver = HERCMONO;
/* set your own here -- or leave detectgraph's settings */

      initgraph(&graphdriver, &graphmode, "c:\\turboc\\");
/* gotcher! the \ needs the \ escape char, so \\ for paths */
      cleardevice();
/* clear screen optional here -- initgraph does it also */
      settextstyle(DEFAULT_FONT,HORIZ_DIR,2);
/* double bitmapped font size */
      setvisualpage(0);
      setactivepage(0);
/* defaults -- so not strictly needed */

      setlinestyle(SOLID_LINE, 0, THICK_WIDTH);
      rectangle(55,20, 340,200);
      drawpoly(sizeof(triangle1)/(2*sizeof(int)), triangle1);
/* triangle1 is in page 0 and is displayed */

      setactivepage(1);
      rectangle(55,20, 340,200);
      drawpoly(sizeof(triangle2)/(2*sizeof(int)), triangle2);
/* triangle2 drawn in page 1 -- not displayed */
      setactivepage(0);
      moveto(50,300);
      outtext("Hit any key..");
      getch();
      setvisualpage(1);
```

▸ *Program 9.6:* *PAGE.C*

```
/* triangles flip a la Spielberg! */

    setactivepage(1);
    moveto(50,300);
    outtext("Hit any key..");
    getch();
    cleardevice();
/* clear graphics screen */

    closegraph();

}
```

► **Program 9.6:** *PAGE.C (continued)*

to acquire the necessary equipment and put some color in your life. Although controlling color in graphics mode is more complex than in text mode, the Turbo C tools do most of the hard work.

The first point to remember is that in a graphics mode each individual pixel has a color attribute. Rather than having a character cell with a foreground and background color (as with the text modes) you now think in terms of a background color for the whole screen plus a color set for the pixel, which I'll call the drawing color. Two rarely used functions can handle individual pixel colors:

unsigned far getpixel(int x, int y);
/ * returns the color value of the pixel at (x,y) */

void far putpixel(int x, int y, int pix_color);
/ * set the pixel at (x,y) to the color value pix_color */

However, you are usually more interested in setting up background and drawing colors.

The values associated with a pixel's color are not usually absolute values— they often index into a table of colors representing the current palette available (the CGA has some exceptions, as you'll see). Most color adapters and monitors permit a wide range of color possibilities, but at any given time only a subset of these is available, namely the current or active palette.

► CGA Color Schemes ►

The palettes for the CGA are as listed in Table 9.9. The CGA mode entries relate to the mnemonic used when you set the mode (see **initgraph( )** in Appendix G). These are the low-resolution CGA modes that allow 320 × 200 resolution and any one of the sets of four-color palettes listed above for the drawing color. (The hi-res 640 × 200 CGA mode is two color only. I'll cover this later.)

You can see from this list that if you set a color value of 1, say, with **set color(1);** the actual pixel color you get depends on which mode you are in. To switch from light green to cyan, for example, you would have to change modes with **setgraphmode(CGA3);** and then set the color to 1 again (since **setgraphmode( )** restores all color settings). The color values 1–3 are the drawing colors. What about the background color? The background color has the value 0, and this can represent any of the sixteen different colors listed in Table 9.10.

To set a CGA background color you use **setbkcolor(color)**, where *color* is any value listed in Table 9.10. So in CGAC1 mode, the following lines would give you light cyan on a red background:

```
setcolor(1);
setbkcolor(RED);
```

CGA Mode Palette		Colors and Values		
		1	2	3
CGAC0	0	Light Green	Light Red	Yellow
CGCA1	1	Light Cyan	Light Magenta	White
CGCA2	2	Green	Red	Brown
CGCA3	3	Cyan	Magenta	Light Gray

► **Table 9.9:** CGA palettes

Mnemonic	Numeric Value
BLACK	0
BLUE	1
GREEN	2
CYAN	3
RED	4
MAGENTA	5
BROWN	6
LIGHTGRAY	7
DARKGRAY	8
LIGHTBLUE	9
LIGHTGREEN	10
LIGHTCYAN	11
LIGHTRED	12
LIGHTMAGENTA	13
YELLOW	14
WHITE	15

► **Table 9.10:** *CGA background colors*

To check the current drawing and background colors, you use **getcolor( )** and **getbkcolor( )**, which are declared as follows:

```
    int far getbkcolor(void);
/* return current background color value */
```

```
    int far getcolor(void);
/* return current drawing colr */
```

► *EGA/VGA Color Schemes* ►

Both the EGA and VGA adapters have a true, user-changeable palette, offering sixteen color values from a total range of sixty-four colors. The functions covered in this section apply equally to both boards, so I will not refer specifically to the VGA. The default palette gives you the sixteen CGA colors listed in Table 9.10 so if you don't do anything to change things with **setpalette( )**, **setcolor(0)** gives black, **setcolor(1)** gives blue, and so on. To manipulate the palette you need to distinguish color indices and actual (or hardware) color numbers. Table 9.11 lists the actual EGA color numbers and their mnemonics as defined in GRAPHICS.H.

As you can guess, it's easier and safer to use the defined names than play around with the numbers.

Mnemonic	Numeric Value
EGA_BLACK	0
EGA_BLUE	1
EGA_GREEN	2
EGA_CYAN	3
EGA_RED	4
EGA_MAGENTA	5
EGA_BROWN	20
EGA_LIGHTGRAY	7
EGA_DARKGRAY	56
EGA_LIGHTBLUE	57
EGA_LIGHTGREEN	58
EGA_LIGHTCYAN	59
EGA_LIGHTRED	60
EGA_LIGHTMAGENTA	61
EGA_YELLOW	62
EGA_WHITE	63

► *Table 9.11:* EGA actual color numbers

The structure **palettetype** and the related function **getpalette( )** are declared as follows in GRAPHICS.H:

```
#define MAXCOLORS 15
struct palettetype {
unsigned char size;
signed char colors[MAXCOLORS + 1];
};
void far getpalette(struct palettetype far *palette);
```

If you call **getpalette( )**, you see can how the palette is currently organized:

```
struct palettetype curr_palette;
...
getpalette(&curr_palette);
/* curr_palette.size gives the maximum index + 1 into the palette, 16 in the
   case of EGA. Each curr_palette.colors[i] gives you the  actual color
   number currently active at index i */
```

The array **colors** is indexed from 0 to **MAXCOLOR** (15). Of course your adapter may have fewer than sixteen colors, so some entries may be unused. The simple function **getmaxcolor( )**, called with no arguments, will return an **int** telling you your real **MAXCOLOR**.

The color at index 0 is by definition the background color. You can change the background color with **setbkcolor( )**, but it works differently from the CGA system. With the EGA, **setbkcolor(N)** will copy the actual color found in **curr_palette.colors[N]** into **curr_palette.colors[0]**. At any given moment, the actual color you get when you use **setcolor(N)** is determined by the entry found in **colors[N]** in the palette structure.

The nice thing is that you can independently change these entries using **setpalette( )** and **setallpalette( )**. This immediately alters the colors being displayed. The pixel values have not altered, but their interpretation by the hardware undergoes a sudden mutation. Look at the following prototypes:

```
void far setpalette(int colornum, int act_color);
/* change palette color indexed at colornum to actual color act_color */

void far setallpalette(struct palettetype far *new_palette_ptr);
/* replace all the current palette structure with the new one found at the
   pointer new_palette_ptr */
```

```
void far setrgbpalette(int colornum,int red, int green, int blue);
  /* included for completeness — sets a mix of red/green/blue for rgb
    signals, a subject beyond the scope of this chapter */
```

As my comments indicate, you can change individual color-number-to-actual-color assignments or you can set up a brand new palette structure. One trick in **setallpalette( )** is that if you put a − 1 in any index position of the new palette structure it tells the system not to alter that entry during the transfer. **set palette( )** and **setallpalette( )** do not return values, but the **graphresult( )** function will return the generic error value − 11 to signal failure.

Although I have mentioned this kind of error checking before, this is a good opportunity to recap the situation. Some graphics routines return values signaling success or failure, but most rely on you calling **graphresult( )** to test if the previous graphics function call worked as planned. The function call **grapherrormsg(*error_code*)**, where *error_code* is the int returned by **graphresult( )**, will display a real, legible error message based on the mnemonics listed under **graphresult( )** in Appendix G.

Although I urge you to make frequent calls on **graphresult( )**, I hope that errors do not intrude too often as you explore the wonderful world of graphics now accessible with Turbo C.

► SUMMARY OF CHAPTER 9 ►

◄► The chief enhancement in Version 1.5 of Turbo C is the graphics library, GRAPHICS.LIB, which contains over 300 new functions.

◄► The basics of video-display technology were covered. Key concepts are raster scanning, mapping video RAM to the screen, display adapters, color and monochrome monitors, text and graphics modes.

◄► Turbo C provides drivers for all the popular graphics boards and has functions that can detect the hardware fitted and initialize the graphics system [**detectgraph( )** and **initgraph( )**].

◄► Text mode and graphics mode have different video mapping schemes, but parallel sets of functions handle most of the bit- and byte-counting operations for you.

◄► The functions can be classified as follows:

Text Modes:	Text Output and Manipulation
	Window and Mode Control
	Attribute Control
	State Query
Graphics Modes:	Systems Control
	Drawing and Filling
	Screen and Viewport control
	Graphics-text output
	Color and Palette control
	Error handling
	State Query

◄► Appendix G has a handy alphabetical listing of all the graphics and text functions with prototypes and brief descriptions.

◄► BGIOBJ can be used to convert driver (.BGI) and font (.CHR) files into .OBJ files. These can be linked into individual programs with TLINK or incorporated into GRAPHICS.LIB using TLIB.

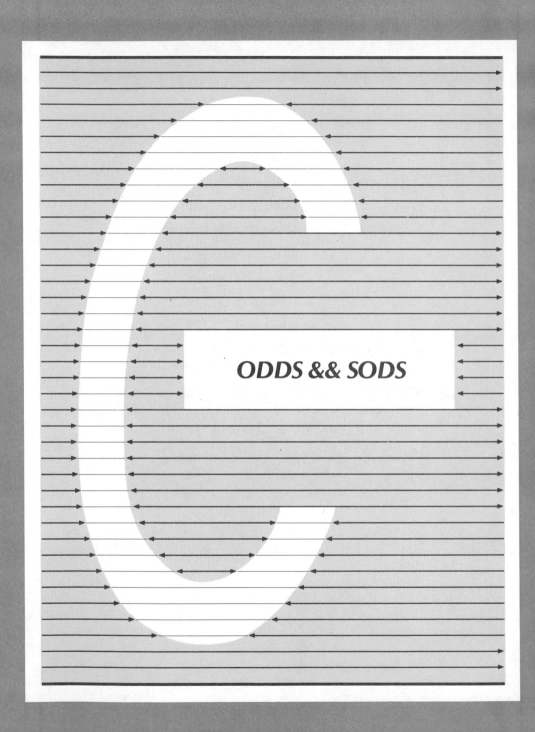

ODDS && SODS

► *CHAPTER 10* ►

This chapter covers several topics that for various reasons did not quite fit in the mainstream of my exposition so far. There were many moments when I had to resist the temptation of making "just another little detour!"

Most of this chapter is devoted to additions and enhancements that became available with Versions 1.5 and 2 of Turbo C (excluding the graphics library covered in Chapter 9 and the integrated debugging facilities covered in Chapter 11). First I cover GREP and explain regular expressions, and then I discuss how and why large programs are divided into separately compilable files. This involves a study of the Project-Make facility as well as a deeper look at the TLIB librarian (new with Version 1.5). The **getopt( )** function, which retrieves switches and options from a command line, will also be revealed.

Finally, I'll present some more advanced topics including the use of recursion and pointers to functions. These will give you some practice in reading C programs, a vital path to honing your writing skills.

► *SUMMARY OF ADDITIONS AND ENHANCEMENTS IN VERSION 1.5* ►

The Turbo C package received a major upgrade from Version 1.0 to 1.5 at the end of 1987. Here is a brief summary of the differences between the two versions.

The main additions are

- ► TLIB.EXE, an object-code librarian

- ► video functions—over 100 new routines that offer powerful and flexible window-based text and graphics facilities (see Chapter 9)

- ► the BGIOBJ utility, which converts graphics drivers and font files to .OBJ files so you can link them into .EXE programs (see Chapter 9)

- ► GREP.COM, a file-search utility based on the UNIX grep program

The enhancements include

- ► new options in the TC integrated environment
- ► extended syntax and features for the TCC.EXE command-line compiler (matching the TC enhancements)
- ► TCINST.EXE installation-customization program
- ► TCCONFIG.EXE (formerly CNVRTCFG) for converting configuration files from and to TC and TCC formats
- ► header-file revisions for the latest ANSI C data and function specifications

► THE GREPS OF WRATH ►

The GREP utility introduced with Versions 1.5 and 2 is based on the UNIX grep command. (Grep is an acronym for global regular expression print.) Turbo C's GREP syntax does not follow all the UNIX rules and adds some new options, so UNIX users should take care.

GREP lets you search selected files for various string matches or mismatches. It turns out to be a valuable programmer's tool as well as being useful in more general contexts. If you have ever wanted to find out which of your programs contain identifiers matching wildcards such as **tax_*_paid** or call the function **init_<*no letter a here*>???(*<arg starting with a, e or x>*)**, you will appreciate the power of GREP over the simple FIND command supplied with DOS.

Given that DOS file names can be unhelpfully cryptic, you may use GREP most often to do tasks such as locating all those .LET files that contain the string "**alimony**". GREP is more than a string-matching routine, however—it gives you a myriad of options for locating sets of characters in different places, and you can also customize it with your own default options. In some ways, you can think of GREP as a miniature programming language.

► The GREP Command Line ►

You set up a search by entering a command based on the following syntax:

C>GREP *[options] string filespec [filespec ... filespec]*

with spaces or tabs between the arguments. For example,

C>GREP overdue *.LET STAN?.*

will locate all files in the current directory with the extension .LET or named STAN? (with any extension) that contain the string **overdue**. Matches are confined to lines in the target file, so **over**<newline character>**due** would not be located. You can switch on the ignore-case option if you want to match **Overdue**, **overDue**, **OVERDUE**, and the like. Here is the command line that you would use to do this.

C>GREP −i overdue *.LET STAN?.*

The −i is one of many such options that will soon be unveiled.

Each file specification can contain complete specifications for drive and path; otherwise the search defaults to the current drive and directory. There are options that allow the search to be extended to lower subdirectories.

Using redirection, you can direct GREP's output to files, ports, or printers; otherwise you get a screen display. With other filter commands you can create many useful pipes not available with the standard DOS FIND command. The type of output you get is determined by the option switches. If you set no options, GREP will simply output each line that contains the search string.

The search string can be either a literal string or a set of so-called regular expressions. Regular expressions contain certain reserved symbols that direct the search. Before I explain these, let's see how the option switches work. Table 10.1 lists the options and explains their actions. The leading minus sign is mandatory. Some find it confusing that −i, for example, turns the i option *on*, but that's UNIX for you. Options can be combined in any way, so −i −l −v, −ilv, −i −lv, and −il −v will each switch on all three options. Certain options can override others, however, and I'll explain this shortly.

Options are turned off with a trailing minus: e.g., −i− will turn off the ignore-case option, giving you case-sensitive searches. By the way, you can use an optional trailing + to switch on an option: −i+ is the same as −i.

► *Literal String Searches*

When the −r (regular expression) option is off, the search pattern is taken literally as a normal string of characters. If the string contains spaces or tabs you must enclose it with quotation marks as in

C>GREP −di "#ifdef __STDC__" \TURBOC*.C

–c   Count only. Displays each file name that has at least one matching occurrence and shows the number of matches in each.

–d   Directories. Extends the search to include the target file specifications in the stated directory and any of the same name in their lower subdirectories. A specification of *.* means search all files in the root directory of the current drive and all files in all subdirectories.

–i   Ignore case. When this switch is on, uppercase and lowercase letters are not distinguished. (This is also known as *case folding*.)

–l   List match files. Once the target string is matched, the file is listed and the search moves on to the next file (if any).

–n   Numbers. Displays line numbers alongside any matching lines.

–r   Regular expression search. The expression for the target string is interpreted as a regular expression rather than as a literal string. The symbols ^ , $, ., *, +, [,], and \ are treated specially unless preceded with the escape character \.

–v   Non-match. Reverses the sense of the search so that lines not containing the search string are displayed or counted.

–w   Write options. Configures GREP by setting selected options as defaults for subsequent invocations of GREP.

–z   Verbose. Combines –c (count), –l (list matches), and –n (line numbers). In addition, all file names are displayed as they are searched, whether a match is found or not.

► *Table 10.1:* GREP option switches

This example would match the whole string regardless of case and would look through all the .C files in \TURBOC and its subdirectories.

► *Regular Expressions*

When the –r option is on, the search pattern is interpreted as a regular expression. (This term originated with Ken Thompson's early UNIX editor called ed; since then regular expressions have spread to sed, grep, awk, and other UNIX commands.) The metacharacters listed in Table 10.2 have nonliteral meanings as shown, while all other characters are taken literally.

Metacharacter	Meaning
^	Matches at start of a line when ^ precedes pattern.
$	Matches at end of a line when $ follows pattern.
.	Matches any character.
*	*expression* * matches zero or more occurrences of *expression* where *expression* is any expression.
+	*expression* + matches one or more occurrences of *expression* where *expression* is any expression.
[...]	Matches any single character in the enclosed string. Ranges are allowed, e.g., [a-zABZ]. All characters inside the brackets have their literal meaning except for ^ when ^ is the first character after the [(see below).
[^...]	Matches any single character provided it is not in the enclosed string following the ^.
\	Escape character. Following metacharacter is treated as literal, e.g., \$ will match a real dollar sign.

► *Table 10.2:* GREP regular expressions

Any combination of these can be devised and juxtaposed to give matching criteria of daunting complexity. The examples in Table 10.3 will help clarify the situation! I assume case-sensitive matches, i.e., that the −i option is off.

► *The GREP Options in Action* ►

The GREP.COM you receive from Borland has all the option defaults set to off, but GREP can modify itself using the −w option. For example, if you always want to ignore case differences, you can use the following command line:

```
C>GREP −w −i
```

GREP will then default to "Ignore case on," that is, case insensitive. If you need to restore case sensitivity for a particular session, you must do so with

Regular Expression	Matches
^Dear	"Dear", "Dears", etc. at the start of any line
sincerely$	"sincerely", "xxsincerely", etc. at the end of any line
^contents$	Any line containing only the string "contents"
^$	Empty lines (newline character only)
i.m	"iAm", "ibm", "Siamese", etc.
HEL*	"HE", "HEL", "HELL", "HELLL", etc.
.*	Every string (= DOS use of *). Note especially the non-DOS interpretation of * as a wildcard.
Pom+	"Pom", "PomPom", "PomPomPom", etc.
[a-z,ABZ]	Any one of "a", "b"..."z", "A", "B", or "Z"
[a-km-z:]	Any lowercase letter (except *l*) followed by a colon
[^0-9]	Any nondigit
[^a--zA--Z]	Any nonalphabetic character
[$.^]	"$", ".", or "^" (since ^ is not the first character and $ and . are not metacharacters inside [ ])
[A--Za--z].*[:%]	Any string starting with an alphabetic character followed by zero or more anythings, and ending with : or %
array[02--9]\[[^2--5]\]	"array7[6]", "array0[0]", "array3[9]", etc. Note that the second [is treated literally because of the backslash.

► **Table 10.3:** *Examples of GREP's regular expressions in use*

Regular Expression	Matches
[^a-zA-Z]stan[^a-zA-Z]	An isolated "stan", so usually finds the word "stan" (however, will also match "stan!" and "8stan-")
" stan "	A better way to find the word "stan"
\\\ *[A-F]:" "*	"\" followed by any number of spaces, followed by any one of "A" to "F", followed by ":" and any number of spaces. This shows two ways of matching spaces. You can escape with \ <space> or enclose <space> with double quotes. The first \ escapes the second \, of course.
^[" "\" ' (]	Any line that starts with space, ", ', or (. The double quotes must be escaped to get a literal match.

► *Table 10.3: Examples of GREP's regular expressions in use (continued)*

the − i− switch:

    C>GREP − i− tax *.C

GREP will then match "tax" but not "Tax" in any .C file in the current drive and directory. Notice that as the GREP line is scanned the rightmost switch may override an earlier switch. In

    C>GREP − d − i− − d− − i tax *.C

The − d and − i− are overridden by the following − d− and − i. You can picture each option being switched on or off from left to right. Recall that − i+ is equivalent to − i.

You obviously need to remember which default options you have set, and it's a good idea to make a backup copy before modifying GREP with − w.

► *THE TLIB OBJECT-CODE LIBRARIAN* ►

You met TLIB.EXE in Chapter 9, in which it was used as a method for incorporating driver and font .OBJ files into GRAPHICS.LIB. TLIB is a full-blown library manager that will help you in other ways as your programs become larger and need to be broken down into separately compiled files of functions. TLIB also makes it easier to incorporate other vendors' .OBJ files into your programs. To appreciate these advantages you need to understand what a library is and how the linker works.

► *What Is a Library?* ►

A library is a file with the extension .LIB that contains a set of .OBJ modules together with lists of identifiers to aid the linker. (TLIB can handle library files with extensions other than .LIB, but Project-Make expects the .LIB, so it's safer to keep to this rule.)

Your Turbo C system comes equipped with complete libraries for each memory model. For example, CS.LIB contains all the object code to support the tiny and small models, CM.LIB supports the medium model, and so on. When you compile/link, Turbo C automatically links CS.LIB, CM.LIB, etc. for you. You may recall from Chapter 9 that GRAPHICS.LIB had to be explicitly linked because it covers all memory models. When you create your own libraries you must also adopt a suitable linking strategy.

► *Why Use Libraries?* ►

Suppose you write a program called MYMAIN.C that calls functions you have coded in files MYFUNCS1.C and MYFUNCS2.C. Presumably, these functions are considered to be of general use; otherwise they might as well reside in MYMAIN.C. One way of proceeding is to precompile the two function files, giving MYFUNCS1.OBJ and MYFUNC2.OBJ. When you compile/link MYMAIN.C, you tell the system to link these .OBJ files. The most convenient way to do this with the IDE is to create a project file, namely an ASCII text file called MYMAIN.PRJ, which contains the lines

```
MYMAIN.C
MYFUNC1.OBJ
MYFUNC2.OBJ
```

The extension .C is optional, but you must add the .OBJ extensions. If they are not in your current directory, you can supply path specifications. The .OBJ files can be listed in any order.

A more sophisticated MYMAIN.PRJ file would be

MYMAIN.C (MYFUNC1.OBJ MYFUNC2.OBJ)
MYFUNC1.OBJ
MYFUNC2.OBJ

which informs Project-Make that MYMAIN.C depends on the two support-ing function programs. The last two lines control the linkage, while the files listed in parentheses spell out the dependencies.

Briefly, this means that Turbo C will automatically recompile/relink MYMAIN.C if either MYFUNC1 or MYFUNC2 has been changed since the last recompile/relink. Project-Make always checks the date/time stamps on various files before deciding what needs to be done to produce a good MYMAIN.EXE.

If any supporting file has changed, certain recompilations or relinks are triggered on the dependent files; otherwise time is saved by avoiding redun-dant processing. In addition to the implicit dependencies, you have given Project-Make two explicit dependencies. Note carefully that the above .PRJ file does not contain any reference to MYFUNC1.C or MYFUNC2.C, so don't expect it to recompile these. It simply checks the date/times of the two function .OBJ files in relation to MYMAIN.C, MYMAIN.OBJ (if it exists) and MYMAIN.EXE (if it exists) to see which is the most current. Another neat fact is that Project-Make also checks the relative date/time of MYMAIN.PRJ! Oth-erwise some vital steps could be missed.

Before we leave the subject of dependencies, consider the very common situ-ation in which you examine your MYFUNC1.C file and find that it starts with a whole bunch of **#include**s and **#define**s, many of which occur also in MYFUNC2. It is meet and proper to consider creating a MYOWN.H header file.

```
/* myown.h – – includes & defines for myfunc1, myfunc2 */
#include <stdio.h>
#include <stdlib.h>
#include <conio.h>
#ifndef BUFSIZ
#define BUFSIZ 512
#endif
/* more of the same */

    extern double anyfunc(char *chptr, struct mine *sptr);
/* and so on */
```

Your function source files can now start with

```
/* myfunc1.c — — set of widget — splining functions */
#include <myown.h>

/* more includes, defines, declarations unique to this module */
/* all your functions come here */
/* end of myfunc1.c */

/* myfunc2.c — — set of widget — extrusion functions */
#include <myown.h>

/* more includes, defines, declarations unique to this module */
/* all your functions come here */
/* end of myfunc2.c */
```

but now it pays to revise MYMAIN.PRJ as follows:

```
MYMAIN.C (MYOWN.H  MYFUNC1.OBJ  MYFUNC2.OBJ)
MYFUNC1.OBJ
MYFUNC2.OBJ
```

widening the dependencies of MYMAIN.C. This is a good idea since even a minor change to MYOWN.H could affect MYMAIN.C.

You might be tempted to add (MYOWN.H) alongside MYFUNC1.OBJ and MYFUNC2.OBJ. Resist the urge, even though the .OBJs do depend on MYOWN.H! Only source files can have explicit dependency lists. The .OBJ lines are there purely to ensure correct linkage. What you can do, though, is create MYFUNC1.PRJ and MYFUNC2.PRJ for use when these two are compiled. MYFUNC1.PRJ would contain

```
MYFUNC1.C (MYOWN.H)
```

and MYFUNC2.PPJ would contain

```
MYFUNC2.C (MYOWN.H)
```

► *On the Make* ►

Whenever you invoke Project-Make for MYMAIN.PRJ, whether you do so directly with F9 or indirectly with Alt-R, the .PRJ file ensures that MYFUNC1.OBJ and MYFUNC2.OBJ are included in the list of files to be linked. (The appropriate C?.LIB is added to this list for you.) You now have MYFUNC.EXE.

You can also compile MYMAIN.C and link in your two function files with a TCC command line:

C>TCC MYMAIN MYFUNC1.OBJ MYFUNC2.OBJ

or you could compile MYMAIN.C separately and then use TLINK with the three .OBJ files as follows:

C>TLINK MYMAIN MYFUNC1 MYFUNC2, MYMAIN

With TLINK the default extension for all files before the comma is .OBJ. The name after the comma determines the name of the .EXE file.

The end result of all three methods is MYMAIN.EXE, all ready to run and amaze your family.

► *Exploiting Your Function Files* ►

So far, so good. But suppose you now write NEWMAIN.C and compile it to NEWMAIN.OBJ. It may or may not call functions in MYFUNC1.OBJ and/or MYFUNC2.OBJ. How should you link NEWMAIN.OBJ? As projects get larger and more complex, you can spend much time poring over your listings trying to remember which functions are in which files so you can decide which .OBJ files need to be linked. Taking the safe and easy way out by always linking all possible .OBJ files has the disadvantage of inflating NEWMAIN.EXE.

TLIB comes to the rescue. If you use TLIB to create a MYFUNC.LIB file from MYFUNC1.OBJ and MYFUNC2.OBJ (and possibly others), you can link NEWMAIN.OBJ with MYFUNC.LIB without worrying about which .OBJ file contains which functions. The linker will pull in only those .OBJ modules needed by NEWMAIN.OBJ. A .LIB file is so organized that TLINK (or any compatible linker) can determine the module in which any referenced function or external variable is located. An added bonus is that the size of the collected .OBJ modules is nearly always smaller than the sum of the individual .OBJ files. (You'll see shortly that there is no need to keep an .OBJ file separately on disk after it's safely incorporated in a library.)

Once they are embedded in MYFUNC.LIB, the .OBJ sets of code are more correctly referred to as *modules* rather than as *files*. As modules within a library they are still referenced by their original .OBJ names (MYFUNC1 and MYFUNC2), but you don't name the drive, path, or extension.

► *What Is a Librarian?* ►

TLIB can create new .LIB files, add modules to existing libraries, and delete modules from existing libraries. It can extract a module from a library and recover the original .OBJ file, and it can also add all the modules of one library to another. Finally, but not least, TLIB lets you examine the contents of a library by creating a list file. These tasks are known as *library maintenance*. The software that performs them is called a librarian or library manager.

► *Creating and Adding to a Library* ►

To create the MYFUNC.LIB file you use TLIB at the DOS command level as follows:

C>TLIB MYFUNC*[.LIB]* + MYFUNC1*[.OBJ]* + MYFUNC2*[.OBJ]*

TLIB assumes the obvious extensions shown as defaults. Wildcards are not allowed. The plus signs immediately before the .OBJ file names indicate additions to the library. If MYFUNC.LIB already exists, the above line would add both .OBJ files to it, otherwise TLIB creates a new file called MYFUNC.LIB and then adds the .OBJ files. This example assumes that all three files are in the current directory. If they are elsewhere, you must specify their drives and paths—but remember that TLIB stores only the module names after stripping off any extraneous rubbish.

You could later add a module called MYFUNC3 to \TB, remove the original MYFUNC2, and add in all the modules from another library called OEM.LIB with one command line:

C>TLIB MYFUNC + \TB\MYFUNC3 − MYFUNC2 + OEM.LIB

Notice the minus sign used for module deletion. No path or extension is needed with a − (delete) action since module names are just module names! If you unnecessarily add paths or extensions, TLIB will quietly remove them. The \TB\ *is* needed for adding MYFUNC3 because TLIB needs to locate the .OBJ file (.OBJ is the default). Inside the library, though, the module retains no clue to its original directory.

You can present these + and − actions in any sequence because TLIB sorts them before processing your requests. The removals are always performed before the additions. The following line appears pointless yet is very common and sensible:

C>TLIB MYFUNC – MYFUNC1 + MYFUNC1

Yes, you are replacing MYFUNC1 with a new version. The following line would have the same effect:

C>TLIB MYFUNC + MYFUNC1 – MYFUNC1

This operation is so common that TLIB allows you to use the following short-hand equivalents:

C>TLIB MYFUNC – + MYFUNC1

and

C>TLIB MYFUNC + – MYFUNC1

If you try to remove a module that isn't there, TLIB will inform you of the irresolvable quandary it faces. Similarly, TLIB balks at adding a module that already exists, forcing you to do the – + trick.

Ah! But what if you remove MYFUNC2 from MYFUNC.LIB but do not have MYFUNC2.OBJ somewhere as a separate file? Alas, unless MYFUNC2 exists within another library, it has now disappeared. If you kept MYFUNC2.C, of course, no lasting harm is done—you can always recompile. TLIB offers *module extraction* as an alternative to recompilation. What TLIB putteth together, TLIB can also pulleth asunder! In

C>TLIB MYFUNC *MYFUNC2

The * (extract) operator recovers the MYFUNC2 module and writes it out to MYFUNC2.OBJ, either creating this file or overwriting any existing file of that name. This recovers the .OBJ file in the exact format it had during the original addition operation. If the requested module is not found, you get a suitable message and no new file is created.

As you may guess, a safe way to remove a module without losing it is to combine * and – as follows:

C>TLIB MYFUNC * – MYFUNC2

This creates MYFUNC2.OBJ and then removes the module MYFUNC2 from MYFUNC.LIB. In this case, indicating the drive and path makes sense if you want to extract the module and save it in another directory. The drive and path would be used by the * but ignored by the – . Again, the order in which you present these actions is irrelevant—the extractions always precede the removals, and any additions are always performed last.

The following lines are all equivalent to the previous example:

```
C>TLIB  MYFUNC  – *MYFUNC2
C>TLIB  MYFUNC  *MYFUNC2  – MYFUNC2
C>TLIB  MYFUNC  – MYFUNC2  *MYFUNC2
```

► *The TLIB Syntax* ►

The full TLIB syntax is

C>TLIB *libfile [/C] [ops_list] [,listfile]*

Libfile can be a full file specification, with the default extension being .LIB. As I mentioned earlier, you should avoid other extensions since both TC and TCC look for .LIB automatically.

► *TLIB Operations List*

The optional *ops_list* is any sequence of file names (with or without drive and paths) preceded by combinations of the action symbols + (add a module), – (delete a module), and * (extract a module), as described earlier. The legal combinations are – *, *– (both extract and then remove) and – +, + – (both remove and then add). Suitable error messages are given if you try to remove or extract a nonexistent module or add an existing module. You should be careful with * since it could overwrite a later .OBJ version with an earlier version without warning.

Only the + action is possible with a library file name. You can add all the modules in one library to another, but you can only remove and extract single modules. To rename a module, you have to extract it, rename the .OBJ file, and then add the renamed file.

► *Listing the TLIB Contents*

The optional file name (*listfile*) appearing after a comma at the end of the command line receives a listing of the library modules in alphabetical order with their sizes in bytes. After each module a list of the public symbols defined in that module appears, also in alphabetical sequence.

These public symbols represent all the external identifiers you studied in Chapter 7: function names, global variables, and **extern**ed variables defined in the original source files. The compiler passes these to the .OBJ files (for direct linking purposes) and TLIB passes them to the .LIB files (for selective linkage).

TLIB listings are only produced if you enter a comma followed by a file name or the device-file names CON (screen display) or PRN (direct printer output). For example, if you are logged into \TURBOC\LIB,

    C>TLIB EMU.LIB, CON

will display the modules in the FP emulation library, as shown in Figure 10.1.

Similarly,

    C>TLIB MYFUNC, MYLIB.PRT

will create a file called MYLIB.PRT that contains the module names and public symbols. You can study this file at your leisure (using GREP, perhaps). You

```
 Sat  1-30 1988 /   5:12:53.75 : C:\
SCREEN00 CAP     4256   1-30-88    5:11a
        1 File(s)   2072576 bytes free

C>erase *.cap

C>tlib \turboc\lib\emu, con
Turbo Lib 1.0  Copyright (c) 1987 Borland International
Publics by module

FMU086          size = 9742
        e086_Entry                          e086_Shortcut
        emws_control                        emws_status

EMU087          size = 1282
        e087_Entry                          e087_Shortcut

EMUINIT         size = 319
        FIARQQ                              FICRQQ
        FIDRQQ                              FIERQQ
        FISRQQ                              FIWRQQ
        FJARQQ                              FJCRQQ
        FJSRQQ                              __EMURESET

C>_
```

► *Figure 10.1:* TLIB listing of EMU.LIB modules

will find it instructive to list the modules in CS.LIB, the small memory model support library, and you will see many familiar names in the symbol list.

In normal, default Turbo C operation, these identifiers retain their upper-case and lowercase source-code spellings but have an underscore (_) pre-pended. When mixing C and case-insensitive Pascal code, as discussed in Chapter 5, you have to use options to suppress the underscore (using Generate underscores...Off in the Options menu or − u − in TCC) and force conversions to uppercase (with the **pascal** modifier). These conversions are important in understanding the /C option in TLIB.

► *The TLIB/TLINK Case-Sensitivity Problem*

The optional /C flag provides compatibility with both case-insensitive languages and non-Turbo C, case-insensitive linkers.

As I mentioned, TLIB maintains a table of all the public symbols (such as function names and global variables) defined in its member modules. This table is consulted by TLINK or some alien linker to determine which modules to pull in. We clearly cannot allow duplicates in any set of tables, so whenever you add a module to a library, TLIB has to check that the new symbols being added are unique. If they are not, an error is signaled and the new module is rejected.

The question arises, Is case relevant? Are the entries **_sum** and **_SUM**, for instance, different? As far as the C language and Turbo C's TLINK linker are concerned, they are indubitably distinct; however, many old-fashioned linkers and languages are case-insensitive and cannot differentiate! Remember that a linker is not really concerned about the origin of the .OBJ files (they can come from almost any high- or low-level language) as long as they follow an agreed format.

If you *omit* the /C flag, you force TLIB to be case-insensitive as a sop to the older regimes. TLIB would therefore reject a new module defining **_sum** (or **sum** if underscore suppression is active) if the symbol **_SUM** (or **SUM**) already existed in that library's symbol table. In Pascal mode, in fact, this would be a genuine error.

In non-Pascal situations, TLIB warns you of possible trouble should you or somebody else try to link with a case-insensitive linker. This feature may not concern you, but it is important for software developers who may have no control over the linkers used by their customers.

Summing up, if you include the /C flag, TLIB becomes case-sensitive and your library is less portable because many linkers match the early single-case computer languages.

If you intend to use only TLINK and case-sensitive languages, you can safely add the /C option; otherwise it is wiser to omit it. Yes, you can use either /c or /C.

Incidentally, if you ever get a long list of **identifier unknown** linker-error messages showing names with underscores, it probably indicates that you failed to include a .LIB file. The likely candidate is GRAPHICS.LIB (since it is outside the normal C?.LIB collection).

► *TLIB Response Files* ►

The final TLIB feature to be covered is the *response file*—an ASCII text file you can create to help you automate repetitive maintenance operations on your libraries. The idea is that if you have a response file called UPDATE.RSP, say, containing the line

```
MYLIB – + NEW.OBJ – + REV.OBJ
```

its contents can be pulled into the command line by typing

```
TLIB  @UPDATE.RSP
```

at the prompt. The leading @ causes the following file name to read into the command line, exactly as if you had typed

```
TLIB  MYLIB – + NEW.OBJ – + REV.OBJ
```

at the prompt. I gave the response file an extension .RSP as a recognition aid—in fact, any extension or none is OK. Apart from saving keystrokes, the response file solves the problem that DOS command lines are limited to 127 characters. A response file can be as long as you like provided that you use a & to indicate a continuation line:

```
MYLIB + – REVISED1.OBJ + – REVISED2.OBJ + – REVISED3.OBJ &
+ NEWONE.OBJ – OLDONE *REVIEW.OBJ
```

The response file need not contain the entire command entry—you can enter some fields by hand and have the rest pulled in from the response file. You can even use several response files in the same command. If REV.RSP was the file holding the previous lines, and you set up files MYPATH and LIBLST to contain

    \TURBOC\NEWLIB\

and

    , LIBLST.LST

respectively, you could type

    TLIB @REV.RSP *−@MYPATH SPECIAL @LIBLIST

at the prompt. The response file shortcut is also available with TLINK, and the syntax is identical.

► *THE getopt( ) UTILITY* ►

You have now seen quite a few command-line switches in action with GREP, TCC, TLINK, and TLIB. It is instructive to see how these options are programmed in C. You saw in Chapter 8 how

    main(int argc, char *argv[ ], char *argenv[ ])

allowed C to access the whole command line. Borland supplies **getopt( )**, a useful function that lets you parse the argument strings in a general way, returning information on what options may have been selected. **main( )** can still access the normal nonoption arguments, but **getopt( )** does the tricky work of picking out options and possible arguments embedded in the options.

Diskette 5 of Version 1.5 has a file called GETOPT.C. It is listed here as Program 10.1 (which you'll see in full shortly) by kind permission of Borland International. I have edited their comments to suit my exposition.

Here is the definition of **getopt( )**.

    int getopt(int argc, char *argv[ ], char *optionS)

This function picks up via **main( )** the number of arguments on the command line in **argc** and the set of string pointers, **argv[ ]** (one for each argument string). You also need to give it a string, **optionS**, which represents all the legal switches allowed for the command. It is this option string that gives **getopt( )** its flexibility—you can set it up for almost any pattern of command line.

► *The Option-String Syntax* ►

The option string is a user-defined string of ASCII characters with the following format:

SW[optLetter]... [argLetter space... argument]... [SW...]...

where *SW* is the switch character, either / or − , according to the current MS-DOS setting of switchar. DOS usually uses / to indicate a switch option, as in

C>CHKDSK A:/F

but to please UNIX programmers it can be changed to − using interrupt 21h function 37h.

Do not confuse the option string with the various strings, including actual options, picked up from the command line. The differences will emerge as I proceed.

The square brackets indicate that an entry can be omitted, and the ellipses indicate that repetitions are possible, including repeats of the basic sequence. (I told you it was a very generalized function.)

optLetter indicates legal alphabetic options, so any option letters encountered during the parse need to match one of the optLetters. *argLetter* indicates that an argument follows each matching occurrence in the command line. In an option string argLetters have a colon immediately following to distinguish them from optLetters. Arguments can contain the switch character; they are delimited by white space, but argLetters and optLetters must not have any preceeding spaces. Uppercase and lowercase letters are distinct.

As an example, suppose the switch character is / (the MS-DOS default). If you set the option string to A:F:PuU:wXZ: then P, u, w, and X are optLetters (because no colons follow them). If these letters are encountered, they are taken as simple on/off switches to be interpreted as you see fit. The letters A, F, U, Z are argLetters. When they are found in the command line **getopt( )**

they will extract the following strings as arguments. With these settings, the following command line

AnyCommand /uPFPi /X /A L *SomeFileName*

would return the following sequence of values:

'u' and 'P' as isolated option letters
'F' as an argLetter with Pi as its argument string
'X' as an isolated option letter
'A' as an argLetter with L as its argument

SomeFileName terminates **getopt( )**. It is not an option and must be processed via ***argv[ ]** along with any subsequent arguments in the usual way.

As this example shows, the first nonoption argument, marked by the absence of a leading switch character, terminates the parsing scan. **getopt( )** returns EOF to signal this and leaves the global **optind** as an index to the next **argv[ ]** string not yet processed. **optind** starts life as 1 (remember that **argv[0]** is the name of the command itself) and moves on as each distinct argument is processed. Within these conventional, space-delimited arguments, of course, **getopt( )** may well uncover a whole bunch of options and option arguments.

There can be any number of option clusters starting with switch characters, but a final, solitary switch is definitely taboo. Duplicate occurrences of optLetters and argLetters are allowed since, as we saw with TLIB, that may be legal and sensible. It is up to the program using **getopt( )** to decide how to handle duplicated options.

If **getopt( )** encounters the sequence *SWSW* (// or − −), these two characters and the rest of the line are ignored, leaving **main( )** to extract the subsequent arguments. This allows you to have nonoption arguments containing the switch character by using the old escape-character approach.

To recap, the option string, ***optionS**, allows valid option and argument letters to be recognized. When an argLetter is discovered, the global **optarg** is set to point at its associated argument string, bypassing any intervening white space. **getopt( )** itself returns the optLetter or EOF if no more remain.

If a switch precedes an unknown letter, **getopt( )** returns a ? and an error message appears via **perror( )** unless the global variable **opterr** has been set to zero (false).

Study GETOPT.C (Program 10.1) carefully to see if you can match its logic with the above description. Then I'll show you an extract from a program called FILECOMP.C that calls **getopt( )**. This should clarify the situation and give you some practice in digesting larger pieces of code than those found in earlier chapters.

► *getopt( ) in Action* ►

The following extract from FILECOMP.C (used with permission of Borland International) shows how **getopt( )** is called repeatedly until all the option switches have been diagnosed. I will not say too much about FILECOMP.C. All you need to know is that it compares two files, like the DOS COMP command, but it provides informative displays of where the files differ. The

```
/*   getopt.c -- Turbo C */

Copyright (c) 1986,1987 by Borland International Inc.
All Rights Reserved.
*/

#include <errno.h>
/* needed for global errno, used by perror() to print error
   messages.  errno is set to a specific value whenever a library
   call fails, giving the reason for failure */

#include <string.h>
/* needed for strchr() */

#include <dos.h>
/* needed for geninterrupt() which calls on DOS via interrupts */

#include <stdio.h>
/* nearly always needed! */

int     optind = 1; /* index of which argument is next */
char    *optarg;        /* pointer to argument of current option */
int     opterr = 1;   /* allow error message  */
/* set to 0 to suppress perror() displays */

static    char    *letP = NULL;
/* remember next option char's location */

static  char    SW = 0;
/* DOS switch character, will be set to '--' or '/' */
/* notice the use of 2 static variables here */

int  getopt(int argc, char *argv[], char *optionS)
{
    unsigned char ch;
    char *optP;
/* local, automatic variables */
```

► *Program 10.1:* GETOPT.C

```
        if (SW == 0) {
            _AX = 0x3700;
            geninterrupt(0x21);
            SW = _DL;
        }
/* get SW using DOS 21h interrupt, function 0x37 */
/* once set, this routine will be skipped */

/* first test if any more args to examine */
    if (argc > optind) {
/* then test if any char left in current arg */
        if (letP == NULL) {
            if ((letP = argv[optind]) == NULL ||
                *(letP++) != SW)  goto gopEOF;
            if (*letP == SW) {
                optind++;  goto gopEOF;

            }
        }
        if (0 == (ch = *(letP++))) {
            optind++;  goto gopEOF;
        }
        if (':' == ch  ||  (optP = strchr(optionS, ch))
                                    == NULL)
            goto gopError;

/* strchr(string, ch) scans a string looking for the first
   occurrence of ch; at first match from left it returns a
   pointer to match.  If no match, it returns NULL */

/* a rare sight of the dreaded goto, used here legitimately to
   exit a loop in terminating or error situation */

        if (':' == *(++optP)) {
            optind++;
            if (0 == *letP) {
                if (argc <= optind)  goto  gopError;
                letP = argv[optind++];
            }
            optarg = letP;
            letP = NULL;
        } else {
            if (0 == *letP) {
                optind++;
                letP = NULL;
            }
            optarg = NULL;
        }
        return ch;
    }
gopEOF:
    optarg = letP = NULL;
    return EOF;

gopError:
    optarg = NULL;
    errno  = EINVAL;
/* perror() will display "Invalid argument: <message>" if opterr
   set to 1 */
    if (opterr)
        perror ("get command line option");
    return ('?');
}

/*************** END of GETOPT() *****************/
```

► **Program 10.1:** *GETOPT.C (continued)*

options dictate how the comparisons are made and how much is displayed. FILECOMP.C is based on the UNIX diff utility and is especially useful when two files are almost the same (such as versions 1.1 and 1.2 of one of your programs).

The command format is

C>FILECOMP *[options] filespec1 filespec2*

The options are

/f	show full lines
/t	expand tabs before comparing
/b	ignore trailing blanks
/w	ignore spaces and tabs
/y	case-insensitive compare

You can combine options, as in /fwy or /f /bw or /f /b, in any order or combination, with or without white space—which explains why **getopt( )** is so useful! The default settings are

no	/f	show just first 34 characters of lines
no	/t	don't expand tabs before comparing
no	/b	don't ignore trailing blanks
no	/w	compare spaces and tabs
no	/y	case-sensitive compare

You clearly can set any defaults you like—**getopt( )** simply tells you what option letters were found in the command line. Program 10.2 is the extract from FILECOMP.C.

► *FUNCTIONS AT WORK* ►

In this final section I want to touch on two important aspects of functions: functions as arguments to other functions and recursive functions. These are big subjects that fill many esoteric volumes, so, like the Winchester readhead, I can only scratch the surface.

```
/* Extracts from FILECOMP.C */

/* Copyright (c) Borland International 1987
   All Rights Reserved. */

#define FULL     0x80      /* sets bit 7 */
#define TABS     0x40      /* sets bit 6 */
#define TRIM     0x20      /* etc.       */
#define WHITE    0x10
#define CASE     0x08
#define BLANK    0x04

#define TRUE     1
#define FALSE    0

    unsigned char flag1 = WHITE;

void givehelp(void)
{
        printf("Usage is: FILECOMP [options] filespec1 filespec2\n");
        printf("Options:\n");
        printf("  /f\tshow full lines.\n");
        printf("  /t\texpand tabs before comparing.\n");
        printf("  /b\tignore trailing blanks.\n");
        printf("  /w\tignore spaces and tabs.\n");
        printf("  /y\tcase insensitive compare.\n");
        printf("filespec2 can be a drive or directory name.\n");
}

/* main program */
int cdecl main(int argc, char *argv[])
/* cdecl allows you to run Pascal mode */
{
        int i,j,k,opt;

        extern int getopt(int argc, char *argv[], char *optionS);
        extern int opterr, optind;
/* declared here but defined in getopt.c */

        if (argc<3) {
                givehelp();
                return 0;
        }
/* typical check on argc = number of arguments */

        /* get options */

        opterr = FALSE;
/* turn off the perror() display -- handle errors yourself */

        while ((opt = getopt(argc, argv, "ftbwy")) != EOF) {

/* sets option string for lowercase optLetters only. Only these
   five choices are valid. No argLetters with colon, so no args

   expected after the option switches. The loop keeps going
   until parse scan reaches first nonopt arg namely filespec1 */

/* opt is set to the letter returned by getopt() -- natural for
   the switch-case mechanism */
```

▸ *Program 10.2:* FILECOMP.C extract

```
                switch (opt) {
                        case '?':
                                printf("Invalid command line option\n");
                                givehelp();
                                return(1);
                        case 'f':
                                flag1 |= FULL; break;
                        case 't':
                                flag1 |= TABS; break;
                        case 'b':
                                flag1 |= TRIM; break;
                        case 'w':
                                flag1 &= ~WHITE; break;
                        case 'y':
                                flag1 |= CASE; break;
                }
        }
/* note how flag1 is progressively set with bitwise OR:
   flag1 = flag1 | FULL sets bit 7; a further option might set
   bit 3, and so on. flag1 reveals all options set and duplicate
   options would be OK */
/* Later in program flag1 is tested with & to decide on strategy  */


/************ rest of main() comes here *************/

/* Following snippet is instructive -- each tab is changed to
   spaces -- the number of spaces is j mod 8 */

/* expand tabs -- called if /t option selected */
void tabex(unsigned char *s1, unsigned char *s2)
{
        int i;
        unsigned char j;
        for (i=j=0; s1[i]; i++) {
                if (s1[i] != '\t') {
                        s2[j++] = s1[i];
                        continue;
                }
                do s2[j++] = ' '; while(j%8 != 0);
        }
        s2[j] = 0;
}

/* How to kill spaces and tabs */
/* input string s1 -- output string s2 less white-space */
void zapwhite(unsigned char *s1, unsigned char *s2)
{
        int i, j;

        for (i=j=0; s1[i]; i++) {
                if (s1[i] != ' ' && s1[i] != '\t')
                        s2[j++] = s1[i];
        }
        s2[j] = 0;
}
```

► **Program 10.2:** *FILECOMP.C extract (continued)*

► *Pointers to Functions* ►

When the compiler meets the declaration of an array such as **char name[30];** you know that the identifier **name** is translated as a pointer (the constant pointer to the **char** at address **&name[0]**). So **name** plays a dual role as array name and pointer.

In the same way, the names of declared functions also play a second role as pointers. The syntax distinguishes between **func(arg);** as a call to **func** and the isolated identifier **func** as a pointer. If you encounter the following declaration:

```
int (*func_ptr)(void);
```

you can deduce that **(*func_ptr)** is playing the role of a function taking no arguments and returning an **int**. C's declaration syntax is based on the "template for action" principle. What the declaration has achieved is similar to the other pointer declarations you have encountered, e.g., **int *ptr;** does not create an **int** but creates an uninitialized variable of type pointer to integer. Similarly, the **func_ptr** declaration creates not a function but an uninitialized variable of type 'pointer to function of type F' where F is 'takes no arg and returns an integer.' Before being used this pointer must be initialized with an appropriate value. If you define

```
int myfunc(void)
{ /* body here */
}
```

then **myfunc** is a respectable candidate for **func_ptr**:

```
func_ptr = myfunc;
i = *func_ptr( );
/* same as i = myfunc( ); */
```

In the first assignment it is tempting but wrong to use **&myfunc** on the right side. This is as wrong as using **&name** rather than the true pointer, **name**. Since **func_ptr** now has a valid, non-NULL value, the indirection is valid and ***func_ptr( )** is a legal invocation of a function.

Function pointers can be used just like other pointers. You can store them in arrays, structures, and unions. For example, you can have

```
struct action_table {
        int (*func1)( );
      float (*func2)( );
      action_table *node;
    } my_table;
```

Here you can store function pointers representing actions to be taken under different circumstances. Saving formulae in spreadsheet cells can be achieved with this approach.

Function pointers can be arguments to functions, and they can be returned as values by functions. Functions cannot return arrays or functions per se, but they can return pointers for these objects. When all the dust from the pointer controversy settles, you can say that the dangers are offset by the power and elegance of being able to pass and effectively return arrays and functions to and from functions.

A simple but instructive example is **qsort( )**, which is prototyped in STDLIB.H as follows:

```
void qsort( void *base, size_t nelem, size_t width,
            int (*fcmp)( ) );
```

The arguments are as follows:

> **base** is the pointer to the first (0th) element of the table to be sorted.
> **nelem** is the number of entries in the table.
> **width** is the size in bytes of each element to be sorted.

Ah ha—what is the final parameter? Yes, it's a pointer to a user-supplied function called the *comparison function*. You tell **qsort( )** how to sort by indicating what you mean by "greater," "equal," and "less than." Your **fcmp( )** must be defined so that **fcmp(ptr1, ptr2)** returns − 1 if ***ptr1** is less than ***ptr2**, 0 if ***ptr1** equals ***ptr2**, and + 1 if **ptr1** is greater than ***ptr2**. **ptr1** and **ptr2** are declared as pointers to elements of the table to be sorted.

The sort, based on C. A. R. Hoare's quicker-sort, is therefore applicable to any numerical or symbolic ordering sequence you can possibly dream up. For simple lexicographic string sorts you can use any of the **strcmp( )** variants in STRING.H because these return the prescribed **int** values. For more complex sorts you write **my_comp( )** and pass **my_comp** as the pointer argument.

► *Recursion* ►

(*Recursive* adj. See *Recursive* [Kelly-Bootle, Stan. *The Devil's DP Dictionary.* New York: McGraw-Hill, 1981.])

C shares a valuable property with most modern structured languages in its support of *recursion* both for functions and data structures.

You saw recursive data structures in Chapter 5 where a structure member was a pointer to its own structure.

I mentioned in Chapter 7 that a function can call any function within its scope, and that this allows **func( )** to call **func( )** recursively. To avoid an infinite regress you need to ensure that each call to **func( )** somehow converges to some measurable, terminating goal. Recursion also occurs when A calls B, B calls C, and C calls A. This is equally allowed in C provided the scoping rules are followed. Recursion offers an elegant solution to many problems where each stage of computation is defined in terms of the same function, although in theory any recursive solution has an equivalent nonrecursive formulation. The classic illustration is **factorial(N)**, which is defined as **(N * factorial(N − 1))** unless **N** equals 0 [factorial(0) is defined as 1]. Another example is the exponentiate or power function, since $X^N = X*(X^{N-1})$. Consider the function **exp(X, N)** for non-negative **N**, defined as follows:

```
double exp(double X, int N)
{
    if (N < 0) return (− 1);              /* error */
    if (N = 0) return (1);
    else return (X*exp(X, N − 1));
}
```

Each time **exp( )** calls itself, the exponent argument is reduced by 1, guaranteeing an end to the sequence. You should try this with different values, noting that for very large values of **N** you may get stack overflow. Program 10.3, MYEXP.C, gives you a bare-bones platform to experiment with.

MATH.H contains the standard power function

```
double pow(double x, double y);
    /* toil and trouble? */
```

for more exotic calculations of x^y. You might want to compare its accuracy with **myexp( )** when **y** is a whole number.

► SUMMARY OF ENHANCEMENTS AND CHANGES IN VERSION 2 ►

As discussed in more detail in Chapter 11, Borland again upgraded the Turbo C package from Version 1.5 to 2 in August 1988. Chapter 11 discusses the integrated debugging facilities of Turbo C 2. Here I'll run through some

```
/* myexp.c - tests recursion */
#include <stdio.h>

double myexp(double X, int N)
{
        if (N < 0) return (-1);
        if (N == 0) return (1);
        else return (myexp(X,N-1)*X);
}

void main()
{
        double x = 0; int n = 0; char ch = '\0';

        do {
          puts("Enter N and X:");
          scanf("%d %lf",&n, &x);
          printf("N=%d, X=%f\n",n,x);
          printf("X^N=%f\n",myexp(x,n));}
        while ((ch = getch()) != 'X');
}
```

► **Program 10.3:** *MYEXP.C*

of the other enhancements and changes you'll find when you step up from Version 1.5 to Version 2.

To accommodate the new features, some of the menu layouts and hot-key assignments have been revised. These changes have been indicated in Chapter 1 but will be explained further in this section and in Chapter 11.

When you run a program from within the IDE, the program returns you to the IDE screen. There is no **hit any key** message on the program output screen (also known as the *user* screen) allowing you to examine your results before returning to the main TC screen. You need to use the new hot-key combination Alt-F5 to toggle between the TC screen and the user screen.

Compiling and linking are faster by 20 to 30 percent, and execution times have been improved using faster functions and floating-point emulations. Also, support for extended memory systems allows you to allocate extra memory to the edit buffer. Up to 64KB additional memory can be provided for compiling and running.

The BGI (Borland Graphics Interface) library has several new functions, including installable drivers and fonts. The routines for EGA and VGA displays have been made faster, and you can now flood-fill elliptical shapes. The Version 2 *.BGI files are all different, so you will have to relink your Version 1.5 graphics programs before they will run correctly under Version 2.

The **gsignal( )** and **ssignal( )** software signal-handling functions have been replaced by the ANSI C-conforming **raise( )** and **signal( )** functions.

A new function, _ _**emit**_ _( ), lets you insert machine code directly into the object code generated by the compiler. This hairy alternative to in-line assembly-language code (using the **asm** keyword) has the advantage that it is available on both the TC (integrated) and TCC (command line) compilers. The **asm** construct works only with TCC. The arguments to _ _**emit**_ _( ) are "literal" bytes representing raw 808x machine instructions rather than the assembly-language mnemonics used with **asm**, so don't expect any gentle error messages!

OBJXREF.COM is a new utility for listing cross-references from a specified set of object and library files. A wide range of reports can be generated, including lists of public names and the modules in which they are defined as well as lists of modules and each of their external references.

Support is now provided for the ANSI C **long double** data type. The **long double** gives you an 80-bit precision compared with the 64-bit precision of **double**. **Long double**s conform to the IEEE 80-bit, double-precision, floating-point standard. The range of a **long double** is 3.4E–4932 to 1.1E+4932, giving an accuracy of approximately 19 significant decimal digits. Of course, you pay in terms of speed and memory usage for this extra precision, so use **long double**s only when your sums really need them. Both the 8087 and 80287 math coprocessors support the 80-bit format. The **printf(**) statement and its variants now accept the input-size modifier **L** to display numbers in **long double** format.

The stand-alone Make utility has been greatly improved to provide *auto-dependencies*. Once you have created a suitable Make file that lists the component *.OBJ and *.H files together with the compiler and linker commands needed to create your final *.EXE file, Make will check the dependencies and the relative date stamps of all files. Make then performs the minimum recompilation and linkage to ensure that all changes are incorporated into your *.EXE file. The improvements in Make stem from the new ways of writing your Make file. You can now incorporate both *explicit* and *implicit* rules regarding dependencies and the actions needed to update the final *.EXE file. Implicit rules can include command-line variables and macros. The Make file can also use C-like directives, such as **!include** and **!if**, as well as C-like numerical and conditional operators. Make can even obey DOS commands, such as **cd** and **copy**, in a Make file, or you can include a complete batch file (*.BAT) so that your action lists can make backups as well as performing the usual recompiles and relinks. So, writing a Make file is very much like writing a C program or UNIX shell script; yes, you can add comments with a preceding #.

The Project-Make facility built into the IDE also offers a new auto-dependency check feature that you can toggle on or off using the new Auto

Dependencies switch in the Project menu. When this feature is on, TC will look at the .OBJ files corresponding to each .C file listed in the .PRJ file. Each .OBJ file compiled by either TC or TCC contains information on any files included in the original source code. TC can therefore check the relative date/time stamps of all the constituent files and automatically recompile any dependent files that may have changed since the last compilation. The auto-dependency feature saves you from having to enter explicit dependencies in the .PRJ file. You can still list explicit dependencies, as discussed later in this chapter in the section entitled "Why Use Libraries?," but these will simply be ignored if you are running with Auto Dependencies on.

The editor has some new features such as block indent/unindent and optimal fill.

THELP.COM lets you access the Turbo C context-sensitive help data from any program. Running THELP.COM loads a RAM-resident TSR (terminate and stay resident) program that can be "popped-up" via the numeric 5 key.

The IDE help support has been extended. F1 still brings up context-sensitive Help windows; in addition, Ctrl-F1 triggers the display of information on the library functions. You simply position the editor cursor on any library function name in your source code, then press Ctrl-F1.

Installing Turbo C has been made easier in Version 2. If you are upgrading from Version 1.5, you can use CINSTXFR.EXE, which guides you through diskette insertion and replaces all the appropriate files while preserving any options you may have saved under Version 1.5. To install Version 2 from scratch, you use INSTALL.EXE. Version 2 comes on six floppies, and even then Borland had to compress (archive) all the example files. An UNPACK utility is provided so that you can restore (unarchive) the *.ARC files at any time. INSTALL will do the unpacking for you if you ask it. INSTALL will also run CINSTXFR for you if you wish, or you may prefer to set up your own directories/subdirectories and copy away.

Note that TCINST.COM has grown to TCINST.EXE. Make sure that your old TCINST is erased, or else you might suffer from a familiar quirk of DOS: If you have two files called AAA.COM and AAA.EXE, typing AAA will invoke AAA.COM.

TC now has additional command-line switches. Version 1.5 offered the /C switch (see Appendix B) whereby

    C>TC /CMYCONFIG

for example, fires up the IDE with the configuration file MYCONFIG.TC replacing the default TTCONFIG.TC. Version 2 allows the following extra switches:

► **The Build Switch, /B** Subject to certain conditions

> C>TC MYPROG /B

will compile and link MYPROG.C, then return to DOS. Any messages generated by the compiler will be displayed on the standard output device. The *B* stands for Build, meaning compile/link regardless of date/stamps and dependencies. The /B switch can be used in conjunction with /C switch so that you can load a special configuration file specifying a project file to be built or a primary file to be compiled/linked—for example:

> C>TC /CMYCONFIG /B

The /B switch is useful when you want to invoke TC in a batch file without displaying the IDE screens and menus.

► **The Make Switch, /M** The /M switch works like the /B switch but invokes a make rather than a build:

> C>TC /CMYCONFIG /M

This means that date/time stamps are tested and only antiquated files are compiled. For both /B and /M, TC searches for a target file in the following sequence: a .PRJ file in the loaded .TC file, then a primary file in the loaded .TC file. In the absence of these, TC looks for a file name in the command line, failing which, TC takes the file currently loaded in the TC editor.

► **The Dual Monitor Switch, /D** The /D switch lets you use two monitors: one for the normal TC screen menu activity (called the *inactive* screen); the other for program output (called the *active* screen). Of course, you'll need two display adapter cards that can coexist, typically one monochrome DA and one color or multifunction board, such as the Everex EGA or the Video-7 VEGA. The main point is that the two boards must access distinct video RAM addresses. When you type a TC /D command, it will appear on the active screen together with subsequent program output, whereas the TC menus will come up on the inactive screen. You can select which monitor is active either by using the DOS MODE command or by using the programs supplied with your graphics adapter board. The /D switch is a godsend for debugging certain graphics programs because you can isolate the IDE activity from the all the weird effects of bugs on the graphics screen.

► SUMMARY OF CHAPTER 10 ►

◄► GREP is a flexible FIND-like utility able to scan sets of files for complex string matches. Matches can be simple strings or UNIX-type regular expressions using ^ (line start), $ (line end), * and + (multiple occurrences), \ (escape), and [...] (ranges).

◄► TLIB is a simple but effective object-code library manager. You can create and maintain .LIB files using command-line option switches and/ or response files. You can + (add), – (remove), or * (extract) .OBJ files to any .LIB file. TLIB also lets you display, print, or write to disk the members of a .LIB file. The /C switch gives you compatibility with case-insensitive languages and linkers. The Turbo C supplied TLINK linker syntax was explained.

◄► You saw how and why libraries are used in C—both for efficiency and control of large projects. Project-Make was also explained in the context of maintaining multifile programs. .PRJ files allow you to express the interdependencies of .C, .OBJ and .H files.

◄► The **getopt( )** function was explained and dissected, throwing more light on the **main(int argc, char *argv[ ], char *argenv[ ])** mechanism for extracting data from a command line. Extracts from FILECOMP.C showed how **getopt( )** is used in a real-life application.

◄► The pointer to function allows you to write "generic" functions such as **qsort( )** that take a function as an argument. The syntactical key is that **func** as an identifier is taken as the pointer to the function, whereas **func(args)** is used to declare, define, or invoke the function.

◂▸ Recursion—I gave you a brief, tantalizing peek at a topic of great importance. Recursive data structures are widely used in C, allowing a **struct** member to point to itself (in a manner of speaking). Recursive functions call themselves directly or indirectly. To avoid infinite loops and exhausted stacks, some tested criterion in the recursion must ensure an exit. The function X^Y (exponentiate) was coded recursively as a simple example.

◂▸ I introduced you to the changes and enhancements (other than the debugging facilities) of Version 2.

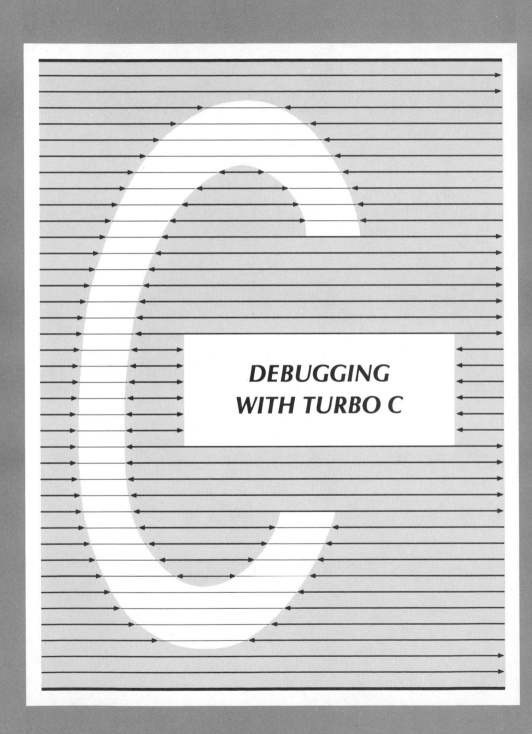

DEBUGGING
WITH TURBO C

► *CHAPTER 11* ►

"Stan, have you considered Chapter 11?" —Don Shaw, CPA

On August 29, 1988, Borland announced a wide range of new and improved products under the slogan "Programming Without Compromise." In fact, Borland chairman and CEO Philippe Kahn described the unveiling as the single most important announcement in Borland's history. In addition to the all-new Turbo macro assembler (TASM) and stand-alone Turbo Debugger, Borland released upgraded versions of existing products: Turbo Pascal 5 and Turbo C 2. Both Turbo Pascal 5 and Turbo C 2 offer built-in source-level debugging, accessible via the IDE (Integrated Development Environment) menus, as well as support for the new, more sophisticated freestanding Turbo Debugger. Borland offers special packaged combinations of these new products; for example, the Turbo C Professional package includes Turbo C 2 plus TASM and the separate Turbo Debugger.

This chapter is devoted to the exciting, new integrated debugging facilities of Turbo C 2. The new version also offers some other enhancements and changes, which are summarized in Chapter 10.

► *THE NEW SOURCE CODE DEBUGGERS* ►

In the ongoing Microsoft/Borland C wars, one of Microsoft's key advantages has been its Quick C integrated debugger and the freestanding Code-View debugger supplied with Microsoft C. Version 2 of Turbo C was clearly aimed at Quick C, whereas Borland's stand-alone Turbo Debugger offers a counterchallenge to CodeView. In fact, the Turbo Debugger supports CodeView-compatible *.EXE files and in addition offers multiple overlapping views (you can observe code and data at CPU or source levels), 386 virtual-86 mode debugging, remote terminal debugging, full data-structure debugging, and session logging.

To avoid confusion, note that the freestanding Turbo Debugger offers features beyond those found in the Version 2 integrated debugger. In fact, the freestanding Turbo Debugger can be used with many languages, both Borland's and otherwise, and is not confined to Turbo C. In the following exposition I will assume that you just have Turbo C 2—however, many of the basic debugging strategies will prove useful if and when you move up to the independent Turbo Debugger.

► *FOR ALL YOU DO, THIS BUG'S FOR YOU!* ►

First, let's step back and consider the nature of the beast. What exactly are bugs, and how can they be squashed? If you have tried any of the examples in this book, you have almost certainly encountered unexpected results from time to time, just as I did when devising the programs! Bugs are the critters that take the blame for a program misbehaving in some way.

The entomological taxonomy of bugs, though, is quite complicated and still the subject of intense computer scientific debate. To say that a program misbehaves implies that you have a firm and formal picture of what constitutes "correct" behavior. A program intended to compute factorial N, for instance, may give erroneous results (or loop forever with no results) if you input too big an N or a negative or fractional value of N. It is even possible to envisage a bizarre factorial N program that works fine for all values of $N < 50$ except for $N = 7$ and $N = 39$.

Is the problem with the program for failing to trap such input, or with the definition of factorial N, or with the limited capacity of your registers, or with the user of the program? Furthermore, the "defect" may not be discovered for many years because it was never subjected to "dubious" input, reminding us that bugs can and do "lurk" undetected simply because it may be impossible to test a large program with all possible input combinations. Testing each module as it is developed is mandatory, of course, but there is no automatic guarantee that your modules will cooperate as planned.

You may have also heard the ironic in-joke that bugs are simply "undocumented features." The truth is that as your program grows in complexity, it becomes increasingly difficult to define exactly how it should behave under all circumstances. Certain nonfatal quirks may surface, and it is often cheaper to change the program specifications than modify the code. There are limits to this, of course. If your factorial program tells you that 4! (pronounced "factorial 4") is 23 rather than 24, no amount of redefinition and redocumentation will save you from the scorn of your potential user base.

Studies of large software projects reveal two frightening facts:

1. As the number of bugs is reduced, it becomes exponentially harder to remove the residual bugs—whence the old saw "Let sleeping bugs lie."

2. The code used to remove bugs, often called a *patch*, has a higher propensity for error than the original code owing to the possibility of subtle side effects.

Remember too that a program can run correctly with a given compiler/ OS/hardware mix and yet fail when ported to some other system. More often than you may imagine, a version change of the OS or compiler, or a change in the parameters and defaults used during compilation/linking, can dramatically affect the behavior of your code. In these cases, where exactly is the "bug"?

► *TYPES OF ERROR* ►

The mere act of typing, whether you are copying from a list or transferring your inward thoughts, is remarkably error-prone. And so is the task of proofreading when you compare two documents. The study of this problem goes back many centuries before the advent of computer programs. Even the most conscientious scribes copying revered manuscripts slipped up occasionally, as any biblical commentary will confirm. Two classes of error are common enough to attract special nomenclature by textual scholars: *dittography* and *haplography*.

With dittography, the scribe, possibly because of some interruption, copies a piece of text for the second time. A modern version of this occurs with word processors when a block of text is wrongly duplicated. Haplography is the opposite problem: When copying text that contains repetitive phrases, the eye moves ahead and a section is inadvertently omitted. It is surprisingly difficult sometimes to spot such aberations (such as the missing *r*) in your own work but not when you are reading someone else's efforts. The actual perception, that is to say, the message sent from eye to brain, of what you have written is so easily colored by what you *intended* to write. It may seem a trite observation, but you may not be the best person to debug your own code. If, however, you are working alone, then you must develop the concentration needed to achieve clinical objectivity.

I have already mentioned the differences between syntactical (compile time) and semantic (run time) errors in a program (Chapter 1). In real life, these two classes of errors can overlap in disconcerting ways. You can sometimes make "syntax" errors that generate legal code with unintended "semantic" side effects.

Gross syntax errors are trapped by the compiler but may generate a rash of "misleading" error messages. This is because the impact of a syntax error may extend beyond its immediate neighborhood. It may take several statements, for example, before a misspelling, such as typing **far** or **fur** in place of **for**, can be diagnosed by the compiler!

There are far more ways of getting a program wrong than there are ways of getting it right, so it is difficult to formulate precise rules for debugging. If the final, erroneous output of the program is your only guide, you need a lot of luck to locate the bug immediately. It can be useful to embed various display statements in a program under development so that intermediate results can be observed. The aim is to work back from the known faulty result to the prime cause or causes.

If the computed value (**a * b / c**) is wrong, for example, you make sure that you did not enter (**a / b * c**), then trace back to see whether **a**, **b**, and **c** were computed correctly. In many cases, these three variables are set from other calculations, and you enter a confusing maze of possibilities. The only advice here is the obvious need for patient, logical detective work with large sheets of plain paper to note the effect of *single* changes to the program. Changing too many parameters at once is a common temptation. In the above example, you might try setting **a = 1** and bypassing the function that computes **a**. This approach involves lots of time editing and recompiling. Source-level debugging offers several time-saving tricks, as you'll shortly see.

Before I show you some real examples, let me explain the principles of the source code debugger and establish some of the jargon you will need.

► *SOURCE-LEVEL DEBUGGING* ►

It is worth stressing, first of all, that debuggers do not actually debug your code! You alone must determine why the program is misbehaving and make the corrections. Apart from locating syntax errors, the compiler, linker, and run-time support system have no innate ability to guess your intentions. It can even be proved that no general metaprogram exists that can detect endless loops. What debuggers can do is allow you to inspect and interact with a program while it is executing, thereby giving you useful clues pointing to the problems.

Before the advent of the source-level debugger, debugging high-level-language run-time errors was a major problem. The most you could expect was a *core dump* showing you the contents of memory and registers at selected moments of execution. The rather gloomy sounding *postmortem* dump was often triggered automatically when the program *abended* (i.e., ended through abortion). Relating pages of obscure octal or hex listings back to your legible source code was a real pain.

The popularity of *interpreters* over compilers can be traced to their obvious advantages in debugging: Each line of code is interpreted and executed immediately, pinpointing most errors for an instant fix. Reduced execution speed, however, is the price to be paid. A compromise that is emerging offers a C interpreter for program development, after which you switch to a compiler to get your final *.EXE.

The source-level debugger still remains the most popular approach to debugging, offering major advantages over the old core-dump approach. First, symbol table data is made available in various ways so that, during execution, variables can be referenced by their original source code names rather than via memory locations.

Second, *breakpoints* can be set at the source code level, allowing you to run a program up to a selected line or statement. When the program stops, you can peek at variables, expressions, and registers and optionally change their values. Finally, you can step through the program, statement by statement, optionally performing function calls as one step or stepping through each statement defining the function. You can then go full-speed ahead to the next breakpoint. Let's see how these maneuvers are performed with the Turbo C 2 menus and hot keys.

► USING THE VERSION 2 INTEGRATED DEBUGGER ►

The Debug and Break/watch menus control various aspects of the new integrated debugger. The first selection needed before you can use the debugger is made with the Debug menu. Fire it up with Alt-D, then select Source debugging. This offers a choice of three settings:

On: Programs compiled/linked in this mode can be debugged using either the integrated debugger or the stand-alone Turbo Debugger.

Standalone: Programs compiled/linked in this mode can be debugged only with the stand-alone Turbo Debugger.

None: Programs compiled/linked in this mode cannot be debugged.

Note the shorthand for uniquely specifying a sequence of menu selections:

D/S/O: selects On

D/S/S: selects Standalone

D/S/N: selects None

Make sure that Debug/Source debugging is on (the default set by Borland).

Next, invoke the Options menu with Alt-O, and select Compiler, then Code generation, then OBJ debug information. The shorthand description of these selections is O/C/C/O. The possible choices are on and off. You need to set OBJ debug information on before proceeding with the following exercise.

The key point here is that the *.OBJ and *.EXE programs you create with these two modes set on carry additional debugging data. This does not affect their normal execution, but once you have debugged a program, you should relink with the D/S/N option set (Debug/Source = None) and the O/C/C/O toggle off to reduce *.EXE file sizes.

To simplify our discourse I will refer to *.EXE programs that have been compiled/linked with both debug options on as debuggable programs.

Now, enter Program 11.1, SIGMA.C, then compile and link it in the usual way. SIGMA.C contains some deliberately instructive errors, ranging from the obvious to the less obvious.

Now type Alt-R to run SIGMA from within the IDE. Notice that Alt-R now brings up a Run menu, whereas under Turbo C 1.0/1.5, Alt-R triggered a run immediately. The new Version 2 Run menu has several run variations, but for

```
/* SIGMA.C purports to sum first n integers: 1+2+...+n */
/* WARNING: this program has deliberate bugs */

#include <stdio.h>

     int sumn(int m);      /* declaration */

     void main()
     {
          unsigned int n;
          printf("\nEnter a number: ");
          scanf("%u", &n);
          printf("\nSigma %u = %lu", n, sumn(n) );
     }


/* Function sumn() */
     int sumn(int m)        /* definition */
     {
          unsigned i;
          long unsigned sum;

          for (i-0; i < m; i++)
               sum =+ i;
          return sum;
     }
```

▶ *Program 11.1:* SIGMA.C

now use the first menu selection, called Run. This corresponds to the Version 1.0/1.5 Alt-R selection. To save you typing R/R, you can use the new hot key Ctrl-F9.

Since you have not yet set any breakpoints, the program will run normally, stopping only for **scanf( )** keyboard input. The user screen will display **Enter a number:**. Type 3 and press Enter. The user screen will flash the result and return to the IDE screen, possibly before you can read the ouput. Use Alt-F5 to toggle back to the user screen. Note that this is a new feature on Version 2.

The final answer should be 3 + 2 + 1 = 6, but SIGMA is not behaving as it should. Run the program again with different input and see if you can discern any pattern in the erroneous output.

The answers given by SIGMA.C are

Sigma 1 = 65536	not so good—should be 1
Sigma 2 = 131073	terrible—should be 3
Sigma 3 = 196610	worse—should be 6

You should always keep a note of the results with simple inputs—such as 1, 2, or 3—then look through the source code first for any obvious errors. The wrong answers here immediately suggest that we have somehow mixed up **signed** and **unsigned** numbers. Because this is an artificial debugging exercise, I will assume that you do not immediately spot the bugs responsible.

To give you some practice with the debugging features, I'll show you first how to *single-step* through the program.

▶ *SINGLE-STEPPING* ▶

Select Step-over from the Run menu, or use the handy hot key F8. The first thing that happens is that Turbo C will check the program's dependencies and, if necessary, recompile/relink to obtain the latest .EXE file. In other words, Step-over (F8) initially behaves just like Run (Ctrl-F9). With Step-over, however, execution is now under the control of the debugger: The program will be executed one step at a time.

Your IDE screen will now show a highlighted band, known as the *execution band*, positioned over the **main( )** line, indicating that you are beginning the debugging session from the start of SIGMA (see Figure 11.1). The execution band always shows you the statement line *about to be executed*. Notice that nonexecutable lines, such as comments and **#include**s are skipped, so the debugger stopped at the first executable line, the function **main( )**.

```
    File   Edit   Run   Compile   Project   Options   Debug   Break/watch
   ──────────────────────────────── Edit ────────────────────────────────
      Line 7     Col 30   Insert Indent Tab Fill Unindent * C:SIGMA.C
              void main()
              {
                      unsigned int n;
                      printf("\nEnter a number: ");
                      scanf("%u", &n);
                      printf("\nSigma %u = %lu", n, sumn(n) );
              }

    /* Function sumn() */
          int sumn(int m)         /* definition */
          {
                  unsigned i;
                  long unsigned sum;

                  for (i=0; i < m; i++)
                          sum =+ i;
                  return sum;
          }
   ─────────────────────────────── Watch ───────────────────────────────



    F1-Help  F5-Zoom  F6-Switch  F7-Trace  F8-Step  F9-Make  F10-Menu
```

▶ *Figure 11.1:* The Edit Screen with execution band on **main( )**

F8 is just one of several ways of initiating a debugging session. You can terminate a debugging session with Run/Program reset, or its hot key, Ctrl-F2.

You should now use Run/Trace-into or, more conveniently, the equivalent hot key, F7, to single-step the program. Notice how the execution band moves through successive lines for each F7 Trace-into operation. Of course, the execution band follows the actual run sequence. This seldom matches the physical sequence of the source code statement, so show no surprise when the band jumps around during **while**, **for**, and other control loops.

Just like F8, F7 can be used to initiate a debugging session. Turbo C will check dependencies and recompile/relink in exactly the same way. So, how do F7 and F8 differ?

► *Tracing and Stepping* ►

F7 (Trace-into) and F8 (Step-over) both single-step in the same way until you reach a statement calling a user-supplied function. As the names imply, F7 single-steps into the function's statements, whereas F8 steps over the function, executing it as a single step. Note that F7 can only trace into a debuggable function—that is, a function whose source code is available to the debugger. Also, of course, the function must have been compiled/linked originally with the debug options on.

For example, a Turbo C-supplied library function such as **printf( )** cannot usually be traced into because it was not compiled in debug mode. As you have seen, this would bloat the library without due cause. Both F7 and F8, then, will simply execute **printf( )** as a single step. Normally, of course, there would be no practical point in stepping through the individual statements of **printf( )** or any other supplied library function. You are really interested in debugging *your* code not Borland's!

If you have purchased the library source from Borland, you may wish to create debuggable versions of standard functions simply as an educational exercise, but for now I will assume that you will always step over standard functions rather than trace into them.

Note the vital difference between the *cursor* position and the execution band position. These two are quite independent. The cursor indicates your current position in the IDE editor, whereas the execution band indicates the next statement to be executed by the debugger. Later on you'll meet the Go to cursor command in the Run menu (hot key F4), which allows you to execute all statements between the execution band and the line holding your current cursor. Also, the cursor lets you edit your code in the usual manner during a debugging session. Remember, though, to use F2 (File/Save) and rebuild (compile/link) before resuming the debugging session. More on this later.

For now, just keep pressing F7 to step line by line, noticing how the execution band follows the source code. When you pass the **printf( )** statement, the user screen will momentarily display the prompt and then return to the IDE screen with the **scanf( )** line highlighted. When you press F7 to execute the **scanf( )** statement, you return automatically to the user screen and the system waits for you to enter a number, just as if you were running normally.

After entering **n**, you are returned to the IDE screen with the execution band on the next line:

```
printf("\nSigma %u = %lu", n, sumn(n) );
```

If you press F7 now, execution of **printf( )** calls the function **sumn( )**. It is important to note that although the execution band tracks line by line, a typical C line may contain several statements, possibly including calls to functions. The debugger will execute these in the correct sequence, as specified by the C syntax.

Because **sumn( )** is a debuggable function and in the same module as **main( )**, you will see the execution band move down into the **sumn( )** source code. Had you used F8, all the steps of the function **sumn( )** would have been invoked in one fell swoop.

As you press F7 to step through **sumn( )**, notice that the single statement within the **for** loop will be invoked as many times as the parameters dictate. In our simple example, the execution band seems to remain on the same statement, **sum = + i;**, but be not alarmed! The statement *is* being executed each time you press F7—indeed, this sequence gives you a useful clue as to whether the **for** loop is correctly coded (in fact, you've probably spotted some gross errors in the **for** loop already).

Keep pressing F7 until the **for** loop terminates; then on through the **return** statement; then back to **main( )**, where the **printf( )** is completed. Again, you will see a momentary flash to the user screen before you land back in the IDE screen. Alt-F5 allows you to inspect the output by toggling you back to the user screen. Jot down the results, then press Ctrl-F2 to end the debugging session.

The foregoing drill was intended to give you a feel for the single-stepping hot keys. However, we have not yet tackled the bugs—we have simply been running a buggy program in slow motion! In the next session, you will learn how to peek and poke or, more politely, how to evaluate and reset expressions at selected points in the run sequence.

► *EVALUATING EXPRESSIONS* ►

Repeat the previous debugging session and enter n = 2, then stop at the **for** loop in **sumn( )**:

```
for (i = 0; i < m; i + +)
    sum =+ i;
return sum;
```

Now select Debug/Evaluate, or use the more convenient hot key Ctrl-F4. Figure 11.2 shows the Edit screen with the Debug menu pulled down, ready for you to select Evaluate. The Evaluate window pops up (see Figure 11.3), displaying three fields as follows:

Evaluate field	Enter the variable or expression to be evaluated.
Result field	The debugger displays the requested value here.
New Value field	You can optionally enter here a new value for the selected variable or expression.

The Evaluate field displays a default expression corresponding to the word at your current cursor position. You can edit or change this expression in various ways.

```
  File   Edit   Run   Compile   Project   Options   Debug   Break/watch
┌──────────────────────── Edit ════════════════════╤══════════════════════╗
│     Line 22    Col 33   Insert Indent Tab         │ Evaluate    Ctrl-F4  │
│     void main()                                   │ Call stack  Ctrl-F3  │
│     {                                             │ Find function        │
│           unsigned int n;                         │ Refresh display      │
│           printf("\nEnter a number: "             │ Display swapping  Smart │
│           scanf("%u", &n);                        │ Source debugging  On │
│           printf("\nSigma %u = %lu",              │                      │
│     }                                             └──────────────────────┘
│ /* Function sumn() */
│     int sumn(int m)          /* definition */
│     {
│           unsigned i;
│           long unsigned sum;               .
│
│           for (i=Ø; i < m; i++)
│                  sum =+ i;
│           return sum;
│     }
└──────────────────────────── Watch ───────────────────────────────────────┘

 F1-Help  F5-Zoom  F6-Switch  F7-Trace  F8-Step  F9-Make  F1Ø-Menu
```

► *Figure 11.2:* The pull-down Debug menu

```
   File    Edit    Run    Compile    Project    Options    Debug    Break/watch
                                         Edit
      Line 22    Col 33    Insert Indent Tab Fill Unindent * C:SIGMA.C
        void main()
        {
            unsigne  ┌─────────────── Evaluate ───────────────┐
            printf(  │  sum                                   │
            scanf("  └────────────────────────────────────────┘
            printf(  ┌─────────────── Result ─────────────────┐
        }            │  2228683310                            │
                     └────────────────────────────────────────┘
/* Function sumn() */┌─────────────── New value ──────────────┐
        int sumn(int m) │                                     │
        {            └────────────────────────────────────────┘

            unsigned i;
            long unsigned sum;

            for (i=0; i < m; i++)
                    sum =+ i;
            return sum;
        }
                              ─────── Watch ───────


   F1-Help   F7-Trace   F8-Step   F10-Menu   TAB-Cycle   ◄─┘-Evaluate
```

► *Figure 11.3:* The Evaluate window

You can exit from and clear the Evaluate window by pressing Esc, or you can simply press F7 or F8, which clears the Evaluate window *and* resumes the single-stepping.

For now, type **sum** in the Evaluate field and press Enter. The value of **sum** will appear in the Result field. I get 2209415726; your value may be different. Can you explain the weird value revealed? Yes, the local variable **sum** has not been initialized. Since the aim is to accumulate $1 + 2 + ...$ in **sum**, clearly we should set **sum** to 0 before the **for** loop.

► Bug Number 1 ►

We have uncovered our first bug—an instructive one to be sure. Most bugs are bugs of omission rather than bugs of commission. Here, we failed to initialize a local variable. The probability that the rubbish found in **sum** will be 0 is too low to form the basis of a sound program! There are four ways to correct this bug:

1. Define **sum** as a **static** variable, so that it is set to 0 automatically.

2. Initialize **sum** in the definition as follows:

    long unsigned sum = 0;

3. Initialize **sum** in the **for** loop as follows:

    for(i = 0,sum = 0; i < m; i + +)

4. As a temporary patch, without changing the source code, you can change the value of **sum** using the New Value field of the Evaluate window.

    Enter **sum** in the Evaluate field, press Enter to get the value, then use the down arrow key to reach the New Value field. You can now enter **0** (or any other constant) and press Enter, then press Esc to get back to the IDE screen. Or you can enter expressions such as **sum + 1** or **sum/(i*3)**, provided that the variables used are currently defined and within the scope of the current function. (Later on, you'll see how to *qualify* out-of-scope variables to make them accessible.) Such expressions are evaluated according to the normal rules of C, then assigned to **sum**. When you resume execution, the new value of **sum** will be in force. If you type a new value then change your mind, you can edit or escape, but once you press Enter, the new value will be assigned. The New Value field, like the Evaluate field, can be scrolled left or right to accommodate long expressions using the left and right arrows and the Home and End keys. Setting new values during a run allows you to probe and test a program in many ways without changing the source code. It is often the only way to deliberately pass invalid-parameter data to a function in order to test your error-trapping routines.

For the moment, though, let's press on without correcting this **sum** initialization bug. I want to reveal another common, diabolical situation in debugging—how one bug can mask the presence of another.

► *Bug Number 2* ►

Press F7 once through the **sum** =+ i; statement, and use Ctrl-F4 again to reevaluate **sum**. The plot gets thicker: **sum** is now 0! Had we not bothered to evaluate **sum** before entering the loop, this result—**sum** equals **0**—might have led to complacency.

Look carefully at the following statement in the **for** loop:

sum =+ i;

Of course—this should read **sum += i;**, as explained in the discussion of compound assignments in Chapter 2. In the early days of C, the compound assignments were actually written =+, =/, and so on. This led to some syntactic ambiguities: Does **sum =+ i;** mean **sum = (+i);** or **sum (=+) i;**? So the compound assignments were revamped from =*op* to *op*=.

Correct this line to show **sum += i;**, and while you are at it, add **sum = 0** in the **for** loop initialization, as discussed in the previous section. Now press F2 to save your changes, then F7 again. Turbo C will cleverly recompile/relink before resuming the Trace-into.

Program 11.2 shows the current state of SIGMA.C.

Alas, you will still find that **n = 1** gives **Sigma 1** as **65536**, yet if you evaluate **sum** just before the **return** statement, you find that **sum** is 0.

This directs our attention to the line

printf("\nSigma %u = %lu", n, sumn(n));

```
/* SIGMA.C purports to sum first n integers: 1+2+...+n */
/* WARNING: this program still has bugs */

#include <stdio.h>

    int sumn(int m);      /* declaration */

    void main()
    {
        unsigned int n;
        printf("\nEnter a number: ");
        scanf("%u", &n);
        printf("\nSigma %u = %lu", n, sumn(n) );
    }


/* Function sumn() */
    int sumn(int m)       /* definition */
    {
        unsigned i;
        long unsigned sum;

        for (i=0,sum=0; i < m; i++)    /* initialize sum */
            sum += i;                  /* was =+ */
        return sum;
    }
```

► *Program 11.2: SIGMA.C (stage 2)*

in **main( )**. Yes, **sumn( )** has been defined as returning an **int**, yet **sum** is a **long unsigned** and the format string uses **%lu** for a **long unsigned** variable. We must either change **sum** to **int** and change the **%lu** to **%d** or, preferably, redefine **sumn( )** to return a **long unsigned**. **Sigma n** would benefit from the larger range, and we know the answer is always nonnegative. You need to alter both the declaration and definition of **sumn( )** to show

```
long unsigned sumn(Int m);
...
long unsigned sumn(int m)
    {
...
```

Program 11.3 shows SIGMA.C after these corrections.

Now use F2 to save your changes, use Ctrl-F2 to reset the program, and rerun it by typing Alt-R/R (or Ctrl-F9). Are we any closer to our elusive target?

Well, now we get the *less* wild results

Sigma 1 = **0**   should be **1**

Sigma 2 = **1**   should be **3**

Sigma 3 = **3**   should be **6**

```
/* SIGMA.C purports to sum first n integers: 1+2+...+n */
/* WARNING: this program still has a bug */

#include <stdio.h>

    long unsigned sumn(int m);    /* declaration */

    void main()
    {
        unsigned int n;
        printf("\nEnter a number: ");
        scanf("%u", &n);
        printf("\nSigma %u = %lu", n, sumn(n) );
    }

/* Function sumn() */
    long unsigned sumn(int m)      /* definition */
    {                              /* return type now matches sum
*/
        unsigned i;
        long unsigned sum;

        for (i=0,sum=0; i < m; i++)   /* initialize sum */
            sum += i;                  /* was =+ */
        return sum;
    }
```

► *Program 11.3:* SIGMA.C *(stage 3)*

The answers are still wrong, but because **Sigma 2** is showing the correct value for **Sigma 1**, and **Sigma 3** gives us the proper value for **Sigma 2**, we can hazard a guess that the **for** loop is terminating too soon. Of course, you might spot the reason for this right away by examining the source, but to reveal more debugging tricks, I will show you how to set up breakpoints and watch windows.

▶ *SETTING AND USING BREAKPOINTS* ▶

Load the latest SIGMA.C (stage 3), if you haven't already done so, press F8 (setting the execution band on **main( )**), then position the cursor on the **for** loop line. Now select Break/watch with Alt-B. The lower part of the menu (see Figure 11.4) shows the breakpoint options

Toggle breakpoint   Ctrl-F8

Clear all breakpoints

View next breakpoint

```
    File   Edit   Run   Compile   Project   Options   Debug   Break/watch
  ┌──────────────────────────── Edit ────────────────┌─────────────────────────┐
  │     Line 22    Col 25   Insert Indent Tab Fill    │ Add watch      Ctrl-F7  │
  │     (                                             │ Delete watch            │
  │            unsigned int n;                        │ Edit watch              │
  │            printf("\nEnter a number: ");          │ Remove all watches      │
  │            scanf("%u", &n);                       │                         │
  │     )   ┌──────── Add Watch ────────┐      su     │ Toggle breakpoint Ctrl-F8│
  │         │ sum                       │             │ Clear all breakpoints   │
  │         └───────────────────────────┘             │ View next breakpoint    │
  │ /* Function sumn() */                             └─────────────────────────┘
  │          long unsigned sumn(int m)         /* definition */
  │          (                                 /* return type now matches sum */
  │                 unsigned i;
  │                 long unsigned sum;
  │
  │                 for (i=0,sum=0; i < m; i++)    /* initialize sum */
  │ ███████████████████ sum += i; ██████████████ /* was =+ */
  │                 return sum;
  │          )
  │ ────────────────────────────── Watch ──────────────────
  │•i: 0
  │ m: 3
    F1-Help  F5-Zoom  F6-Switch  F7-Trace  F8-Step  F9-Make  F10-Menu  →-More text
```

▶ *Figure 11.4:* The Break/watch menu with Add Watch selected

Selecting T will set a breakpoint on the line where the current cursor is situated, namely, the **for** loop. Escape back to the Edit screen and note that each character of the breakpoint line is individually highlighted. The hot key Ctrl-F8, of course, allows you to toggle a breakpoint more conveniently without leaving the Edit screen.

You really cannot confuse a breakpoint highlight with an execution band because the latter illuminates the whole line in a band of reverse video. Be warned, however, that when an execution band passes over a breakpoint line, the execution band temporarily "swamps" the highlight on the breakpoint line.

If you now select Run/Run (or press Ctrl-F9), the program will run at normal speed, stopping for **scanf( )** input and then coming to rest at the breakpoint line, with the execution band and breakpoint line coinciding. You can now evaluate expressions (with Ctrl-F4) or use F7 (Trace-into), F8 (Step-over), Ctrl-F9 (Run), or F4 (Run until cursor position—also known as Go to cursor). Turbo C will always monitor your dependencies, so if you have changed any constituent module, a recompile/relink occurs.

If you edit a file with breakpoints and then try to continue the debugging session, you get the prompt **Source modified, rebuild Y/N?** As you might guess, it can be tricky for Turbo C to maintain breakpoints during certain edits—for example, when you delete a breakpoint line. Note, though, that if you use F2 to save a file, load another file, then reload the original file, it will retain any previously set breakpoints. This is a great help when you are debugging across several different modules. But if you leave the IDE, the breakpoints disappear. You can also clear breakpoints individually by positioning the cursor and using the Ctrl-F8 toggle. Or you can clear all your breakpoints using Break/watch/Clear all breakpoints (there is no hot key for this operation). One minor warning: Before you compile, it is possible (but pointless) to set breakpoints on nonexecutable lines, such as comments and **#defines**. Once you have compiled/linked and started debugging, however, Turbo C *knows* what's going on and will disallow invalid breakpoints.

The View next breakpoint submenu selection simply moves the cursor to the next breakpoint without execution. "Next" is determined by the order in which the breakpoints were set, not the order in which they might be encountered during program execution.

Play around with the breakpoint facilities by setting and clearing breakpoints and running in different modes.

Because we have narrowed down the remaining bug (or bugs) in SIGMA.C to the **for** loop, it would be nice if we could monitor all the involved variables—namely, **m**, **i**, and **sum**—without having to flip to and from the Evaluate window. Well, there is such a feature, known as the Watch window. Let's see how it works.

► THE WATCH WINDOW AND WATCH EXPRESSIONS ►

The Watch window allows you to peek at any number of variables or expressions as your program is running. It works rather as if you had selected a whole set of expressions in the Evaluate field of the Evaluate window, except that the debugger constantly monitors your list and displays each value as the program unfurls.

To invoke the Watch mechanism select Break/watch/Add watch, or use the hot key Ctrl-F7 (see Figure 11.4). A box appears into which you type the name of the expression to be watched. As with the Evaluate field, the default expression appearing in the box is the word (if any) over the editor cursor. You can edit this word or type a new word, which then appears in the Watch window at the bottom part of the IDE screen (the area usually occupied by the Message window when you are not debugging) together with its current value.

Each time you invoke Ctrl-F7 and add a watch expression, that expression joins the previous list in the Watch window. If you add too many watch expressions, they will scroll down out of sight, just as error messages can disappear from an active Message window.

To help you keep track of the Edit, Message, and Watch windows in Version 2, the Version 1.5 hot keys have been supplemented as follows:

F6   toggles the active window from Edit to Watch when debugging but toggles the active window from Edit to Message when compiling/linking.

F5   zooms and unzooms the active window.

Alt-F6   toggles between the Watch and Message windows, provided one or the other is active.

Warning: Alt-F6 has an entirely different function if the Edit window is active: It reloads the previously loaded file!

► *Editing the Watch Expressions* ►

So, if the Watch window overflows, you can use F6 and F5 to get a full screen's worth. When the Watch window is active, you can edit and delete from the watch expression list in a natural way. The Home, End, up arrow, and down arrow keys move you around the Watch window, highlighting the selected watch expression. You then invoke the Watch editor with Break/watch/Edit watch. An Edit box appears containing the selected watch expression. You then retype the expression and press Enter; the edited watch expression then replaces the previous version in the Watch window.

You can delete a watch expression by highlighting it, then selecting Break/watch/Delete or, alternatively, by using Ctrl-Y or Del. To delete all your watch expressions, you can save time by selecting Remove all watches from the Break/watch menu.

► *WATCHING THE LOOP* ►

To get the feel of all this, load and use F8 on the latest version of SIGMA.C. Press Ctrl-F7 (Add watch) and enter **m**. Repeat this for **i** and **sum**, and see how the expressions build up in the Watch window at the bottom of your screen (see Figure 11.4). Now, depending on where the execution band is, you may find that some or all of your variables are out of scope. If so, you'll see, for example:

sum: 'Undefined symbol 'sum'

If the variable is in scope, you will see, for example:

sum: 0

as is shown in Figure 11.5.

Now press F7 (Trace-into), enter **n = 3** at the **scanf( )** statement, then use F7 to trace into the **for** loop. You will observe the three variables' values in the Watch window. The variable **m**, of course, will remain equal to **3**, the value passed from **main( )**. Now for some serious debugging! Note the values of **i** and **sum** as

```
   File    Edit    Run   Compile   Project   Options   Debug   Break/watch
 ──────────────────────────────── Edit ────────────────────────────────────
     Line 22    Col 25   Insert Indent Tab Fill Unindent * C:SIGMA.C
       {
               unsigned int n;
               printf("\nEnter a number: ");
               scanf("%u", &n);
               printf("\nSigma %u = %lu", n, sumn(n) );
       }

/* Function sumn() */
       long unsigned sumn(int m)        /* definition */
       {                                /* return type now matches sum */
               unsigned i;
               long unsigned sum;

               for (i=0,sum=0; i < m; i++)    /* initialize sum */
██████████████████████sum += i;████████████████████/* was =+ */█████
               return sum;
 ──────────────────────────────── Watch ───────────────────────────
 •sum: 0
  i: 0
  m: 3


 F1-Help  F5-Zoom  F6-Switch  F7-Trace  F8-Step  F9-Make  F10-Menu
```

► *Figure 11.5: The Watch list shows sum = 0.*

you use F7 to step through the **for** loop. The bug will be readily exposed:

    loop 1:   m = 3, i = 0, sum = 0

    loop 2:   m = 3, i = 1, sum = 1

    loop 3:   m = 3, i = 2, sum = 3

The loop now exits with **sum = 3** and i = 3 because (i < m) is now false.

► *Bug Number 3* ►

It should be clear (at long last!) that the loop is ending too soon: The condition (i < m) terminates the loop after **Sigma (m-1)** has been accumulated. The easiest fix is to change the loop condition to (i <= m). (See Chapter 4 for more details on the **for** loop). Alternatively, you could change the initializer to i = 1, but if so, you must watch out for the special case n = 0 (see later).

Change SIGMA.C as shown in Program 11.4. If you still have a breakpoint on the **for** statement, you can Ctrl-F9 (triggering a rebuild), enter **n = 3** at the **scanf( )**, then run up to that breakpoint. Now use F7 to step through the loop. You should see the following more promising sequence in the Watch window:

loop 1: $m = 3, i = 0, sum = 0$

loop 2: $m = 3, i = 1, sum = 1$

loop 3: $m = 3, i = 2, sum = 3$

loop 4: $m = 3, i = 3, sum = 6$

The loop now exits with **sum = 6** and $i = 4$ because ($i <= m$) is now false. Try a few other values of **n** to convince yourself that SIGMA is now correct.

There still remains a "philosophical" problem with SIGMA. How do we define **Sigma n** for $n <= 0$? **Sigma 0** could reasonably be defined as **0** (the sum of the first 0 integers); if so, then SIGMA.C works for **n = 0**. For **n < 0**, it would be wiser to say that **Sigma n** is *undefined*. Because **n** has been declared an **unsigned int**, SIGMA.C as it stands would generate misleading rubbish for **n < 0**. I will leave you to revamp SIGMA.C to trap negative input. Hint: change **n** to **signed int** to allow the test if n<0.

SIGMA.C was a short, artificially doctored program to illustrate debugging some common errors. Turbo C comes with a more complex example, WRDCNT.C, that you should try, but be warned that Borland's earlier users' guide has a few textual errors when describing the Debug menu operations.

```
/* sumn() sums first n integers: 1+2+...+n */
#include <stdio.h>

        long unsigned sumn(int m);

        void main()
        {
        unsigned int n;
        printf("\nEnter a number: ");
        scanf("%u", &n);
        printf("\nSigma %u = %lu", n, sumn(n) );
        }

        long unsigned sumn(int m)
        {
        unsigned i;
        long unsigned sum;

        for (i=0,sum=0; i <= m; ++i)
                sum += i;
        return sum;
        }
```

▶ *Program 11.4: SIGMA.C (stage 4)*

► SUMMARY OF DEBUGGING COMMANDS ►

Table 11.1 provides a brief summary of the debugging commands provided with Version 2.

Menu Sequence	Hot Key	Function
Run/Run	Ctrl-F9	Run program until breakpoint
Run/Program reset	Ctrl-F2	Reset program and end debugging session
Run/Go to cursor	F4	Run program from execution band to current cursor
Run/Trace-into	F7	Single-step, including functions
Run/Step-over	F8	Single-step over functions
Run/User screen	Alt-F5	Toggle between Edit and user screens
Debug/Evaluate	Ctrl-F4	Pop up Evaluate window
Debug/Call stack	Ctrl-F3	Display call stack
Debug/Find function	none	Display a function definition
Debug/Refresh display	none	Restore Edit screen
Debug/Display swapping	none	Smart/Always/None
Debug/Source debugging	none	On/Standalone/None
Break/watch/Add watch	Ctrl-F7	Add watch expression
Break/watch/Delete watch	none	Delete watch expression
Break/watch/Edit watch	none	Edit watch expression

► **Table 11.1:** *Debugging commands*

Menu Sequence	Hot Key	Function
Break/watch/Remove all watches	none	Clear all watch expressions
Break/watch/Toggle breakpoint	Ctrl-F8	Turn breakpoint on/off
Break/watch/Clear all breakpoints	none	Turn off all breakpoints
Break/watch/View next breakpoint	none	Move cursor to next breakpoint
Options/Compiler/Code generation/OBJ debug information	none	On/Off
none	F5	Zoom/unzoom active window
none	F6	Switch active window
none	F10	Toggle menu/active window
none	Ctrl-F1	Context function help
none	Alt-F6	Switch Watch/Message windows (if active)
none	Alt-F6	Reload previous file (if Edit window active)

► **Table 11.1:** *Debugging commands (continued)*

► *VARIABLES AND THEIR QUALIFICATIONS* ►

I have mentioned several times that expressions to be evaluated or watched may contain variables outside the scope of the current function or module. Clearly, if you have several variables each legally named—say, **count** in different scopes—the debugger needs some help in determining which one you want to evaluate. Turbo C offers a trick known as *qualification* that will be familiar to Pascal and Modula-2 programmers. The basic idea is to create a unique expression by appending the name of the function or module (or both) to the target variable. The syntax is

[.*module_name.*]*function_name.variable_name*

where *module_name* is optional and the various elements are separated by
.'s (periods).

For example, to evaluate the static variable **count** in the function **random**
in the module called **exmod**, you would enter

.exmod.random.count

in the Evaluate field. If the target variable **sum** (static or auto) is in the same
module but in a different function, say—**sumn( )**—you need only enter

sumn.sum

► EVALUATION FORMATS ►

Finally, there are several options available to format the evaluations you
see in the Result field. Fortunately, these are not as complex as the **printf( )**
format specifiers. The general syntax is

expression[*,repeat_count*],[*format_char*]

Here, *repeat_count* is an integer specifying the number of consecutive variables to be evaluated (such as elements of an array). *format_char* is a single
letter indicating the format, as follows:

C	Character display.
S	String display.
D	Decimal display.
H or X	Hexadecimal display.
F*n*	Floating point (with *n* significant digits where $2 <= n <= 18$).
M	Memory dump starting with the address of the target expression. Can be used in conjunction with D, C, S, H, or X.
P	Pointer display in segment:offset format with additional information such as the variable pointed at.
R	Structure and union displays with field names and values.

You can evaluate arrays, structures, and unions. For example, if your program contained the following declarations:

```
struct {
    int  cusno;
    char cusname[25];
} customer = { 1000, "Kelly" };

int checks[4] = {100, 101, 102, 103};

int *int_ptr = checks;

main( )

{
...
}
```

you could display the following evaluations:

Evaluate Field	Result Field
checks	{100, 101, 102, 103}
checks[1],2	101, 102
checks[1],1H	0x65
customer	{ 1000, "Kelly\0\0\0\..\0" }
customer,R	{ cusno: 1000, cusname:"Kelly\0\0\0\..\0" }
int_ptr	DS:0200
int_ptr,P	DS:0200 [_checks]

► WHAT NEXT? ►

As you have seen, the Turbo C package provides an inexhaustible treasure of features to help you develop your own programs quickly and effectively. An area I have barely touched on is the brilliant integration of C and assembly-language tools in Turbo C. This answers the common criticism that C is inefficient for certain time-critical tasks. TCC lets you examine the assembly-language source of your C code and lets you embed your own optimized in-line, low-level code wherever this is needed.

In spite of all the layers of complexity and potential frustration, programming in general (and coding in C in particular) has no rival as an activity in which your skill and patience can bring such rich rewards—not only financially in a rapidly growing, programmer-hungry marketplace but also at a personal-achievement level.

By the time this book appears it is likely that Borland will have launched further support products to simplify the creation of programs for database management, text editors, and telecommunications.

If you have stayed the course this far, I dare to hope that your appetite has been whetted for a deeper study of C. Appendix H lists some useful resources for consolidation and more advanced work. To do serious work with Turbo C you definitely need to purchase the run-time library source code—a software bargain rivaled only by the Turbo C package itself. Currently priced at $150, the run-time library source comes on two diskettes, but when the .ARC files are UNPACKed you have over 1.5 MB of C and assembly-language source that will teach you more about professional programming than any set of books I know of.

Having said that, there are a few books you should have. From the hundreds of works on C available, I recommend the three listed in Appendix H.

Although there is much to learn, I have tried to ensure that you will not have too much to unlearn. When a language passes a certain threshold of usage, there is very little that can dislodge it—as shown by BASIC, Cobol, and Fortran. C has certainly achieved this degree of immortality, so good C programmers will never be short of job opportunities.

To some programmers, the ANSI C standard, like all standards, threatens a rather moribund immortality without the fun of diversity and innovation. Yet C has already been postincremented with the arrival of Bjarne Stroustrup's C++, which comes from the same AT&T Bell Labs that gave us the original K&R C. Mastery of Turbo C will prepare you for this bright future.

APPENDICES

► APPENDIX A ►
ASCII CODE CHART

HEX DIGITS 1st / 2nd	0-	1-	2-	3-	4-	5-	6-	7-	8-	9-	A-	B-	C-	D-	E-	F-
0		►		0	@	P	`	p	Ç	É	á	▒	└	┴	α	≡
1	☺	◄	!	1	A	Q	a	q	ü	æ	í	▓	┴	╥	β	±
2	☻	↕	"	2	B	R	b	r	é	Æ	ó	▓	┬	╥	Γ	≥
3	♥	‼	#	3	C	S	c	s	â	ô	ú		├	╙	π	≤
4	♦	¶	$	4	D	T	d	t	ä	ö	ñ	┤		╘	Σ	⌠
5	♣	§	%	5	E	U	e	u	à	ò	Ñ	╡	┼	╒	σ	⌡
6	♠	▬	&	6	F	V	f	v	å	û	ª	╢	╞	╓	µ	÷
7	•	↨	'	7	G	W	g	w	ç	ù	º	╖	╫	╫	τ	≈
8	◘	↑	(	8	H	X	h	x	ê	ÿ	¿	╕	╚	╪	Φ	°
9	○	↓	)	9	I	Y	i	y	ë	Ö	⌐	╣	╔	┘	Θ	∙
A	◎	→	*	:	J	Z	j	z	è	Ü	¬	║	╩	┌	Ω	·
B	♂	←	+	;	K	[	k	{	ï	¢	½	╗	╦	█	δ	√
C	♀	∟	,	<	L	\	l	|	î	£	¼	╝	╠	▄	∞	ⁿ
D	♪	↔	-	=	M	]	m	}	ì	¥	¡	╜	═	█	φ	²
E	♫	▲	.	>	N	^	n	~	Ä	₧	«	╛	╬	█	ε	■
F	☼	▼	/	?	O	_	o	⌂	Å	ƒ	»	┐	┴	▄	∩	

► **Table A.1:** *U.S. ASCII table*

HEX DIGITS 1st / 2nd	0-	1-	2-	3-	4-	5-	6-	7-	8-	9-	A-	B-	C-	D-	E-	F-
0		►		0	@	P	`	p	Ç	É	á	▒	└	ð	Ó	-
1	☺	◄	!	1	A	Q	a	q	ü	æ	í	▓	┴	Đ	β	±
2	☻	↕	"	2	B	R	b	r	é	Æ	ó	▓	┬	Ê	Ô	=
3	♥	‼	#	3	C	S	c	s	â	ô	ú		├	Ë	Ò	¾
4	♦	¶	$	4	D	T	d	t	ä	ö	ñ	┤	─	È	õ	¶
5	♣	§	%	5	E	U	e	u	à	ò	Ñ	Á	┼	ı	Õ	§
6	♠	▬	&	6	F	V	f	v	å	û	ª	Â	ã	Í	µ	÷
7	•	↨	'	7	G	W	g	w	ç	ù	º	À	Ã	Î	þ	¸
8	◘	↑	(	8	H	X	h	x	ê	ÿ	¿	©	╚	Ï	Þ	°
9	○	↓	)	9	I	Y	i	y	ë	Ö	®	╣	╔	┘	Ú	¨
A	◎	→	*	:	J	Z	j	z	è	Ü	¬	║	╩	┌	Û	·
B	♂	←	+	;	K	[	k	{	ï	ø	½	╗	╦	█	Ù	¹
C	♀	∟	,	<	L	\	l	|	î	£	¼	╝	╠	▄	ý	³
D	♪	↔	-	=	M	]	m	}	ì	Ø	¡	¢	═	─	Ý	²
E	♫	▲	.	>	N	^	n	~	Ä	×	«	¥	╬	█	¯	■
F	☼	▼	/	?	O	_	o	⌂	Å	ƒ	»	¬	░	▄	´	

► **Table A.2:** *Multilingual ASCII table*

► *APPENDIX B* ►
INSTALLATION SUMMARY

This appendix gives a quick, "get-you-started" Turbo C installation guide followed by a discussion of the many facilities for customizing your development environment.

► *GETTING STARTED* ►

Have you already made backup copies of all your Turbo C diskettes? If not, do so now.

► *Hardware Needs* ►

You need an IBM PC, PC/XT, PC/AT, or PS/2 or genuine compatible with PC-DOS (or MS-DOS) 2.0 or later with at least 384KB of RAM.

Although you can run most of Turbo C with two floppy drives (or even with one drive if you forgo the TCC command-line compiler and don't mind swapping disks), a hard disk with one or two floppies makes life so much sweeter. You got a bargain with Turbo C, so treat yourself to a 20MB hard disk—they are cheaper now than many C compilers and certainly cheaper than floppy drives were five years ago.

► *Rapid Installation* ►

The simplest way to install Turbo C on a hard-drive system is to use the INSTALL batch file supplied on the IDE (integrated development environment) diskette. (With Version 1.0 you have to create your directories with MKDIR and then type a few COPY commands.)

Although you can put the various Turbo C files almost anywhere, the sensible thing to do is to follow Borland's suggestion of having a working directory \TURBOC on your hard disk with subdirectories containing the following files:

> \TURBOC holds *.EXE, *.TCH, *.COM, *.C, *.BGI, *.CHR, *.PRJ
> \TURBOC\LIB holds *.ASI, *.ASM, *.BAT, *.LIB, *.OBJ
> \TURBOC\INCLUDE holds *.H (except STAT.H)
> \TURBOC\INCLUDE\SYS holds STAT.H

(The * is the DOS wildcard symbol matching every file name.) In this scheme \TURBOC is called the working directory.

Assuming you have a floppy drive A and a hard disk drive C, you can achieve the above configuration as follows:

1. Boot up and get the A> prompt.

2. Place the IDE diskette into drive A.

3. Type INSTALL A: C:\TURBOC and press Enter.

(Vary the A: and C: arguments if your drives are different.)

The batch file will prompt you to insert each of the five Turbo C diskettes as it proceeds. INSTALL creates the directories and subdirectories for you, then copies the files listed above.

▸ *Change Your PATH* ▸

Next, add C:\TURBOC to the PATH command in your AUTOEXEC.BAT:

> PATH C:\;C:\BOOK;A:\;C:\TURBOC

(Note the semicolon separators.)

This change, which will not become effective until your next boot, is optional but worthwhile since it allows you to run Turbo C from directories other than \TURBOC.

▸ *TCINST.EXE—Setting the IDE Defaults* ▸

Before you start using the Turbo C IDE you have to set certain basic environmental characteristics and values as defaults. The important defaults tell

TC where to find things by listing the directories (paths) of include files needed during compilation and .LIB files needed during linkage. Versions 1.5 and later allow multiple directories for the .LIB file search; Version 1.0 allows a single library directory.

You can set these defaults in several ways but for now I'll show you the simplest—the TCINST installation/customization program. It is a .COM file in Version 1.0 but has grown to TCINST.EXE in Versions 1.5 and later. The differences will emerge later, but they do not affect the following instructions except as noted.

1.   Log to the working directory with CD \TURBOC (be sure that you have TCINST.EXE there—if not, reread and repeat the INSTALL instructions).

2.   Type TCINST TC.EXE to bring up the main TCINST menu (see Figure B.1).

3.   Select Turbo C directories. Select the submenus and enter the paths shown in step 4.

4.   Set \TURBOC\INCLUDE in the Include directories.
     Set \TURBOC\LIB in the Library directories.

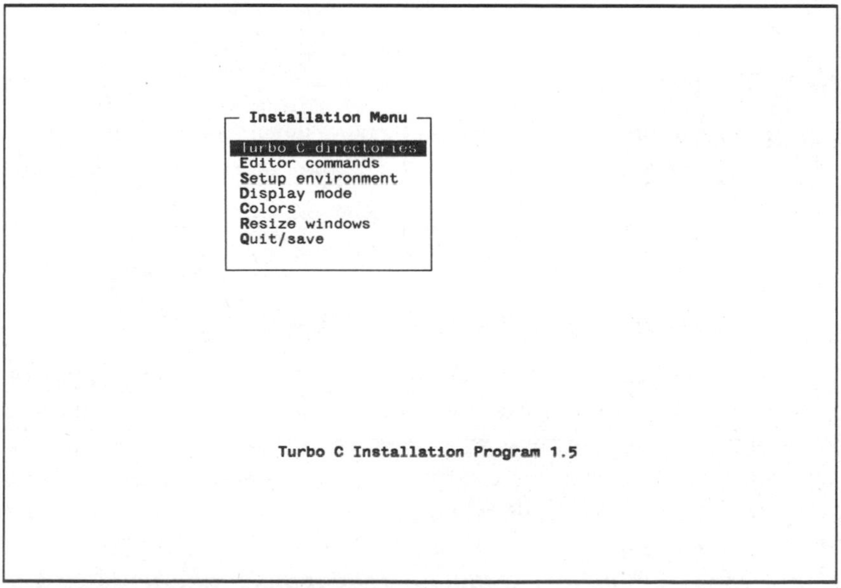

```
                  ┌─ Installation Menu ─┐
                  │ Turbo C directories │
                  │ Editor commands     │
                  │ Setup environment   │
                  │ Display mode        │
                  │ Colors              │
                  │ Resize windows      │
                  │ Quit/save           │
                  └─────────────────────┘




             Turbo C Installation Program 1.5
```

► *Figure B.1:* TCINST.EXE main menu (Version 1.5)

Set \TURBOC in the **O**utput directory.
Set \TURBOC in the **T**urbo C directory.
Set TCPICK.TCP in the **P**ick file name.

5. Escape back to main TCINST menu and select the **S**etup Environment Option menu. Check that **C**onfig auto save is toggled ON (Version 1.5 only). If not, toggle it ON.

6. Escape to main TCINST menu. Quit and answer Y(es) to the question, "Save changes to TC.EXE? (Y/N)?"

I'll explain the significance of these settings in the section entitled Advanced Default Management later in this appendix. For now, notice that all the above choices, except for the Turbo C directory selection, match choices offered in the IDE menu.

The general idea is that TCINST sets the default defaults, as it were, which you can change during a session in several ways. In addition to using the TC menu directly, you'll see later that you can use *configuration files* to override some of the TCINST defaults for some or all TC runs. The exception mentioned earlier is important: the Turbo C directory can only be set and changed by TCINST. It tells TC where to find the help file, TCHELP.TCH, and the default configuration file TCCONFIG.TC (to be explained anon).

► *Testing, Testing...* ►

Type TC and press Enter. You should see the IDE main menu. Press F1 to check that the help file is installed correctly, then press ALT-X or Files/Quit to exit.

► *An Introduction to Configuration Files* ►

Because Config auto save was ON, you will now find that a configuration file called TCCONFIG.TC has been created. This non-ASCII file encodes most of your TCINST settings. Briefly, if you make changes to your defaults from the IDE menu, you can save them with the Store option command or let TC save them automatically when you exit. If you don't give TC a specific configuration file name (with the default extension being .TC), TC uses the default name TCCONFIG.TC. When you next run TC, you can tell it to read a given configuration file, but if you don't, TC will read TCCONFIG.TC to pick up the defaults found there. TC.EXE is not physically changed by a .TC file—it simply behaves that way!

To know exactly what defaults are in force you need to combine the two separate influences: how TCINST has changed TC.EXE (permanent), and the contents of the configuration file that TC.EXE has just read (temporary). In the case of those defaults alterable by both TCINST and a .TC file, the .TC file has the last word; its influence overrides the TCINST default settings even though TC.EXE itself retains the TCINST defaults. Table B.1, which you'll see shortly, lists the TCINST defaults and indicates which of them are also influenced by a .TC file.

► *Other TCINST.EXE Features* ►

As you probably noticed while running TCINST, there were many other parameters and options open to change. The largest choice involves personalizing the TC editor (see Figure B.2). This comes with quasi-WordStar key/command preassignments that I personally find acceptable. If you just cannot bear the WordStar commands, do what you have to do. The Editor menu selection brings up the Install Editor screen. From this you can remap

```
                          Install Editor
   Command name           Primary                     Secondary

   New Line             * <CtrlM>                    · <CtrlM>
   Cursor Left          * <CtrlS>                    · <Lft>
   Cursor Right         * <CtrlD>                    · <Rgt>
   Word Left            * <CtrlA>                    · <CtrlLft>
   Word Right           * <CtrlF>                    · <CtrlRgt>
   Cursor Up            * <CtrlE>                    · <Up>
   Cursor Down          * <CtrlX>                    · <Dn>
   Scroll Up            * <CtrlW>
   Scroll Down          * <CtrlZ>
   Page Up              * <CtrlR>                    · <PgUp>
   Page Down            * <CtrlC>                    · <PgDn>
   Left of Line         * <CtrlQ><CtrlS>             · <Home>
   Right of Line        * <CtrlQ><CtrlD>             · <End>
   Top of Screen        * <CtrlQ><CtrlE>             · <CtrlHome>
   Bottom of Screen     * <CtrlQ><CtrlX>             · <CtrlEnd>
   Top of File          * <CtrlQ><CtrlR>             · <CtrlPgUp>
   Bottom of File       * <CtrlQ><CtrlC>             · <CtrlPgDn>
   Move to Block Begin  * <CtrlQ><CtrlB>
   Move to Block End    * <CtrlQ><CtrlK>             ·

   CtrlS-select  PgUp-PgDn-page  Ctrl-modify  R-restore factory defaults  ESC-exit
   F4-Key modes:  (*)-WordStar-like  (I)-Ignore case  (·)-Verbatim
```

► **Figure B.2:** *Editor menu*

keystrokes to text-edit functions in a self-explanatory way. If you get mixed up, you can Restore all key settings to the factory defaults.

The Setup Environment menu used in step 5 above also gives you various editor default choices like Insert mode on/off, Screen size, Autoindent mode on/off, and so on. I'll return to these later in this appendix.

▶ Pick Files

The TCINST menu allows you to set a default Pick-file name. The factory default is TCPICK.TCP. The latter defines a file where TC will save data on the state of the editor for each file in your Pick list. Pick files also keep track of all the file names you have been loading by maintaing a *Pick list*. The Pick list is accessed via the File/Pick list menu. The Pick list shows you the most recently loaded files, which is useful if you are editing several files in one session. The Pick file lets you switch the file being edited, edit another file, then return to the original file exactly where you left off.

▶ Moving On ▶

For the moment, let's leave all the other TCINST settings at their factory defaults—they represent sensible choices for the beginner. Many defaults can be changed via the IDE menu, or you can use TCINST again. If you ever get confused over the state of TC.EXE just copy from the original distribution version and start again.

You are now ready for some Turbo C action. Once you have gained more experience you will be in a better position to personalize your TC.EXE to suit your programming style. The rest of this appendix explains how defaults and .TC files work and how TCINST can be used to further customize your TC.EXE.

▶ ADVANCED DEFAULT MANAGEMENT ▶

A default is usually defined as some value or environmental characteristic that the system will implicitly assume in the absence of any contrary input. I need to extend this definition to include the two additional cases in which the default is "no default—input must be supplied" and "default value requires confirmation."

Some defaults, like the small memory model default, can be far-reaching, generating a whole slew of further defaults (such as pointer sizes and run-time library selections), while others are quite specific and local, like a Project-Make file name or a default path to a file.

You should be aware of the difference between *changing* a default and *overriding* a default. Many Turbo C features can be temporarily or locally modified by overriding a default. A typical example is the declaration **unsigned char ch;** when the default is signed **char**. This affects **ch** but not the default.

The general rule is that a default is set for the most frequently used disposition in order to reduce typing. For instance, the .OBJ file name defaults to the .C name, and pointers default to **near** in the smaller memory models.

Often, though, it is safer to be redundant, as in the case of **char** declarations. Declaring all **char**s explicitly as **signed** or **unsigned** makes your code default-dependent and (possibly) more portable.

► *Default Management* ►

With literally thousands of option permutations flying about, the user needs some help in managing defaults. Perfectly valid programs can suddenly misbehave when compiled, linked, or executed under inappropriate conditions. Turbo C provides many useful features to help you keep track of your defaults, rather as Project-Make watches out for file dependencies.

TCINST uses the following syntax:

C>TCINST *[/C] [path]*

The /C switch here is only needed if you have a color monitor and want the TCINST menus to be displayed in color. Without the switch you will get black and white. The *path* entry is only needed if TC.EXE is not located in your current directory. It is not unusual for Turbo C users to keep several distinct copies of TC.EXE (in different directories, of course), each customized differently with TCINST for different applications. By adding the *path* argument they can access these variants.

When you ran TCINST earlier it actually modified TC.EXE so that from now on when TC fires up it will carry the paths, and any other settings you entered, as built-in defaults. Table B.1 lists the options available from TCINST and indicates the default defaults built into the original TC.EXE.

Default Choice	Set via TCINST or .TC
Turbo C Directories Option	
Include directories	both [none]
Library directories	both* [none]
Output directory	both [none]
Turbo C directories	TCINST only [none]
Pick file name	both* [TCPICK.TCP]
Editor Command Option	
Special menu for keystroke changes	TCINST only [factory]
Setup Environment Option	
Backup source file	both [on]
Edit auto save	both** [off]
Config auto save	both* [on]
Zoom state	both [off]
Insert mode	TCINST only [on]
Autoindent mode	TCINST only [on]
Use tabs	both (.TC sets tab size)[on]
Screen size	both [hardware dependent]
Display Mode Option	
Default	TCINST only [on]
Color	TCINST only [hardware dependent]
Black and white	TCINST only [hardware dependent]
Monochrome	TCINST only [hardware dependent]
Resize Windows Option	
Up down arrow adjustments	TCINST only [factory]

► *Any IDE menu items not listed above are .TC only.*
  * *new or modified with Version 1.5*
  ** *name changed with 1.5, same function*
  [ ] *indicates default default*

► **Table B.1:** *TCINST.EXE and .TC options (Versions 1 and 1.5)*

(The TCC command-line compiler, by the way, has different default strategies and configuration files that are outside the scope of this book.)

The defaults you have set up so far with TCINST might be called the sensible minimal set to run TC. In theory, only the Turbo C directory needs TCINST since there's no other way to set that. Without it the TC help system cannot be invoked. But we could have set the include and library directories from the IDE Options menu.

TC will create or update the standard configuration file, TCCONFIG.TC, when you exit, provided that you leave the Config auto save option in its default ON state. TC will refer to this configuration file next time you run TC in order to reestablish your environmental defaults. A .TC file can only affect some of the defaults, as indicated in Table B.1.

► *IDE Configuration Files* ►

To understand the finer points of environmental control you must know a little more about default selection and configurations files. As your projects become more ambitious you may want to keep several configuration files, each preset for particular sessions.

The TC you now have has certain built-in defaults, some from the factory and some that you entered. You can look on these as now providing a new set of default defaults.

For example, Turbo C will assume until you say otherwise that you want the small memory model, that all **char**s are signed, that your code will be optimized for size, that your ouput code will go to the current directory, that your help file is in \TURBOC, that your .LIB files are in \TURBOC\LIB, that you want to backup your source code, and so on.

► *Recap of Setting and Changing Defaults* ►

To recap, there are three interrelated ways of changing the TC defaults: the IDE menu, the TCINST.EXE utility, and configuration files.

The menu method is the one described in Chapter 1: you pull down a particular menu, confirm or enter a value, or toggle a switch. This sets the environment for the current session. The new defaults, though, may or may not be "remembered." The other two methods offer more permanent control.

TCINST.EXE, the Turbo C installation program, customizes your IDE by directly changing TC.EXE. This is the only way of setting and changing certain defaults (such as the location of the Turbo C directory, your preferred editor keyboard, and color-monitor assignments). TCINST.EXE is a large program with its own Turbo C-like menu. You used just a small section of this menu during the installation sequence earlier in this appendix.

Configuration files are optional files that are stored and read by TC.EXE to alter your defaults temporarily. TC.EXE itself is not modified. Configuration files usually have the extension .TC and can be used to override some of the TCINST.EXE settings for particular IDE sessions.

There is a special CTOPAS.TC file on the IDE distribution disk for mixed C and Pascal work—if you need any other configuration files, you have to create them yourself using the Store menu command or make sure that the Config auto save toggle is ON.

► *Keeping Your Options* ►

During your first session with the TCINST.EXE-modified TC you can change any or all of the menu defaults. Your program might need the huge memory model with **unsigned char** as the default, for example. Under Version 1.0, unless you specifically saved these settings using the Store options command, they would be lost when you exited TC. Your next encounter with TC would start again with the original default options. If you did store them, a .TC configuration file would be created and called TCCONFIG.TC by default. The next session with TC would pick up the default settings from TCCONFIG.TC.

The difference in Versions 1.5 and later is that you have a new Options menu item—the Config auto save toggle. If this is toggled OFF, the old and new versions work the same. You must use Store to create or update your configuration file. If Config auto save is toggled ON, Versions 1.5 and later will create or update a .TC file automatically whenever you use Run, exit to DOS, or Quit.

The auto saved file takes its name from the last .TC file loaded or retrieved. In the absence of any such file name, the auto save is to TCCONFIG.TC.

In my suggested install procedure, I recommended that Config auto save should default to ON, but there's nothing to stop you toggling it OFF during a session if you don't want to save a particular bunch of defaults.

Whether Config auto save is on or not, you can use the Store option. When you save your defaults you can provide a name such as MYCON-FIG.TC, or you can use the default name TCCONFIG.TC.

How do you recover these saved configurations? The **R**etrieve command in the Options menu lets you pull in any .TC file to switch defaults in midstream. Alternatively, you can provide a .TC file name to replace the TCCONFIG.TC when you invoke TC. The latter method requires the /C option.

► *The TC.EXE /C Option* ►

If you just enter TC or TC FILENAME at the prompt, the system first looks for TCCONFIG.TC in various places (I'll explain where and how in a moment). If TCCONFIG.TC is found, TC assumes any defaults that are stored in it, otherwise TC assumes all the default defaults. However, if you invoke TC with the /C option, as in

C>TC /CMYCONFIG

or

C>TC /CMYCONFIG FILENAME

a search is made for a configuration file called MYCONFIG.TC. Note that there is no space between /C and MYCONFIG. If MYCONFIG.TC is not found, you get a warning message and TC fires up with its own defaults—it does not bother to search for TCCONFIG or any other .TC file. If MYCON-FIG.TC is found, TC.EXE assumes all its defaults during the session (or until you change them in some way).

The /C option lets you call up specific configuration files for different TC sessions. It also provides a trick method of ignoring a TCCONFIG.TC and getting back to your TC defaults—you use /C with a nonexistent .TC file name!

As mentioned, you can also load or switch configuration files during a session using Restore from the Options menu. The window shows you the previously loaded .TC file (or *.TC the first time round). You type the name of the .TC file you need (or press Enter to confirm) and TC.EXE switches the defaults accordingly. Restore can give you a directory listing to help you select a .TC file (the same method used when loading source files).

► *Configuration Files and TCCONFIG.EXE* ►

Configuration files are not ASCII text files like .PRJ files, so you cannot create or modify them with a text editor. TCC configuration files, however, are ASCII text, which opens the door to another way of generating TC configuration files. Turbo C provides a utility called TCCONFIG.EXE that will convert TCC configuration files (the default extension is .CFG) to TC format and vice versa. This is a great help when you want to use the IDE for program development and then switch to the command-line compiler for compiling/linking (some jobs can only be done with TCC). The TCC and TC defaults overlap so an exact correlation may not be possible. The TCC options are beyond the scope of this book.

► *Configuration-File Searching Methodology*

Do I have your attention now? I am about to reveal how TC.EXE looks for configuration files. You can guess why it is important—you can have any number of .TC files in different directories, and some may have the same name; indeed, you may have several files called TCCONFIG.TC. When TC looks for TCCONFIG.TC in the absence of a /C switch, which file gains control of your default schema?

Configuration files store search-path information for files—so there is a whiff of recursive Zen in the air! Must we find something in order to know where it is located?

The solution for /C switched .TC files such as /CMYCONFIG has to be quite mundane—TC looks only in the current directory (if it's not there, you fire up with the defaults found in TC.EXE).

For TCCONFIG.TC searches, TC looks first in the current directory. Then, if not found, TC looks in a directory known as the *Turbo C directory* provided that you have previously designated one. If you haven't defined a Turbo C directory, or if the one defined has no TCCONFIG.TC, you start up with the defaults found in TC.EXE. How do you designate a Turbo C directory? You will recall that it can only be done with TCINST.EXE, the utility that actually changes TC.EXE. Further, the Turbo C directory can only be altered using TCINST.

The alternative of allowing a .TC file to determine its own search path could lead to great uncertainty. A TCCONFIG.TC in \MYDIR might give you a search path of \YOURDIR, while the TCCONFIG.TC in \YOURDIR might say the search path is \MYDIR.

► *APPENDIX C* ►
printf( ) AND scanf( ) FORMATS

► *THE printf( ) FAMILY* ►

All the **printf( )** variants send formatted data to some device or destination: the screen, the standard output device (**stdout**), a specified stream, or a specified string or buffer. Once you understand how **printf( )** works, the variants follow quite naturally.

Here is a brief summary of each variant with its prototype as defined in STDIO.H or CONIO.H. The notation , ... is the official ANSI C prototyping syntax to indicate a variable number of arguments of undetermined data type. (I have omitted the _Cdecl modifier for clarity.) All these functions return the total number of bytes outputted, but this number is rarely used.

► *printf( )*

int printf (const char *format, ...); outputs to stdout. A more helpful syntax is

    printf("[text][%format][text][%format]...",[arg1,arg2,...]);

where each **%format** is matched with an **argN**. The arguments can be constants, variables or expressions.

► *cprintf( )*

int cprintf (char *format, ...); outputs to console. LFs are not translated as newline characters.

► *fprintf( )*

int fprintf (FILE *fp, const char *format, ...); outputs to stream **fp**.

► *sprintf( )*

int sprintf (char *buffer, const char *format, ...); outputs to buffer (NUL-terminated string).

► *vprintf( )*

int vprintf (const char *format, va_list arglist); outputs to stdout with arguments from **va_arg** array.

► *vfprintf( )*

int vfprintf (FILE *fp, const char *format, va_list arglist); outputs to stream **fp** with arguments from **va_arg** array.

► *vsprintf( )*

int vsprintf (char *buffer, const char *format, va_list arglist); outputs to buffer (NUL-terminated string) with arguments from **va_arg** array.

The **V**... variants allow you to supply variable-argument functions that use the formatting features of **printf( )**. They are listed here for completeness but are beyond the scope of this book.

► *The printf( ) Family Format String* ►

The **char *format** indicates a special string that you supply to control formatting, i.e., how each argument is converted and displayed. For each argument to be formatted there must be a corresponding element in the format string.

The format string can contain any number of the following groups of items:

1. Literal text (displayed unchanged)

2. Format specifications—a sequence of symbols preceded by **%**

A format specification (FS) looks like this.

% [flags] [width] [.precision] [F ¦ N ¦ h ¦ l] type

where ¦ means select one only, and the square brackets indicate that the enclosed item is optional. The *[F ¦ N ¦ h ¦ l]* is called the *size field*.

A minimal FS would be **%d** with type **d** indicating that a single integer argument would be converted to ASCII and displayed as follows:

```
printf("%d",my_int);              /* display my_int - no newline */

printf("%d\n",my_int);            /* display my_int plus newline */

printf("This = %d\n",my_int);     /* display This = my_int plus newline */
```

► *The Conversion-Type Field*

Although appearing last in the syntax list, the conversion type is the main element (and often the only one you need). It specifies the data type of the argument to be converted. In the absence of any overriders from the other fields (see below), you will get the following conversions:

Type	Input	Output
"d"	integer	signed decimal integer
"i"	integer	signed decimal integer
"o"	integer	unsigned octal integer
"u"	integer	unsigned decimal integer
"x"	integer	unsigned hex with "a", "b", etc.
"X"	integer	unsigned hex with "A", "B", etc.
"f"	FP	signed decimal: *[–]dd...d.dddddd.* (all FP arguments can be float or double)
"e"	FP	signed scientific: *[–]d.dddd e [+ ¦ –]ddd*
"E"	FP	signed scientific: *[–]d.dddd E [+ ¦ –]ddd*
"g"	FP	signed: either "f" or "e" depending on size
"G"	FP	signed: either "f" or "E" depending on size
"c"	char	Single character display
"s"	*char	Sequence of characters until NUL or precision limit reached. The pointer argument is taken as **near** or **far** depending on the memory model.

"%"		"%%" needed to display "%"
"n"	*int	Special argument to capture number of characters displayed. The pointer argument is taken as **near** or **far** depending on the memory model.
"p"	pointer	Displays near pointers as *OOOO* (offset only). Displays far pointers as *SSSS:OOOO* (segment:offset). The pointer argument is taken as **near** or **far** depending on the memory model. Size field may override.

► *The Size Field*

The next thing to look for is the optional size field, a single letter in front of the type field used to indicate a **short** or **long** integer argument or a **near** or **far** pointer argument. There are four possibilities:

Size	Action
"F"	Affects pointer arguments only: treats them as **far**. Used only with %p, %n, and %s.
"N"	Affects pointer arguments only: treats them as **near**. Used only with %p, %n, and %s.
"h"	For **d**, **i**, **o**, **u**, **x**, **X**: treat as a **short int**. Overrides the default size for numeric input.
"l"	For **d**, **i**, **o**, **u**, **x**, **X**: treat as a **long int**. Overrides the default size for numeric input. For **e**, **E**, **f**, **F**, **g**, **G**: treat as a **long double**. Overrides the default size for FP numbers.

► *Size and Type Examples*

Typical combinations encountered are

"%ld" for decimal **long int**
"%lf" for decimal **long double**. (Note that "%f" works with both **float** and **double**.)
"%lu" for decimal **unsigned long int**
"%hd" for decimal **short int**
"%ho" for octal **unsigned short int**

► *The Flags Field*

This is a sequence of characters controlling the following features:

" – " Left justification: pad with spaces to right. If omitted, right justification: pad left with spaces or zeroes.

" + " If a signed value is being formatted, always show a leading sign symbol (" + " or " – ").

blank Omit " + " if value is >= 0. Always show " – " if value is < 0.

"#" Specifies an "alternative form" conversion (see below) usually involving whether 0's or decimal points will appear.

► *The Width Field*

This field contains either a number or a "*".

"*N*" At least *N* characters will appear. If less are needed, pad right or left according to the flag field (see above).

"0*N*" At least *N* characters will appear. If less are needed pad left with zeros.

"*" The argument preceding the one to be formatted contains the width field to be used, i.e., you supply an extra argument *N* or 0*N*.

► *The Precision Field*

The precision field, if present, always starts with a period. It governs the maximum number of characters to be displayed and the minimum number of digits to be displayed.

Precision Field	Action
none	Default precision depending on the type. 1 for d, i, o, u, x, X; 6 for e, E, f. All significant figures for g, G. Until NUL for s. c types are unaffected.
".0"	Use default for d, i, o, u, x, X. Omit decimal point for e, E, f.

" .N"   For **d**, **i**, **o**, **u**, **x**, **X** at least *N* digits will display. Left pad with 0 if
            necessary. No truncation ever. For **e**, **E**, **f** you get *N* digits after
            the decimal point. The last digit is rounded. For **g**, **G** types you
            get at most *N* significant digits. For **c** types there is no effect.
            For **s** types no more than *N* characters will appear.

"*"   As for width, the field is to be found in the argument list pre-
            ceding the value to be converted.

► The "#" Alternative Forms

As noted earlier, # appearing in the flags field modifies the conversion.
Here's how.

Type Field	Effect of # Flag
c, s, d, i, u	No effect
o	0 prepended to a nonzero argument
x, X	0x or 0X prepended to argument
e, E, f	Always display a decimal point
g, G	As with e and E, but trailing zeroes will not be removed

► Examples of printf( ) ►

I'll divide my examples into appropriate categories.

► Characters and Strings

Given **char ch** = 'A'; and **char name[5]** ="Stan";:

```
printf("ch = %c",ch); displays ch = A
printf("ch = %5c",ch); displays ch = ssssA (leading spaces)
printf("ch = %-5c",ch); displays ch = Assss (trailing spaces)
printf("ch = %05c",ch); displays ch = 0000A
printf("Name = %s",name); displays Name = Stan
printf("Name = %6s",name); displays Name = ssStan
printf("Name = %*s",6,name); displays Name = ssStan
                            (* means "take next int arg as width")
```

printf("Name = %06s",name); displays **Name = 00Stan**
printf("Name = % – 6s",name); displays **Name = Stan*ss***
printf("Name = %.3s",name); displays **Name = Sta**
(a small precision truncates)

printf("Name = %2s",name); displays **Name = Stan**
(a small width never truncates)

► *Integers*

Given int i = 453;, int j = – 89; and long int li = 78998:

printf("i = %d",i); displays i = 453
printf("i = %2d",i); displays i = 453
printf("i = %3d",i); displays i = 453
printf("i = %4d",i); displays i = *s*453
printf("i = % – 5d",i); displays i = 453*ss*
printf("i = % + d",i); displays i = +453
printf("i = % + 05d",i); displays i = +0453
printf("i = % + – 6d",i); displays i = +453*ss*

printf("i = %5.1d",i); displays i = 453 (precision ignored)
printf("i = %.6d",i); displays i = 000453

printf("i = %o",i); displays i = 705 (octal)
printf("i = %#o",i); displays i = 0705 (leading 0 octal)
printf("i = %05o",i); displays i = 00705 (pad octal)
printf("i = %x",i); displays i = 1c5 (hex)
printf("i = %X",i); displays i = 1C5 (hex)
printf("i = %#x",i); displays i = 0x1c5 (hex)
printf("i = %06x",i); displays i = 0001c5 (hex)

printf("j = %d",j); displays j = – 89
printf("j = % + d",j); displays j = – 89
printf("j = %2d",j); displays j = – 89
printf("j = %4d",j); displays j = *s* – 89
printf("j = % – 5d",j); displays j = – 89*ss*
printf("j = %06d",j); displays j = – 00089
printf("j = %.8",j); displays j = – 000089

```
printf("li = %ld",li); displays li = 78998
printf("li = % + ld",li); displays li = + 78998
printf("li = %8ld",li); displays li = sss78998
printf("li = %08ld",li); displays li = 00078998
printf("li = %.8ld",li); displays li = 00078998
printf("li = % − 8ld",li); displays li = 78998sss
```

► Floating Point

The type "%f" works with **float** or **double** arguments since **floats** are converted to **double** before formatting is performed. Assuming that **float height** or **double height** contains 2500.3498537,

```
printf("Height = %T",height);
```

will display as shown below given the listed width/precision/type combinations

Combinations	Screen Display and Notes
"%f"	Height = 2500.349854 (default = "%.6f" rounded)
"%.0f"	Height = 2500 (no decimal point)
"% + .0f"	Height = + 2500 (sign always shown " + " or " − ")
"% .0f"	Height = 2500 (sign only if " − ")
"%.1f"	Height = 2500.3 (rounded)
"%.2f"	Height = 2500.35 (rounded)
"%.3f"	Height = 2500.350 (rounded)
"%6.2f"	Height = 2500.35 (width ignored—too small)
"%9.2f"	Height = ss2500.35 (pad blanks to 9 columns)
"%09.2f"	Height = 002500.35 (pad zeroes to 9 columns)
"%14f"	Height = sss2500.349854 (same as "%14.6f")
"%14.0f"	Height = sssssssss2500 (no decimal point)
"%#14.0f"	Height = sssssssss2500. ("#" gives decimal point)
"% − 6.2f"	Height = 2500.35 (width ignored—too small)
"% − 9.2f"	Height = 2500.35ss (pad right spaces to 9 columns)

"%−09.2f"	Height = 2500.35*ss* (zero is ignored)
"%−14f"	Height = 2500.349854*sss* (default is "%−14.6f")
"%−14.0f"	Height = 2500*ssssssssss* (no decimal point)
"%−#14.0f"	Height = 2500.*ssssssssss* ("#" gives decimal point)

(If **height** were declared as **long double** you would replace each "f" in the above with **lf**. The displays would be the same.)

"%e"	Height = 2.5003499e+003 (default = %.6e)
"%.3e"	Height = 2.500e+003
"%.3g"	Height = 2.500e+003
"%15.4E"	Height = *ssss*2.5003E+003 (leading spaces)
"%015.4E"	Height = 00002.5003E+003
"%+015.4E"	Height = +0002.5003E+003
"%−15.4e"	Height = 2.5003e+003*ssss* (trailing spaces)
"%−+15.4E"	Height = +2.5003E+003*sss* (trailing spaces)

(Exponent always displays sign symbol and 3 digits. Mantissa is always d.dddd....)

► *THE scanf( ) FAMILY* ►

The functions in the **scanf( )** family all perform formatting operations on input from the keyboard, standard input (**stdin**), a stream, or a string. The formatted data is placed in arguments given by **&arg1**, **&arg2**, and so on. Their prototypes from STDIO.H are listed below. (I have omitted the **_Cdecl** modifier for clarity.)

► *scanf( )*

int scanf (const char *format, ...); accepts input from **stdin**. Returns number of input characters successfully converted.

► *cscanf( )*

  int cscanf (const char *format, ...); accepts input from keyboard.

► *fscanf( )*

  int fscanf (FILE *fp, const char *format, ...); accepts inputs from stream **fp**.

► *sscanf( )*

  int sscanf (const char *buffer, const char *format, ...); accepts data from buffer.

► *vscanf( )*

  int vscanf (const char *format, va_list arglist); accepts data from **stdin**— uses arguments from **va_arg** array.

► *vfscanf( )*

  int vfscanf (FILE *fp, const char *format, va_list arglist); accepts data from stream **fp**—uses arguments from **va_arg** array.

► *vsscanf( )*

  int vsscanf (const char *buffer, const char *format, va_list arglist); accepts data from buffer—uses arguments from **va_arg** array.

  The **V**... variants allow you to supply variable-argument functions that use the formatting features of **scanf( )**. They are listed here for completeness but are beyond the scope of this book.

► *The scanf( ) Format String* ►

  The format string is used to control how each input packet is converted, formatted, and saved in the matching argument. The rules generally follow a similar pattern for **printf( )** but in the opposite direction, as it were! For example, "%d" takes a decimal integer and converts it to an **int**. The matching argument must be a pointer to **int**, say, **&int_arg**, whereupon **int_arg** will receive the converted value:

```
int int_arg;

scanf("%d",&int_arg);
/* if you key in 345, int_arg will receive 345 */
```

Staying with this simple case, two inputs would be handled as follows:

```
int int_arg1, int_arg2;

scanf("%d%d",&int_arg1, &int_arg2);
/* if you key in 345 whitespace 67,
   int_arg1 will receive 345 and int_arg2 will get 67 */
```

The idea is that **scanf( )** parses the input received under the control of the format string. The format string can hold groups of the following objects:

1. Format specifications signaled by the "%" symbol.

2. Literal text: any symbols, including white space, other than "%". The function of these is *not* to display [as with **printf( )**], but to *match* and discard identical characters being keyed. Any mismatch here causes **scanf( )** to terminate.

Any white space in a literal section serves to discard any amount of white space being keyed, but other literals must be matched on a one by one basis. As soon as you key a character other than white space it enters the **scanf( )** parser. It either matches a literal in the format string and gets discarded or starts a conversion process depending on the next "%" sequence encountered. Subsequent keystrokes contribute to the input until one of several events occurs:

1. If it's a stream input, EOF may be reached.

2. A white space is encountered.

3. An inappropriate character is keyed, for example, an alphabetic in a numeric field.

4. The number of characters exceeds a specified width.

In the simple case above, I keyed 345 followed by a space. This told **scanf( )** to process the input, and since there was a "**%d**" in situ the conversion was made to decimal. The same happened when I entered the second number, 67, followed by a new line. Again the conversion was triggered, this time with the second "**%d**". Each packet of input, therefore, must match something in the format string. In the next example, I alter **scanf( )** to accept two fixed field numbers separated by /

```
int int_arg1, int_arg2;

scanf("%3d/%2d",&int_arg1, &int_arg2);
/* if you key in 345/67 return
   int_arg1 will receive 345 and int_arg2 will get 67 */
```

The format string now converts three digits, discards the /, and then converts two digits.

Two important warnings: you must use pointer arguments, and you must balance the format string with the number and type of entries. Unpredictable calamities will occur otherwise.

The syntax of the format string is

% [*] [width] [F ¦ N ¦ h ¦ l] type

Let's look at the type first—there are important differences from **printf( )**.

Type	Input	Output Argument
"d"	decimal integer	int *arg
"D"	decimal integer	long int *arg
"o"	octal integer	int *arg
"O"	octal integer	long int *arg
"i"	any integer	int *arg
"I"	any integer	long int *arg

"u"	unsigned decimal	**unsigned int *arg**
"U"	unsigned decimal	**unsigned long int *arg**
"x"	hex integer	**int *arg**
"X"	hex integer	**long int *arg**
"e"	FP	**float *arg**
"E"	FP	**double *arg**
"f"	FP	**float *arg**
"g"	FP	**float *arg**
"G"	FP	**double *arg**
"s"	string	**char array[ ]** (Allow for final NUL)
"c"	character	**char *arg** (if width is given use **char arg[*width*]**.) Converts next character input including white space. Use "**%1c**" to skip one white space character.
"%"		No conversion with "%%". The second "%" is stored.
"n"	none	**int *arg** will store the number of successful characters up to the "%n".

► Selective Conversion

You can use regular expressions as explained in Chapter 10 to allow ranges of input to be matched and converted. For example,

"%[A – Z]" will catch all uppercase input.
"[^ a – c]" will catch all ASCII except "a", "b", and "c".

► *Assignment Suppression*

A "%*T" combination (where "*" is not the pointer sign!) causes the matching input field of type *T* to be scanned but discarded.

► *Width Specifier*

This sets the number of characters to be scanned and converted.

► *Size and Type Modifiers*

The *[N¦F¦h¦l]* field works like **printf( )**, allowing you to override the default or declared size of the argument.

Size	Action
"F"	Treat argument pointer as **far**.
"N"	Treat argument pointer as **near**.
"h"	For **d, i, o, u, x, X**: convert to **short int**. Ignored for **D, I, O, U, X**.
"l"	For **d, i, o, u, x, X**: convert to **long int**. Ignored for **D, I, O, U, X**. For **e, f**: convert to **double**.

► *APPENDIX D* ►
COMPUTER MATH BASICS

► *NUMBER SYSTEMS* ►

The decimal integer (whole number) 562 represents $5 \times 10^2 + 6 \times 10^1 + 2 \times 10^0$.

$X^n = X \times X \times ...$ (n factors)
$X^0 = 1$ for all X because $X^m/X^n = X^{m-n}$
$X^{-n} = 1/X^n$
$X^n \times X^m = X^{m+n}$

The *base* of decimal notation is 10. This means that the contribution of C_n, the nth numeral from the right, is $C_n \times 10^n$ (n starts from 0 not 1, so you often see the strange notation 0th position). C_n is a numeral in the range 0–9.

More generally, a number Z in base B notation is expressed as $Z = C_n \times B^n + C_{n-1} \times B^{n-1} + ... + C_1 \times B^1 + C_0 \times B^0$ where each C_i is in the range 0 to $(B-1)$.

If $B > 9$ you have to invent extra symbols to represent the decimal values 10, 11,and so on.

The most common bases used in computer math are 2 (binary notation), 8 (octal), and 16 (hexadecimal or hex).

► *Binary* ►

If the base is 2, the only permitted values for C_i are 0 and 1. The bit is the basic "binary digit" taking the values 0 (off, clear, or reset) and 1 (on or set).

Counting up in binary goes 0, 1, 10, 11, 100, 101, 110, 111, 1000, and so on. Decimal 12 = binary 1100 = $2^3 + 2^2 + 0 + 0 = 8 + 4 + 0 + 0 = 12$.

► *Octal* ►

When the base is 8, only the numerals 0–7 are used:

Decimal 12 = octal 014 = $1 \times 8^1 + 4 \times 8^0$

C distinguishes octal constants with a leading 0, which is why the octal equivalent of decimal 12 is 014. (This convention can easily trap the unwary.)

► *Hexadecimal* ►

If the base is 16, you need six more symbols than with decimal notation.

Hex	Decimal
A	= 10
B	= 11
C	= 12
D	= 13
E	= 14
F	= 15

Decimal $123 = 7 \times 16^1 + 11 \times 16^0 =$ hex 7B. C uses 0x to distinguish hex constants from decimal and octal constants, for example, hex 0x56 = $5 \times 16^2 + 6 \times 16^0 = 86$ decimal.

► *STORAGE CONVENTIONS* ►

Most computers store numbers internally in binary form in fixed units of 4 (nibble), 8 (byte), 16 (word), or 32 (long word) bits. Numbers are usually stored without a specific + or − symbol to indicate whether they are positive or negative. (One exception is binary-coded decimal (BCD), in which 4 bits are used to encode each decimal digit or sign.)

► *UNSIGNED AND SIGNED NUMBERS* ►

Distinguishing postive and negative numbers relies on special modes and conventions. In *unsigned mode* all values are taken as positive, and you simply add up all bit values as powers of 2. In *signed mode* various conventions can apply to signal a negative value.

The most common conventions are *one's complement* and *two's complement*, where the most significant bit (MSB) in position 3, 7, 15, or 31 is a *sign bit*: 0 for positive, 1 for negative. These conventions evaluate binary numbers to decimal values as shown in Table D.1. The table just lists nibbles, but bytes, words, and long words follow the same pattern.

Two's complement is used on the IBM PC family and most other systems. One's complement is quite rare, but C does not specify any particular internal number representation. Note that one's complement has two ways of recording 0 (+0 and −0), whereas two's complement has a unique 0 but

Binary	Signed		Unsigned
	One's Complement	Two's Complement	
0111	7	7	7
0110	6	6	6
0101	5	5	5
0100	4	4	4
0011	3	3	3
0010	2	2	2
0001	1	1	1
0000	0	0	0
1111	−0	−1	15
1110	−1	−2	14
1101	−2	−3	13
1100	−3	−4	12
1011	−4	−5	11
1010	−5	−6	10
1001	−6	−7	9
1000	−7	−8	8

► **Table D.1:** *Decimal values of nibbles*

more negative numbers than positive numbers (+8 is outside and −8 is inside the legal range of a nibble). From here on, signed numbers will be assumed to be in two's complement format.

► BYTE, WORD, AND LONG WORD RANGES ►

It is vital to have a feel for the legal ranges of groups of bits in the various modes since they are directly related to C's integer data types.

char (1 byte)

unsigned range: 0 to +255 decimal

                          0 to +0377 octal

                          0 to +0xFF hex

signed range: −128 to +127 decimal

                          −0200 to +0177 octal

                          −0x80 to +0x7F hex

(short) int (2 bytes)

unsigned range: 0 to +65535 decimal

                          0 to +0177777 octal

                          0 to 0xFFFF hex

signed range: −32768 to +32767 decimal

                          −0100000 to +077777 octal

                          −0x8000 to +0x7FFF hex

long (4 bytes)

unsigned range: 0 to +4294967295 decimal

                          0 to +037777777777 octal

                          0 to +0xFFFFFFFF hex

signed range: -2147483648 to $+2147483647$ decimal

-020000000000 to $+017777777777$ octal

$-0x80000000$ to $+0x7FFFFFFF$ hex

► CARRY AND OVERFLOW ►

Unsigned addition follows the normal rules until you reach the upper limits. If you add 1 to 0xFFFF the answer flips to 0x0000, but the carry bit "emerging" from the top is stored by the CPU in a condition code register (CCR). The C language does not mandate any specific warning—it assumes all unsigned calculations are performed modulo 2^n where n is the number of bits in the data type. The modulo or remainder operator is explained in Chapter 3.

Signed arithmetic in two's complement format does not suffer from carry. It so happens that the sums turn out correctly if you ignore the carry:

Decimal		**Binary**
5		0101
+ −3		+ 1101
2	ignore carried 1	0010 (decimal 2)

However, signed arithmetic can suffer from overflow, meaning that a number can be generated that exceeds the signed range for the data type:

Decimal	**Binary**
4	0100
+ 5	+ 0101
9	1001 (decimal −7 in signed mode)

In this example $+9$ is not expressible in 4 bits. C mandates that overflow create "an undefined result," leaving the implementor to decide on the appropriate action. The CPU's CCR has a flag to indicate overflow.

If you mix signed and unsigned arithmetic, several subtle errors can arise. For example, **ch** = −**128** is legal for a signed **char**, but if you negate it with −**ch** the result is not +128 since that would exceed +127, the maximum valid value for signed **chars**.

► *FLOATING-POINT FORMAT* ►

The basic FP notation expresses any number *X*, integral or fractional, as

$$X = M \times B^n$$

where *M* is called the *mantissa*, *B* is the *base,* and *n* is the *exponent*. In base 10, you could write $3.7 = 37 \times 10^{-1}$ or $3.7 = 0.37 \times 10^1$, so there is no unique FP expression for a given number.

In base 10, this notation is shortened to *X* = *MEn* or *Men*, e.g., 3.7 = 37E−1 = 3.7E1 = 37e−1 = 37e1 = 0.37E2 and so on. This is called *scientific* or *E* notation.

Internally, base 2 is used. In base 2 the "decimal" point is really a binary point, so 0.1 (binary) = $\frac{1}{2}$ = 1×2^{-1}. Bits to the right of a binary point represent $\frac{1}{2}$, $\frac{1}{4}$, $\frac{1}{8}$, and so on. Multiplying by 2 is equivalent to shifting the binary point to the left; dividing by 2 is the same as shifting the binary point to the right. This follows the familiar operation with decimal points and powers of 10.

C has two FP formats: single precision (**float**) and double precision (**double**). (A third format, **long double**, exists, but in Turbo C this is the same as **double**, as allowed by the ANSI C standards.)

► *The float Format* ►

The data type **float** takes up four bytes (32 bits) as follows:

sign bit	1 bit (0 = positive, 1 = negative)
exponent	8 bits (range 0–255, but 127 is subtracted from this field to give actual exponents in the range − 127 to + 128. This is called "excess 127 format.")
mantissa	23 bits to the right of the binary point with an implied 1.0 to the left, so effectively 24 bits (see below)

To ensure a unique internal representation for each FP number, the exponent is adjusted so that the mantissa has a single 1 before its binary point. For example, 2 is stored as $(1.0) \times 2^1$ rather than as $(0.1) \times 2^2$. This *normalization* means that the 1 in front of the binary point need not be stored! (It is always there, so why waste a bit?) Nor do you waste space with leading 0's—just shift left until you hit the first 1. If you don't find a 1, then you have a zero FP. Zero FP's are stored specially with 0's in all positions. (If the normal rules were applied to a **float** with 32 0's, they would give a value of $+1.0 \times 2^{-127}$, which is small but nonzero! A zero mantissa with a zero exponent therefore needs special decoding to give a true zero.)

For nonzero FP numbers the *implied bit* is added back before the mantissa is used in a calculation. So, although there are 23 bits in the mantissa, it really provides a precision of 24 significant bits.

The largest mantissa value is 1.11111... (23 1's after the binary point). This is approximately equal to 2, so the largest **float** is approximately 2×2^{128} or 3.4E+38. The smallest positive **float** has a mantissa of 1.0000...01 and exponent -127, so its value is approximately $1 \times 2^{-127} = 1.0E-38$. The smallest negative **float** is $-3.4+38$.

The "excess 127" trick in the exponent gives a wider range for the absolute value of large numbers: 2^{128} compared with 2^{-127} for small numbers. A simple signed, or "excess 128," exponent would reverse this, giving 2^{127} for large and 2^{-128} for small numbers. The IBM BASIC FP format uses the latter, a fact that you might find invaluable one rainy night.

The 32 bits thus allocated for a **float** have fields that straddle byte boundaries. The resulting bit twiddling adds to the FP-management overhead and stresses the advantage of a dedicated math coprocessor such as the 8087. Although C has bit-field operators, emulating the 8087 by software is one area where the speed and tightness of assembly language is essential.

► *The double Format* ►

Double-precision values take 8 bytes (64 bits) allocated as follows:

sign bit	1 bit (0 = positive, 1 = negative)
exponent	11 bits (range 0–2048, but 1023 is subtracted from this field to give actual exponents in the range -1023 to $+1024$. This is called "excess 1023 format.")
mantissa	52 bits to the right of the binary point with an implied 1.0 to the left, so effectively 53 bits

Following the same logic as for **float**, you can see that the ranges for **double** are thus:

Maximum positive: 2×2^{1024} = 1.8E308 (approximately)

Minimum negative: = $-$1.8E308

Minimum positive: 1×2^{-1023} = 1.0E$-$309 (approximately)

► *FP Constants* ►

C treats the constant **2** as an **int** and **2.0** or **2.** as a **double** even though a **float** would be adequate. To force **2.0** into the smaller **float** format, use **2.0F**. This saves RAM but not CPU cycles since **float**s are internally promoted to **double**s before any expression is evaluated. You can also use scientic notation for FP constants.

► *FP Precision* ►

The enormous range of **double** variables disguises the true precision available. The width of the mantissa, effectively 53 bits, is the real guide. When you add FP numbers their exponents must be adjusted so that their true binary points are aligned. This often leads to the loss of significant figures in the smaller number as it is shifted to the right. In an extreme case, adding *B* to *A* will not alter *A*! **float** gives you the equivalent precision of 7 decimal places, while **double** boosts this to about 17 places.

Programmers need to be constantly aware of the precision of the numbers used in expressions. It is quite easy to have a variable **x** holding, say, 1.999999 that is displayed as 2.00000 (**printf( )** rounds up for display purposes only), yet the conditional test **if (x == 2.0) {...}** fails. Testing for equality between FP numbers is nearly always hazardous, and even testing for **y > x** will sometimes deceive you. It is useful to define a constant, **EPSILON**, representing the smallest significant number for the precision being aimed at. If you are using numbers with only 3 reliable decimal places, you could set **EPSILON** to 0.0005. You would then test **if (fabs(x − y) < EPSILON) {...}**. Numbers differing by less than **EPSILON** are effectively equal.

► *ABSOLUTE VALUES* ►

fabs( ) gets you the absolute value (also known as the modulus) of an FP number or expression by setting the sign bit to zero. In other words, fabs(− 2.0) equals **fabs(2.0)** equals 2.0.

There are variants of the function **fabs( )** for other data types, for example, int **abs(int_arg)** is the variant for **int**s. **abs(− 1)** returns + 1, but **abs(− 32768)** will not work! Why not? Because + 32768 is not a valid **int**, as I warned you earlier. **long labs(long_arg)** gives you the absolute value of a **long int**. The macro **cabs(Z)** returns the absolute value of the complex number Z. The **struct complex** is declared as

```
struct complex {
    double X, Y;
};
```

The variable Z would be written as $Z = X + iY$, (where i is one of the square roots of − 1) in traditional mathematics. X represents the *real* component and Y the *imaginary* component of the complex number Z. **cabs( )** returns mod Z, written $|Z|$, which is the distance from (0,0) to (X,Y) in the complex plane, namely the positive square root of $(X^2 + Y^2)$. The calculation is achieved like this

```
#define cabs(z) (hypot ((z).x, (z).y))
```

► *GENERAL MATHEMATICAL FUNCTIONS* ►

Turbo C offers all the standard mathematical functions specified by the ANSI C draft. Their declarations can be found in MATH.H, STLIB.H, and FLOAT.H. Appendix G gives their prototypes.

It is also worth knowing that MATH.H defines mnemonics for all the important mathematical constants, such as e (the base of natural logarithms), greek *pi*, and so on, to 18 decimal places:

```
#define M_E    2.71828182845904524
#define M_PI   3.14159265358979324
```

In addition to logarithmic functions (both natural and base 10), and exponential and power routines, Turbo C offers the usual trigonometric functions **cos( )**, **sin( )**, **tan( )**, their inverses **acos( )**, **asin( )**, **atan( )**, and their hyperbolic cousins **cosh( )**, **sinh( )**, and **tanh( )**. They all take and return **double** values. These routines are invaluable for many graphics and image-processing applications, which are unfortunately beyond the range of this book.

What is worth knowing, in general terms, is how Turbo C handles FP errors. The function **_matherr( )** is called internally whenever an FP error is detected:

```
double _matherr (_mexcep why, char *fun, double *arg1p,
                 double *arg2p, double retval);
```

Typical errors include illegal arguments (*domain* errors) and illegal return values (*range* errors). Many of the standard math functions have singularities, for example, **tan(x)** increases rapidly as *x* approaches 90 degrees, at which value it is officially infinite. An enumeration **typedef** in MATH.H gives you the following mnemonics:

```
typedef enum
{
    DOMAIN = 1,        /* argument domain error : log (−1) */
    SING,              /* argument singularity : pow (0, −2)) */
    OVERFLOW,          /* overflow range error : exp (1000) */
    UNDERFLOW,         /* underflow range error : exp (−1000) */
    TLOSS,             /* total loss of significance : sin(10e70) */
    PLOSS,             /* partial loss of signif. : not used */
} _mexcep;
```

_matherr( ) fills an exception structure giving you the function name, an error code, and, if possible, the offending values:

```
struct exception
{
    int       type;
    char      *name;
    double    arg1, arg2, retval;
};
```

If these values are above **MAXDOUBLE** or below **MINDOUBLE**, **_matherr( )** substitutes **HUGE_VAL** (the FP equivalent to infinity) or 0, respectively. **_matherr( )** then calls **matherr( )**, a user-modifiable function that you set up to handle the errors,

```
int matherr (struct exception *e);
```

where **e** is a pointer to the exception structure filled by **_matherr( )**.

► USEFUL LIMITS ►

I conclude this brief survey of computer math with some excerpts from LIMITS.H. They are worth studying, especially the section handling limits for signed and unsigned **char**—the compiler needs to know what defaults have been set. Notice, too, that the spirit of C's portability is enshrined in this kind of code.

```
#define CHAR_BIT 8

#if (((int)((char)0x80)) < 0)
#define CHAR_MAX          0x7F
#define CHAR_MIN          0x80
#else
#define CHAR_MAX          0xFFU
#define CHAR_MIN          0x00
#endif

#define SCHAR_MAX         0x7F
#define SCHAR_MIN         0x80
#define UCHAR_MAX         0xFFU

#define SHRT_MAX          0x7FFF
#define SHRT_MIN          ((int)0x8000)
#define USHRT_MAX         0xFFFFU

#define INT_MAX           0x7FFF
#define INT_MIN           ((int)0x8000)
#define UINT_MAX          0xFFFFU

#define LONG_MAX          0x7FFFFFFFL
#define LONG_MIN          ((long)0x80000000L)
#define ULONG_MAX         0xFFFFFFFFUL
```

► APPENDIX E ►
PRECEDENCE AND ASSOCIATIVITY TABLE

Table E.1 groups Turbo C's operators according to their precedence and direction of association and gives examples of the operators in use. Operators in the same group have equal precedence. In the absence of grouping parentheses, operators of equal precedence are grouped according to the associativity rule of that group (left to right or right to left). The *higher* the group, the *lower* the precedence.

Group 1 (associates left to right)	
( )	Function arguments: **func(arg1, arg2)**
[ ]	Array elements: **array[20]**
.	struct,**union** member: **player.name**
–>	struct,**union** pointer member: **sptr –>name**
Group 2 (associates right to left)	
!	Logical NOT: **!FULL**
~	One's complement: **~i**
–	Unary minus: **– x**
++	Increment: **i ++ ; ++j**
––	Decrement: **i –– ; ––j**
&	Address of: **ptr = &x**
*	Indirection: ***ptr**
(type)	Type cast: **(char) x**
sizeof	Size (in bytes): **sizeof(int)**

► *Table E.1: Precedence and associativity of Turbo C's operators*

Group 3 (associates left to right)

*	Multiply: **x * 4**
/	Divide: **y / z**
%	Remainder: **tab % 8**

Group 4 (associates left to right)

+	Add: **a + b**
−	Subtract: **a − b**

Group 5 (associates left to right)

<<	Left Shift: **x << 2**
>>	Right Shift: **z >> i**

Group 6 (associates left to right)

<	Less than: **if (x < y)**
<=	Less than or equal: **while (a <= 2)**
>	Greater than: **if (x > max)**
>=	Greater than or equal: **while (j >= k)**

Group 7 (associates left to right)

==	Equality: **if (x == y)**
!=	Inequality: **while (x != y)**

Group 8 (associates left to right)

&	Bitwise AND: **x & y**

Group 9 (associates left to right)

^	Bitwise exclusive OR: **x ^ y**

▸ *Table E.1: Precedence and associativity of Turbo C's operators (continued)*

Group 10 (associates left to right)	
¦	Bitwise OR: x ¦ y

Group 11 (associates left to right)	
&&	Logical AND: **x && y**

Group 12 (associates left to right)	
¦ ¦	Logical OR: **x ¦ ¦ y**

Group 13 (associates right to left)	
?...:	Conditional: **x ? y : z**

Group 14 (associates right to left)	
=	assignment: **i = j**
*=	* assignment: **k *= 2 (k = k*2)**
/=	/ assignment: **m /= n (m = m/n)**
%=	% assignment: **i %= d (i = i%d)**
+=	+ assignment: **x += y (x = x + y)**
−=	− assignment: **w −= x (w = w − x)**
<<=	<< assignment: **z <<= 2 (z = z<<2)**
>>=	>> assignment: **z >>= 3 (z = z>>3)**
&=	& assignment: **a &= b (a = a&b)**
^=	^ assignment: **c ^= d (c = c^d)**
¦=	¦ assignment: **e ¦= f (e = e¦f)**

Group 15 (associates left to right)	
,	Comma expressions: **exp1, exp2, exp3**

► **Table E.1:** *Precedence and associativity of Turbo C's operators (continued)*

► *APPENDIX F* ►
8088/8086 REGISTERS: LOW-LEVEL STUFF

► *PREAMBLE* ►

How much do you really need to know about the CPU in your PC? For writing reasonably sized programs entirely in Turbo C, the answer is, "Very little, but it never hurts to have a general feel for what's going on inside!"

If your program size exceeds certain limits or if you want to do some macho low-level programming with Turbo C's pseudo register variables or assembly language in order to improve control and speed, then you must become more (and more) familiar with your CPU's architecture and instruction set.

The term *systems programming* is often used to describe delving into the chip's registers or tapping directly into DOS, as opposed to *applications programming*, in which you usually rely on the standard functions to hide the inner details. Turbo C blurs this distinction somewhat by providing intermediate tools. For instance, you can call DOS and BIOS services directly without needing a great deal of knowledge of how interrupts work.

This appendix gives you an introductory overview of the 808x registers and their role in Turbo C. It may help you decide how much deeper you want to swim.

Creating large programs requires some knowledge of the Turbo C memory models, which in turn calls for an understanding of the 808x addressing modes.

► *MEMORY ADDRESSING AND THE 808X* ►

Turbo C, like other C compilers for the IBM PC family, has to accommodate the architectural quirks of the Intel 808x and 80x86 families of CPUs, in particular the segment:offset addressing scheme (see Figure F.1).

As shown, the effective address comes out 20 bits wide, giving a 1MB (2^{20}) address space of overlapping 64KB segments, but two 16-bit values, a segment and an offset, are needed to address each byte. Let's see how registers are used to store these.

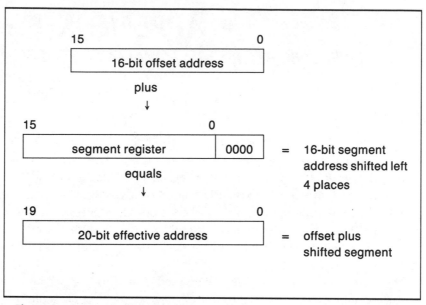

► *Figure F.1:* Segment:offset addressing

► *Segment Registers* ►

A register can be viewed as a small, superfast storage device built into the CPU. The 808x has 14 registers, each 16 bits wide. Most machine instructions use these registers in one way or another for arithmetic, control, and memory access.

Your PC keeps track of code, data, stack, and "extra" segments by storing their current segment addresses in four special-purpose registers:

CS   code segment register
DS   data segment register
SS   stack segment register
ES   extra segment register

► *Pointer and Index Registers* ►

The offset values from which the effective address is calculated can come from a variety of registers. Typical arrangements are shown below.

CS + IP (instruction pointer) = instruction address, e.g., pointer to a
function

DS + BX (base register) = address of data in RAM, e.g., a static variable

SS + SP (stack pointer) = address of data on stack, e.g., a local variable

ES + DI (destination index) = address of a string in RAM

(DS is also often combined with an index register, either SI [source index] or DI [destination index]. SS can also be combined with BP [base pointer].)

The above is just a selection of the many ways the offset value is derived. For a fixed segment address, the offset register can index any byte of the 64 kilobytes associated with that segment address, which is often called the *base address*.

► *Data Registers* ►

The 808x has four 16-bit data registers, each of which can also be treated as two 8-bit registers. AX, for example, is a 16-bit accumulator that can also be referenced as AH (high byte) and AL (low byte). The other registers have specialized duties: CX is for loop counting, BX is for indexing, and DX is for arithmetic and I/O, but these roles can vary depending on the instruction.

The complete register disposition is shown in Figure F.2.

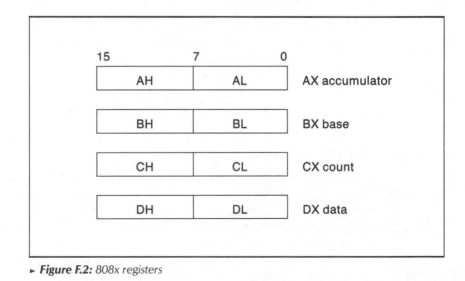

► *Figure F.2: 808x registers*

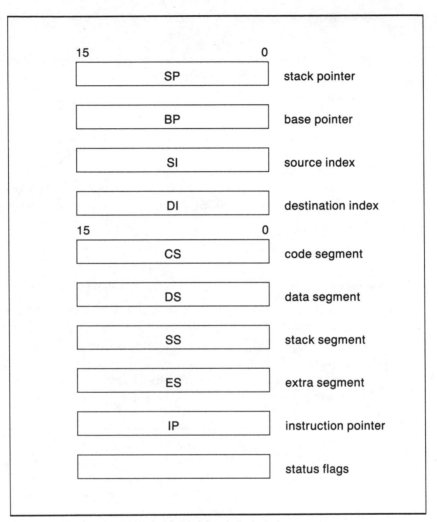

► *Figure F.2:* 808x registers (continued)

► *Instruction Pointer* ►

The IP is the approximate equivalent of the PC (program counter) in other CPUs. When added to the CS it gives the execution address of the next instruction. Because of the built-in instruction pipeline, this is not quite the "next-fetch-address" found in conventional program counters (since the instruction has already been fetched!).

► *Status Flags* ►

The status flags register uses 9 of the 16 bits to flag various processor or arithmetical states: carry, parity, auxiliary carry, zero, sign, trap (single-step mode), interrupt enable, direction (for string increment/decrement), and overflow. The other 7 bits are unused.

► *Pointers and the Memory Models* ►

Pointers to data can be simple 16-bit objects (called *near* pointers) provided that your data fits in one 64KB segment. This is because the segment part of the address is fixed and you need specify only the offset in order to get the effective address of an operand. Similarly, pointers to functions can be 16-bit near pointers if your code fits in a 64KB segment. In order to exceed these limits for either data, code, or both, two additional types of 32-bit pointers, known as *far* and *huge* pointers, are needed to specify both the segment and offset values.

Turbo C offers six memory models: tiny, small, medium, compact, large, and huge. Each of these determines a default pointer type for data and code references.

The default model is small and uses near pointers for data and code, allowing you a 64KB maximum for data and a 64KB maximum for code. You need not fret about pointer size unless you exceed either limit.

Even when you have programs beyond the limits, you can let Turbo C adjust the pointer types by selecting the appropriate memory model. You do this via the IDE Options/Model submenu or by adding – mx to the TCC command line, where x can be t, s, m, c, l, or h (the first letter of the memory model needed).

Each memory model gives you one of the four following combinations: (near-data, near-data), (near-data, far-code), (far-data, near-code), or (far-data, far-code).

The default pointer type, near or far, may not always be the most economical. If you understand how pointers relate to your code and data segments, you can safely use the type modifiers **near** and **far** to override the defaults. The **huge** modifier is always needed explicitly. Huge pointers are normalized to allow simpler arithmetic. Far pointers cannot readily be compared for size since the same effective address can have many segment:offset representations (see Chapter 5).

The basic principle here is that near pointers can only access data in the current segment, and near functions can only be called from within their own code segment.

The reason Turbo C provides you with separate start-up .OBJ files and run-time libraries for each memory model is that functions and pointer arguments need to be declared as near or far for optimum performance. (The tiny and small models, though, share the same library—CS.LIB).

You will find in Chapter 9 that the graphics library, GRAPHICS.LIB, is used for all models. Its functions are all declared as far for this reason. (Also, a graphics function may have to access video memory outside the near pointer range.)

► *Pseudovariables for Register Access* ►

Turbo C is unique in offering direct programmer access to registers without the need for assembly language. The so-called pseudovariables **_CS**, **_DS**, **_ES**, and **_SS** can be used in C expressions to represent the current values in the four segment registers. They are not true variables since many C operators are not applicable. For example, you cannot write **&_CS** to get the address of the code segment address! All the other registers, except for IP and status flags, are available in the mnemonic form **_AH**, **_AL**, **_AX**, and so on.

You can read from and write into registers using the pseudovariables as though they were global variables declared as **unsigned int** (the 16-bit registers like **_AX**) or as **unsigned byte** (the 8-bit, "half" registers like **_AL**).

```
char ch = '\n';
int i = 34;
_AH = ch;
_BX = i + 3;
_DX = _BX;
ch = _BL;
```

Two caveats: You need to know what you are doing! Changing **_CS** without due cause and attention is guaranteed to haunt you. Further, most function calls change most registers, so you cannot expect your register assignment to survive very long.

```
_AX = 629;
puts("\nYou are here");
/* AX no longer = 629 */
```

Some registers are not changed (either unused or saved and restored) by function calls, namely _CS, _BP, _SI, and _DI. Still, care is needed since **SI** and **DI** are the likely candidates for being assigned to variables of storage class **register** (see Chapter 7).

Pseudovariables are useful when calling low-level systems routines. (**mytab( )** in Chapter 6 explained one approach using **Int86( )** with **union REGS**.) You select the service code via **_AH** and then slot in the prescribed register values before calling **geninterrupt(0x10)**, which triggers the INT 10h ROM-BIOS service.

To scroll up a window using INT 10h, service 5, you need to set seven registers before the call:

```
_AH = 5;                         /* service code to AH */
_AL = lines_to_scroll;
_BH = filler_attribute;
_CH = upper_row;
_CL = left_column;
_DH = lower_row;
_DL = right_column;
geninterrupt(0x10);              /* call INT 10h service */
```

The DOS reference books list hundreds of such services, so it's easy to tap the resources of DOS directly and build up your own set of functions. Many INT calls return values by setting a register. All you need is a line after the call as in

```
unsigned char *disk_status;
...
_AH = 0x01;           /* service code 1, INT 13h */
geninterrupt(0x13);
*disk_status = _AL;
/* AL returns 1 (bad command); 3 (write – protect violation) etc */
```

You will probably be reinventing the wheel, of course, since Turbo C has most of these routines neatly dressed up in the library somewhere.

Nonetheless, it's a good way to become familiar with the ROM-BIOS services before attempting to improve Turbo C.

► ASSEMBLY LANGUAGE AND TURBO C ►

For more advanced control, you can combine assembly-language code with Turbo C in two distinct ways. First, using MASM (the official Microsoft macro assembler) or TASM (Borland's Turbo assembler), you write and assemble your code to an .OBJ module, then TLINK it with Turbo C .OBJ files.

Second, you can supply *in-line* assembly code, which turns out to be simpler but slightly less versatile than linking full-blown assembled modules. In-line assembly code, as the name implies, is written directly into the C source. You need to prefix each such line with the keyword **asm** (non-ANSI C) to give the compiler fair warning. The code following an **asm** is treated as a line of normal 808x assembly code until either a newline character or semicolon is reached:

```
asm mov ax,my – int – var;       /* you can use C variables! */
asm xor di,di;                   /* you must use C style comments.
                                    MASM style comments are illegal */

puts("\nThis is normal Turbo C");
```

Since I am not teaching assembly language here, I cannot go into much detail. Suffice it to say that the **asm** lines are embedded in the assembly code that Turbo C is producing from the C code, creating an .ASM file. Turbo C then invokes the Microsoft assembler MASM (so you need to make it available) to produce the final .OBJ file. The advantages of being able to mix assembly-language symbols and normal C variables, including structures, should be obvious. Less obvious are the savings compared with independent assembly modules, which need countless housekeeping details to set up for TLINK and memory-model compatibility.

Programs with **asm** sections need a special directive called **#pragma**. ANSI C introduced this as way of sending nonportable information to the compiler. If **#pragma** is not defined on a particular system it is just ignored. Turbo C uses two **#pragma** directives:

```
    #pragma inline
/* Advanced warning of asm lines ahead */
```

```
        #pragma warn +pro
/* Turn on warning to report any function without a prototype.
   There are several variants, e.g., -pro will cancel warnings */
```

► *APPENDIX G* ►
COMPLETE FUNCTION REFERENCE

PROTOTYPES OF STANDARD FUNCTIONS

► *abort* ►

abort   abnormally terminates a process

Prototype   void abort(void);

Prototype in   stdlib.h
                    process.h

► *abs* ►

abs   absolute value

Prototype   int abs(int i);

Prototype in   stdlib.h (**abs, labs**)
                    math.h (**cabs, fabs**)

► *absread* ►

absread   reads data

Prototype   int absread(int *drive*,int *nsects*, int *sectno*, void **buffer*);

Prototype in   dos.h

► *abswrite* ►

abswrite   writes data

Prototype   int abswrite(int *drive*, int *nsects*, int *sectno*, void **buffer*);

Prototype in   dos.h

► *access* ►

access   determines accessibility of a file

Prototype   int access(char *filename*, int *amode*);

Prototype in   io.h

► *acos* ►

acos   trigonometric function

Prototype   double acos(double *x*);

Prototype in   math.h

► *allocmem* ►

allocmem   allocates DOS memory segment

Prototype   int allocmem(unsigned *size*, unsigned *seg*);

Prototype in   dos.h

► *_argc, _argv* ►

_argc, _argv   count of command-line arguments
                    array of command-line arguments

Prototype   extern int_argc;
                    extern char**_argv;

Prototype in   dos.h

► *asctime* ►

asctime   converts date and time to ASCII

Prototype   #include <time.h>
                    char *asctime(struct tm *tm*);

Prototype in   time.h

► *asin* ►

asin   trignometric function

Prototype   double asin(double *x*);

Prototype in   math.h

► *assert* ►

assert   tests a condition and possibly aborts

Prototype   #include <assert.h>
                  #include <stdio.h>
                  void assert(int *test*);

Prototype in   assert.h

► *atan* ►

atan   trigonometric arctangent function

Prototype   double atan(double *x*);

Prototype in   math.h

► *atan2* ►

atan2   trigonometric function

Prototype   double atan2(double *y*, double *x*);

Prototype in   math.h

► *atexit* ►

atexit   registers termination function

Prototype   #include <stdlib.h> int atexit(atexit_t *func*)

Prototype in   stdlib.h

► *atof* ►

atof	converts a string to a floating point number
Prototype	double atof(char *nptr*);
Prototype in	math.h
	stdlib.h

► *atoi* ►

atoi	converts a string to an integer
Prototype	int atoi(char *nptr*);
Prototype in	stdlib.h

► *atol* ►

atol	converts a string to a long
Prototype	long atol(char *nptr*);
Prototype in	stdlib.h

► *bdos* ►

bdos	MS-DOS system call
Prototype	int bdos(int *dosfun*, unsigned *dosdx*, unsigned *dosal*);
Prototype in	dos.h

► *bdosptr* ►

bdosptr	MS-DOS system call
Prototype	int bdosptr(int *dosfun*, void *argument*, unsigned *dosal*);
Prototype in	dos.h

► *bioscom* ►

bioscom   communications I/O

Prototype   int bioscom(int *cmd*, char *byte*, int *port*);

Prototype in   bios.h

► *biosdisk* ►

biosdisk   hard disk/floppy I/O

Prototype   int biosdisk(int *cmd*, int *drive*, int *head*, int *track*, int *sector*, int *nsects*, void **buffer*);

Prototype in   bios.h

► *biosequip* ►

biosequip   checks equipment

Prototype   int biosequip(void);

Prototype in   bios.h

► *bioskey* ►

bioskey   keyboard interface

Prototype   int bioskey(int *cmd*);

Prototype in   bios.h

► *biosmemory* ►

biosmemory   returns memory size

Prototype   int biosmemory(vold);

Prototype in   bios.h

► biosprint ►

biosprint   printer I/O

Prototype   int biosprint(int *cmd*, int *byte*, int *port*);

Prototype in   bios.h

► biostime ►

biostime   returns time of day

Prototype   long biostime(int *cmd*,long *newtime*);

Prototype in   bios.h

► brk ►

brk   changes data-segment space allocation

Prototype   int brk(void *endds*);

Prototype in   alloc.h

► bsearch ►

bsearch   binary search

Prototype   #include <stdlib.h>
                 void *bsearch(const void *key*, const void *base*, size_t
                 nelem, size_t *width*, int(*fcmp*)(const void*,const void*));

Prototype in   stdlib.h

► cabs ►

cabs   absolute value of complex number

Prototype   #include <math.h>
                 double cabs(struct complex *znum*);

Prototype in   math.h

► *calloc* ►

calloc	allocates main memory
Prototype	#include <stdlib.h>
	void *calloc(size_t *nelem*, size_t *elsize*);
Prototype in	stdlib.h and alloc.h

► *ceil* ►

ceil	rounds up
Prototype	double ceil(double *x*);
Prototype in	math.h

► *cgets* ►

cgets	reads string from console
Prototype	char *cgets(char *string*);
Prototype in	conio.h

► *chdir* ►

chdir	changes working directory
Prototype	int chdir(char *path*);
Prototype in	dir.h

► *_chmod* ►

_chmod	changes access mode of file
Prototype	#include <dos.h>
	int _chmod(char *filename*, int *func* [,int *attrib*]);
Prototype in	io.h

► *chmod* ►

chmod	changes access mode of file
Prototype	#include <sys\stat.h>
	int chmod(char *filename*,int *permiss*);
Prototype in	io.h

► *chsize* ►

chsize	changes file size
Prototype	int chsize(int handle, long size);
Prototype in	io.h

► *_clear87* ►

_clear87	clears floating-point status word
Prototype	unsigned int_clear87 (void);
Prototype in	float.h

► *clearerr* ►

clearerr	resets error indication
Prototype	#include <stdio.h>
	void clearerr(FILE *stream*);
Prototype in	stdio.h

► *_close* ►

_close	closes a file handle
Prototype	int_close(int *handle*);
Prototype in	io.h

▶ *close* ▶

close   closes a file handle

Prototype   int close(int *handle*);

Prototype in   io.h

▶ *_control87* ▶

_control87   manipulates floating-point control word

Prototype   unsigned int _control87(unsigned int *newvals*, unsigned int *mask*);

Prototype in   float.h

▶ *coreleft* ▶

coreleft   returns a measure of unused memory

Prototype   in the tiny, small, and medium models:
                   unsigned coreleft(void);
                   in the compact, large, and huge models:
                   unsigned long
                   coreleft(void);

Prototype In   alloc.h

▶ *cos* ▶

cos   trigonometric function

Prototype   double cos(double *x*);

Prototype in   math.h

▶ *cosh* ▶

cosh   hyperbolic functions

Prototype   double cosh(double *x*);

Prototype in   math.h

► *country* ►

country	returns country-dependent information
Prototype	#include <dos.h>
	struct country *country(int *countrycode*, struct country
	countryp);
Prototype in	dos.h

► *cprintf* ►

cprintf	sends formatted output to the console
Prototype	int cprintf(const char *format*[,*argument*, ...]);
Prototype in	conio.h

► *cputs* ►

cputs	sends a string to the screen
Prototype	int cputs(const char *string*);
Prototype in	conio.h

► *_creat* ►

_creat	creates a new file or rewrites an existing one
Prototype	#include <dos.h>
	int _creat(char *filename*, int *attrib*);
Prototype in	io.h

► *creat* ►

creat	creates a new file or rewrites an existing one
Prototype	#include <sys\stat.h>
	int creat(char *filename*, int *permiss*);
Prototype in	io.h

► *creatnew* ►

creatnew	creates a new file
Prototype	#include \<dos.h\>
	int creatnew(char *filename*, int *attrib*);
Prototype in	io.h

► *creattemp* ►

creattemp	creates a new file or rewrites an existing one
Prototype	#include \<dos.h\>
	int creattemp(char *filename*, int *attrib*);
Prototype in	io.h

► *cscanf* ►

cscanf	performs formatted input from console
Prototype	int cscanf(char *format*[,*argument*, ...]);
Prototype in	conio.h

► *ctime* ►

ctime	converts date and time to a string
Prototype	char *ctime(long *clock*);
Prototype in	time.h

► *ctrlbrk* ►

ctrlbrk	sets control-break handler
Prototype	void ctrlbrk(int(*fptr*)(void));
Prototype in	dos.h

▶ *delay* ▶

delay	suspends execution for interval (milliseconds)
Prototype	void delay(unsigned milliseconds);
Prototype in	dos.h

▶ *difftime* ▶

difftime	computes difference between two times
Prototype	#include <time.h>
	double difftime(time_t *time2*, time_t *time1*);
Prototype in	time.h

▶ *directvideo* ▶

directvideo	direct output to video RAM flag
Prototype	extern int directvideo;
Prototype in	conio.h

▶ *disable* ▶

disable	disables interrupts
Prototype	#include <dos.h>
	void disable(void);
Prototype in	dos.h

▶ *div* ▶

div	divides two integers, returning quotient and remainder
Prototype	#include <stdlib.h>
	div_t div(int numer, int denom);
Prototype in	stdlib.h

► *dosexterr* ►

dosexterr   gets extended error

Prototype   #include <dos.h>
                   int dosexterr(struct DOSERR *eblkp);

Prototype in   dos.h

► *dostounix* ►

dostounix   converts date and time to UNIX time format

Prototype   #include <dos.h>
                   long dostounix(struct date *dateptr, struct time *timeptr);

Prototype in   dos.h

► *dup* ►

dup   duplicates a file handle

Prototype   int dup(int handle);

Prototype in   io.h

► *dup2* ►

dup2   duplicates a file handle

Prototype   int dup2(int oldhandle, int newhandle);

Prototype in   io.h

► *ecvt* ►

ecvt   converts a floating-point number to a string

Prototype   char *ecvt(double value, int ndigit, int *decpt, int *sign);

Prototype in   stdlib.h

► *eof* ►

eof	detects end-of-file
Prototype	int eof(int *handle*);
Prototype in	io.h

► *exec...* ►

exec... functions that load and run other programs

Prototype int execl(char **pathname*, char **arg0*, *arg1*, ...,argn, NULL);
int execle(char **pathname*, char **arg0*,*arg1*, ..., *argn*, NULL, char **envp[ ]*);
int execlp(char **pathname*, char **arg0*, *arg1*, ..., *argn*, NULL);
int execlpe(char **pathname*, char **arg0*, *arg1*, ..., *argn*, NULL, char **envp[ ]*);
int execv(char **pathname*, char **argv[ ]*);
int execve(char **pathname*, char **argv[ ]*, char **envp[ ]*);
int execvp(char **pathname*, char **argv[ ]*);
int execvpe(char **pathname*, char **argv[ ]*, char **envp[ ]*);

Prototype in process.h

► *_exit* ►

_exit	terminates program
Prototype	void _exit(int *status*);
Prototype in	process.h

► *exit* ►

exit	terminates program
Prototype	void exit(int *status*);
Prototype in	process.h

► *exp* ►

exp	exponential function; returns e^x
Prototype	double exp(double *x*);
Prototype in	math.h

► *fabs* ►

fabs	absolute value
Prototype	double fabs(double *x*);
Prototype in	math.h

► *farcalloc* ►

farcalloc	allocates memory from the far heap
Prototype	void far *farcalloc(unsigned long *nunits*, unsigned long *unitsz*);
Prototype in	alloc.h

► *farcoreleft* ►

farcoreleft	returns measure of unused memory in far heap
Prototype	long farcoreleft(void);
Prototype in	alloc.h

► *farfree* ►

farfree	frees a block from far heap
Prototype	void farfree(void far *block*);
Prototype in	alloc.h

► *farmalloc* ►

farmalloc	allocates from far heap
Prototype	void far *farmalloc(unsigned long *size*);
Prototype in	alloc.h

► *farrealloc* ►

farrealloc	adjusts allocated block in far heap
Prototype	void far *farrealloc(void far *block*, unsigned long *newsize*);
Prototype in	alloc.h

► *fclose* ►

fclose	closes a stream
Prototype	#include <stdio.h>
	int fclose(FILE *stream*);
Prototype in	stdio.h

► *fcloseall* ►

fcloseall	closes open streams
Prototype	int fcloseall(void);
Prototype in	stdio.h

► *fcvt* ►

fcvt	converts a floating-point number to a string
Prototype	char *fcvt(double *value*, int *ndigit*, int *decpt*, int *sign*);
Prototype in	stdlib.h

► *fdopen* ►

fdopen   associates a stream with a file handle

Prototype   #include <stdio.h>
           FILE *fdopen(int *handle*, char *type*);

Prototype in stdio.h

► *feof* ►

feof   detects end-of-file on stream

Prototype   #include <stdio.h>
           int fflush(FILE *stream*);

Prototype in stdio.h

► *ferror* ►

ferror   detects errors on stream

Prototype   #include <stdio.h>
           int ferror(FILE *stream*);

Prototype in stdio.h

► *fflush* ►

fflush   flushes a stream

Prototype   #include <stdio.h>
           int fflush(FILE *stream*);

Prototype in stdio.h

► *fgetc* ►

fgetc   gets character from stream

Prototype   #include <stdio.h>
           int fgetc(FILE *stream*);

Prototype in stdio.h

► *fgetchar* ►

fgetchar   gets character from stream

Prototype   int fgetchar(void);

Prototype in   stdio.h

► *fgetpos* ►

fgetpos   gets the current file pointer

Prototype   #include <stdio.h>
                             int fgetpos(FILE*stream, fpos_t,*pos);

Prototype in   stdio.h

► *fgets* ►

fgets   gets a string from a stream

Prototype   #include <stdio.h>
                             char *fgets(char *string, int n, FILE *stream);

Prototype in   stdio.h

► *filelength* ►

filelength   gets file size in bytes

Prototype   long filelength(int handle);

Prototype in   io.h

► *fileno* ►

fileno   gets file handle

Prototype   #include <stdio.h>
                             int fileno(FILE *stream);

Prototype in   stdio.h

► *findfirst* ►

findfirst	searches disk directory
Prototype	#include <dir.h>
	#include <dos.h>
	int findfirst(char *pathname*, struct ffblk *ffblk*, int *attrib*);
Prototype in	dir.h

► *findnext* ►

findnext	fetches files which match **findfirst**
Prototype	#include <dir.h>
	int findnext(struct ffblk *ffblk*);
Prototype in	dir.h

► *floor* ►

floor	rounds down
Prototype	double floor(double *x*);
Prototype in	math.h

► *flushall* ►

flushall	clears all buffers
Prototype	int flushall(void);
Prototype in	stdio.h

► *fmod* ►

fmod	calculates *x* modulo *y*, the remainder of *x/y*
Prototype	double fmod(double *x*, double *y*);
Prototype in	math.h

► fnmerge ►

fnmerge	makes new file name
Prototype	#include <dir.h> void fnmerge(char *path*, char *drive*, char *dir*, char *name*, char *ext*);
Prototype in	dir.h

► fnsplit ►

fnsplit	splits a full path name into its components
Prototype	#include <dir.h> int fnsplit(char *path*, char *drive*, char *dir*, char *name*, char *ext*);
Prototype in	dir.h

► fopen ►

fopen	opens a stream
Prototype	#include <stdio.h> FILE *fopen(char *filename*, char *type*);
Prototype in	stdio.h

► FP_OFF ►

FP_OFF	gets a far address offset
Prototype	#include <dos.h> unsigned FP_OFF(void far *farptr*);
Prototype in	dos.h

► *FP_SEG* ►

FP_SEG   gets far address segment

Prototype   #include <dos.h>
                    unsigned FP_SEG(void far *farptr*);

Prototype in dos.h

► *_fpreset* ►

_fpreset   reinitializes floating-point math package

Prototype   void _fpreset( );

Prototype in float.h

► *fprintf* ►

fprintf   sends formatted output to a stream

Prototype   #include <stdio.h>
                    int fprintf(FILE *stream*, char *format*[, *argument*, ...]);

Prototype in stdio.h

► *fputc* ►

fputc   puts a character on a stream

Prototype   #include <stdio.h>
                    int fputc(int *ch*, FILE *stream*);

Prototype in stdio.h

► *fputchar* ►

fputchar   puts a character on *stdout*

Prototype   int fputchar(char *ch*);

Prototype in stdio.h

► *fputs* ►

fputs	puts a string on á stream
Prototype	#include <stdio.h>
	int fputs(char*string, FILE*stream);
Prototype in	stdio.h

► *fread* ►

fread	reads data from a stream
Prototype	#include <stdio.h>
	int fread(void *ptr*, int *size*, int *nitems*, FILE *stream*);
Prototype in	stdio.h

► *free* ►

free	frees allocated block
Prototype	void free(void *ptr*);
Prototype in	stdlib.h and alloc.h

► *freemem* ►

freemem	frees a previously allocated DOS memory block
Prototype	int freemem(unsigned *seg*);
Prototype in	dos.h

► *freopen* ►

freopen	replaces a stream
Prototype	#include <stdio.h>
	FILE *freopen(char *filename*, char *type*, FILE *stream*);
Prototype in	stdio.h

► *frexp* ►

frexp	splits a double number into mantissa and exponent
Prototype	double frexp(double *value*, int *eptr*);
Prototype in	math.h

► *fscanf* ►

fscanf	performs formatted input from a stream
Prototype	#Include <stdio.h>
	int fscanf(FILE *stream*, char *format*[, *argument*, ...]);
Prototype in	stdio.h

► *fseek* ►

fseek	repositions a file pointer on a stream
Prototype	#include <stdio.h>
	int fseek(FILE *stream*, long *offset*, Int *fromwhere*);
Prototype in	stdio.h

► *fsetpos* ►

fsetpos	positions the file pointer on a stream
Prototype	#include <stdio.h>
	int fsetpos(FILE *stream, const fpos_t *pos);
Prototype in	stdio.h

► *fstat* ►

fstat	gets open file information
Prototype	#include <sys\stat.h>
	int fstat(char *handle*, struct stat *buff*)
Prototype in	sys\stat.h

► *ftell* ►

ftell	returns the current file pointer
Prototype	#include <stdio.h>
	long ftell(FILE *stream);
Prototype in	stdio.h

► *fwrite* ►

fwrite	writes to a stream
Prototype	#include <stdio.h>
	int fwrite(void *ptr, int size, int nitems, FILE *stream);
Prototype in	stdio.h

► *gcvt* ►

gcvt	converts floating-point number to string
Prototype	#include <dos.h>
	char *gcvt(double value, int ndigit, char *buf);
Prototype in	stdlib.h

► *geninterrupt* ►

geninterrupt	generates software interrupt
Prototype	#include <dos.h>
	void geninterrupt(int intr_num);
Prototype in	dos.h

► *getc* ►

getc	gets character from stream
Prototype	#include <stdio.h>
	int getc(FILE *stream);
Prototype in	stdio.h
	conio.h (getch, getche, ungetch)

► *getch* ►

getch   gets character from console, no echoing

Prototype   int getch(void);

Prototype in conio.h

► *getchar* ►

getchar   gets character from stream

Prototype   #include <stdio.h>
                    int getchar(void);

Prototype in stdio.h

► *getche* ►

getche   gets character from keyboard, echoes to screen

Prototype   int getche(void);

Prototype in conio.h

► *getcurdir* ►

getcurdir   gets current directory for specified drive

Prototype   int getcurdir(int *drive*, char **direc*);

Prototype in dir.h

► *getcwd* ►

getcwd   gets current working directory

Prototype   char *getcwd(char **buf*, int *n*);

Prototype in dir.h

▸ *getdate* ▸

getdate   gets MS-DOS date

Prototype   #include <dos.h>
                     void getdate(struct date *dateblk);

Prototype in   dos.h

▸ *getdfree* ▸

getdfree   gets disk free space

Prototype   #include <dos.h>
                    void getdfree(int drive, struct dfree *dfreep);

Prototype in   dos.h

▸ *getdisk* ▸

getdisk   gets current drive

Prototype   int getdisk(void);

Prototype in   dir.h

▸ *getdta* ▸

getdta   gets disk transfer address

Prototype   char far *getdta(void);

Prototype in   dos.h

▸ *getenv* ▸

getenv   gets string from environment

Prototype   char *getenv(char *envvar);

Prototype in   stdlib.h

► *getftime* ►

getftime   gets file date and time

Prototype   #include <dos.h>
                int getftime(int *handle*, struct ftime **ftimep*);

Prototype in dos.h

► *getpass* ►

getpass   reads a password

Prototype   char *getpass(char **prompt*);

Prototype in conio.h

► *getpsp* ►

getpsp   gets the program segment prefix

Prototype   unsigned getpsp(*void*);

Prototype in dos.h

► *gets* ►

gets   gets a string from a stream

Prototype   char *gets(char **string*);

Prototype in stdio.h (**fgets, gets**)
                conio.h (**cgets**)

► *gettime* ►

gettime   gets system time

Prototype   #include <dos.h>
                vold gettlme(struct time **timep*);

Prototype in dos.h

► *getw* ►

getw gets integer from stream

Prototype #include <stdio.h>
int getw(FILE *stream);

Prototype in stdio.h

► *gmtime* ►

gmtime converts date and time to Greenwich Mean Time

Prototype #include <time.h>
struct tm *gmtime(long *clock);

Prototype in time.h

► *int86* ►

int86 general 8086 software interrupt interface

Prototype #include <dos.h>
int int86(int intr_num, union REGS *inregs, union REGS *outregs);

Prototype in dos.h

► *int86x* ►

int86x general 8086 software interrupt interface

Prototype #include <dos.h>
int int86x(int intr_num, union REGS *inregs, union REGS *outregs, struct SREGS *segregs);

Prototype in dos.h

► *intdos* ►

intdos general MS-DOS interrupt interface

Prototype #include <dos.h>
int intdos(union REGS *inregs, union REGS *outregs);

Prototype in dos.h

► *intdosx* ►

intdosx   general MS-DOS interrupt interface

Prototype   #include <dos.h>
                 int intdosx(union REGS *inregs*, union REGS *outregs*,
                 struct SREGS *segregs*);

Prototype in dos.h

► *intr* ►

intr   alternate 8086 software interrupt interface

Prototype   #include <dos.h>
                 void *intr(int intr_num*, struct REGPACK *preg*);

Prototype in dos.h

► *is...* ►

is...   character classification macros

Prototype   #include <ctype.h>
                 int isalpha(int *ch*);
                 int isalnum(int *ch*);
                 int isascii(int *ch*);
                 int iscntrl(int *ch*);
                 int isdigit(int *ch*);
                 int isgraph(int *ch*);
                 int islower(int *ch*);
                 int isprint(int *ch*);
                 int ispunct(int *ch*);
                 int isspace(int *ch*);
                 int isupper(int *ch*);
                 int isxdigit(int *ch*);

Prototype in io.h

► *isatty* ►

isatty   checks for device type

Prototype   int isatty(int *handle*);

Prototype in io.h

► *itoa* ►

itoa	converts an integer to a string
Prototype	char *itoa(int *value*, char *string*, int *radix*);
Prototype in	stdlib.h

► *kbhit* ►

kbhit	checks for recent keystrokes
Prototype	int kbhit(void);
Prototype in	conio.h

► *labs* ►

labs	gives long absolute value
Prototype	long labs(long *n*);
Prototype in	stdlib.h

► *ldiv* ►

ldiv	divides two longs, returns quotient and remainder
Prototype	#include <stdlib.h> ldiv_t ldiv(long lnumer,long ldenom):
Prototype in	stdlib.h

► *lfind* ►

lfind	performs a linear search
Prototype	#include <stdlib.h> void *lfind(const void *key*, const void *base*, size_t*pnelem, size_t *width*, int(*fcmp)(const void*, const void*));
Prototype in	stdlib.h

► *localtime* ►

localtime	converts date and time to a structure
Prototype	#include <time.h>
	struct tm *localtime(long *clock);
Prototype in	time.h

► *log* ►

log	logarithm function in(x)
Prototype	double log(double x);
Prototype in	math.h

► *log10* ►

log10	logarithm function $\log^{10}(X)$
Prototype	double log10(double x);
Prototype in	math.h

► *_lrotl* ►

_lrotl	rotates an unsigned long value to the left
Prototype	unsigned long _lrotl(unsigned long lvalue, int count);
Prototype in	stdlib.h

► *_lrotr* ►

_lrotr	rotates an unsigned long value to the right
Prototype	unsigned long _lrotr(unsigned long lvalue, int count);
Prototype in	stdlib.h

► *lsearch* ►

lsearch   linear search

Prototype   #include <stdlib.h>
void *lsearch(const void *key, void *base, size_t *pnelem,
size_t width, int(*fcmp)(const void*,const void*));

Prototype in stdlib.h

► *lseek* ►

lseek   moves read/write file pointer

Prototype   #include <io.h>
long lseek(int *handle*, long *offset*, int *fromwhere*);

Prototype in io.h

► *ltoa* ►

ltoa   converts a long to a string

Prototype   char *ltoa(long *value*, char *string*, int *radix*);

Prototype in stdlib.h

► *malloc* ►

malloc   allocates main memory

Prototype   #include <stdlib.h>
void*malloc(size_t *size*);

Prototype in stdlib.h and alloc.h

► *mem...* ►

mem...   manipulates memory arrays

Prototype in string.h
mem.h

► *mkdir* ►

mkdir   creates a directory

Prototype   int mkdir(char *pathname*);

Prototype in   dir.h

► *mktemp* ►

mktemp   makes a unique file name

Prototype   char *mktemp(char *template*);

Prototype in   dir.h

► *modf* ►

modf   splits into integer part and fraction

Prototype   double modf(double *value*, double *lptr*);

Prototype in   math.h

► *movedata* ►

movedata   copies bytes

Prototype   void movedata(int *segsrc*, int *offsrc*, int *segdest*, int *offdest*,
                   unsigned *numbytes*);

Prototype in   mem.h
                   string.h

► *movmem* ►

movmem   moves a block of bytes

Prototype   void movmem(void *source*, void *destin*, unsigned *len*);

Prototype in   mem.h

► *nosound* ►

nosound   turns PC speaker off

Prototype   void nosound(void);

Prototype in   dos.h

► *_open* ►

_open   opens a file for reading or writing

Prototype   #include <fcntl.h>
                   int_open(char *pathname,int access);

Prototype in   io.h

► *open* ►

open   opens a file for reading or writing

Prototype   #include <fcntl.h>
                   #include <sys\stat.h>
                   int open(char *pathname, int access[,int permiss]);

Prototype in   io.h

► *putc* ►

putc   outputs a character to a stream

Prototype   #include <stdio.h>
                   int putc(int ch, FILE *stream);

Prototype in   stdio.h

► *putch* ►

putch   puts character on screen

Prototype   int putch(int ch);

Prototype in   conio.h

► *putchar* ►

putchar	puts character on a stream
Prototype	#include <stdio.h> int putchar(int *ch*);
Prototype in	stdio.h

► *putenv* ►

putenv	adds string to current environment
Prototype	int putenv(char **envvar*);
Prototype in	stdlib.h

► *puts* ►

puts	puts a string on a stream
Prototype	int puts(char **string*);
Prototype in	stdio.h (**fputs and puts**) conio.h (**cputs**)

► *putw* ►

putw	puts character or word on a stream
Prototype	#include <stdio.h> int putw(int *w*, FILE **stream*);
Prototype in	stdio.h

► *qsort* ►

qsort	sorts using the quick sort routine
Prototype	void qsort(void **base*, int *nelem*, int *width*, int(**fcmp*)( ));
Prototype in	stdlib.h

► *rand* ►

rand   random number generator

Prototype   int rand(void);

Prototype in stdlib.h

► *random* ►

random   random number generator

Prototype   #include <stdlib.h>
               int random(int num);

Prototype in stdlib.h

► *randomize* ►

randomize   initializes random number generator

Prototype   #include <stdlib.h>
               void randomize(void);

Prototype in stdlib.h

► *_read* ►

_read   reads from file

Prototype   int_read(int *handle*, void *buf*, int *nbyte*);

Prototype in io.h

► *read* ►

read   reads from a file

Prototype   int read(int *handle*, void *buf*,unsigned *nbyte*);

Prototype in io.h

► *realloc* ►

realloc   reallocates main memory

Prototype   #include <stdlib.h>
void *realloc(void *ptr,size_t newsize);

Prototype in   stdlib.h, alloc.h

► *registerbgidriver* ►

registerbgidriver   registers linked-in graphics driver code

Prototype   #include <graphics.h>
int registerbgidriver(void(*driver)(void));

Prototype in   graphics.h

► *registerbgifont* ►

registerbgifont   registers linked-in stroked font code

Prototype   #include <graphics.h>
int registerbgifont(void (*font)(void));

Prototype in   graphics.h

► *rename* ►

rename   renames a file

Prototype   int rename(char *oldname, char *newname);

Prototype in   stdio.h

► *rewind* ►

rewind   repositions a stream

Prototype   #include <stdlo.h>
int rewind(FILE *stream);

Prototype in   stdio.h

► *rmdir* ►

rmdir   removes directory

Prototype   int rmdir(char *pathname*);

Prototype in dir.h

► *_rotl* ►

_rotl   rotates a value to the left

Prototype   unsigned _rotl(unsigned value,int count);

Prototype in stdlib.h

► *_rotr* ►

_rotr   rotates a value to the right

Prototype   unsigned _rotr(unsigned value,int count);

Prototype in stdlib.h

► *setdate* ►

setdate   sets MS-DOS date

Prototype   #include <dos.h>
                 void setdate(struct date *dateblk*);

Prototype in dos.h

► *setdisk* ►

setdisk   sets current disk drive

Prototype   int setdisk(int *drive*);

Prototype in dir.h

► *setftime* ►

setftime   gets file date and time

Prototype   #include <io.h>
          int setftime(int *handle*, struct ftime **ftimep*);

Prototype in io.h

► *setmem* ►

setmem   assigns a value to memory

Prototype   void setmem(void **addr*, int *len*, char *value*);

Prototype in mem.h

► *setmode* ►

setmode   sets mode of open file

Prototype   int setmode(int *handle*, unsigned *mode*);

Prototype in io.h

► *settime* ►

settime   sets system time

Prototype   #include <dos.h>
          void settime(struct time **timep*);

Prototype in dos.h

► *sleep* ►

sleep   suspends execution for interval

Prototype   unsigned sleep(unsigned *seconds*);

Prototype in dos.h

► *sound* ►

sound	turns PC speaker on at specified frequency
Prototype	void sound(unsigned frequency);
Prototype in	dos.h

► *spawn...* ►

spawn...   functions that create and run other programs

Prototype
```
#include <process.h>
int spawnl(int mode, char *pathname, char *arg0, arg1,
...,argn, NULL);
int spawnle(int mode, char *pathname, char *arg0,
arg1,...,argn,NULL,char *envp[ ]);
int spawnlp(int mode,char *pathname, char
*arg0,arg1,...,argn,NULL;
int spawnlpe(int mode,char *pathname, char
*arg0,arg1,...,argn, NULL,char *envp[ ]);
int spawnv(int mode, char *pathname,char *argv[ ]);
int spawnve(int mode, char *pathname,char *argv[ ], char
*envp[ ]);
int spawnvp(int mode, char *pathname,char *argv[ ]);
int spawnvpe(int mode, char *pathname, char *argv[ ],char
*envp[ ]);
```

Prototype in   process.h

► *sprintf* ►

sprintf	sends formatted output to a string
Prototype	int sprintf(char *string, char *format[,argument, ...]);
Prototype in	stdio.h

► *sqrt* ►

sqrt	calculates square root
Prototype	double sqrt(double x);
Prototype in	math.h

► *srand* ►

srand	initializes random number generator
Prototype	void srand(unsigned *seed*);
Prototype in	stdlib.h

► *sscanf* ►

sscanf	performs formatted input from a string
Prototype	int sscanf(char **string*, char **format*[,*argument*,...]);
Prototype in	stdio.h

► *stat* ►

stat	gets information about open file
Prototype	#include <sys\stat.h> int stat(char **pathname*, struct stat **buff*)
Prototype in	sys\stat.h

► *stime* ►

stime	sets time
Prototype	int stime(long **tp*);
Prototype in	time.h

► *stpcpy* ►

stpcpy	copies one string into another
Prototype	char **stpcpy*(char **destin*, char **source*);
Prototype in	string.h

► *str...* ►

str...	family of string manipulation functions

Prototype			
char	*	stpcpy(char *destin*, char *source*);
char	*	strcat(char *destin*, char *source*);
char	*	strchr(char *str*, char *c*);
int		strcmp(char *str1*, char *str2*);
char	*	strcpy(char *destin*, char *source*);
int		strcspn(char *str1*, char *str2*);
char	*	strdup(char *str*);
int		stricmp(char *str1*, char *str2*);
int		strcmpi(char *str1*, char *str2*);
unsigned		strlen(char *str*);
char	*	strlwr(char *str*);
char	*	strncat(char *destin*, char *source*, int *maxlen*);
int		strucmp(char *str1*, char *str2*, int *maxlen*);
char	*	strncpy(char *destin*, char *source*, int *maxlen*);
int		strnicmp(char *str1*, char *str2*, unsigned *maxlen*);
int		strncmpi(char *str1*, char *str2*, unsigned *maxlen*);
char	*	strnset(char *str*, char *ch*, unsigned *n*);
char	*	strpbrk(char *str1*,char *str2*);
char	*	strrchr(char *str*,char *c*);
char	*	strrev(char *str*);
char	*	strset(char *str*,char *ch*);
int		strspn(char *str1*,char *str2*);
char	*	strstr(char *str1*, char *str2*);
double		strtod(char *str*,char * *endptr*);
long		strtol(char *str*,char * *endptr*,int *base*);
char	*	strtok(char *str1*, char *str2*);
char	*	strupr(char *str*);

Prototype in string.h

► *strerror* ►

strerror	returns pointer to error message string
Prototype	char *strerror(int errnum);
Prototype in	string.h

► *_strerror* ►

_strerror	returns pointer to error message string
Prototype	char *_strerror(const char *string);
Prototype in	string.h

► *strtoul* ►

strtoul	converts a string to an unsigned long
Prototype	unsigned long strtoul(const char *str,char **endptr,int radix);
Prototype in	stdlib.h

► *swab* ►

swab	swaps bytes
Prototype	void swab(char(from, char *to, int nbytes);
Prototype in	stdlib.h

► *system* ►

system	issues an MS-DOS command
Prototype	int system(char *command);
Prototype in	stdlib.h

► *tan* ►

tan	trigonometric tangent function
Prototype	double tan(double *x*);
Prototype in	math.h

► *tell* ►

tell	gets current position of file pointer
Prototype	long tell(int *handle*);
Prototype in	io.h

► *time* ►

time	gets time of day
Prototype	long time(long **tloc*);
Prototype in	time.h

► *tmpfile* ►

tmpfile	opens a binary "scratch" file
Prototype	#include <stdio.h> FILE *tmpfile(void);
Prototype in	stdio.h

► *tmpnam* ►

tmpnam	creates a unique file name
Prototype	char *tmpnam(char *sptr);
Prototype in	stdio.h

► *toascii* ►

toascii   translates characters to ASCII format

Prototype   int toascii(int *c*);

Prototype in   ctype.h

► *_tolower* ►

_tolower   translates characters to lowercase

Prototype   #include <ctype.h>
                 int _tolower(int *c*);

Prototype in   ctype.h

► *tolower* ►

tolower   translates characters to lowercase

Prototype   int tolower(int *c*);

Prototype in   ctype.h

► *_toupper* ►

_toupper   translates characters to uppercase

Prototype   #include <ctype.h>
                 int _toupper(int *c*);

Prototype in   ctype.h

► *toupper* ►

toupper   translates characters to uppercase

Prototype   int toupper(int *c*);

Prototype in   ctype.h

► *ultoa* ►

ultoa   converts an unsigned long to a string

Prototype   char *ultoa(unsigned long *value*, char *string*, int *radix*);

Prototype in   stdlib.h

► *ungetc* ►

ungetc   pushes a character back into input stream

Prototype   #include <stdio.h>
                   int ungetc(char *c*, FILE *stream*);

Prototype in   stdio.h

► *ungetch* ►

ungetch   pushes a character back to the keyboard buffer

Prototype   int ungetch(int *c*);

Prototype in   conio.h

► *unlink* ►

unlink   deletes a file

Prototype   int unlink(char *filename*);

Prototype in   dos.h

► *_write* ►

_write   writes to a file

Prototype   int _write(int *handle*, void *buf*,unsigned *nbyte*);

Prototype in   io.h

► *write* ►

write	writes to a file
Prototype	int write(int *handle*, void **buf*, int *nbyte*);
Prototype in	io.h

► *DESCRIPTIONS OF GRAPHICS FUNCTIONS* ►

► *arc* ►   ► *graphics* ►

arc	draws a circular arc
Prototype	#include <graphics.h>
	void far arc(int x, int y, int *stangle*, int *endangle*, int *radius*);
Prototype in	graphics.h

► *Description*

This function draws a circular arc on a graphics screen, using the current drawing color and line style. The center is at the coordinates given by *x* and *y*, and the radius is given by *radius*. The parameters *stangle* and *endangle* specify the starting and stopping angles in degrees, where 0 degrees is at the 3 o'clock position, 90 degrees is at 12 o'clock, and so on.

For example, the following code draws an arc and connects the endpoints:

```
struct arccoordstype arccoords;

arc (100,100,0,180,75);
getarccoords (&arccoords);
line (arccoords.xstart,arccoords.ystart,
arccoords.xend,arccoords.yend);
```

See also **getarccoords( )**, **line( )**

► *bar* ►   ► *graphics* ►

bar	draws a bar
Prototype	#include <graphics.h>
	void far bar(int *left*, int *top*, int *right*, int *bottom*);
Prototype in	graphics.h

► *Description*

This graphics function draws a bar on the screen by filling the specified rectangular area with the current fill color and fill pattern. It does not draw an outline around the bar (to draw an outline, you can use **bar3d( )** with a *depth* value of 0). The first two parameters give the coordinates of the upper-left corner of the bar, and the second two parameters specify the lower-right corner.

bar( ) could be used, for example, to construct bar charts. The following code draws a vertical bar:

```
bar (50,50,75,150);
```

See also **bar3d( )**

► *bar3d* ►   ► *graphics* ►

bar3d	draws a 3-D bar
Prototype	#include <graphics.h> void far bar3d(int *left*, int *top*, int *right*, int *bottom*, int *depth*, int *topflag*);
Prototype in	graphics.h

► *Description*

bar3d( ) draws the outline for a three-dimensional bar on a graphics screen, using the current drawing color and line style, and then fills the enclosed area with the current fill color and pattern. The first four parameters give the upper-left and lower-right corners of the bar, and the *depth* parameter specifies the depth in pixels. You should set *topflag* to 1 if you want a top drawn on the box and to 0 if you do not want a top.

This function can be used to create attractive three-dimensional bar charts. The following lines generate a bar that is filled with slanted lines:

```
setfillstyle (LTSLASH_FILL,1);
bar3d (50,50,75,150,5,1);
```

See also **bar( )**, **setfillstyle( )**

► *circle* ►   ► *graphics* ►

circle   draws a circle

Prototype   #include <graphics.h>
                  void far circle(int *x*, int *y*, int *radius*);

Prototype in graphics.h

► *Description*

circle( ) draws a circle on the graphics screen with a center given by *x* and *y* and a radius specified by *radius*. The function uses the current drawing color and line style. For example, the following line draws a circle in the center of the screen, with a radius of 75 pixels:

circle (getmaxx ( ) / 2, getmaxy ( ) / 2, 75);

See also getmaxx( ), getmaxy( )

► *cleardevice* ►   ► *graphics* ►

cleardevice   clears the graphics screen

Prototype   #include <graphics.h>
                  void far cleardevice(void);

Prototype in graphics.h

► *Description*

This function clears the entire graphics screen and moves the current position to (0,0). You should use the function **clearviewport( )** to clear only the current viewport on a graphics screen and **clrscr( )** to clear the screen when you are in a text mode.

See also **clearviewport( )**, clrscr( )

► *clearviewport* ►   ► *graphics* ►

clearviewport   clears the current viewport

Prototype   #include <graphics.h>
                    void far clearviewport(void);

Prototype in   graphics.h

► *Description*

This function clears only the current viewport on a graphics screen and moves the current position (CP) to (0,0). You should use **cleardevice( )** to clear the entire graphics screen or **clrscr( )** to clear the screen when you are in a text mode.

See also **cleardevice( )**, **clrscr( )**, **getviewsettings( )**

► *closegraph* ►   ► *graphics* ►

closegraph   shuts down the graphics system

Prototype   #include <graphics.h>
                    void far closegraph(void);

Prototype in   graphics.h

► *Description*

You should call **closegraph( )** when you have finished using the Turbo C graphics routines. This function releases the memory allocated by the graphics system and restores the screen to the video mode that was active before **initgraph( )** was called.

See also **initgraph( )**

► *clreol* ►   ► *text* ►

clreol   clears to end of line in text windows

Prototype   void clreol(void);

Prototype in   conio.h

► Description

You should use this function only when you are in a text mode. It clears all characters from the cursor position to the end of the line within the current text window. **clreol( )** does not move the cursor.

See also **clrscr( )**, **delline( )**, **window( )**

► *clrscr* ►   ► *text* ►

clrscr   clears text mode windows

Prototype   void clrscr(void);

Prototype in conio.h

► Description

clrscr( ) should be used only in a text mode. This function clears the current window and places the cursor at position (1,1) within this window. To clear the entire screen, the current window must be defined to encompass the full screen. To clear a graphics screen, use either **cleardevice( )** or **clearviewport( )**.

See also **cleardevice( )**, **clreol( )**, **clearviewport( )**, **delline( )**, **window( )**

► *delline* ►   ► *text* ►

delline   deletes line in text window

Prototype   void delline(void);

Prototype in conio.h

► Description

You should use **delline( )** only in a text mode. This function deletes the line containing the cursor and fills the gap by moving up all lines that are below it. **delline( )** affects only lines within the current text window.

See also **clreol( )**, **window( )**

► *detectgraph* ►   ► *graphics* ►

detectgraph   determines graphics driver and mode to use by checking
the hardware

Prototype   #include <graphics.h>
void far detectgraph(int far *graphdriver*, int far *graphmode*);

Prototype in   graphics.h

► *Description*

This function determines the type of graphics adapter installed in the computer and the highest resolution graphics mode supported by the adapter. **detectgraph( )** assigns the graphics adapter type to *graphdriver* and the graphics mode to *graphmode*. Constant definitions for all graphics adapter types and modes are furnished in the header file graphics.h. If **detectgraph( )** detects none of the supported graphics adapter types, it assigns a value of − 2 to *graphdriver*.

For example, the following code will print the current video adapter type and highest resolution mode:

```
int graphdriver;
int graphmode;
...
detectgraph (&graphdriver,&graphmode);
printf ("driver = %d; mode = %d", graphdriver,
        graphmode);
```

See also initgraph( )

► *drawpoly* ►   ► *graphics* ►

drawpoly   draws the outline of a polygon

Prototype   #include <graphics.h>
void far drawpoly(int *numpoints*, int far *polypoints*);

Prototype in   graphics.h

► *Description*

This function draws a sequence of connected line segments on the graphics screen and can be used to construct a polygon. The first parameter, *num-points*, gives the number of endpoints, and the second parameter, *polypoints*, contains the address of a sequence of integer pairs that specify each endpoint. The function uses the current drawing color and line style and draws a line segment from the first endpoint to the second endpoint, from the second endpoint to the third, and so on through the last endpoint. For example, the following code draws a triangle:

```
int triangle [ ] =
    {
    300,100,
    400,190,
    200,190,
    300,100
    };
...
drawpoly (4, triangle);
```

Note that to draw a closed figure consisting of three lines, this example must specify four endpoints. You do not need to draw a polygon with this function—you can construct any sequence of connected line segments.

See also **fillpoly( )**

► *ellipse* ►   ► *graphics* ►

ellipse   draws an elliptical arc

Prototype   #include <graphics.h >
               void far ellipse(int *x*, int *y*, int *stangle*, int *endangle*, int
               xradius, int *yradius*);

Prototype in graphics.h

► *Description*

This function draws an elliptical arc on the graphics screen, using the current drawing color and line style. The first two parameters specify the *x* and *y* coordinates of the center of the ellipse, and **stangle** and **endangle** give the starting and ending angles of the arc in degrees, where 0 degrees is at the 3 o'clock position, 90 degrees is at 12 o'clock, and so on. The parameters **xradius** and **yradius** provide the lengths of the horizontal and vertical axes (that is, one half the total horizontal and vertical dimensions).

For example, the following command draws an elliptical arc that consists of half an ellipse:

    ellipse (300,200,0,180,100,50);

► *fillpoly* ►   ► *graphics* ►

fillpoly	draws and fills a polygon
Prototype	#include <graphics.h>
	void far fillpoly(int *numpoints*, int far *polypoints*);
Prototype in	graphics.h

► *Description*

This function draws a polygon using the current drawing color and line style and then fills the polygon using the current fill color and pattern. See the description of **drawpoly( )** for an explanation of the parameters.

► *floodfill* ►   ► *graphics* ►

floodfill	flood-fills a bounded region
Prototype	#include <graphics.h>
	void far floodfill(int x, int y, int border);
Prototype in	graphics.h

► *Description*

This function fills the area on a graphics screen surrounding the point given by *x* and *y* with the current fill color and pattern until a border consisting of the color border is encountered. Note that to fill a discrete area of the screen, the surrounding border must be continuous; if there are any gaps, the filling will leak out, possibly encompassing the entire screen. **floodfill( )** returns − 7 if an error occurs. For compatibility with future versions of the graphics package, Borland recommends that you use **fillpoly( )** whenever possible.

For example, the following code draws a circle and then fills the area with cross-hatching.

```
circle (360,174,200);
setfillstyle (HATCH_FILL,1);
floodfill (360,174,1);
```

Note that although this example specifies the coordinates of the center of the circle, any point within the circle could have been chosen.

See also **fillpoly( )**

► *getarccoords* ►   ► *graphics* ►

getarccoords gets coordinates of the last call to **arc**

Prototype   #include <graphics.h>
                void far getarccoords(struct arccoordstype far *arccoords);

Prototype in   graphics.h

► *Description*

getarccoords( ) loads the **arccoordstype** structure with information regarding the last call to **arc( )**. This structure is defined in graphics.h as follows:

```
struct arccoordstype
    {
    int x, y;
    int xstart, ystart, xend, yend;
    };
```

See the example given under the description of **arc( )**.

See also **arc( )**

► *getaspectratio* ►   ► *graphics* ►

getaspectratio   returns the current graphics mode's aspect ratio

Prototype   #include <graphics.h>
                       void far getaspectratio(int far *xasp*, int far *yasp*);

Prototype in   graphics.h

► *Description*

This graphics function returns the relative horizontal and vertical spacings between pixels on the screen. The relative horizontal spacing is assigned to *xasp* and the relative vertical spacing to *yasp*. On a CGA system, for example, the horizontal spacing is less than the vertical spacing; therefore the value assigned to *xasp* is smaller than that assigned to *yasp* (in high-resolution graphics, there are 640 pixels across the screen but only 200 from top to bottom). Note that the function does not actually return the aspect ratio; rather, you must calculate the ratio from the relative values that are returned (by performing a division).

This function can be used to specify horizontal and vertical pixel dimensions that will generate equal dimensions on the screen. For example, the following code uses **getaspectratio( )** to generate a rectangle that will appear on the screen with four equal sides:

```
int xasp, yasp;
int xdim, ydim;
...
getaspectratio (&xasp,&yasp);
xdim = 200;
ydim = (200L * xasp) / yasp;
rectangle (0,0,xdim,ydim);
```

► *getbkcolor* ►   ► *graphics* ►

getbkcolor   returns the current background color

Prototype   #include <graphics.h>
                   int far getbkcolor(void);

Prototype in   graphics.h

► *Description*

This function returns the current background color used in graphics modes. For VGA, EGA, and low-resolution CGA graphics modes, the background color is the color displayed for a pixel value of 0 (in other words it is color number *0* in the current palette). The following colors are available in these modes (the constants are defined in graphics.h):

Constant	Numeric Value
BLACK	0
BLUE	1
GREEN	2
CYAN	3
RED	4
MAGENTA	5
BROWN	6
LIGHTGRAY	7
DARKGRAY	8
LIGHTBLUE	9
LIGHTGREEN	10
LIGHTCYAN	11
LIGHTRED	12
LIGHTMAGENTA	13
YELLOW	14
WHITE	15

The values returned by this function for two-color graphics modes, such as high-resolution CGA and Hercules graphics, seem to be meaningless (they only reflect the last value passed to **setbkcolor( )**; see the description of setbkcolor( )).

See also **setbkcolor( )**

► *getcolor* ►   ► *graphics* ►

getcolor   returns the current drawing color

Prototype   #include <graphics.h>
                      int far getcolor(void);

Prototype in   graphics.h

► Description

This function returns the color used to draw objects in graphics modes. The possible return values range from 0 to the maximum color value supported by the graphics mode (returned by **getmaxcolor( )**). The return value represents the actual pixel value written to video memory. For VGA, EGA, and low-resolution CGA graphics modes, a pixel value is an index into the current color palette; therefore, for these modes the actual color corresponding to the value returned by **getcolor( )** depends upon the current palette. For example, if the video mode is CGAC1 (CGA palette 1), then a pixel value of 2 indicates light magenta. The default EGA palette (which can be modified) contains the 16 basic colors listed in the descriptions of **getbkcolor( )** and **getpalette( )**. See the detailed explanation of color palettes in the *Turbo C Additions and Enhancements* manual. (In a Hercules graphics mode, the only pixel values are 0 for black and 1 for white. For high-resolution CGA graphics, the actual color that corresponds to a pixel value of 1 depends upon the value passed to the **setbkcolor( )** function.)

See also **getmaxcolor( )**, **setbkcolor( )**

► *getfillpattern* ►   ► *graphics* ►

getfillpattern   copies a user-defined fill pattern into memory

Prototype   #include <graphics.h>
                      void far getfillpattern(char far *upattern);

Prototype in   graphics.h

► Description

This function copies the current user-defined fill pattern, if one has been defined, into the 8-byte array **upattern**. **getfillpattern( )** allows you to save a user-defined fill pattern so that it can later be restored. See the explanation of **setfillpattern( )** for a description of how a user-defined fill pattern is created.

See also **getfillsettings( )**, **setfillpattern( )**, **setfillstyle( )**

► *getfillsettings* ►   ► *graphics* ►

getfillsettings gets information about current fill pattern and color

Prototype   #include <grahics.h>
              void far getfillsettings(struct fillsettingstype far *fillinfo);

Prototype in graphics.h

► *Description*

This function returns the current graphics fill pattern and fill color. The fill pattern and color are those used to fill areas of the graphics screen by the functions **bar( )**, **bar3d( )**, **fillpoly( )**, **floodfill( )**, and **pieslice( )**.

getfillsettings( ) returns these values by assigning the fields of a **fillsettingstype** structure, which is defined in graphics.h as follows:

```
struct fillsettingstype
    {
    int pattern;
    int color;
    };
```

The ***pattern*** field contains a code for one of the following predefined patterns:

Constant	Pattern Number	Type of Pattern
EMPTY_FILL	0	background color
SOLID_FILL	1	solid color
LINE_FILL	2	horizontal lines
LTSLASH_FILL	3	/// pattern
SLASH_FILL	4	/// pattern (thick lines)
BKSLASH_FILL	5	\\\ pattern (thick lines)

LTBKSLASH_FILL	6	\\\ pattern
HATCH_FILL	7	light cross hatch
XHATCH_FILL	8	heavy cross hatch
INTERLEAVE_FILL	9	interleaving lines
WIDE_DOT_FILL	10	sparse dots
CLOSE_DOT_FILL	11	densely packed dots
USER_FILL	12	user-defined fill pattern

If the value **USER_FILL** is returned, then the current fill pattern is user-defined. User-defined patterns are created through the function **set fillpattern( )**.

The *color* field identifies the color value used to fill areas. See the description of **getcolor( )** for an explanation of color values.

See also **getfillpattern( )**, **setfillpattern( )**, **setfillstyle( )**

► *getgraphmode* ►   ► *graphics* ►

getgraphmode   returns the current graphics mode.

Prototype   #include <graphics.h>
                    int far getgraphmode(void);

Prototype in   graphics.h

► *Description*

This function returns the current graphics mode. A list of all graphics modes supported by Turbo C is provided in the description of the function **initgraph( )**.

getgraphmode( ) is useful for saving the graphics mode set by **initgraph( )**, so that this mode may later be restored by calling **setgraphmode( )**. Note that you must call **initgraph( )** before you can successfully call **getgraph mode( )**. See the description of **setgraphmode( )** for a program example.

See also **getmoderange( )**, **initgraph( )**, **restorecrtmode( )**, **setgraphmode( )**

► *getimage* ►   ► *graphics* ►

getimage	saves a bit image of the specified region into memory.
Prototype	#include <graphics.h>
	void far getimage(int *left*, int *top*, int *right*, int *bottom*, void far *bitmap*);
Prototype in	graphics.h

► *Description*

This function saves a rectangular area of a graphics screen in the buffer pointed to by the parameter *bitmap*. The first two parameters specify the upper-left corner of the area, and the second two parameters give the lower-right corner. To determine the correct buffer size, you should first call the function **imagesize( )**. To write the block of data back to the screen, use the function **putimage( )**. (Note that the function uses the first two words of the buffer to hold the width and height of the rectangle.)

As an example, the following code writes a rectangle in the upper-left corner of the screen and then copies the block to another location, using **get image( )** to save the image in a buffer and then **putimage( )** to write the image to the new position:

```
char *bitmap;
...
rectangle (0,0,50,75);
bitmap = malloc (imagesize (0,0,50,75));
getimage (0,0,50,75,bitmap);
putimage (100,0,bitmap,COPY_PUT);
```

See also **imagesize( )**, **putimage( )**

► *getlinesettings* ►   ► *graphics* ►

getlinesettings	gets the current line style, pattern, and thickness
Prototype	#include <graphics.h>
	void far getlinesettings(struct linesettingstype far *lineinfo*);
Prototype in	graphics.h

► *Description*

This function returns the current line style and thickness used by graphics drawing functions. The returned values are assigned to the **linesettingstype** structure pointed to by the parameter *lineinfo*. This structure is defined in graphics.h as follows:

```
struct linesettingstype
    {
    int linestyle;
    unsigned upattern;
    int thickness;
    };
```

The *linestyle* field is set to one of the following possible line styles:

Constant	Numeric Value	Meaning
SOLID_LINE	0	solid line
DOTTED_LINE	1	dotted line
CENTER_LINE	2	center line
DASHED_LINE	3	dashed line
USERBIT_LINE	4	user-defined line style

A center line is one consisting of alternate long and short line segments. If the value **USERBIT_LINE** is returned, then the current line style is user-defined (via the function **setlinestyle( )**); in this case, the *upattern* field contains the bit pattern corresponding to the line style (see **setlinestyle( )**).

The field *thickness* provides the current line thickness and is assigned one of the following values:

Constant	Numeric Value	Meaning
NORM_WIDTH	11	1 pixel wide
THICK_WIDTH	33	3 pixels wide

The following are examples of functions that use the line settings returned by getlinesettings( ): arc( ), circle( ), drawpoly( ), ellipse( ), line( ), lineto( ), pieslice( ), and rectangle( ).

See also **setlinestyle( )**

► *getmaxcolor* ►   ► *graphics* ►

getmaxcolor   returns maximum color value

Prototype   #include <graphics.h>
                   int far getmaxcolor(void);

Prototype in   graphics.h

► *Description*

This function returns the highest color number available for the current graphics mode. For each mode the available colors are numbered beginning with 0 and ending with the value returned by **getmaxcolor( )**. Therefore, if **getmaxcolor( )** returns *n*, there are *n*+1 colors available in the current mode. For VGA, EGA, and low-resolution CGA graphics modes, the color value is an index into the current palette. Consequently, for these modes, the value returned by **getmaxcolor( )** is also the size of the palette minus 1. See the explanation of **getcolor( )** for a description of color values.

See also **getcolor( ), getpalette( ), setcolor( )**

► *getmaxx* ►   ► *graphics* ►

getmaxx   returns maximum *x* screen coordinate

Prototype   #include <graphics.h.>
                   int far getmaxx(void);

Prototype in   graphics.h

► Description

    This function returns the maximum horizontal screen coordinate for the current graphics mode. Because horizontal coordinates are given in terms of pixel numbers beginning with 0, the value returned by **getmaxx( )** equals the number of horizontal pixels minus 1. For example, in a Hercules graphics mode, **getmaxx( )** returns 719 (Hercules resolution is 720 × 348 pixels).

    Using **getmaxx( )** in conjunction with **getmaxy( )** provides a convenient means for writing code that does not depend upon the particular graphics mode. For example, the following function call draws a circle in the center of the screen that has a radius equal to one-third the height of the screen and should produce consistent results with any graphics mode:

    circle (getmaxx ( ) / 2, getmaxy ( ) / 2, getmaxy ( ) / 3);

See also **getmaxy( )**

► *getmaxy* ►   ► *graphics* ►

getmaxy   returns maximum *y* screen coordinate

Prototype   #include <graphics.h>
                  int far getmaxy(void);

Prototype in graphics.h

► Description

    This function returns the maximum vertical screen coordinate for the current graphics mode. See the description of **getmaxx( )** for an explanation and a programming example.

    See also **getmaxx( )**

► *getmoderange* ►   ► *graphics* ►

getmoderange   gets the range of modes for a given graphics driver

Prototype   #include <graphics.h>
                  void far getmoderange(int *graphdriver*, int far **lomode*, int far **himode*);

Prototype in   graphics.h

► Description

This function returns the range of graphics modes available under a specified graphics driver. You should set *graphdriver* to the number of the driver; **getmoderange( )** will then assign the lowest mode number to **lomode* (generally 0) and the highest mode number to **himode*. If you pass an invalid driver through the *graphdriver* parameter, **getmoderange( )** will set both **lomode* and **himode* to − 1.

The numbers and corresponding constant definitions for all graphics and modes are listed under the description of **initgraph( )**.

See also **getgraphmode( )**, **initgraph( )**

► *getpalette* ►   ► *graphics* ►

getpalette   returns information about the current palette

Prototype   #include <graphics.h>
                void far getpalette(struct palettetype far *palette);

Prototype in   graphics.h

► Description

This function returns information regarding the color palette for the current graphics mode and the current graphics driver. The function assigns the fields of the **palettetype** structure pointed to by the *palette* parameter. **palettetype** is defined in graphics.h as follows:

```
#define MAXCOLORS 15

struct palettetype
     {
     unsigned char size;
     signed char colors[MAXCOLORS + 1];
     };
```

The *size* field is assigned the number of colors in the current palette and the *colors* array is loaded with a list of the actual color numbers in the current palette. Note that these color numbers are the actual raw color numbers and should not be confused with the color values passed to functions such as **setcolor( )**, which are actually indices into the current color palette.

See the description of **getcolor( )** for an explanation of colors and palettes.

For EGA and VGA systems, one of 64 possible color values can be assigned to a given palette element. The colors in the default EGA palette are the same as those available in CGA systems and have the following numeric values (constants are defined in graphics.h):

Constant	Numeric Value
EGA_BLACK	0
EGA_BLUE	1
EGA_GREEN	2
EGA_CYAN	3
EGA_RED	4
EGA_MAGENTA	5
EGA_BROWN	20
EGA_LIGHTGRAY	7
EGA_DARKGRAY	56
EGA_LIGHTBLUE	57
EGA_LIGHTGREEN	58
EGA_LIGHTCYAN	59
EGA_LIGHTRED	60
EGA_LIGHTMAGENTA	61
EGA_YELLOW	62
EGA_WHITE	63

For CGA and Hercules graphics modes, the **getpalette( )** function does not seem to return meaningful values.

See also **getbkcolor( )**, **getcolor( )**, **getmaxcolor( )**, **setallpalette( )**, **setpalette( )**

► *getpixel* ►   ► *graphics* ►

getpixel   gets the color of a specified pixel

Prototype   #include <graphics.h>
                  int far getpixel(int *x*, int *y*);

Prototype in   graphics.h

► *Description*

getpixel( ) returns the value of the pixel at the location given by the coordinates *x* and *y*. Note that the return value is the actual number written to video memory, which is an index into the current color palette. See the description of getcolor( ) for an explanation of color values.

See also getcolor( ), putpixel( )

► *gettext* ►   ► *text* ►

gettext   copies text from text-mode screen to memory

Prototype   int gettext(int *left*, int *top*, int *right*, int *bottom*, void *destin*);

Prototype in   conio.h

► *Description*

This function can be used only in text mode. It copies a block of screen data to *destin*. The first two parameters give the column and row coordinates of the upper-left corner of the block, and the second two parameters give the coordinates of the lower-right corner. Note the following:

   ► The coordinates are absolute positions on the full screen (they are not window-relative).

   ► The target buffer must be large enough to contain the data. Because each character on the screen requires 2 bytes of storage (one for the character and one for the attribute), the size of the buffer in terms of the parameters is given by the following expression:

(right − left + 1) * (bottom − top + 1) * 2

► gettext( ) returns 1 if successful and 0 if an error occurs.

Once the screen information has been stored in the buffer, it can be written back to the screen, optionally at a different location, using the function **puttext( )**. The function **movetext( )** provides an alternative means for moving screen data immediately from one location on the screen to another.

See also **movetext( )**, **puttext( )**

► *gettextinfo* ►   ► *text* ►

gettextinfo   gets text mode video information

Prototype   #include <conio.h>
                void gettextinfo(struct text_info *inforec*);

Prototype in   conio.h

► *Description*

This function supplies a wealth of information on the current state of the text mode screen. The function assigns values to the fields of a **text_info** structure, the address of which is passed as a parameter. This structure is defined in conio.h as follows:

```
struct text_info
    {
    unsigned char winleft;          /* left coordinate of window */
    unsigned char wintop;           /* top coordinate of window */
    unsigned char winright;         /* right coordinate of window */
    unsigned char winbottom;        /* bottom coordinate of window */
    unsigned char attribute;        /* current text attribute */
    unsigned char normattr;         /* normal attribute */
    unsigned char currmode;         /* current text mode */
    unsigned char screenheight;     /* number of rows on screen */
    unsigned char screenwidth;      /* number of columns on screen */
    unsigned char curx;             /* x coordinate in window */
    unsigned char cury;             /* y coordinate in window */
    };
```

► *gettextsettings* ►   ► *graphics* ►

gettextsettings   returns information about the current text settings

Prototype   #include <graphics.h>

             void far gettextsettings(struct textsettingstype far
textinfo);

Prototype in   graphics.h

► *Description*

This function returns the current settings for text displayed in graphics modes. The information is returned by assigning the fields of a **textsettings type** structure, the address of which is passed to **gettextsettings( )**. This structure is defined in graphics.h as follows:

```
struct textsettingstype
    {
    int font;          /* current graphics character font */
    int direction;     /* horizontal or vertical direction */
    int charsize;      /* size of text characters */
    int horiz;         /* justification for horizontal characters */
    int vert;          /* justification for vertical characters */
    };
```

The first three parameters are set by the function **settextstyle( )**, and the last two are set by **settextjustify( )**.

The *font* field can have one of the following values (constants are defined in graphics.h):

Constant	Numeric Value	Meaning
DEFAULT_FONT	0	default: 8×8 bit-mapped font
TRIPLEX_FONT	1	stroked triplex font
SMALL_FONT	2	stroked small font
SANS_SERIF_FONT	3	stroked sans serif font
GOTHIC_FONT	4	stroked gothic font

DEFAULT_FONT is the default font and is built into the graphics library; the characters in this font are based upon an 8 × 8-pixel bit map, and as the characters are enlarged they become coarser. The remaining fonts are often read at run time from corresponding font files (which have a .CHR extension). These fonts are based upon vector graphics and retain their resolution when enlarged.

The *direction* field specifies whether the text is to be displayed horizontally or vertically. It should be assigned one of the following values:

Constant	Numeric Value	Meaning
HORIZ_DIR	0	default: horizontal text
VERT_DIR	1	vertical text

The *charsize* field specifies a magnification factor for the graphics characters. A value of 1 signifies the default size (for **DEFAULT_FONT** this is an 8 × 8-pixel matrix); a value of 2 indicates a magnification of 2 times the default size; and so on. If *charsize* is assigned 0, then the font size is regulated by calling **setusercharsize( )**; this option, however, affects the stroked fonts only. Use the functions **textheight( )** and **textwidth( )** to determine the actual size of a string displayed on the screen.

The *horiz* field specifies the style of justification used for horizontal text. It can be assigned one of the following values:

Constant	Numeric Value	Meaning
LEFT_TEXT	0	default: left-justified text
CENTER_TEXT	1	centered text
RIGHT_TEXT	2	right-justified text

Finally, the *vert* field specifies the style of justification used for vertical text. It can be assigned one of the following values:

Constant	Numeric Value	Meaning
BOTTOM_TEXT	0	bottom-justified text
CENTER_TEXT	1	centered text
TOP_TEXT	2	default: top-justified text

Note that justification is performed relative to the current position (CP); for example, bottom-justified vertical text would begin at the current position and extend upward.

See also **settextstyle( )**, **settextjustify( )**, **textheight( )**, **textwidth( )**

► *getviewsettings* ►   ► *graphics* ►

getviewsettings   returns information about the current viewport

Prototype   #include <graphics.h>
                       void far getviewsettings(struct viewporttype far *viewport*);

Prototype in   graphics.h

► *Description*

   getviewsettings( ) returns information about the current graphics viewport. The function assigns values to the fields of a **viewporttype** structure, the address of which is passed as a parameter. This structure is defined in graphics.h as follows:

```
struct viewporttype
     {
     int left, top, right, bottom;
     int clip;
     };
```

The first four fields give the coordinates of the current viewport. The viewport is a rectangular area on the screen that serves as a reference frame for many graphics functions. For example, all x and y coordinates passed to drawing functions are relative to the upper-left corner of the current viewport; also, functions such as **getimage( )**, **putimage( )**, and **clearviewport( )** affect only the area within the current viewport. However, the coordinates passed to certain functions, such as **getviewsettings( )** and **setviewport( )**, use absolute screen coordinates rather than viewport-relative coordinates. When a viewport is defined, the current position (CP) is assigned to the position (0,0) with respect to the new viewport. The default viewport established by **initgraph( )** and **setgraphmode( )** is the entire graphics screen.

If the *clip* flag is nonzero, then all portions of drawings that extend beyond the dimensions of the current viewport are eliminated, or clipped.

See also **clearviewport( )**, **setviewport( )**

► *getx* ►   ► *graphics* ►

getx   returns the current position's x coordinate

Prototype   #include <graphics.h>
                  int far getx(void);

Prototype in graphics.h

► Description

This function returns the **x** coordinate of the current position (CP) on the graphics screen. The current position is a reference point used by many graphics functions, such as **lineto( )**, **moverel( )**, and **outtext( )**, and is relative to the current viewport. The current position can be set through the function **moveto( )**.

As an example, the following code saves the current position, sets the current position to another value, and then restores the original position:

```
int cpx, cpy;
...
cpx = getx ( );                    /* save current position */
cpy = gety ( );
moveto (getmaxx ( )/2,getmaxy ( )/2);
settextjustify (CENTER_TEXT,TOP_TEXT);
outtext ("This is centered on the screen.");
moveto (cpx,cpy);                  /* restore current position */
settextjustify (LEFT_TEXT,TOP_TEXT);
outtext ("This string starts at the original current position.");
```

See also **gety( )**, **moveto( )**

► *gety* ►   ► *graphics* ►

gety	returns the current position's *y* coordinate
Prototype	#include <graphics.h>
	int far gety(void);
Prototype in	graphics.h

► *Description*

This function returns the *y* coordinate of the current position (CP) on the graphics screen. See the description of the analogous function **getx( )** for an explanation.

► *gotoxy* ►   ► *text* ►

gotoxy	positions cursor in text window
Prototype	void gotoxy(int x, int y);
Prototype in	conio.h

► *Description*

This function positions the cursor on the screen in a text mode. The *x* and *y* parameters specify the desired column and row positions. Rows and columns are numbered beginning with 1 and are relative to the current window. If you pass a coordinate outside the current window, the function will do nothing.

See also **wherex( )**, **wherey( )**

► *graphdefaults* ►   ► *graphics* ►

graphdefaults	resets all graphics settings to their defaults
Prototype	#Include <graphics.h>
	void far graphdefaults(void);
Prototype in	graphics.h

▶ *Description*

This function resets all graphics settings to their default values. Specifically, **graphdefaults( )**:

- ▶ sets the current viewport to the entire screen (see **getviewsettings( )**)

- ▶ sets the current position to (0,0) (see **getx( )** and **gety( )**)

- ▶ sets the current palette to the default colors (see **getpalette( )**)

- ▶ sets the drawing color and background color to the default values (see **getcolor( )** and **getbkcolor( )**)

- ▶ sets the fill pattern and color to the default values (see **getfillpattern( )** and **getfillsettings( )**)

- ▶ sets graphics text to the default font and justification style (see **gettext settings( )**)

▶ *grapherrormsg* ▶   ▶ *graphics* ▶

grapherrormsg   returns an error message string

Prototype   #include <graphics.H.
                  char far*far grapherrormsg(int errorcode);

Prototype in graphics.h

▶ *Description*

This function returns a pointer to a descriptive string that corresponds to a graphics error code. You can call the function **graphresult( )** immediately after calling any graphics function to obtain an error status code. You can then pass this error code to **grapherrormsg( )** to obtain a string that describes the error condition. See the description of **graphresult( )** for a list of the error status codes and corresponding error strings returned by **grapherrormsg( )**.

See also **graphresult( )**

► _graphfreemem ►   ► graphics ►

graphfreemem   user-modifiable graph memory deallocation

Prototype   #include <graphics.h>
                   void far _graphfreemem(void far *ptr*, unsigned *size*);

Prototype in   graphics.h

► Description

This function is used internally by the functions of the Turbo C graphics library for freeing memory that has been allocated through the function **_graphgetmem( )**. If you want to take control over the dynamic allocation of memory by the Turbo C graphics library, you should write your own versions of **_graphgetmem( )** and **_graphfreemem( )**.

See also **_graphgetmem( )**

► graphgetmem ►   ► graphics ►

graphgetmem   user-modifiable graphics memory allocation

Prototype   #include <graphics.h>
                   void far * far _graphgetmem(unsigned *size*);

Prototype in   graphics.h

► Description

This function is used internally by the functions of the Turbo C graphics library for dynamically allocating memory. **_graphgetmem( )** is declared in graphics.h not so that you can call it from your program but rather so that you can write an alternative routine that replaces the original function. You should provide your own version of this routine if you want to control the allocation of memory for the graphics library. You can also control the routine for freeing this memory by writing a replacement for the **_graphfreemem( )** function.

See also **_graphfreemem( )**

► *graphresult* ►   ► *graphics* ►

graphresult   returns an error code for the last unsuccessful graphics
                 operation

Prototype   #include <graphics.h>
                 int far graphresult(void);

Prototype in   graphics.h

► Description

This function returns an error status code for the last graphics function that was called. You can then pass the error status to the function **graph errormsg( )** to obtain a string describing the error condition. The following are the error status codes reported by **graphresult( )** and the corresponding strings returned by **grapherrormsg( )** (the constants are defined in graphics.h as fields of the enumeration type **graphics_errors**):

Constant	Value	Descriptive String
grOk	0	no error
grNoInitGraph	–1	(BGI) graphics not installed
grNotDetected	–2	graphics hardware not detected
grFileNotFound	–3	device driver file not found
grInvalidDriver	–4	invalid device driver file
grNoLoadMem	–5	not enough memory to load driver
grNoScanMem	–6	out of memory in scan fill
grNoFloodMem	–7	out of memory in flood fill
grFontNotFound	–8	font file not found
grNoFontMem	–9	not enough memory to load font
grInvalidMode	–10	invalid graphics mode for selected driver
grError	–11	generic graphics error
grIOerror	–12	graphics I/O error
grInvalidFont	–13	invalid font file

| grInvalidFontNum | –14 | invalid font number |
| grInvalidDeviceNum | –15 | invalid device number |

Note that after you call **graphresult( )**, the graphics error status is reset to 0; therefore, you can obtain a meaningful error status only the first time you call this function.

The following code illustrates the use of **graphresult( )** and **graph errormsg( )**:

```
int graphdriver = DETECT;
int graphmode;
int errorstat;
...
initgraph (&graphdriver,&graphmode,"");
errorstat = graphresult ( );
if (errorstat)
    {
    restorecrtmode ( );
    printf (grapherrormsg (errorstat));
    exit (1);
    }
...
```

See also **grapherrormsg( )**

► *highvideo* ►   ► *text* ►

highvideo   selects high intensity text characters

Prototype   void highvideo(void);

Prototype in   conio.h

► *Description*

Calling this function turns on the high-intensity display attribute for all subsequent screen output through direct-video display functions such as **cprintf( )**. Note that **highvideo( )** affects only the foreground color (or monochrome attribute) of subsequent output and does not alter data already dislayed on the screen.

See also **lowvideo( )**, **normvideo( )**

► *imagesize* ►   ► *graphics* ►

imagesize   returns the number of bytes required to store a bit image

Prototype   #include <graphics.h>
                  unsigned far imagesize(int *left*, int *top*, int *right*, int *bottom*);

Prototype in   graphics.h

► *Description*

This function returns the buffer size, in bytes, required to store a rectangular block of graphics data on the screen using the function **getimage( )**. The first two parameters specify the upper-left corner of the area, and the second two parameters give the lower-right corner. Once you have determined the necessary buffer size, you should call **getimage( )** to copy the graphics data into the buffer and then call **putimage( )** to write the data back to the screen. Note that the size returned by **imagesize( )** includes the two words used by **getimage( )** and **putimage( )** to store the width and height of the screen area. If the required size is equal to or greater than 64KB, **imagesize( )** returns the value 0xffff. See the description of **getimage( )** for a programming example.

See also **getimage( )**, **putimage( )**

► *initgraph* ►   ► *graphics* ►

initgraph   initializes the graphics system

Prototype   #include <graphics.h>
                  void far initgraph(int far **graphdriver*, int far **graphmode*,
                  char far **pathtodriver*);

Prototype in   graphics.h

► *Description*

You should call **initgraph( )** before using any of the graphics display functions. This function:

- ► loads the appropriate graphics driver from a disk file

- ► places the system in the requested graphics mode

- ► sets all graphics settings to their default values (see **graphdefaults( )**)

Note that the first two parameters passed to **initgraph( )** are the addresses of integer variables. Therefore, you cannot pass numeric constants but rather must first declare integers, assign appropriate values, and then pass the addresses of the integers.

The first parameter, *graphdriver*, specifies the graphics driver. The following are the available drivers (constants are defined in graphics.h):

Constant	Value	Description
DETECT	0	auto-detect the adapter type
CGA	1	Color Graphics Adapter (CGA)
MCGA	2	Multicolor Graphics Array (MCGA)
EGA	3	Enhanced Graphics Adapter (EGA)
EGA64	4	EGA with 64KB RAM
EGAMONO	5	EGA with monochrome monitor
IBM8514	6	IBM-8514 graphics card
HERCMONO	7	Hercules Monochrome Graphics card
ATT400	8	AT&T 400-line Graphics Adapter
VGA	9	Video Graphics Array (VGA)
PC3270	10	3270 PC Graphics Adapter

You must use the appropriate driver for the type of graphics adapter installed in the machine. However, if you pass a value of **DETECT** = 0, then the **initgraph( )** function will automatically detect the type of adapter and load the appropriate driver. (Note, however, that auto-detect will not work with the IBM-8514 graphics adapter; you must specify the **IBM8514** driver explicitly.) Note that if you specify the auto-detect option, **initgraph( )** will assign the value of the selected driver to ***graphdriver**.

The second parameter, *graphmode*, allows you to choose one of the graphics modes supported by the selected graphics driver. The following are the graphics modes supported by each of the drivers (constants are defined in graphics.h):

Constant	Value	Description
CGA driver		
CGAC0	0	320×200 palette 0^*, 1 page
CGAC1	1	320×200 palette 1^*, 1 page

CGAC2	2	320×200 palette 2*, 1 page
CGAC3	3	320×200 palette 3*, 1 page
CGAHI	4	640×200, 1 page

MCGA driver

MCGAC0	0	320×200 palette 0*, 1 page
MCGAC1	1	320×200 palette 1*, 1 page
MCGAC2	2	320×200 palette 2*, 1 page
MCGAC3	3	320×200 palette 3*, 1 page
MCGAMED	4	640×200, 1 page
MCGAHI	5	640×480, 1 page

EGA driver

| EGALO | 0 | 640×200, 16 color, 4 pages |
| EGAHI | 1 | 640×350, 16 color, 2 pages |

EGA64 driver

| EGA64LO | 0 | 640×200, 16 color, 1 page |
| EGA64HI | 1 | 640×350, 4 color, 1 page |

EGAMONO driver

| EGAMONOHI | 3 | 640×350 64KB on card, 1 page 256KB on card, 4 pages |

HERCMONO driver

| HERCMONOHI | 0 | 720×348, 2 pages |

ATT400 driver

ATT400C0	0	320×200 palette 0*, 1 page
ATT400C1	1	320×200 palette 1*, 1 page
ATT400C2	2	320×200 palette 2*, 1 page
ATT400C3	3	320×200 palette 3*, 1 page

ATT400MED	4	640×200, 1 page
ATT400HI	5	640×400, 1 page

VGA driver

VGALO	0	640×200 16 color, 4 pages
VGAMED	1	640×350 16 color, 2 pages
VGAHI	2	640×480 16 color, 1 page

PC327 driver

PC3270HI	0	720×350, 1 page

IBM8514 driver

IBM8514LO	0	640×480, 256 colors
IBM8514HI	1	102×768, 256 colors

*These four predefined palettes contain the following colors:

Palette		Colors		
	0	1	2	3
0	background	light green	light red	yellow
1	background	light cyan	light magenta	white
2	background	green	red	brown
3	background	cyan	magenta	light gray

Note that if you have chosen the auto-select feature by passing **DETECT** as the first parameter, then you do not need to assign a value to *graphmode*. In this case, initgraph( ) will automatically select the highest resolution mode supported by the driver and assign the number of this mode to *graphmode*.

The final parameter, *pathtodriver*, specifies the path to the directory containing the graphics driver files (files with the .BGI extension). **initgraph** first looks in this directory, and then in the current directory. If you assign this parameter a Null value (""), then only the current directory is searched. The function **settextstyle( )** also searches the path specified by this parameter for its font files (*.CHR).

► *insline* ►   ► *text* ►

insline   inserts blank line in text window

Prototype   void insline(void);

Prototype in   conio.h

► *Description*

This function can be used in text mode only. It inserts a blank line within a text window at the current cursor position. All lines within the current window that are below the inserted line scroll down, and the bottom line in the window disappears.

See also **clreol( )**, **delline( )**, **window( )**

► *line* ►   ► *graphics* ►

line   draws a line between two specified points

Prototype   #include <graphics.h>
void far line(int *x0*,int *y0*,int *x1*,int *y1*);

Prototype in   graphics.h

► *Description*

This function draws a line in graphics mode from the point specified by the first two parameters to the point specified by the second two parameters (relative to the viewport). The line is drawn using the current line style and thickness and the current drawing color. The current position (CP) is not updated.

See also **getcolor( )**, **getlinesettings( )**, **linerel( )**, **lineto( )**

► *linerel* ►   ► *graphics* ►

linerel   draws a line a relative distance from the current position
(CP)

Prototype   #include <graphics.h>
void far linerel(int *dx*,int *dy*);

Prototype in   graphics.h

► Description

This function draws a line in graphics mode from the current point (CP) to a point that is a specified distance away. The parameter *dx* gives the horizontal distance, and *dy* gives the vertical distance. The line is drawn using the current line style and thickness and the current drawing color. The CP is moved to the end of the line drawn.

See also **getcolor( )**, **getlinesettings( )**, **line( )**, **lineto( )**

► *lineto* ►   ► *graphics* ►

lineto   draws a line from the CP to (x,y)

Prototype   #include <graphics.h>
                   void far lineto(int *x*,int *y*);

Prototype in graphics.h

► Description

This function draws a line in graphics mode from the current point (CP) to the point specified by the parameters *x* and *y*. The line is drawn using the current line style and thickness and the current drawing color. The CP is moved to the specified point at the end of the line drawn.

► *lowvideo* ►   ► *text* ►

lowvideo   selects low-intensity characters

Prototype   void lowvideo(void);

Prototype in conio.h

► Description

lowvideo( ) works only in text mode. Calling this function turns off the high-intensity display attribute for all subsequent screen output through direct-video display functions such as **cprintf( )**. Note that **lowvideo( )** affects only the foreground color (or monochrome attribute) of subsequent output and does not alter data already dislayed on the screen.

See also **highvideo( )**, **normvideo( )**

► *moverel* ►   ► *graphics* ►

moverel	moves the current position (CP) a relative distance
Prototype	#include <graphics.h>
	void far moverel(int *dx*,int *dy*);
Prototype in	graphics.h

► *Description*

This function moves the current graphics point (CP) by the specified displacement. The parameter *dx* gives the horizontal displacement, and *dy* gives the vertical displacement.

See also **moveto( )**

► *movetext* ►   ► *text* ►

movetext	copies text on-screen from one rectangle to another
Prototype	int movetext(int left, int top,int right,int bottom,int newleft,int newtop);
Prototype in	conio.h

► *Description*

This function applies to text mode only. It moves a rectangular block of screen data from one position to another. The first two parameters, *left* and *top*, give the column and row coordinates of the upper-left corner of the source block, and the second two parameters, *right* and *bottom*, give the lower-right corner. The last two parameters, *newleft* and *newtop*, specify the upper-left corner of the target location. Note that all coordinates are absolute (not window-relative); therefore, this function ignores the current text window. If successful, **movetext( )** returns 1, and if an error occurs, it returns 0.

► *moveto* ►   ► *graphics* ►

moveto   moves the CP to (x,y)

Prototype   #include <graphics.h>
                    void far moveto(int x,int y);

Prototype in graphics.h

► *Description*

This function moves the current graphics point (CP) to the position specified by the parameters *x* and *y*.

See also **moverel( )**

► *normvideo* ►   ► *text* ►

normvideo   selects normal intensity characters

Prototype   void normvideo(void);

Prototype in conio.h

► *Description*

This function restores the default text mode display attributes that were in effect when the program began running. Both the foreground and background attributes are restored. The function alters the display attributes only for characters that are subsequently displayed; it does not affect data already written to the screen.

See also **highvideo( )**, **lowvideo( )**

► *outtext* ►   ► *graphics* ►

outtext   displays a string in the viewport

Prototype   #include <graphics.h>
                    void far outtext(char far *textstring);

Prototype in graphics.h

► *Description*

The **outtext( )** function displays a string in graphics mode at the current position (CP). The characters are displayed according to the current font, direction, size, and justification style set by **settextjustify( )** and **settextstyle( )**. See the description of **gettextsettings( )** for an explanation of these settings. Note that if the text is displayed horizontally and is left-justified, then the current point (CP) will be moved to the end of the string.

See also **gettextsettings( )**, **outtextxy( )**, **settextjustify( )**, **settextstyle( )**, **textheight( )**, **textwidth( )**

► *outtextxy* ►   ► *graphics* ►

outtextxy   sends a string to the specified location

Prototype   #include <graphics.h>
                   void far outtextxy(int *x*,int *y*,char far *textstring*);

Prototype in   graphics.h

► *Description*

This function is the same as **outtext( )** except that it displays text at the point specified by the *x* and *y* parameters and does not move the current graphics point (CP).

See also **outtext( )**

► *pieslice* ►   ► *graphics* ►

pieslice   draws and fills in pie slice

Prototype   #include <graphics.h>
                   void for pieslice(int *x*,int *y*,int *stangle*,int *endangle*,int *radius*);

Prototype in   graphics.h

► *Description*

This function draws a pie-slice-shaped figure in graphics mode using the current drawing color and filling the figure with the current fill pattern and color. The *x* and *y* parameters specify the center of the encompassing circle and *radius* its radius. *stangle* and *endangle* give the starting and stopping angles in degrees, where 0 is at the 3 o'clock position and 90 is at 12 o'clock.

See also **arc( )**, **getlinesettings( )**

► *putimage* ►   ► *graphics* ►

putimage	puts a bit image onto the screen
Prototype	#include <graphics.h>
	void far putimage(int *x*,int *y*,void far *bitmap*,int *op*);
Prototype in	graphics.h

► *Description*

putimage( ) writes a buffer containing graphics data saved by the function **getimage( )** to a given location on the screen. The first two parameters give the upper-left corner of the target location, and *bitmap* supplies the address of the buffer containing the data saved by **getimage( )**. The parameter *op* specifies the manner in which **putimage( )** combines the data in the buffer with the data already on the screen; the following are the possible values for *op:*

Constant	Value	Action
COPY_PUT	0	overwrite the existing pixels
XOR_PUT	1	XOR with existing bits
OR_PUT	2	OR with existing bits
AND_PUT	3	AND with existing bits
NOT_PUT	4	invert data and overwrite existing pixels

Options 0 and 4 simply overwrite the existing screen data at the target location. The other options combine each bit in the buffer with each bit on the screen using a specific logical operator. For example, by calling **putimage( )** with the XOR option, you can display a figure on top of an image on the screen and then restore the original image by calling **putimage( )** a second time. (The XOR operator causes each 1 bit in the buffer to toggle the corresponding bit on the screen; this feature is useful for producing animation effects.)

If the entire rectangle specified by **getimage( )** is unable to fit on the screen at the target location, **putimage( )** has no effect. See the description of **getimage( )** for a programming example.

See also **getimage( )**, **imagesize( )**

► *putpixel* ►   ► *graphics* ►

putpixel   plots a pixel at a specified point

Prototype   #include <graphics.h>
                   void far putpixel(int *x*,int *y*,int *pixelcolor*);

Prototype in   graphics.h

► *Description*

This function plots a point in a graphics mode at the coordinates given by *x* and *y* and using the color specified by *pixelcolor*. Note that *pixelcolor* should contain the actual number that is written to video memory and is an index into the current color palette. See the description of **getcolor( )** for an explanation of color values.

See also **getcolor( )**, **getpixel( )**

► *puttext* ►   ► *text* ►

puttext   copies text from memory to screen

Prototype   int puttext(int *left*,int *top*,int *right*,int *bottom*,void *source*);

Prototype in   conio.h

► *Description*

The **puttext( )** function is effective only in text mode. It displays a block of text that has been saved in a buffer by the function **gettext( )**. The first four parameters specify the target location on the screen and are absolute screen coordinates. The parameter *source* is the address of the buffer containing the data. See the function **gettext( )** for more details.

See also **gettext( )**

► *rectangle* ►   ► *graphics* ►

rectangle   draws a rectangle

Prototype   #include <graphics.h>
                   void far rectangle(int *left*,int *top*,int *right*,int *bottom*);

Prototype in   graphics.h

► *Description*

This graphics function draws a rectangle on the screen using the current drawing color and line style and thickness. The first two parameters specify the coordinates of one corner of the rectangle, and the second two parameters give the position of the opposite corner.

See also **arc( )**, **bar( )**, **getlinesettings( )**

► *restorecrtmode* ►   ► *graphics* ►

restorecrtmode   restores the screen mode to its pre-**initgraph** setting

Prototype   #include <graphics.h>
                   void far restorecrtmode(void);

Prototype in   graphics.h

► *Description*

You should use this function only when you are in graphics mode; it allows you to escape temporarily to text mode. To return to graphics mode, you can call **setgraphmode( )**. If you want to end the graphics mode permanently, call **closegraph( )**, which frees all allocated memory. Note that when you escape to text mode, all graphics data is erased from the screen; either you can regenerate this data when you return to graphics mode, or you can save and restore the screen data using the functions **getimage( )** and **putimage( )**.

See also **closegraph( )**, **getimage( )**, **setgraphmode( )**, **putimage( )**

► *setactivepage* ►   ► *graphics* ►

setactivepage   sets active page for graphics output

Prototype   #include <graphics.h>
               void far setactivepage(int *pagenum*);

Prototype in   graphics.h

► *Description*

This graphics function allows you to set the current active page for graphics modes that support multiple pages. All graphics output is sent to the current active page. The visual page is the page that is currently being displayed on the screen and can be set by calling **setvisualpage( )**. By default, the active page and visual page are the same, and therefore all graphics output becomes immediately visible. By maintaining separate visual and active pages, however, you can gradually build up a graphics display in an active page that is not visual and then quickly display the entire screen by calling **set visualpage( )** to switch visual pages. See the description of graphics modes under **initgraph( )** to determine the number of pages available for a given graphics mode.

See also **initgraph( )**, **setvisualpage( )**

► *setallpalette* ►   ► *graphics* ►

setallpalette   changes all palette colors as specified

Prototype   #include <graphics.h>
               void far setallpalette(struct palettetype far *palette*);

Prototype in graphics.h

► Description

This function is useful for modifying several palette colors or the entire palette under EGA and VGA graphics modes. You should first assign the fields of a **palettetype** structure to indicate the number of palette entries and the desired palette colors and then pass the address of this structure to **setall palette( )**. See the description of **getpalette( )** for the layout of **palettetype( )**, and the description of setpalette for an explanation of the color values you may assign. This function is useful only for CGA and EGA graphics modes, which allow you to dynamically reset any element of the current palette.

► *setbkcolor* ►   ► *graphics* ►

setbkcolor   sets the current background color using the palette

Prototype   #include <graphics.h>
           void far setbkcolor(int *color*);

Prototype in graphics.h

► Description

This function sets the current background color used in graphics modes. For VGA, EGA, and low-resolution CGA graphics modes, the background color is the color displayed for a pixel value of 0, or, in other words, it is color number 0 in the current palette. The following colors are available in these modes (the constants are defined in graphics.h):

Constant	Color Number
BLACK	0
BLUE	1
GREEN	2
CYAN	3
RED	4
MAGENTA	5
BROWN	6

LIGHTGRAY	7
DARKGRAY	8
LIGHTBLUE	9
LIGHTGREEN	10
LIGHTCYAN	11
LIGHTRED	12
LIGHTMAGENTA	13
YELLOW	14
WHITE	15

You can pass either a numeric value or use one of the predefined constants. Note that because of a perversity of the BIOS interface, **setbkcolor( )** actually sets the foreground color used by the high-resolution CGA mode. This function has no effect in the Hercules graphics mode.

See also **getbkcolor( )**

► *setcolor* ►   ► *graphics* ►

setcolor   sets the current drawing color using the palette

Prototype   #include <graphics.h>
                 void far setcolor(int *color*);

Prototype in   graphics.h

► *Description*

This function sets the current drawing color to the value given by *color*. The numbers you may assign to this parameter range from 0 to the maximum color value supported by the graphics mode (returned by **getmax color( )**). For VGA, EGA, and low-resolution CGA graphics modes, the color value is an index into the current palette and is the same as the number returned by **getcolor( )**. See the explanation of **getcolor( )** for a description of color values.

See also **getcolor( )**

► *setfillpattern* ►   ► *graphics* ►

setfillpattern   selects a user-defined fill pattern

Prototype   #include <graphics.h>
               void far setfillpattern(char far *upattern*,int *color*);

Prototype in   graphics.h

► *Description*

This function allows you to create a user-defined fill pattern. The parameter ***upattern*** points to an 8-byte array that specifies the pattern of pixels that will be used to fill areas of the screen. Each bit equal to 1 represents an on pixel, and each bit equal to 0 represents an off pixel. The total pattern you specify is 8 pixels wide and 8 pixels high; this pattern is repeated throughout the filled area. The pattern given by the second byte goes under the pattern specified by the first byte, the pattern given by the third byte goes under that given by the second, and so on. For example, the following code fills a circle with a checkered pattern:

```
char pattern [ ]  =
    {
    0xf0,0x0f,0xf0,0x0f,0xf0,0x0f,0xf0,0x0f
    };
...
circle (360,174,200);
setfillpattern (pattern,1);
floodfill (360,174,1);
```

You can temporarily store a user-defined fill pattern by calling the function **getfillpattern( )**. The function **setfillstyle( )** also allows you to set the current fill style; however, with this function you must use one of the predefined fill patterns.

► *setfillstyle* ►   ► *graphics* ►

setfillstyle   sets the fill pattern and color

Prototype   #include <graphics.h>
               void far setfillstyle(int pattern,int color);

Prototype in   graphics.h

► Description

This function sets the current graphics fill pattern and fill color. See the description of the function **getfillsettings( )** for an explanation of the predefined fill patterns and a list of values you can assign to the *pattern* parameter. Note, however, that you should not assign a value of **USER_FILL**; rather, you must use the function **setfillpattern( )** to create a user-defined fill pattern. Also, see the description of **getcolor( )** for an explanation of the color values you can assign to the parameter *color;* all the predefined patterns are drawn in the color specified by this parameter except **EMPTY_FILL**, which uses the current background color.

If one of the values you pass to **setfillstyle( )** is invalid, the function **graphresult( )** will return − 11 and the current fill pattern and color will not be altered.

See also **getcolor( )**, **getfillpattern( )**, **getfillsettings( )**, **fillpoly( )**, **floodfill( )**

► *setgraphbufsize* ►   ► *graphics* ►

setgraphbufsize   changes the size of the internal graphics buffer

Prototype   #include <graphics.h>
                     unsigned for setgraphbufsize(unsigned bufsize);

Prototype in   graphics.h

► *setgraphmode* ►   ► *graphics* ►

setgraphmode   sets the system to graphics mode,clears the screen

Prototype   #include <graphics.h>
                     void far setgraphmode(int mode);

Prototype in   graphics.h

► Description

This function switches the system into the graphics mode specified by the parameter *mode*. You may specify any mode available under the current graphics driver. See the description of the **initgraph( )** function for a list of supported modes (also, the function **getmoderange( )** returns the range of valid graphics modes for a given driver). The graphics mode is initially set by **initmode( )**. You might want to use **setgraphmode( )** in the course of your program for the following two reasons:

► to switch into graphics mode other than the one set by **initgraph( )**

► to restore the original graphics mode after you have temporarily switched into text mode using the function **restorecrtmode( )**

As an example, the following code draws a graphics figure, saves the graphics mode set by **initgraph( )**, temporarily switches into text mode, and then restores the original graphics mode with a call to **setgraphmode( )**:

```
int graphmode;
...
circle (360,174,200);                 /* create a graphics image */
delay (3000);
graphmode = getgraphmode ( );   /* save graphics mode */
restorecrtmode ( );                    /* switch into text mode */
printf ("The system is temporarily in text mode");
delay (3000);
setgraphmode (graphmode);       /* restore original graphics mode */
circle (360,174,200);                 /* restore graphics image */
```

Note that when the system switches into text mode, the screen data is lost and must be restored after returning to graphics mode. You must call **initgraph( )** before you may successfully call **setgraphmode( )**.

See also **getgraphmode( )**, **getmoderange( )**, **initgraphmode( )**, **restorecrtmode( )**

► *setlinestyle* ►   ► *graphics* ►

setlinestyle   sets the current line width and style

Prototype   #include <graphics.h>
                    void far setlinestyle(int *linestyle*,unsigned *upattern*,int *thickness*);

Prototype in graphics.h

► Description

This function sets the current line style and thickness used by graphics drawing functions. The parameter *linestyle* should be given one of the following values:

Constant	Numeric value	Meaning
SOLID_LINE	0	solid line
DOTTED_LINE	1	dotted line
CENTER_LINE	2	center line
DASHED_LINE	3	dashed line
USERBIT_LINE	4	user-defined line style

You should pass one of the first four constants if you want to select a predefined line style. If you want to define your own line style, pass the value **USERBIT_LINE**; in this case the next parameter, *upattern*, should contain a sequence of on and off bits representing the pattern of on and off pixels used for drawing the line. For example, the value 0x0f0f will create a dashed line. Note that if you are not assigning a user-defined line style (that is, *linestyle* is not equal to **USERBIT_LINE**), the value assigned to *upattern* is ignored.

The parameter *thickness* should be given one of the following values:

Constant	Numeric Value	Meaning
NORM_WIDTH	1	one pixel wide
THICK_WIDTH	3	three pixels wide

Note that passing a value of 2 has the same effect as passing 1 (**NORM_WIDTH**), and lines will be drawn only 1 pixel wide.

If you pass an invalid value to **setlinestyle( )**, **graphresult( )** will return a value of − 11 and the current line style will be unaltered. See the description of **getlinesettings( )** for a list of functions that are affected by this command. The following lines of code display the two line thicknesses by drawing both horizontal and vertical lines in each thickness:

```
setlinestyle (SOLID_LINE,0,NORM_WIDTH);
line (0,0,0,50);
line (0,100,50,100);
setlinestyle (SOLID_LINE,0,THICK_WIDTH);
line (25,0,25,50);
line (0,125,50,125);
```

See also **getlinesettings( )**

► *setpalette* ►   ► *graphics* ►

setpalette	changes one palette color
Prototype	#include <graphics.h>
	void far setpalette(int *index*,int *actual_color*);
Prototype in	graphics.h

► *Description*

This function changes the colors in the current color palette. The parameter ***index*** should contain the index of the palette entry you want to change, and ***actual_color*** should be assigned the raw color number for the new color you want to assign. The change is made immediately on-screen.

For EGA and VGA systems, one of 64 possible color values may be assigned to a given palette element (0 through 63). The colors in the default EGA palette are the same as those available in CGA systems and have the following numeric values (constants are defined in graphics.h):

Constant	Numeric Value
EGA_BLACK	0
EGA_BLUE	1
EGA_GREEN	2
EGA_CYAN	3

EGA_RED	4
EGA_MAGENTA	5
EGA_BROWN	20
EGA_LIGHTGRAY	7
EGA_DARKGRAY	56
EGA_LIGHTBLUE	57
EGA_LIGHTGREEN	58
EGA_LIGHTCYAN	59
EGA_LIGHTRED	60
EGA_LIGHTMAGENTA	61
EGA_YELLOW	62
EGA_WHITE	63

For the low-resolution CGA modes, you may change only palette entry 0, which is the background color. Modifying palette entry 0 has the same effect as calling the function **setbkcolor( )**. Under these modes, the only way to change the other palette colors is to switch to another of the four predefined color palettes; to change to another palette, you must switch to the appropriate mode (using **setgraphmode( )**—see **initgraph( )** for a list of these modes).

Note that for the high-resolution CGA mode, modifying palette entry 0 changes the foreground color (because of the same system perversity that causes **setbkcolor( )** to alter the foreground color for this mode). Also, this function has no effect under the Hercules graphics mode.

See also **getpalette( )**, **setallpalette( )**

► *settextjustify* ►   ► *graphics* ►

settextjustify   sets text justification

Prototype   #include <graphics.h>
void far settextjustify(int *horiz*,int *vert*);

Prototype in   graphics.h

► Description

This function sets the current style of justification used for displaying horizontal and vertical graphics characters. See the description of the function **gettextsettings( )** for an explanation of these settings and a list of possible values.

See also **gettextsettings( )**

► *settextstyle* ►   ► *graphics* ►

settextstyle   sets the current text characteristics

Prototype   #include <graphics.h>
void far settextstyle(int *font*,int *direction*,int *charsize*);

Prototype in   graphics.h

► Description

This function sets the font, direction, and character size used for graphics mode text display. See the description of **gettextsettings( )** for an explanation of these settings and a list of possible values.

See also **gettextsettings( )**

► *setusercharsize* ►   ► *graphics* ►

setusercharsize   user-defined character magnification factor for stroked fonts

Prototype   #include <graphics.h>
void far setusercharsize(int *multx*,int *divx*,int *multy*,int *divy*);

Prototype in   graphics.h

► Description

This graphics function allows you to control the size and proportions of text displayed using stroked fonts only. The first two parameters specify the horizontal multiplication factor, where *multx* is the numerator and *divx* is the divisor. For example, if *multx* is set to 2 and *divx* is set to 3, then the multiplication factor is 2/3. Similarly, *multy* and *divy* specify the vertical multiplication factor.

Before using this function, you must call **settextstyle( )**, setting the *charsize* field to 0. Note that **settextstyle( )** also allows you to modify the character size, but you can specify only a single integral multiplier.

See also **gettextsettings( )**, **settextstyle( )**

► *setviewport* ►

setviewport   sets the current viewport for graphics output

Prototype   #include <graphics.h>
                 void far setviewport(int *left*,int *top*,int *right*,int *bottom*,int
                 clipflag);

Prototype in   graphics.h

► *Description*

This function defines the current viewport on the graphics screen. The first four parameters are the dimensions of the rectangle on the screen that constitutes the viewport. The last parameter, *clipflag*, should be set to a nonzero value if you want drawings to be clipped at the viewport boundaries and should be set to zero if you do not want clipping. See the description of **get viewsettings( )** for more information on viewports and clipping.

See also **getviewsettings( )**

► *setvisualpage* ►   ► *graphics* ►

setvisualpage   sets the visual graphics page number

Prototype   #include <graphics.h>
                 void far setvisualpage(int *pagenum*);

Prototype in   graphics.h

► *Description*

This graphics function sets the video page that is currently displayed and is useful only for graphics modes that support multiple pages. See the description of **setactivepage( )** for an explanation of how this function is used.

See also **setactivepage( )**

► *textattr* ►   ► *text* ►

textattr   sets text attributes

Prototype   void textattr(int *attribute*);

Prototype in   conio.h

► *Description*

You can use this function only when you are in a text mode. It allows you to set both the foreground and background colors (or monochrome display attributes) used for screen output. **textattr( )** does not affect characters already displayed on the screen but only those subsequently written using a direct console output function, such as **cprintf( )**. See the explanation of display attributes in Chapter 9.

See also **textbackground( )**, **textcolor( )**

► *textbackground* ►   ► *text* ►

textbackground selects new text background color

Prototype   void textbackground(int *color*);

Prototype in   conio.h

► *Description*

This text mode function allows you to set the background color (or monochrome display attribute) to be used for screen output. **textbackground( )** does not affect characters already displayed on the screen but only those subsequently written using a direct console output function, such as **cprintf( )**. See the explanation of display attributes in Chapter 9.

See also **textattr( )**, **textcolor( )**

► *textcolor* ►   ► *text* ►

textcolor   selects new character color in text mode

Prototype   #include <conio.h>
                     void textcolor(int *color*);

Prototype in conio.h

► *Description*

This text mode function allows you to set the foreground color (or mono-chrome display attribute) to be used for screen output. **textcolor( )** does not affect characters already displayed on the screen but only those subsequently written using a direct console output function, such as **cprintf( )**. See the explanation of display attributes in Chapter 9.

See also **textattr( )**, **textbackground( )**

► *textheight* ►   ► *graphics* ►

textheight   returns the height of a string, in pixels

Prototype   #include <graphics.h>
                     int far textheight(char far *textstring*);

Prototype in graphics.h

► *Description*

This graphics function returns the height (in pixels) of a string displayed on the screen. **textheight( )** incorporates the current font size and multiplication factor into its calculation of the height.

See also **textwidth( )**

► *textmode* ►   ► *text* ►

textmode	puts screen in textmode
Prototype	void textmode(int *mode*);
Prototype in	conio.h

► *Description*

You should call this function to change to another text mode only when you are already in a text mode. If you are in a graphics mode and you want to return permanently to text mode, call **closegraph( )**; if you want to return temporarily to text mode, call **restorecrtmode( )**. The following are the possible values you can pass to this function (constants are defined in conio.h):

Constant	Value	Description
LASTMODE	– 1	return to last active text mode
BW40	0	black and white, 40 columns
C40	1	color, 40 columns
BW00	2	black and white, 80 columns
C80	3	color, 80 columns
MONO	7	monochrome, 80 columns

See also **closegraph( )**, **restorecrtmode( )**

► *textwidth* ►   ► *graphics* ►

textwidth	returns the width of a string, in pixels
Prototype	#include <graphics.h> int far textwidth(char far *textstring*);
Prototype in	graphics.h

► *Description*

This graphics function returns the width (in pixels) of a string displayed on the screen. **textwidth( )** incorporates the string length, the current font size, and the multiplication factor into its calculation of the height.

See also **textheight( )**

► *wherex* ►   ► *text* ►

wherex   gives horizontal cursor position within windows

Prototype   int wherex(void);

Prototype in   conio.h

► *Description*

This function can be used only in text mode. It returns the current horizontal (column) position of the cursor within the text window.

See also **wherey( )**

► *wherey* ►   ► *text* ►

wherey   gives vertical cursor position within windows

Prototype   int wherey(void);

Prototype in   conio.h

► *Description*

This function can be used only in text mode. It returns the current vertical (row) position of the cursor within the text window.

See also **wherex( )**

► *window* ►   ► *text* ►

window   defines active text mode windows

Prototype   void window(int *left*, int *top*, int *right*, int *bottom*);

Prototype in   conio.h

► *Description*

This function defines the current text mode window on the screen. The first two parameters specify the column and row coordinates of the upper-left corner of the window, and the second two coordinates give the lower-right corner. If you pass invalid coordinates, the function will have no effect. By default, the current window encompasses the entire screen.

See also **gettextinfo( )**

► APPENDIX H ►
TURBO C RESOURCE LIST

► BOOKS ►

Harbison, Samuel P., and Steele, Guy L. Jr. *C: A Reference Manual*. 2nd ed. Englewood Cliffs, N.J.: Prentice-Hall Inc., 1987.

Kernighan, Brian W., and Ritchie, Dennis M. *The C Programming Language*. Englewood Cliffs, N.J.: Prentice-Hall Inc., 1978.

Young, Michael J. *Systems Programming in Turbo C*. Alameda, Calif.: SYBEX, 1988. (This book has a comprehensive bibliography.)

► FONTS ►

Multi-Lingual Scholar and specialized software for exotic alphabets. Gamma Productions Inc., 710 Wilshire Boulevard, Santa Monica, CA 90401; (213) 394-8622.

► MAGAZINES ►

The following have regular coverage of C topics with source-code listings:

BYTE. One Phoenix Mill Lane, Peterborough, NH 03458; (603) 924-9281. (See especially "A C Language Primer" by James Joyce in the August 1983 issue.)

Computer Language. 500 Howard Street, San Francisco, CA 94105; (415) 397-1881. (See especially Programming On Purpose, the monthly column by P. J. Plauger and Bit by Bit by Stan Kelly-Bootle.)

Dr. Dobb's Journal of Software Tools. 501 Galveston Dr., Redwood City, CA 94063; (415) 366-3600.

Structured Language World. 175 Fifth Avenue, New York, NY 10010.

UNIX REVIEW. 500 Howard Street, San Francisco, CA 94105; (415) 397-1881. (See especially the monthly column C Advisor by Eric P. Allman and Ken Arnold.)

► *MISCELLANEOUS* ►

The C Users' Group, *The C User's Journal,* 2120 W. 25th St., Ste. B, Lawrence, KS 66046; (913) 841-1631.

► *MISCELLANEOUS SOFTWARE PRODUCTS* ►

Complete set of software tools with source code, separate library for each memory model. There are two diskettes and the price is $29.50. The tools are fully described in *Systems Programming in Turbo C* (see above). Michael J. Young, P.O. Box 5068, Mill Valley, CA 94942.

C Programmer's Tool Box, Volumes I and II. A variety of productivity aids and utilities. MMC AD Systems, P.O. Box 360845, Milpitas, CA 95035; (408) 263-0781.

C-scape/ Look & Feel. Interface management system including screens, menus, help support, data capture/verification. Oakland Group, 675 Massachusetts Avenue, Cambridge MA 02139; (800) 233-3733.

The Heap Expander. Interface for expanded heaps up to 8 MB. The Tool Makers, P.O. Box 8976, Moscow, ID 83843; (208) 883-4979.

PEGA Functions. EGA toolkit with 90 enhanced graphics functions. Prototype Systems Ltd., 637 17th Street, Boulder, CO 80302; (800) 628-2828, extension 493.

Screen Maker. Code generator for text files and input/output screens. SoftScience Corp., P.O. Box 42905, Tucson, AZ 85733-2905; (800) 453-5000.

Turbo C Tools. Function Support for Turbo C including strings, screens, graphics, windows, menus, keyboards, files, printers, memory management, interrupt service support, intervention code, utilities, and macros. Blaise Computing Inc., 2560 Ninth Street, Suite 316, Berkeley, CA 94710; (415) 540-5441.

Vitamin C. Screen painter/code generator; window/data, entry/menu manager; help handler. Creative Programming, P.O. Box 112097, Carrollton, TX 75011; (214) 416-6447.

(All the above product names are trademarks of the suppliers.)